THE FINANCIAL TIMES
GUIDE TO
MANAGEMENT
AND
FINANCE

THE FINANCIAL TIMES GUIDE TO

MANAGEMENT

AND

FINANCE

An A-Z of Tools, Terms and Techniques

RICHARD KOCH

FINANCIAL TIMES

PITMAN PUBLISHING

PITMAN PUBLISHING
128 Long Acre, London WC2E 9AN

A Division of Longman Group Limited

First published in 1994

© Richard Koch 1994

British Library Cataloguing in Publication Data
A CIP catalogue record for this book can be obtained from the British Library.

ISBN 0 273 60851 7

1 3 5 7 9 10 8 6 4 2

Typeset by PanTek Arts, Maidstone, Kent.
Printed and bound by Bell and Bain Ltd., Glasgow

*The Publishers' policy is to use paper manufactured
from sustainable forests.*

To the memory of Bruce Henderson;
and for Bill Bain, Iain Evans and Jim Lawrence,
colleagues from whom I learnt more than
100 per cent of what I now know about business.
And for Sté, with love, always.

ACKNOWLEDGEMENTS

The idea for this Guide came from Mark Allin and his publishing colleagues, and I thank them for their encouragement: especially Rod Bristow, Trish Denoon, Sally Green, Kate Salkilld and Richard Stagg. I was also carried along by the enthusiasm shown for the project by my friend Marian Clarke, who also supervised the production.

Those who read a draft of the text and made useful comments were: Michael Bishopp, Andrew Campbell, Jane Carmichael, Charles Coates, Robin Field, Paul Judge, Bryan Mayson, David Norton, Jamie Reeve, Anthony Rice and Clive Richardson. Goodness only knows why they are willing to give valuable time critiqueing and enriching my books, but long may it continue, and my heartfelt thanks to them. I would also like to thank David Woodvine for his eagle-eyed proof-reading.

I am very grateful for the practical help and intellectual stimulation provided by OC & C Strategy Consultants' partners and associates throughout the writing process. Without OC & C's input, the Guide would have been much less comprehensive and even more idiosyncratic.

Towards the end of compiling this Guide, there was an important change in my life that I had neither wanted nor expected. But the message of the Guide is clear: change is good and must be welcomed, in life as in management. In their different ways many friends pointed this out, and pushed me out on my voyage of discovery. I am particularly indebted to Marian Clarke, Dominique and Robin Field, Liz Johnstone, Bryan Mayson, Andy and Chris Outram, Jamie Reeve, Anthony Rice, Mary Saxe-Falstein, Selma Jeevanjee, Patrick Weaver and Michael Yaxley for their insight and practical help.

INTRODUCTION

WHO THIS GUIDE IS FOR

It is written for (i) managers anywhere around the world and (ii) MBA and other business students. It has two uses for either group:

- as a pleasurable summary of anything important in management thinking and practice;
- as a reference work that will provoke thought as well as provide information.

While having the benefits of dictionary format, this is quite unlike any other management dictionary, for eight reasons:

1. It is up-to-date, reflecting state-of-the-art 1994 thinking, and includes many words used by practical managers but not recorded in conventional dictionaries.
2. It is chatty and fun to read, whether you want to look up a single entry or just browse through. It is intended to be the sort of book you want in your briefcase for a relaxed but enlightening read whenever you have a spare minute or hour on a plane or train.
3. It is practical and comes from the world of practical managers rather than academia, including many expressions used in business that are not used or reported on elsewhere.
4. It is also conceptual, and includes all important management ideas that have ever been developed and used. It includes a summary of the world's most important management thinkers from 1850 to 1994, including a number of new 'stars' not referred to by other guides.
5. It is opinionated, telling you what is important and what is not, or, for those already having opinions, providing a thought-provoking comparison with them.
6. It reports and synthesises an overall philosophy of management, while being fair to and reporting fully other perspectives.
7. It is global in its vocabulary, reach and outlook, drawing examples from and contrasts between practice in Japan, the other Asian countries, America, the different European countries and elsewhere. Japanese management techniques cast their light throughout the guide, though it also offers Western managers ways to win that it will be difficult for the Japanese to replicate.
8. It takes a broad view of management, including finance, culture, technology and psychology, pointing out the public policy implications and the role of industrial policy, while also cutting out broad swathes of academic and useless economic theories that obstruct insight but are all too present in conventional dictionaries and guides.

It is also at least as authoritative as the dull-and-worthy, out-of-date works it replaces. By being comprehensive as well as topical, it is intended to be the first management book that you will turn to on 99 per cent of the queries you have, and more useful than any other single book that you may refer to or use.

These claims may seem large and extravagant, but put them to the test: dip into the Guide and start reading anywhere, and see if you agree.

A note on comprehensiveness, order, acronyms, cross-references and people

- **Comprehensiveness:** I have actually included any words I could find that managers around the world actually use, whether colloquial or 'proper', and any useful management concepts whether or not they are yet in wide currency. I have excluded the following: words (like 'computer') that everyone understands anyway; economic concepts (like 'marginal utility') that are never used by managers, for the simple reason that they are useless; and words that refer to national and often transient institutions (like ACAS or the Price Commission) or to one country's legislation (like a TESSA).

- **Order:** this is strictly alphabetical, for example, 'marketing' comes between 'market imperfections' and 'marketing-led', with a host of terms starting with the word 'market' followed by another word (e.g. 'market intelligence', 'market leader', 'market maker') coming afterwards. The rule adopted is that to start with letters nearest 'a' for each succeeding letter, regardless of how many words are involved. Hyphens are ignored for alphabetical ranking purposes.

- **Acronyms:** many words are mainly known or referred to by their acronyms (e.g. 'PE ratio', 'P&L', 'R&D') and are listed in the strict alphabetical order of the acronym, rather than by the order of the full words (not 'price earnings ration', 'profit and loss statement', 'research and development'). Where someone may reasonably know the full word but not the acronym, this is cross-referenced. Where acronyms are used, but most people use the full term (e.g. 'Natural Language Processing' or 'Purchasing Power Parity') they are listed under the full term rather than the acronym, again with cross-referencing where required.

- **Cross-references:** words that are defined elsewhere appear in SMALL CAPITALS every time that they are mentioned in an entry. The curious reader may then look up the other entry. Where I consider it important for the general reader to look up the cross-reference, I say 'see also SMALL CAPITALS', usually at the end of the entry. I know how irritating it can be, however, to be shunted around a dictionary, so I have generally given a short definition even if there is a cross-reference with a fuller explanation.

- **People:** management thinkers are listed by their surnames. I have tried to select only those who have something to say to today's managers and who are actually worth reading on their key subjects. Many may find my choice eclectic but it is intended to focus on people whose ideas are useful and distinctive (for instance, I exclude John Humble, because everything important in him can be found in Peter Drucker, but I include some little-known but important thinkers like Michael Goold, Ira Magaziner, Reg Revans and Fons Trompenaars). I have included some important managers-with-ideas and consultants, like Marvin Bower, Bruce Henderson, Konosuke Matsushita, and Alfred Sloan, and those like Alvin Toffler and Charles Handy whose concerns range widely on social issues that are affecting management profoundly, in addition to mainstream business academics. My apologies to the many thinkers, consultants, business leaders and academics I have omitted.

How you can help to update the Koch

It is intended that this work be updated annually to keep it fully abreast of new thinking and vocabulary. Inevitably, also, this first edition will have missed a number of key words. You can render a service to the world of management (and to my publishers and me) by writing to me with your suggestions (and even definitions) for new words. If you enjoy reading this guide and find it useful, please do take the trouble to send your suggestions to me by fax on 071 240 5771. Thank you for your help.

Happy reading!

Richard Koch
August, 1994

A

ABC ANALYSIS, ACTIVITY-BASED COSTING

This is a recent and important method of ensuring that all costs, and especially INDIRECT COSTS and OVERHEADS, are properly allocated to particular products. Traditional costing methods allocated indirect costs via COST CENTRES, which was an imprecise method. This did not matter so much when direct costs were the majority of the COST STRUCTURE, but today many products comprise a greater amount of indirect than DIRECT COST. Using the old methods tended to under-allocate cost to special products and services using a lot of indirect cost, resulting in AVERAGE COSTING and AVERAGE PRICING, i.e. pricing standard products too high and SPECIALS too low. ABC avoids this by allocating indirect costs better by identifying the COST DRIVERS for each activity.

ABC works as follows:

1. The ACTIVITIES and OBJECTS (usually products, but sometimes customers or other relevant definitions of what is provided) are defined. This can be a lengthy and challenging process, overturning previous views of relevant categories for defining profit. For example, if a customer demands being supplied with two products, or special terms, it is more relevant to look at customer than individual product profitability.
2. The cost drivers (what determines cost, for example, the number of work orders) are defined in relation to each activity.
3. The costs are then allocated to each object and compared to PRICE REALISATION to determine profitability.

ABC can be turned into an accounting system, but it is really a way of analysing PRODUCT LINE PROFITABILITY at a point in time. Since the cost drivers and activities can change, ABC analysis needs to revisited periodically to ensure that the previous data and insights are still valid. ABC should lead to changed decisions about pricing, product and customer focus, MARKET SHARE policy and other actions that can raise profitability.

ABM (Activity-Based Management)

An extension of ABC (activity-based costing) which makes it a whole philosophy of management by taking in consideration of customers' needs and working out where the extra cost of special products or services can be fully or more than fully recovered from customers. ABM has not yet achieved anything like the popularity of ABC, but it is a logical outgrowth of it and the focus on customer utility is very useful. See also COMB ANALYSIS.

ABOVE-THE-LINE PROMOTION

Marketing spending such as advertising, addressed to a mass audience (or segments thereof) rather than targeted at individuals, and always involving an advertising agency. Contrast BELOW-THE-LINE promotion.

ABSENTEEISM

Unauthorised absence from work.

ABSORPTION

1. A method of cost accounting that makes each product absorb a certain amount of overhead to arrive at a full cost for each product. This method will understate the true costs if the budgeted quantity of the product is not sold. **2.** A cost which is not charged to clients but which is absorbed into overall overheads, as when a project overruns its cost but the excess cannot be charged. Used especially in professional service firms.

ACCELERATED DEPRECIATION

A method of DEPRECIATION that makes higher charges to the profit and loss statement for an asset during the early years of its life. This results in lower stated profits (and lower immediate tax payable) than alternative methods; it is also usually more realistic.

ACCEPTING HOUSE

Nowadays a posh synonym for a MERCHANT BANK. Technically, a British financial institution that guarantees to honour BILLS OF EXCHANGE.

ACCOUNTABILITY

1. A manager's responsibility for undertaking certain tasks for which he or she will be personally and solely on the line to deliver. **2.** Sometimes used also to denote the task itself for which the above applies. In either case a stress on accountabilities is usually a healthy corrective to working styles where the concept of TEAMWORK is perverted to avoid individual responsibility for action. Assuming accountability for an action does not eliminate teamwork but simply means that one person is focused on each objective and ultimately responsible for its success or failure. Executives and their bosses should know what each person is accountable for. See also MANAGEMENT BY OBJECTIVES (MbO), which is a method (some would say an extreme method) of tying down accountabilities.

ACCOUNT EXECUTIVE

A salesman in a professional services or other firm who has overall responsibility for selling to, liaising with and satisfying a particular customer. Often large national accounts (such as for leading retailers) will be handled by account executives, while smaller accounts will be dealt with by regional salesmen.

ACCOUNTING PERIOD
The time between two consecutive BALANCE SHEET DATES.

ACCOUNTS PAYABLE
Amounts owed to suppliers of goods and services (CREDITORS).

ACCOUNTS RECEIVABLE
Amounts owed to a firm by its customers (DEBTORS).

ACCRUAL
An expense that has been incurred and not yet paid, but that must be recorded as an expense in a monthly or quarterly profit and loss calculation.

ACCRUAL RATE
Normally, the rate a pension increases in value annually, for example by one-sixtieth.

ACCRUALS CONCEPT
Under this concept revenues and expenses are recognised when goods are delivered or expenses incurred, rather than when payment is made. Most business is accounted for in this way, as opposed to a CASH BASIS.

ACCUMULATED AMORTISATION/DEPRECIATION
The total amortisation or depreciation of an asset since it was bought.

ACCUMULATED PROFIT
See RETAINED EARNINGS.

ACID TEST RATIO
See CURRENT RATIO.

ACORN (A Classification Of Residential Neighbourhoods)
Thirty-nine categories of area from which to assess likely income and lifestyle. Also useful for deciding where to site retail outlets.

ACQUISITION MANAGEMENT
See POST-ACQUISITION MANAGEMENT.

ACQUISITIVES
Collective noun for companies that grow mainly by acquisition rather than simply by organic expansion. Contrast ORGANICS. A study in 1993 of UK corporate performance showed that on average between 1984 and

1992 British-based 'acquisitives' grew faster than 'organics' in terms of turnover (18% for the acquisitives versus 8% for the organics), pre-tax profits (18% against 9%), and earnings per share (10% against 7%), and had higher average return on equity (21% against 15%). Interestingly, the average PE RATIO of acquisitives in 1993 was actually lower than for organics, indicating that the stock market thought the earnings of acquisitives of lower quality than those of organics, despite the superior track record. The lower rating for acquisitives was, however, a reversal of the relative ratings between 1986 and 1990, when acquisitives were more appreciated. Provided they can continue to out-perform, the rating of acquisitives will probably rebound. See also CONGLOMERATE.

ACTION LEARNING
An alternative to classroom-based management learning, action learning presents managers with real business issues from their own or another organisation, and invites the best solutions. A good method to enhance problem-solving abilities. See also CASE STUDY METHOD and REVANS.

ACTION RESEARCH
Study of group dynamics invented by Kurt LEWIN.

ACTIVE LEARNING
On-the-job, part-time or sandwich training.

ACTIVE STOCK
Share traded frequently.

ACTIVITIES
A term used in ACTIVITY-BASED COSTING denoting work done, such as planning budgeting, estimating, buying raw materials, invoicing, selling and marketing.

ACTIVITY CHART
A record of work tasks undertaken by a person or a machine at a WORK STATION, broken down into five stages: (1) operation; (2) transportation; (3) inspection; (4) unscheduled delays; (5) storage. A traditional method for reducing delays and improving production flows.

ACTIVITY VALUE ANALYSIS
See AVA.

ACTUARIAL SURPLUS
When a pension fund has contributions exceeding what it is calculated it

will have to pay out. The pension fund is thus OVERFUNDED. There are sometimes disputes as to whom the surplus belongs to: the pensioners or the company.

ACTUARY

A specialist analyst who calculates insurance risk data and pricing.

ADAIR, JOHN (b. 1934)

British pioneer of 'action-centred leadership' who stressed the role of leadership in management and showed that leadership skills could be taught. Stressed the importance of companies having a sense of direction and the role of teamwork. Claimed that action-centred learning was to management what Einstein was to relativity theory, which one charitably assumes demonstrates a sense of humour on his part.

ADDED VALUE

See VALUE ADDED.

ADHOCRACY

Invented by Warren BENNIS in 1968 and popularised by Alvin TOFFLER. Crudely the opposite of BUREAUCRACY: an adhocracy is an organisation that disregards the classical principles of management where everyone has a defined and permanent role. Adhocracies are usually fun to work in, chaotic, task and project team based, disrespectful of authority if not accompanied by expertise, and fast changing. Adhocracy suits cultures and individuals used to thinking for themselves and willing to tolerate ambiguity. Adhocracy is most suited to workforces that are highly educated and motivated and where the work requires creativity and responsiveness to unpredictable and volatile customer needs. Most car plants are not adhocracies, most advertising agencies are.

MINTZBERG supplies a more formal definition: 'Highly organic structure, with little formalisation of behaviour, high horizontal job specialisation, based on formal training; a tendency to group the specialists in functional units for housekeeping purposes, but to deploy them in small market-based teams to do their work.' (*Structure in Firms*).

ADJACENT SEGMENT

A product or product-customer combination that is 'close' or similar to another one and that could be served by a company with relatively little extra effort. Marketing executives often list their adjacent segments as a prelude to deciding which new customers to target or new business areas to enter. For example, a local newspaper serving one area may decide to enter another area (the adjacent segment) either by extending the coverage of its existing paper or by bringing out an additional edition. Entering an adjacent

5

segment is normally a more sensible step than going after a more distant segment (in this case, a distant newspaper area).

The skill in describing and evaluating adjacent segments lies in thinking about dimensions of the adjacency that may not be obvious. It is easy to think of a geographically adjacent market, but the newspaper may also be adjacent to other segments if it can use its skills, cost base or market franchise to enter that market. In this case, local radio, local magazines, or even the promotion of concerts may be adjacent segments for the newspaper.

In choosing adjacent segments it is important to avoid potential new segments that are already dominated by existing competitors, or that are themselves adjacent to other segments controlled by powerful players. For instance, a pet accessory maker may think that pet food is an adjacent segment, but if it is already dominated by a large and well-run pet food manufacturer he should steer clear. A better bet may be to enter an adjacent segment unrelated to pets, for example the manufacture of leather belts (if these have high cost sharing with making cat and dog collars) or other accessories that have high cost sharing with existing operations. See also ANSOFF MATRIX.

ADMINISTRATION

1. The process of managing, especially managing overheads. **2.** A half-way house between normal trading and INSOLVENCY, where accountants are appointed ADMINISTRATORS to run the company, if possible revive it, and if not, sell off assets and pay as much as possible to the CREDITORS.

ADMINISTRATORS

Accountants appointed to run insolvent companies. See ADMINISTRATION.

ADR (American Depository Receipt)

Share certificate issued to Americans in a foreign stock. The ADRs can be traded in the USA as though they were a normal domestic share, and receive dividends in dollars.

ADVANCE/DECLINE RATIO

The number of stocks rising in a day divided by the number falling. A useful indicator of market trends to put alongside the change in a stock market index, especially used in the USA.

ADVERTISED RECRUITMENT

Hiring process using a recruitment agency that places advertisements for the position in the press and screens applicants. Usually for middle-level jobs where it is not economic to use a HEADHUNTER.

AFFILIATE

1. Sister company, linked by some partial common ownership, but not a SUBSIDIARY of the other company. **2.** Organisation linked to another by common interest rather than ownership.

AFFINITY GROUP

An informal grouping of executives and sometimes outside contractors who have a common interest or complementary skills in developing new products or services of a particular type. The affinity group may have a perpetually revolving membership of up to a dozen people charged with solving a particular problem; each member has some 'affinity' with the others even though they may be drawn from different departments, countries or organisations. This form of knowledge development is also found in universities, which are often good sources of members of the group. Affinity groups started in the USA in the aerospace and other high-technology industries, but are now increasingly used in any business where the pursuit and application of new knowledge is key.

AGEING OF DEBTORS

Also called 'age analysis' or 'age profile of debtors', this groups DEBTORS according to how long it is that the invoices have remained unpaid, usually into periods of 30 days (0–30, 31–60, etc.). The longer the time period, the less certain it is that the invoices will ever be paid.

AGEISM

Dreadful word to describe and castigate discrimination against people on grounds of age (e.g. refusing to hire people over 50 because they are too near retirement).

AGENCY

Role of an AGENT.

AGENT

Someone who works on behalf of someone else, the 'PRINCIPAL'. Managers are agents for shareholders, stockbrokers are agents for their clients, and so forth. These agency relationships can be fraught if the agent puts his interests in front of those of the principal, as often happens, particularly if the principal's interests are not carefully defined.

AGREED BID

A TAKEOVER BID that secures the agreement of incumbent management and a majority of the board of directors. Note, however, that agreed bids do not always succeed, because the ultimate decision makers are the shareholders, who may not vote to support a bid even if the directors recommend it, particularly if a higher offer comes along.

Agreed Bid sounds harmonious but such bids are not necessarily in the interests of either the company or its shareholders, particularly if the support of top managers has been won by assuring them of continued office or lucrative pay-offs. Contrast HOSTILE BID.

AGGREGATED REBATE

See OVERRIDER.

AGGRESSIVE PRICING

Not a very useful expression because managers use it in two opposite senses, according to whether one is being aggressive towards competitors or customers.

1. The correct usage is the former, that is, aggressively low pricing in order to increase market share and put pressure on the high-cost, marginal, competitor. **2.** Also used to indicate high pricing or the attempt to maintain industry-wide high profit margins: always a mistake for the leading or low-cost competitor. See PRICE UMBRELLA and OPPORTUNITY/VULNERABILITY MATRIX.

AI (Artificial Intelligence)

The process of developing computer systems to replicate human intelligence and provide a ready-made base of data and thinking which enables less experienced people to deal effectively with a variety of situations encountered.

One of the most valuable applications of AI is in the provision of EXPERT SYSTEMS, which boil down the knowledge of experts and enable non-experts to make the sort of decisions an expert would make. For example, an expert system may enable an engineer who is not an expert in geology to make the decision on where to drill for oil, having fed into the computer system a mass of complex data about the lie of the land in the area. The expert system will have been designed by experts to take into account a huge variety of data and go through the reasoning process and interrogation of data that the human expert would do. Expert systems can take a long time and be expensive to build, but once this investment has been made they can save enormous amounts and ensure that better decisions are taken by fewer and less qualified personnel.

Other applications of AI include ROBOTICS, speech/voice recognition, machine vision (simulating human vision), and Natural Language Processing (computers communicating in English for example).

AI has had and will increasingly have important economic and social consequences in decentralising decision-making and pushing it down to levels which may previously have been tightly controlled, as well as making it possible to use fewer employees. For example, the workers in an oil refinery who were previously 'operatives', doing what they were told by supervisors, can now use simple expert systems to control large sections of plant. One by-product can be that whole levels of management become unnecessary. See DELAYERING.

ALLFINANZ
Combination of banking and insurance services in one financial institution.

ALGORITHM
A procedure or set of rules to solve a problem. Usually describes a computer program but can be applied to human problem-solving.

ALLIANCE
See STRATEGIC ALLIANCE.

ALLOCATION
The allocation and attributing of overhead costs to products, usually inaccurately.

ALLOTMENT
Nothing to do with agriculture. Rather the process of allocating shares in a NEW ISSUE to shareholders who have applied for them, implying a scaling-down of the number asked for in the event of oversubscription.

ALLOTTED (ISSUED) SHARE CAPITAL
The amount of the AUTHORISED SHARE CAPITAL that has actually been issued to investors.

ALPHA COEFFICIENT, ALPHA
See CAPITAL ASSET PRICING MODEL.

ALPHA STOCK
The British name for a blue-chip share on the stock market. An alpha stock is in a big company and the shares are traded in volume every day.

ALTERNATE DIRECTOR
A person allowed to deputise for a given board director.

AMALGAMATION
Old-fashioned word for MERGER.

AMBULANCE STOCKS
Racy shares recommended by a broker to a client in the hope of making large gains, usually after the broker has recommended a set of poor perform-

ing shares. The ambulance trip will either restore the client-broker relationship to health or kill it.

AMORTIZATION

The amount deducted each year from the BOOK VALUE of an INTANGIBLE ASSET. Similar to DEPRECIATION, except that the latter applies to tangible fixed assets.

ANALYST

1. One of the modern breed of number crunchers inside a bank, stock broker, or commercial firm. The breed collect facts, analyse them (usually with the help of a computer and/or calculator) and make judgement about the value of companies, business STRATEGY, or the direction of markets. Useful if kept in the basement. 2. An executive whose mental orientation is driven by facts, analysis and logic: see TYPE TWO EXECUTIVE.

ANNUITANT

Person receiving an ANNUITY.

ANNUITY

An investment paying a predictable annual income, often until the investor dies.

ANSOFF, H IGOR (b. 1918)

Russian-American engineer, mathematician, military strategist and operations researcher who wrote the highly acclaimed *Corporate Strategy* in 1965. The book is quite readable and provides a model for deriving a corporate strategy. The model assumes that the purpose of a firm is to maximise long-term profitability (return on investment) and then gives a host of checklists and charts for deriving objectives, assessing SYNERGY between different parts of the firm (functions and businesses), appraising the firm's COMPETENCE profile and deciding how to expand (how to diversify, how to assess whether entry to an industry is likely to give the desired ROI, whether to acquire or go for organic growth, and how to weight alternatives taking into account a large number of highlighted factors). He stresses the need for a 'common thread' for all a company's businesses if it is to add value to them.

Rereading *Corporate Strategy* today is a disappointing exercise. The book has not aged well, the methodology overwhelms the substance, and it is difficult to gain much insight from the mechanistic procedures suggested. The concept of competitive advantage is only introduced systematically on page 161 (out of a total of 191 pages in my edition) and is then only given four-and-a-half pages. On the other hand the book's checklists are useful for analysts who want to know whether they have looked at everything they should, for example in conducting an industry analysis. The ANSOFF

MATRIX is definitely a useful framework for considering expansion into new areas.

Since 1965 Ansoff has written at least five full-length books on strategic management. The later Ansoff is much more contingent in his prescriptions.

ANSOFF MATRIX

As shown in Figure 1, this gives four options for increasing sales.

Box 1, selling more of existing products in existing markets, is a low risk, market share gain strategy. To be useful, this must specify how this objective is to be attained, for example by enlarging the sales force, increasing advertising or cutting price.

Box 2 implies product development to sell new (or modified) products to existing customers: fine as long as the firm has a good track record of new product development and provided the new products share enough costs and skills with the existing products, and do not face a very strong incumbent competitor (see also ADJACENT SEGMENT).

Figure 1 The Ansoff Matrix for business development

Box 3 takes existing products and sells them to new markets or customers. This is clearly sensible if the new markets can be cultivated at relatively little extra cost, but can be risky if a new market requires investment in fixed cost (for example, a new sales force), if the customers have different requirements, or if there are entrenched competitors.

Box 4 – new products to new markets – is the highest risk strategy: the segments being entered are not adjacent to the existing business and it is almost like starting a new business from scratch. The presumption is that Box 4 strategies are inherently unsound and should only be taken either in desperation or because there is a compelling short-term opportunity not being exploited by others.

ANTI-DUMPING

Government restrictions on imports (tariffs or quotas) to prevent goods being sold cheaper in export markets than in home markets. High-cost businessmen very often complain of dumping when in fact foreign producers have lower costs and can profitably export and sell below the cost for the home producer. When you hear the word 'dumping' there is a very good chance that the speaker's operations are grossly high cost.

ANTI-TRUST

American anti-monopoly legislations dating from 1890. Originally had beneficial effects in disrupting price rigging and anti-consumer behaviour. Now tends to prohibit market-share enhancement that would in many cases lower costs and displace high-cost competitors, to the benefit of consumers.

APOLLO

One of Charles HANDY's four GODS OF MANAGEMENT. In 1978 Handy made a breakthrough in thinking about organisational styles by gracing four typical ways of running companies with the names of Greek gods. Apollo represents 'role culture', being the god of order and rules. This CULTURE assumes that reason should prevail and that tasks can be parcelled out logically. An ORGANISATION CHART that has a series of boxes describing jobs and that is a classic pyramid represents 'Apollonian' thinking. Everyone knows their role and works on their delegated activities according to their JOB DESCRIPTION.

Apollo represents BUREAUCRACY in the pure sense invented by Max WEBER rather than the modern pejorative sense. The Apollo style can be the most efficient way of running firms operating in a stable and predictable environment. Everyone can be given their individual ACCOUNTABILITIES and a system like MANAGEMENT BY OBJECTIVES can ensure that individuals are treated fairly according to their performance rather than the personal opinion or liking of their bosses. Because responsibilities are clear and fixed, many people find the Apollo style easy to deal with, secure and stress-free.

Life insurance companies, monopolies, state industries, the civil service and local government are good examples of Apollo cultures. Private companies operating in slow-changing industries with protected market positions may also exemplify Apollo. This style is unlikely to be effective, however, where there is rapid technological or market change or where TEAMWORK is vital. Nor does it suit creative, restless or questioning individuals, or those who like the firm to be highly personal.

APPLICATIONS SOFTWARE

Computer programs tailored to particular uses, for example for accounts departments, personnel managers, schools etc. Useful and growing.

APPRAISAL

Process of assessing individuals and giving feedback on performance. A good appraisal system should work on a yearly or more frequent cycle and be a two-way process.

APPRENTICESHIP

Formal on-the-job vocational training for young people leading to a qualification in return for a period of low pay.

ARBITRAGE

1. Technically, the process whereby someone buys in one market while simultaneously (or shortly thereafter) selling at a higher price in another market, thereby making a profit and also ironing out MARKET IMPERFECTIONS. Examples would include a trader who notices that different stockbrokers are pricing the same share differently, a currency trader who can buy (say) South African Rands cheaply in America and sell them at a slightly higher price in Johannesburg, or someone who buys stock exchange futures and sells the underlying shares today. The difference in price is usually very small but sufficient to cover the transaction costs and, if the volume is high, return a nice profit. **2.** Used imprecisely to indicate any activity where a gain can be made through superior market knowledge or by bridging the gap between one person's perspective and another's. For example a merchant banker may refer to 'client arbitrage' if he knows that X will sell an asset at a lower price than Y will buy it: the banker will then arrange the deal and take a fee. This is not technically arbitrage, because the banker never owns the asset or pays out his own money, but is in common use. Arbitrage can also be a verb, used either technically or loosely, meaning to act as a middle-man or go-between.

ARBITRAGEUR

Someone who engages in ARBITRAGE, but especially a stock market operator who buys a block of shares in the hope of stimulating a TAKEOVER BID and selling out the stake at a substantial profit. In this latter sense the arbitrageur is engaging in a different and more ethically suspect practice than the trader who is merely smoothing MARKET IMPERFECTIONS by taking a small and instant profit. The more greedy type of arbitrageur is often called an 'arb' and fell into disrepute during the MERGER MANIA of the late 1980s, especially in the US. Those who have met real-life 'arbs' can testify that they are usually distasteful and egotistical, and often unethical, though dedicated adherents of capitalism may claim that they serve a useful social function by helping to remove incompetent management. See also GREENMAIL, an ethically indefensible practice engaged in by some 'arbs'.

ARBITRATION
The setting of industrial or legal disputes by an arbitrator, an expert and neutral third party.

ARGYRIS, CHRIS (b. 1923)
American ORGANISATION DEVELOPMENT guru and one of the first to stress the importance of matching the goals of the individual with those of the firm. Humanistic, rooted in psychology, rather academic but well worth reading.

ARMS-LENGTH PRICE
A normal commercial price which unrelated buyers and sellers would converge on. Normally used when a transaction takes place between two related parties (e.g. in the same firm) and usually also when a truly commercial price is difficult to establish. The phrase 'arms-length' should always arouse suspicion, because they may not be what they claim.

ARTEFACTS
The external manifestation of a firm's CULTURE, like Mars' white coats and time-clocks.

ARTICLES OF ASSOCIATION
Document laying down rules for running a company, rights of shareholders and duties of directors. Desperately boring but important in private companies: many shareholders have discovered that they are constrained from sensible commercial action (e.g. buying out a minority shareholder with whom they are in dispute) because of particular clauses in the articles.

ARTIFICIAL INTELLIGENCE
See AI.

'A' SHARES
Shares that receive dividends but have restricted or no voting rights. Increasingly rare.

ASSENTED SHARES

Shares which have accepted a TAKEOVER BID.

ASSET-BACKED SECURITY

When a financial institution issues a security backed by assets placed in trust, which provide comfort that interest and principal will be repaid.

ASSET COVER

A firm's ASSETS divided by its DEBT: hence the number of times debt is covered by assets.

ASSET MANAGEMENT

1. The business of financial institutions in managing other people's money.
2. Getting the best return from assets owned, whether by individuals, commercial firms or financial institutions.

ASSETS

Property, plant, buildings, raw materials, finished goods, cash or anything else of value owned by a business, and recorded on its BALANCE SHEET. Often classified into FIXED ASSETS which are for the firm's long term use and CURRENT ASSETS like raw materials that are of short term use.

ASSET STRIPPER

A generally pejorative term applied to an investor or manager who takes over a company and sells off assets, especially property, that are not essential for the business's core activities. Asset strippers of the pure variety first became common in the 1950s and 1960s, but are now less common in the USA and UK as managements have pre-empted takeovers by selling the most flagrant surplus assets and as the value of companies has risen to take account of the value of their assets. There is still theoretical scope for asset stripping in many European countries (Germany is a particularly fertile potential field) but the companies are often protected by family control against takeover. In the Anglo-Saxon countries the asset stripper has evolved into the 'break-up merchant' or ARBITRAGEUR who may take over a CONGLOMERATE and sell off unrelated subsidiaries, thus realising cash by selling whole companies rather than individual assets. In contrast to the pure asset stripper, his more modern cousin will often seek to cut costs in the companies that are retained, eliminating surplus labour in particular. See also BREAK-UP VALUE.

ASSET STRUCTURE

The breakdown of assets in a BALANCE SHEET by category, which will help determine whether there is scope for further LEVERAGE (GEARING).

ASSET TURN

Also called 'asset turnover', 'asset utilisation' and 'ratio of sales to capital employed'. The ratio of a firm's revenues to its assets and therefore a measure of efficiency if compared to other firms of a similar ilk. A high asset turn does not necessarily indicate that a firm is efficient: it is a useful diagnostic measure but not a sufficient proof of virtue.

ASSET VALUE PER SHARE

The total net value of a firm's ASSETS less its LIABILITIES, divided by the number of shares. When compared with the share price, it can indicate the extent to which the company is being valued on its assets rather than its earnings: it can sometimes explain why a company may be on a high PRICE EARNINGS RATIO, if there is strong asset support. The usefulness of this measure is, however, diluted by two considerations: (1) the value shown in the balance sheet may not be an adequate reflection of the market value or the BREAK-UP VALUE; and (2) most companies are valued by analysts and investors much more on their earnings than on their asset position.

ASSOCIATES

1. Employees, members of a firm, 2. See ASSOCIATED COMPANY.

ASSOCIATED COMPANY, ASSOCIATED UNDERTAKING, ASSOCIATE

Company where there is a significant cross-shareholding, either directly or via a parent. Generally applies to a shareholding of 20–49% in the associate, which is enough to give the company holding the stake influence but not control.

AT BEST

When an investor tells his stockbroker to buy or sell shares at the best available market price, without setting a minimum or maximum to be paid. Often results in the broker executing the deal without excessive effort to obtain the best price.

ATHENA

One of Charles HANDY's four GODS OF MANAGEMENT, representing a task-oriented way of running companies. Athena was a young warrior goddess, the patron saint of craftsmen and explorers. Athena firms have a problem-solving CULTURE, are not hierarchical, respect professional expertise and encourage TEAMWORK, creativity and energy. They tend to work in project teams which may be dismantled once a problem is solved and be reassembled, perhaps with different membership, to attack a new challenge. The teams are like guerilla commando units rather than massed armies.

Athena firms are most appropriate to 'knowledge industries' and professional firms, to times of expansion, and to people who think for themselves and can tolerate ambiguity and rapid change. The Athena culture may fit badly and be vulnerable if a firm hits a crisis, stops growing or if the work becomes more routine. See also ADHOCRACY, which has many elements of Athena.

ATM (automatic teller machine)
Bank cash machine, often called 'hole in the wall'

ATTITUDE SURVEY
1. Research on what employees think about a company, its managers and its policies, and the extent to which they are committed to the firm. Can be a very useful diagnostic tool when trying to change a firm's culture and increase the extent of employee identification with it. **2.** Research on customers' and potential customers' attitudes towards a firm and its products (often called 'attitude research').

AUDIT
1. External inspection of a company's books by a firm of independent accountants (the AUDITORS) to see that they give a TRUE AND FAIR VIEW of the business. **2.** by extension, any systematic inspection of a particular aspect of a firm's operations, even if carried out by internal staff: see for example INTERNAL AUDIT, ENVIRONMENTAL AUDIT and HUMAN RESOURCES AUDIT.

AUDIT TRAIL
1. Originally used by accountants to denote the primary documents like invoices and ledger entries that can be used to check a firm's accounts. **2.** More interestingly, used by any analyst to indicate a clear set of documents from which it is apparent what data have been used to draw particular findings, so that assumptions can be checked easily and if necessary adjustments made in the light of newer or more accurate data.

AUFSICHTSRAT
German supervisory board; the executive board is the *VORSTAND*.

AUTHORISED SHARE CAPITAL
The total number of shares the directors of a company have been authorised by the shareholders to issue. Contrast ALLOTED SHARE CAPITAL.

AUTHORITARIAN MANAGEMENT
Style which relies upon formal power, reward and punishment, and see little value in consultation or EMPOWERMENT. See THEORY X. Very out of fashion and generally only mentioned in order to condemn it. Has merit in emergencies and in simple, predictable businesses.

AUTOMATIC TELLER MACHINE
See ATM.

AUTONOMY
Independent self-determination for an individual or a group or division within a firm, associated respectively with respect for the individual and DECENTRALISATION. Not necessarily a good thing if it encourages lack of contribution to the whole.

AVA (Activity Value Analysis)
A cost-cutting process that looks at the value being provided by any activity. A precursor of BPR (Business Process Re-Engineering).

AVAL
European guarantee (usually by a bank) to pay a BILL OF EXCHANGE or other such trade finance document.

AVERAGE COSTING
A term coined by the Boston Consulting Group to indicate inadequately accurate costing systems that average costs across products or services taking in reality quite different amounts of cost, especially indirect and over-head costs. For example, a SPECIAL or one-off product for a particular customer may cause unusual levels of cost in terms of specification, selling, quality control and so forth yet when the costing is done be charged no more for these elements of cost than standard products. It is almost always true that traditional cost-centre-based methods of costing understate the cost of top-of-the-line and special products and services and overstate the cost of high-volume standard products. This can be very damaging if (as usual) it leads to AVERAGE PRICING. The way in which average costing and pricing works is illustrated in Figure 2. See also ACTIVITY-BASED COSTING, which is a good way to avoid the perils of average costing.

AVERAGE MANAGEMENT
Managing by averages, providing what the average consumer wants, rather than what is wanted by each market SEGMENT or local market. A sure route to failure.

AVERAGE PRICING
Traditional costing systems understate the cost of producing SPECIAL or one-off products. This AVERAGE COSTING leads to average pricing, which as the name suggests means failing to charge enough of a price premium for top-of-the-line or special products, and conversely charging too much for standard products (because the prices of the two types of product are aver-aged rather than sharply differentiated).

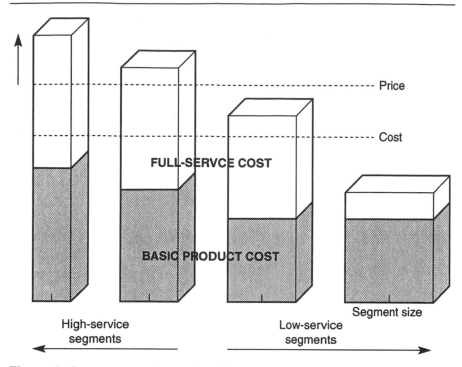

Figure 2 Average costing and pricing

Average pricing is still rife, to a much greater extent than most managers realise. They may charge more for higher specification products, but rarely enough to reflect the real (but hidden) extra cost. For example, a firm making coin mechanisms for vending machines made a special one for the London tube (metro/subway) system. In tendering for the business the firm put in what they considered a very high price, so that the managers believed the work to be highly profitable. After the contract had been completed, a consulting study using ABC ANALYSIS (activity-based costing) showed that it had been highly unprofitable, because of the extra time of engineers and service people needed. 'If we had understood then about average costing and average pricing,' the managers concluded, 'we would have charged 30 per cent more for the work.'

Average pricing is dangerous, not just because of losses on special products, but because it can also lead to loss of market share through over-pricing on the high-volume, standard products. A producer who just concentrates on the latter, 'commodity' business may be able to have a much lower overhead structure, lower prices, and higher profits. Over time the specialist may gain market share of this profitable business and leave the high-overhead, broad-line producer with a higher share of the unprofitable business. If costs are not correctly allocated and prices set accordingly the commercial consequences can be dire.

AVERAGING, AVERAGING DOWN, AVERAGING UP

Buying more shares after they fall or rise in value, producing an average cost closer to the current market price. Averaging down is usually a mistake made by novice investors: more often than not, the price continues falling, and the investor is throwing good money after bad. Averaging up is less practised but often a very good idea.

B

BACKLOG
Unfulfilled orders or work that has piled up.

BACK-TO-BACK LOAN
1. A loan issued in parallel with another, so that the identity of the seller is concealed from the buyer in a credit arrangement. **2.** A loan where there is no real risk because another party is guaranteeing it.

BACK-UP
Duplicates of computer files to guard against their mysterious disappearance.

BACKWARDATION
1. When a product's price for immediate delivery is higher than for future delivery. **2.** When stock prices are in turmoil and certain brokers' OFFER prices are lower than other brokers' BID prices, enabling the very quick-footed investor to make an instant profit.

BACKWARD INTEGRATION
The process whereby a company competes with its suppliers by setting up as a producer earlier in the VALUE CHAIN than it had previously done: for example, a retailer deciding to manufacture some of the products he sells. Backward integration is usually bad news for suppliers. The backward integrator has a guaranteed market for his production, and therefore his risk in investing in a manufacturing facility is lower than for a merchant supplier. Moreover, the backward integrator usually focuses on a few high-volume products where he can attain a low-cost position, leaving the non-integrated producers to supply lower volume and often less profitable products. Backward integration is not always a sensible strategy, as the skills required are often very different, but it should always be considered.

BAD BUSINESSES
Those that have such weak strategic positions and/or irredeemably poor operational performance that they will never be capable of being turned around, however talented the new management and however much cash is aimed at them. Bad businesses have usually been starved of cash and good management and is too late to restore them to health. Human nature often refuses to recognise that a loss-maker is a bad business, thus throwing good money after bad. When faced with a loss-maker, always ask: Is this simply a bad business? See also TURNAROUNDS.

BAD DEBT

Money owed by a customer that is written off, that is, it is assumed that it will never be paid.

BALANCED BOOK

When a trader balances sales and purchases so that he is indifferent whether the market goes up or down. Also called a SQUARE BOOK. See LONG POSITION.

BALANCED MANAGEMENT SKILLS

The idea that management must ensure that all functions such as marketing, operations and finance are in balance to meet customer needs, and that one function is not relied on and the others neglected. Frank Cokayne quotes the example of the professional football market in the UK, where millions of pounds are paid for the transfer of players, yet minimum acceptable standards of organisation, seating, catering and toilet facilities are not met at the football grounds. If a relatively small proportion of funds were diverted by the industry as a whole from transfer to the facilities available to spectators, the available market would be greatly increased. This would ensure a BALANCED PRODUCT OFFERING.

BALANCED PRODUCT OFFERING

Marketeers and managers must ensure that a product package meets reasonable standards under three headings: (i) functional properties (performance/ design/value); (ii) availability (accessibility/presentation/pleasant environment); and (iii) identity (brand presentation/recognition/ perception/meeting expectations). In the entry immediately above the example of the UK professional football market is given: it clearly fails on the availability criterion.

BALANCE SHEET

Statement of a company's ASSETS and the CLAIMS over those assets at a particular date. The balance sheet is the most important financial statement (even more important than the PROFIT & LOSS STATEMENT), although wreathed in mystery for many practising businessmen. The importance of understanding balance sheets cannot be overstated. It is actually not that difficult either, despite accountants' restrictive practices that make it appear so.

A balance sheet is just a list of a firm's assets and liabilities together with their value. An example is given in Figure 3.

Fixed assets of just over £4.2m are the assets the company uses on a long-term, continuing basis: in this case the freehold of the factory and all the machinery in it. The current assets are things expected to be turned into cash within one year, mainly WORK IN PROGRESS, ACCOUNTS RECEIVABLE and STOCKS. The total or 'gross' assets are these two categories together, £6.653m in the example.

From these gross assets must be deducted the claims on the firm: what it owes. The current liabilities in this case are the firm's overdraft and its ACCOUNTS PAYABLE. The long-term liabilities are in this case amounts owed

```
                    CREST FOODS PLC

            Balance sheet at 31 December ,1994

                                    £000
    Assets
        Fixed assets                4,215
        Current assets              2,438
        Total assets                          6,653

    Liabilities
        Current liabilities        (2,005)
        Long-term liabilities      (2,500)
        Total liabilities                    (4,505)

    Net assets                                2,148


    Shareholders' equity

        Capital invested             250
        Retained profit            1,898

        Total shareholders' equity            2,148
```

Figure 3 Balance sheet

to a bank in the form of medium-term loans. Once the total liabilities are deducted, it can be seen that the firm has NET ASSETS of £1.148m. Of this amount, £250,000 was put into the firm originally by its shareholders as share capital, and the rest, £898,000, is the retained profit made by the firm in its history to date, after paying taxes and dividends.

It is useful to display a balance sheet in a graphical form, as in Figure 4.

BALLOON LOAN, BALLOON PAYMENT
A loan where interest and repayments are made in large, irregular amounts ('balloons') towards the end of a loan's life, instead of in regular, small instalments.

BANANAGRAM
Popular name for a very useful OPPORTUNITY/VULNERABILITY MATRIX, because the yellow-coloured central band resembles a banana. See this entry.

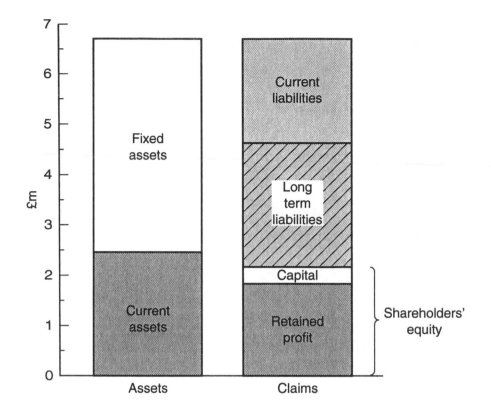

Figure 4 Crest Foods Plc, Graphical Balance Sheet at 31 December 1994
Source: Rice, Anthony (1993) *Accounts Demystified*, Institute of Management/Pitman
Publishing (1993)

BANKER'S DRAFT
A cheque guaranteed by a bank, enabling instant payment.

BANKROLL
To finance a project.

BANKRUPT
See BANKRUPTCY.

BANKRUPTCY
When a person (the BANKRUPT) or firm cannot pay its debts and comes
under the control of a court.

BAR CODES

The small vertical lines on most grocery and some other consumer goods (about the size of a stamp) enabling the product to be scanned at the point of sale and automatically deducted from stock.

BARGAIN

A share transaction.

BARONS

Powerful heads of part of an organisation: usually the heads of a function, country, product area or division. Barons aim to maximise their power and keep their part of the firm (their BARONY) as independent as possible of the CENTRE and other baronies. Barons are a particularly marked feature of European firms, but are often found in US ones as well. Barons are a menace to the corporation and ought to be removed. See FEUDALISM and GLOCALISATION.

BARONY

See BARONS.

BARRIERS TO ENTRY

Obstacle making it difficult or impossible for competitors to enter a particular business SEGMENT. Barriers sometimes exist naturally but astute managers will try to raise these barriers and introduce new ones in order to restrict competition amongst their customers. It is worthwhile reflecting from time to time on what can be done to raise barriers, by examining a checklist of potential barriers (see Figure 5).

	Barrier to Entry	Comment
1.	Investment scale	**Building a bigger or better plant, service network or retail outlet** can discourage competitors from trying to compete with you, especially if your installed customer base means it would take longer for them to get the scale of business to cover the cost of the initial investment, or if your investment gives you a lower cost base than existing competitors
2.	Branding	**Making your product or service synonymous with superior and consistent quality,** whether or not a 'brand' in the conventional sense is used
3.	Service	**Providing such a high level of service** that customers will be naturally loyal and not want to switch to competitors
4.	Building in 'Cost to Switch'	**Locking customers in,** for example by promotional schemes such as 'Air Miles' where customers are saving up for incentives and will not want to switch to another supplier, or by giving OVER-RIDING

Figure 5 Barriers to entry

25

Barrier to Entry	Comment
	DISCOUNTS once a level of sales has been triggered, or even by supplying equipment (such as freezer cabinets for newsagents selling icecream) which can be withdrawn if a competitor's product is bought, or in professional services by knowing so much about a client's business that it would take another supplier too long to 'come up to speed'
5. **Locking up distribution channels**	**Buying or having a special relationship with distributors** that makes it difficult or impossible for a new supplier to get his product to the ultimate consumer: a policy followed for many years with great success, for example, in petrol retailing, where the superior siting of major oil companies' service stations helped them sell their oil
6. **Locking up sources of raw material supply**	**Obtaining the best (or all) the product from its source** either by owning the raw material (as with many large dairy companies) or by having a special relationship with suppliers, or by paying them more
7. **Property/ Location**	**Obtaining the best sites** can be crucial in businesses as diverse as oil production and retailing. It is worth asking from time to time whether the desired location might change in the future and then moving to lock up suitable new sites, as for example in edge of town/out of town superstores
8. **Expertise/hiring the best people**	**Knowing how best to do something that is important to customers** is an under-rated barrier. The key thing is to locate the functional expertise that is most important and then make sure that your firm is better than any other at this. For example, in mass market retailing the buying and merchandising function is crucial, and Marks & Spencer has a huge advantage because it has the best buyers and best relationships with suppliers. Hiring in the best people available to an industry can be a winning tactic, although only if the people can fit into the culture or the culture can be adapted to make best use of the newcomers
9. **Proprietary expertise/ patents**	**The logical extension to 8 above** in many businesses is a patent and in some businesses such as pharmaceuticals patents are hugely important in leading to much higher margins than would otherwise apply. Intellectual property can apply to a surprising range of businesses and it is worth checking whether anything your firm possesses can be patented
10. **Lowest cost producer**	**One of the very best barriers is to be able to produce a particular product or service for a particular market at a lower cost than competitors**, usually by having larger scale in that SEGMENT than competitors and defending that relative advantage ferociously. To be most effective the cost advantage should be passed through in the form of lower prices, although spending more than competitors can match in terms of advertising, sales force or research can also be effective ways of using a cost (and margin) advantage to build barriers

Figure 5 Continued

Barrier to Entry	Comment
11. Competitive response	**Making it clear to competitors that you will defend 'your patch'**, if necessary by 'crazy' actions, is a very effective barrier to entry. If a competitor ignores the warnings and enters, the response must be immediate and crushing, for example by dropping prices to their potential customers
12. Secrecy	**Sometimes a profitable market is relatively small** and its existence or profitability may not be known by competitors. **Keeping these segments well hidden from competitors** can be very important, if necessary by obscuring or playing down their importance to your firm. Conversely, someone seeking to enter a new market should invest properly in information about all potential customers.

Figure 5 Continued

BARRIERS TO EXIT

Exit barriers are undesirable forces that keep too many competitors in a market, and lead to OVER-CAPACITY and low profitability, because it is thought too expensive for a firm to leave the business. Barriers to exit may be real or imagined, economic or illusory, as Figure 6 illustrates. In general, barriers to exit are given too much thought and barriers to entry too little.

Barrier to Exit	Comment
1. Redundancy costs	**The cost of paying off employees** may be very heavy and much larger than the annual loss in a business. If a company is strapped for cash, it may find it easier to carry on in the short-term and hope that others in the business will remove capacity first, thus postponing and perhaps removing the need to spend cash laying off the workforce. More of a problem in the US than most developing countries, more in the UK than the US, and more in most Continental countries than the UK, because of higher statutory redundancy provisions
2. Investment write-offs	**Exiting from a business may cause a write-off of expensive plant and machinery that can only be used in that business.** This leads to a feeling that the investment is being wasted and to a large one-time loss going through the PROFIT AND LOSS STATEMENT and a reduction of net assets in the BALANCE SHEET. This reason is, however, usually a very bad one for not exiting from a lossmaking

Figure 6 Barriers to exit

Barrier to Entry	Comment
	business, since it refers to paper entries and not to industrial reality. A business which ought to have a write-off but does not is no more valuable, and probably less valuable, than a business that bites the bullet. The stock market understands this, and often large losses and write-offs from exiting a business lead to an increase in share price, as investors are relieved by management's realism and look forward to the elimination of losses in the business
3. **Real disengagement costs**	Leaving a business may sometimes lead to real, one-off costs other than labour ones; for example, a quarry may have to pay to restore the countryside to its previous glory, or a shop may have to carry out improvements before leaving. Recently one of the most serious disengagement costs has been long leases on property which cannot be re-let at rates as high as the business is paying, and which would still need to be paid once the business has closed
4. **Shared costs**	Often leaving one loss-making business is difficult because it would leave another profit-making business with higher costs, where these are shared between the two. For example, a factory may make two products and have shared overhead (and sometimes labour) costs, or a sales force may sell two products to the same customers. Very often, however, shared costs are an excuse for inaction. The proper answer, wherever possible (and however painful) is to slim down the overheads for the profitable business to what is necessary for that business after exiting the unprofitable one
5. **Customers require a 'package'**	**Customers sometimes value the provision of multiple products by the same supplier** and would be reluctant or unwilling to buy from one that just supplies the profitable products. For instance, a supermarket that refused to sell loss leaders such as baked beans or milk might find itself short of customers. Very often, however, this claim is a spurious excuse, and customers would continue to buy a narrower product range provided this has a real advantage to them
6. **Non-economic reasons**	Barriers to exit are very often openly non-economic, as when a government or trade union requires the business to be kept open and has the power to enforce this. More covert non-economic reasons include management ego or emotional attachment to a business, fear (normally unfounded or exaggerated) that it will affect a business's image and relationships in the trade, or simply opting for the line of least resistance. Non-economic reasons are increasingly becoming discredited, although they can work to your advantage when you are less sentimental than your competitors or when they face less economically numerate governments

Figure 6 Continued

BARTER

To exchange goods or services for others rather than for cash.

BASIS POINT

One hundredth of a percentage point: for example, the difference in yield between an investment paying 3.5% and 3.99% is 49 basis points (99 minus 50).

BASIS PRICE

The price at which a PUT or CALL OPTION can be exercised. Also called the EXERCISE PRICE or STRIKE PRICE.

BASKET, BASKET OF CURRENCIES

A mix of (usually major) currencies used to create artificial, but often useful, new currencies. See SDR.

BATCH

Group of items produced in one go.

BATCH PROCESSING

Production of discrete job lots rather than continuous flow production.

BATCH SIZE

The number of items produced in each batch. Optimum batch size depends on the level of demand, the SET-UP COST, and the stock-keeping cost.

BAYESIAN PROBABILITY

A formula invented 200 years ago by Thomas Bayes and useful for calculating a new probability estimate based on recent experience.

BCG (the Boston Consulting Group)

US-originated international consulting firm and the most important contributor to ideas on business STRATEGY in the last 30 years. Founded in 1964 by Bruce HENDERSON, BCG went through its most creative period from about 1967 to 1973, when it invented the BCG MATRIX (more properly, the Growth/Share Matrix) and the Experience Curve. More recently it has innovated with TIME-BASED COMPETITION and CUSTOMER RETENTION. BCG's ideas have been far more influential than any other consultancy and it has probably added more to our stock of useful knowledge about business than any business school or university. In my opinion only HANDY, OHMAE, PORTER and PETERS can rival HENDERSON and his successors at BCG in terms of cumulative insight given. See HENDERSON for an assessment of his legacy.

BCG MATRIX

The Boston Consulting Group BCG has invented several matrices, having consultants trained to think in terms of two-by-two displays, but the most famous and useful one is the GROWTH/SHARE MATRIX, invented in

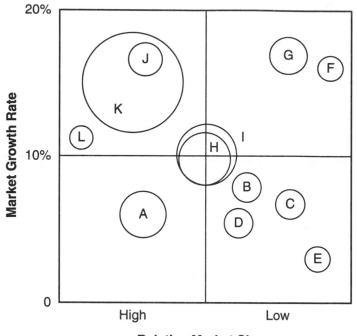

Figure 7 Engulf & Devour Plc, Growth/Share Matrix

the late 1960s and still of great importance today. It measures market growth and relative market share for all the business a particular firm has. An example is shown in Figure 7.

It is important to define the axes properly. The horizontal axis is of fundamental importance and measures the market share that a firm has in a particular business *relative to the share enjoyed in that business by its largest competitor*. Thus if Engulf & Devour Plc has a 40% market share in Business A and its nearest competitor has a 10% market share, its relative market share ('RMS') is 400% or 4 times (written as 4.0x). In Business B, Engulf & Devour may have a 5% share and the leading competitor 10%, in which case Engulf & Devour's relative market share is 50% or 0.5x. Note that absolute market share (for example, 20% of a market) means little, because it could mean a relative market share of 0.33% (if the dominant competitor has 60% market share), or of 10.0x (if the rest of the market is very fragmented and the next largest player only has 2%).

The vertical axis is the growth rate of the market in which the business competes. Much confusion surrounds the precise definition of this market growth rate. The correct definition is the *expected future annual growth rate* (over the next five years) *in volume* (units of production) *of the market as a whole*, not of the particular Engulf & Devour business.

Before going on, it is important to understand the reasons why BCG and I think that the axes are significant. The relative market share is key because a business that is larger than its competitors (has a high relative market share, over 1.0x) *ought to have lower costs, or higher prices, or both, and therefore higher profitability* than a competitor in that business with a lower share. This is generally, although not always, true, as confirmed by data bases such as the PIMS studies.

It is also logical: a business with higher volume ought to be able to spread its fixed costs over more units, and therefore have lower fixed and overhead costs, as well as make better use of any expensive machinery or people that are the best for that particular business. The higher share business may also be able to charge a higher price, either because it has the best brand or because it has the best distribution or simply because it is the preferred choice of most people. Since price minus cost equals profit, the higher share competitor should have the highest margins, or be ploughing back his advantage in the form of extra customer benefits that will reinforce his market share advantage.

Note that we say that the higher share competitor *ought* to have lower costs or higher prices. It does not necessarily follow, since he may squander his potential advantage by inefficiency, sharing costs with unprofitable products, or by having poorer customer service than a rival. Where the higher share player does not have profits higher than competitors there is usually an unstable competitive relationship which can create both opportunity and vulnerability in that market (see the OPPORTUNITY/VULNERABILITY MATRIX).

In some cases having a higher share of a business does not confer any benefit or potential benefit, for example where a one-man plumbing business faces a ten-man plumbing business, and the costs of labour are the same for everyone. Many people have claimed that the importance of market share, and the value of the Growth/Share Matrix, have been greatly overstated, and produce examples of cases where larger businesses are *less* profitable than smaller businesses, or where there is no systematic difference in profitability according to scale. On detailed examination, however, there are few individual business segments where it is not or cannot be a real advantage to be larger, all other things being equal. The qualification in the last phrase is absolutely crucial: relative market share is not the only influence on profitability, and it may be overwhelmed by different competitors' operating skills or strategies or random influences on profitability.

One of the major causes of confusion is that businesses are often not defined properly, in a sufficiently disaggregated way, before measuring market share. The niche player who focuses on a limited product range or customer base is playing in just one segment from the broad line supplier, who may be playing in several segments and may actually not be very large in any one segment despite appearing to have a high overall market share. For example, a national supermarket chain may be bigger than competitors who have regional chains, but the relevant basis of competition may be local scale and customer awareness. See BUSINESS SEGMENT and SEGMENTATION for the importance of correct business definition and some hints on how to do it.

If businesses are defined properly, the higher share competitor should have an advantage at least nine times out of ten. It therefore follows that the further to the left a business is on the BCG Matrix, the stronger it should be.

What about the vertical axis: the growth rate of the market? BCG claimed that there was a real difference between high growth businesses (where demand is growing at 10% or more) and lower growth ones, because of greater fluidity in the former: that is, if the market is growing fast, there is more opportunity to gain market share. This is logical, both because more new business is up for grabs, and because competitors will react much more vigorously to defend their absolute share (to avoid a loss of turnover) than to defend loss of relative share, which they may not even notice in a fast changing market.

Having understood these points, we can go on to characterise the four quadrants of the BCG Matrix (see Figure 8).

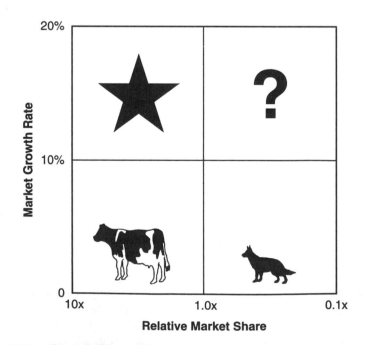

Figure 8 The Growth/Share Matrix four quadrants

The bottom left-hand box contains the CASH COWS (also called GOLD MINES in some early versions of the matrix: in many ways a better name). These businesses have high relative market share (they are by definition market leaders) and therefore ought to be profitable. They are very valuable and should be protected at all costs. They throw off a lot of cash, which can be reinvested in the business, used elsewhere in the business portfolio, used to buy other businesses, or paid out to shareholders.

The top left box comprises STARS: high relative market share businesses in high growth markets. These are very profitable but may need a lot of cash to maintain their position. This cash should be made available. Whatever it takes to hold or gain share in star businesses should be undertaken. If they hold RMS, star businesses will become cash cows when the market growth slows down, and therefore hugely valuable over a long time. But if star businesses lose relative market share, as they are often allowed to do, they will end up as DOGS and be of limited value.

The top right box holds QUESTION-MARKS (sometimes called WILDCATS): low RMS positions but in high growth markets. In this case 'question mark' is a very good description of the business, since it has an uncertain future, and the decision on whether to invest in the business is both important and difficult. If a question-mark does not improve its relative market share – that is, if it remains a follower – it will end life as a DOG. On the other hand, if the volatility that market growth bestows is used and investment made in a question-mark to drive it into a leadership position, the business will migrate to being a star (profitable) and ends its days as a cash cow (very profitable and very cash positive). The problem is that question-mark businesses very often turn into CASH TRAPS, as money can be invested without any guarantee (and in some cases much chance) of attaining a leadership position. A business that is invested in heavily without ever attaining market leadership (like much of the British computer industry) will simply be an investment in failure and a gross waste of money.

The bottom right box is the DOG kennel. Dogs are low relative market share positions in low growth businesses. The theory therefore says that they should not be very profitable and should not be able to gain share to migrate into cash cows. Given that the majority of most firm's businesses may be in this box, this is not a very cheerful notion.

In fact, the greatest weakness in the BCG theory relates to dogs, largely because of this fatalism. The entry later on DOGS puts the case for their defence and stresses the ways in which dogs can often be made valuable parts of a firm's business portfolio. Briefly, dogs *can* migrate into cash cows, by re-segmenting the business or simply by having greater customer responsiveness than the market leader. Even if leadership is not possible, it is usually worthwhile to improve market share position within the dog category. A business with a relative market share of 0.x (70% of the leader) may be quite profitable, highly cash positive, and quite different from a business with an RMS of only 0.3x (30% of the leader).

Nevertheless, it may be true that there is limited room for manoeuvre with dog businesses, and they will generally be less attractive than stars or cash cows.

BCG superimposed on the Growth/Share Matrix a theory of cash management (sometimes confusingly called PORTFOLIO MANAGEMENT) which is intriguing and makes some useful points, although it is also somewhat flawed. The theory looks at the cash characteristics of each of the quadrants (Figure 9).

BCG's theory then came up with an hierarchy of uses of cash, numbered from 1 to 4 in their order of priority (Figure 10).

1. The best use of cash, we can agree, is to defend cash cows. They should not need to use cash very often, but if investment in a new factory or technology is required, it should be made unstintingly.

2. We can also agree that the next call on cash should normally be in stars. These will need a great deal of investment to hold (or gain) relative market share.

3. The trouble begins here, with BCG's third priority, to take money from cash cows and invest in question-marks. The bastardised version of the theory stressed this cash flow in particular. BCG countered by stressing that investment in question-marks should be selective, confined to those cases where there was a real chance of attaining market leadership. With this qualification, BCG's point is sensible.

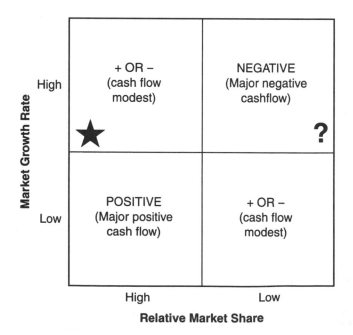

Figure 9 The Growth/Share Matrix cash characteristics

4. The lowest priority was investment in dogs, which BCG said should be minimal or even negative, if they were run for cash. This may be a sensible prescription, but the problem is that the dog kennel may contain a large range of breeds with different qualities, and a differentiated cash strategy is generally required within the dog kennel.

One real weakness of the BCG cash management theory, however, as BCG came to realise, was the assumption that the portfolio had to be in balance in respect of cash on an annual or three year basis. In fact, the cash invested in the overall business portfolio does *not* have to equal the cash generated. Surplus cash can be invested outside of the existing portfolio, either by acquiring new businesses, by entering them from scratch, or by reducing debt or giving cash back to the shareholders. Conversely, if a business needs to invest more cash (for example, in an important and cash-guzzling star) than the business portfolio is generating, it should go out and raise the cash from bankers and/or shareholders to fund the cash gap. The business portfolio should not be thought of as a closed system.

The second major weakness of BCG views on cash, and one not fully realised until much later, was the implicit assumption that *all* businesses should be managed from the CENTRE in a cashbox-plus-strategic-control way. See MANAGEMENT STYLES for a refutation of this view. BCG's theory

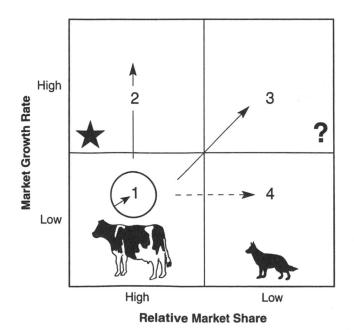

Figure 10 How to use the cash

was immensely attractive to chairmen and chief executives seeking a sensible role for the Centre, and probably did a great deal more good than harm, but it is only a small minority of businesses that are actually run in this way. Indeed, the recent work by GOOLD and CAMPBELL largely divides businesses into those that are run by FINANCIAL CONTROL and those that follow STRATEGIC CONTROL or STRATEGIC PLANNING. These are two very different approaches, the former decentralised, the latter more centralised, and it is difficult to combine the two styles, as BCG's approach assumed. Perhaps, in the future, someone will devise a method of control which does incorporate the strong points of both styles, but it will take much more than a two-by-two matrix to realise this vision.

The BCG Matrix marked a major contribution to management thinking. From the mid to late 1970s BCG tended to retreat too much under the weight of critical comment, and the matrix is not much used today. It is well overdue for a revival. Anyone who tries to apply it thoughtfully to his or her business will learn a lot during the process.

BDI (Brand Development Index)

BDI measures the penetration of a product in a particular region relative to its penetration in a (country) market as a whole. If IBM has 35% of its French sales in the Paris region and that region contains only 25% of the population, then the BDI for that region will be 140 (35 divided by 25 times 100%). The index can help to identify areas (for example, provincial France) where distribution is patchy and where improved distribution could be expected to lead to greater sales.

BDP (Best Demonstrated Practice)

BDP is a form of BENCHMARKING which compares the cost and output performance of one part of an organisation with performance elsewhere in the firm. A very valuable technique that has helped to take out billions of pounds of cost in Britain and elsewhere in the past 15 years.

BEAR

A stock market analyst or investor who expects the market to fall. One who holds the opposite view is a BULL.

BEARER SECURITY

A bond or stock certificate that does not have to be registered in an owner's name and is as good as cash (and equally vulnerable to theft).

BEAR HUG

An approach made to a company indicating that a BID is about to be made.

BEAR MARKET

Period during which the stock market falls or stagnates.

BEAR POSITION

Selling shares, currency or commodities short, that is, selling goods not possessed in the hope that the market will fall and the goods can be bought at a lower price and then delivered to the original buyer, thus making a profit. Expensive if the market rises instead of falling.

BEAUTY CONTEST

A competition for business whereby two or more suppliers of professional services are invited to make a proposal. Also sometimes used when two rival trade unions are attempting to gain recognition from an employer.

BED AND BREAKFASTING

Selling shares and then buying them back the following day or a few days later, usually to create a tax loss or utilise a tax break.

BEHAVIOUR STANDARDS

The policies and behaviour patterns that underpin a firm's distinctive COMPETENCES and its value system. One of the four elements (PURPOSE, STRATEGY, VALUES and BEHAVIOUR STANDARDS) that comprise a firm's MISSION. See MISSION and VALUES.

BELBIN, R M

Important British academic whose pioneering work on TEAMWORK (in his 1981 book, *Management Teams*) came to two key conclusions:

1. that teams composed of the brightest and most accomplished managers did not perform anywhere near the best; they suffered from 'too many cooks', and
2. that the most effective teams, especially when change is rapid, require eight different roles:

   - the CHAIRMAN, a sound, balanced, articulate co-ordinator who listens well and draws the whole group in
   - the SHAPER, an impatient, outgoing spur to action, who gets everyone going
   - the PLANT, the most fertile source of brilliant new ideas, but also an introvert who will switch off if not called upon and listened to
   - the MONITOR-EVALUATOR, the cynic of the group, a cold fish who is the analyst clutching a calculator, taking data and dissecting them, and spotting logical flaws
   - the RESOURCE-INVESTIGATOR, the popular networker, reporting on ideas from elsewhere and bringing in new contacts: the salesman, diplomat and introducer
   - the COMPANY WORKER who organises what needs to be done, allocates tasks and co-ordinates the admin

- the TEAM WORKER, the glue binding the team together, unassertive, supportive, popular and collaborative
- the COMPLETE FINISHER who follows through and ensures that everyone meets their deadlines

BELLS AND WHISTLES

Product features added on to PLAIN VANILLA, basic products, to make them more attractive. For example, an investment trust may issue ordinary shares with detachable WARRANTS that can be sold separately.

BELLWEATHER

A share in a BLUE CHIP COMPANY that usually can be relied upon to move in the same direction as the market.

BELONGING

An important consumer proposition for branded goods: buy Brand Y and you will belong to a 'club' you want to belong to. Heinz has a long track record in exploiting belonging, as in 'A million housewives every day open a can of beans and say "Beanz means Heinz".'

BELOW-THE-LINE PROMOTION

Activities such as PR, mail order, point-of-sale promotions, demonstrations or discounts targeted at individuals rather than a mass audience. May or may not involve an advertising or other specialist agency. Contrast ABOVE-THE-LINE PROMOTION.

BENCHMARK

Originally used in relation to computers to mean a standard set of computer programs used to measure computer output and speed. Now used much more widely to mean the product of benchmarking, that is, a measure of productivity of one department or activity compared to that achieved in other operating units or organisations. See BENCHMARKING.

BENCHMARK GOVERNMENT BONDS

Bonds that are typical or highly traded and that give an indication of price changes for bonds of that particular nationality generally.

BENCHMARKING

One of the key management words of the 1990s, although relying on techniques developed over the past 30 years, benchmarking is the detailed study of productivity, quality and value in different departments and activities in relation to performance elsewhere. The basic idea is to take or build up a DATABASE of relevant performance drawn up from looking at similar activities in other parts of the firm and in other firms, and compare the performance of the unit being reviewed with the range of experience elsewhere. A very simple example would be to compare the number of words and number of errors made by copy typists in one department within a firm with comparable performance elsewhere in other departments and with average performance in other firms. If one department was substantially below the average, it ought to be possible to find ways of raising the performance to that level.

Arthur Andersen and other accounting and consulting organisations offer ready-made benchmarking databases (available in Arthur Andersen's case on a CD-ROM) which enable instant comparison of any activity with their own database, drawn from a huge research effort. Such comparisons are usually helpful but never conclusive, because most tasks are much more complicated and difficult to compare than the copy typist example above.

In most cases benchmarks need to examined on a basis tailored to an individual firm and bearing in mind the particular objectives of the study. There are three different techniques that can be used in benchmarking:

1. **Best Demonstrated Practice** (see BDP), a technique used successfully for the last 15 years, is the comparison of performance by units within one firm. For example, the sales per square foot of toothpaste in a chemists in Leeds can be compared with the same statistic for the Huddersfield store within the same chain, as can the unit cost of electricity, security, or any other cost item cut any way that is relevant. BDP usually throws up large variances, some of which can be explained by lack of comparability, but much of which is due to superior techniques or simply greater efficiency at one site. That site can then be used as a challenge to lever up all other sites' performance.

2. **Relative Cost Position** (see RCP): RCP analysis looks at each element of the COST STRUCTURE (e.g. manufacturing labour) per dollar of sales in firm X compared to the same thing in competitor Y. Good RCP analysis is very hard to do but very valuable, as much for its insight into competitors' strategies as for cost reduction.

3. **Best Related Practice** (see BRP) is like BDP, but takes the comparisons into related (usually not competing) firms, where direct comparisons can often be made by co-operation between firms to collect and compare data.

Different benchmarking exercises may have different overall objectives, which can be any mix of the following:

- **cost reduction,** very often the primary goal
- **output enhancement,** which will also reduce unit costs, but where the main interest is in increasing output to meet market opportunities without expensive investment in new infrastructure
- **quality or service enhancement,** with the main focus on improving the customer proposition and increasing customers' perceived value

- **decision on where to locate extra production and/or investment**, where BDP is used partly or mainly to tell which is really the lowest cost facility amongst several owned by the firm
- **decision on whether to sub-contract manufacture** or contract out overhead functions
- **decisions on streamlining the organisation or re-organising** parts of it

Benchmarking may be a self-contained exercise or a prelude to more detailed analysis of activities and costs, which could involve one or more of the following techniques: ABC (Activity-Based Costing), BPR (Business Process Re-engineering, perhaps the management buzz-word of the decade to date), PBB (Priority-Based Budgeting) and CHANGE MANAGEMENT. Benchmarking alone normally leads to some 'quick wins', that is, clear improvement steps, but leaves unresolved exactly what to do in some other areas, which is where these other techniques may help. Benchmarking is rarely a panacea or an instant solution but it is nearly always useful, at least as a first step.

BENEFICIAL INTEREST
Something that is owned and can be used by the owner at his discretion.

BENEFICIAL OWNER
The ultimate owner of a share rather than the NOMINEE in whose name it is registered.

BENNIS, WARREN (b. 1925)
Probably the best writer on leadership. American industrial psychologist who stressed the impact that leaders and their expectations could have on their people. In his 1985 book, *Leaders: the Strategies for Taking Charge* (co-authored by Burt Nanus), Bennis studied 90 leaders from different professions and identified four common characteristics of the successful leaders: (i) vision as the bridge between the present and the future; (ii) communication, 'the management of meaning'; (iii) trust, the 'emotional glue binding followers and leaders'; (iv) self-management, and the refusal to give in to failure.

Bennis believes that it is possible for people to learn to become leaders, and that the key initial step is to learn to be themselves and to be true to their nature. Bennis is well worth reading, and unlike some other writers on leadership has a well-developed sense of humour.

BEST DEMONSTRATED PRACTICE
See BDP.

BEST EFFORTS
A legal phrase requiring an organisation to do its utmost to secure a particular objective. A very strong phrase and one to which you should try to avoid being committed. 'Reasonable efforts' is much less stringent.

BEST FIT APPROACH
See REGRESSION ANALYSIS.

BEST PRACTICE
The most efficient and/or highest quality examples of similar work, derived either from inside or outside a firm. See also BDP (Best Demonstrated Practice).

BETA COEFFICIENT
See CAPITAL ASSET PRICING MODEL.

BID
1. A takeover offer for a company, to attempt to take over a company.
2. The price at which shares may be bought (usually slightly higher than the MID-MARKET PRICE quoted in newspapers or on screens: see SPREAD), to offer to buy shares at a particular price (as in, 'I bid 300p').

BID-OFFER SPREAD
See SPREAD.

BIG BANG
The day when a financial market is liberalised and restrictions removed. Often refers to the UK stock exchange's reforms on 27th October, 1986.

BILL OF EXCHANGE
A financial document, equivalent of a cheque, used in international trade finance whereby a borrower agrees to pay a certain sum (usually for goods received) in three months' time. The bill of exchange may be guaranteed by an ACCEPTING HOUSE and either held to maturity or sold to a financial institution at a small discount to the face value.

BIMODAL DISTRIBUTION
A FREQUENCY DISTRIBUTION that has two MODES. For example, the two most frequently purchased wines on a wine list may be the cheapest at £6 and the third cheapest at £9: this is a bimodal distribution.

BIOTECHNOLOGY
The use of biological materials and processes, promising a revolution in parts of the health care and food industries and in materials technology for all industries. Biotechnology relies heavily on computer simulation and modelling techniques. It may change the pace and nature of both economic growth and ecological control in the next century, and may even replace large chunks of the current pharmaceuticals industry. If the biotechnology industry becomes as important as its protagonists claim, it will change our concept of the way that organisations should be organised. The biotechnology industry is extremely specialised and nearly every major advance has

come from tiny, unique 'companies' that are really complex networks of individuals co-operating across conventional boundaries of firms and academia. It is impossible to imagine a conventionally organised biotechnology multinational. This is likely to give national competitive advantage in biotechnology to countries like the USA, UK and other European nations whose culture encourages creative networks cutting across normal firm boundaries. Therefore, although Japan has aimed at becoming a world leader in biotechnology, this appears to be very unlikely.

BIT
A measure of computer capacity which is a contraction of binary digit. There are eight bits in a BYTE.

BLACK BOX
When a non-expert uses technical equipment (like a computer system) and follows instructions by rote to achieve a desired effect, without knowing how it works.

BLACK KNIGHT
Bearer of a hostile bid. Contrast GREY KNIGHT and WHITE KNIGHT.

BLACK MONDAY
Usually refers to 19th October, 1987, when world stock markets crashed.

BLACK THURSDAY
The start of the Great Crash, 24th October, 1929.

BLACK TUESDAY
Tuesday 29th October, 1929, the day the US stock market fell the most in percentage terms.

BLIND TEST
Consumer research where a panel of consumers comments on products without knowing which brand they are. It would be more fun to blindfold the testers, but the usual way is to remove labels from the products.

BLOCK TRADING
Large-scale stock trading.

BLUE-CHIP COMPANY
Large company with excellent credit rating. Also used to describe the shares of such companies ('blue chips'). Derives from casinos where the largest denomination chips used to be blue. Blue-chip companies are meant, notwithstanding the derivation, to be low risk.

BLUE COLLAR
Shop floor rather than WHITE COLLAR employee. Unhelpful and increasingly obsolete distinction. See SINGLE STATUS FIRM.

BOARD OF DIRECTORS
The body of those legally responsible for conducting an organisation's affairs. See DIRECTOR and EXECUTIVE BOARD.

BOND
1. a long-term loan to a company or government. Bonds carry a fixed or variable interest rate (COUPON) and these may be traded on a secondary market, fluctuating in value according to current interest rates and the financial status of the company/government concerned. A synonym for LOANSTOCK.
2. The certificate for the loan.

BONDED WAREHOUSE
Place for storing goods where duty only has to be paid when the goods leave the warehouse.

BONUS ISSUE
Issue of additional shares to shareholders to improve liquidity. See also SCRIP ISSUE.

BOOK VALUE
The value of an ASSET as recorded in a company's books. The book value is often different from the current MARKET VALUE.

BOOMERANG EFFECT
Marketing ploy that backfires, such as Hoover's recent air ticket fiasco.

BOTTLENECK
A part of a factory or office process that is likely to suffer from too little capacity relative to demand and therefore to hold up production. A simple example is a fast-growing office that only has one photocopier, so that a queue develops; or a car plant may have relatively few expensive testing machines and these become a bottleneck. One way of dealing with bottlenecks is to invest in more machinery, but a cheaper alternative may to ensure that the bottleneck can be fed with a stream of input even during relatively slack times, for example by creating a BUFFER STOCK of three days' production waiting at the bottleneck for any time when it is not being used (so that even if production is disrupted, the bottleneck can still be used). Bottleneck analysis, a subset of OPT (Optimised Production Technology), is a systematic process of analysing work in progress and shortages compared to surpluses, and software is available to help factories do this efficiently.

BOTTOM

To get to the bottom of an issue, to sort out what is really going on. Useful shorthand often used by gritty managers.

BOTTOM LINE

1. Profit, that is, the bottom line on the P&L STATEMENT, as in 'all the additional sales revenue drops down to the bottom line'. **2.** By extension, what really matters, the heart of the matter.

BRILLIANT PEBBLES

Metaphor derived from Ronald Reagan's star wars programme; in its industrial application it means a form of CORPORATE VENTURING, making many small bets on different entrepreneurial ventures in the hope that a few at least will prove big winners. Making many small investments rather than a few big ones.

BOUGHT DEAL

Way that companies raise capital, usually for acquisitions, where it auctions an issue of new shares to an investment bank or broker, who then sells them on to large institutions for a slightly higher price. Alternative to a placing (see VENDOR PLACING) or a RIGHTS ISSUE. Originated in the USA but now quite frequent in the UK too.

BOUGHT LEDGER

The accounting book or department within a firm dealing with its payments.

BOURSE

Stock exchange.

BOUTIQUE

A small, specialist firm focused on a particular part of a product range. Generally used in respect of consultancies or financial services companies.

BOWER, MARVIN

The real founder of MCKINSEY, who gave it its backbone and values in the 1940s and has kept watch over the Firm's soul ever since. Bower was a lawyer by background and his great innovation was to think that management consulting – up to then a rather fly-by-night and ad hoc activity – could become a profession comparable to the law. Professionalism was partly a matter of high intelligence and codification of all useful knowledge relating to management science, but it was far more than that: it was anchored in the quality and integrity of the client-professional relationship. Bower insisted that McKinsey should put the client's interests first, rather than those of McKinsey or of the individual consultant. Client service, client confidentiality, client responsiveness and integrity in telling the client the truth, as perceived by the professional, were all drummed into the Firm by

Bower. He made McKinsey the most prestigious and envied firm in management consulting throughout the world, based on his ethic of professionalism. Bower, who is now over 90, still has a desk at MCKINSEY, and is deeply revered. Since his retirement a generation ago, he has still been influential, stopping in its tracks all discussion of 'selling out' by taking the Firm public or selling to another firm. He regards his heritage as largely intact, though insiders say that he worries about the materialism and concern for high earnings of the top professionals today. See MCKINSEY.

BPR (Business Process Re-engineering)

A new way of rethinking what a company does and redesigning its processes from first principles in order to produce dramatic improvements in cost, quality, speed and service. BPR is the hottest management concept of the 1990s so far. Its advocates claim that Re-engineering (which they spell, incorrectly, without a hyphen) will be for the 1990s what Strategy was for the 1970s and Quality for the 1980s. This is certainly true as far as consulting revenues are concerned. But BPR is not just a management fad and deserves to be taken seriously. Many leading US companies (such as Eastman Kodak, Ford and Texas Instruments) have used BPR to change their way of doing business, leading to cost reductions in excess of 25%, and in some specific areas of up to 90%.

BPR claims to reinvent the way that companies do business, from first principles, by throwing out the view that firms should be organised into functions and departments to perform tasks, and paying attention instead to processes. A process here is a set of activities that in total produce a result of value to a customer, for example, developing a new product. Who is in charge of this? In the non-BPRed company the answer is 'no-one', despite the involvement of a large number of traditional functions such as R&D, marketing.

The essence of BPR is reversing the task specialisation built into most management thinking since Adam Smith's 1776 pin factory, and focusing instead on completing a total process with value to customers in one fell swoop. A good example is IBM Credit, which used to take seven days to process applications for credit for people wishing to buy computers. Before BPR, there were five separate specialist stages through which an application progressed: logging the credit request; credit checking; modifying the standard loan covenant; pricing the loan; and compiling a quote letter. Experiments then proved that the actual work involved only took 90 minutes; the real delay was caused by having different departments that did the work in stages and had to pass it on to each other. The solution hit upon was to replace the specialists with generalists called deal structures who handled all the steps in the process. The average turnaround time was reduced from seven days to four hours, and productivity was increased 100 times.

'Doing' BPR means taking a clean sheet of paper and asking fundamental questions like: Why do we do this at all? How does it help to meet customer needs? Could we eliminate the task or process if we changed something else? How can we get away from specialisation, so that several jobs are combined into one?

'BPRed' companies have thrown away their 'assembly lines', particularly in respect of clerical and overhead functions. One person, such as a 'customer service representative', may for example act as the single point of contact for a customer, taking care of selling, order taking, finding the equipment to be purchased, and delivering it personally. Performance improvement comes from eliminating the expense and misunderstandings implicit in 'handoffs' from one part of the organisation to another, as well as eliminating internal overheads necessary to manage the complexity brought on by task specialisation.

The process claims several benefits:

1. Customers can deal with a single point of contact (the 'case manager').
2. Several jobs can be combined into one, where the primary need to satisfy the customer is not lost in organisational complexity.
3. Workers make decisions, compressing work horizontally (that is, doing without supervisors and other overhead functions that are necessary as a result of specialisation), resulting in fewer delays, lower overhead costs, better customer response, and greater motivation of staff through EMPOWERMENT.
4. The steps in the process are performed in a sensible order, and removing specialisation enables many more jobs to be done in parallel, as well as lowering the need for rework.
5. Processes can be adapted easily to cope with work of greater or less complexity, instead of forcing everything to go through the same lengthy work steps.
6. Work can be performed where it makes most sense, which is often not by specialists.
7. Checks and controls and reconciliations can be reduced without loss of quality.

Like all forms of radical change, BPR often fails: objective estimates are that this is so in almost 75% of cases. The most frequent causes of failure are lack of top management commitment, an insufficiently broad canvas on which to operate (as when parts of the organisation refuse to take the effort seriously), and lack of readiness to adapt corporate CULTURE. Nevertheless, BPR has achieved such stunning results in many documented cases that it cannot be ignored. In the most successful cases it is clear that BPR as a technique was the catalyst for more far reaching changes in culture and standards.

Two points about BPR are not sufficiently well made by its protagonists, for obvious reasons. One is that certain types of company and business are more likely to benefit from BPR than others. The most susceptible companies are those where manufacturing is a relatively small part of the COST STRUCTURE, where overheads are a large part, where customer needs have been neglected, and where the potential benefits of information technology (IT) have not yet been exploited.

The other point is that BPR is not a Do-It-Yourself technique : serious attempts at BPR nearly always involve help from consultants. As BPR has boomed, so too has the supply of consultant help, but often at the expense of quality. Many consultants reduce BPR to cost reduction techniques or re-badge their existing methodologies under the BPR banner, without having the imagination and creativity required for effective BPR. The likely result is that as most companies come to undertake some form of BPR, most will become disillusioned, and the technique itself may fall into disrepute.

BRAINSTORMING

Collective way of generating new ideas for business by allowing all partici-pants to contribute any possible thoughts, however unconventional, before these ideas are rationally evaluated. Ideas feed off each other and a group can generate far more ideas than any individual.

BRAND

A visual design and/or name that is given to a product or service by an organisation in order to differentiate it from competing products and which assures consumers that the product will be of high and consistent quality. Examples include manufacturers' brands such as Coca-Cola and Ford, retailers' brands such as St Michael or Sainsbury's, and even a brand which is synonymous with a whole company like British Airways or Air Canada. Firms often create 'sub-brands' or new brands within a particular category, such as Diet Coke or Club Europe.

Branding goes back to the time when medieval guilds required tradesmen to put trademarks on their products to protect themselves and buyers against inferior imitations. Nowadays virtually everything has been branded. Consumers prefer brands because they dislike uncertainty and need quick reference points. A brand is particularly powerful if it can gain a SLOT IN THE BRAIN and be identified either with whole product categories ('hoovers' for vacuum cleaners or 'filofax' for personal organiser) or with particular attributes (a Rolls Royce will always be high quality, a Mars bar will supply energy, Avis will always try harder). Many brands have helped companies remain market leaders in particular products throughout the last 60 years, including Bird's in custard, Heinz in soup and tomato ketchup, Kellogg's in cornflakes, McVitie's in digestive biscuits, Schweppes in mixers, Colgate in toothpaste, Kodak in film, Gillette in razors, and Johnson's in floor polish.

Despite the longevity of brands, it is always possible to develop new, pow-erful brands, although this requires a real new product advantage and usually very heavy investment in advertising and other marketing (there are excep-tions to the latter requirement, such as Filofax, Laura Ashley and Walkers

Crisps, where a cult develops almost spontaneously, but they are few and far between). Examples of strong new brands include Flora, Ariel, Canon, Sony, Heineken, Diamond White cider, Mr Kipling and (regrettably) *The Sun*.

Brands have seven major advantages for suppliers:

1. They can help to build *consumer loyalty* and thus give a higher and more enduring market share.
2. Most brands involve a *price premium* which can be very substantial and which greatly exceeds the extra cost in terms of superior ingredients and marketing. The most profitable food companies in the UK in terms of return on sales are Kellogg's and Walkers Crisps, whose sales are exclusively branded. Cider is another recent UK industry where clever branding and product innovation turned a low-price industry into one with high prices. Market research has often asked consumers what they would pay for a particular new product, both unnamed, and with a trusted brand name, and it is not unusual for the latter to attract a 30% price premium in the research.
3. By virtue of their premium price (which widens margins for wholesalers and retailers as well as the manufacturer) and consumer pull, brands can make it easier for manufacturers to gain *vital distribution*. This is particularly crucial for new products and for smaller suppliers.
4. Brands can sometimes *change the balance of power* between different parts of an industry. The development of manufacturers' grocery brands between 1918 and 1960 helped to put manufacturers in the driving seat and give them higher margins than retailers. In the past 25 years consolidation in food retailing and the development of retailers' (own label) brands has handed higher margins to retailers and enabled them to introduce new products from smaller suppliers, including some high margin innovations such as chilled ready meals.
5. Brands can make it easier to *introduce new products* and get consumers to try them, so that often a new product will use some of the BRAND EQUITY in an existing brand by using it while adding a differentiating sub-brand, such as Miller Lite or Guinness Draught Bitter.
6. Closely associated with point 5, branding facilitates the *creation of new market segments* within an established product category: for instance, low-calorie or low-fat versions of almost any food or drink product, the creation of at least three classes of airline travel, or longer lasting products such as Duracell.
7. Finally, the combination of trust and razzmatazz that brands carry can enable whole industries to defy the MARKET MATURITY stage of the alleged PRODUCT LIFE CYCLE, taking a fusty and declining market and injecting *new growth into an industry*. Besides the cider and stout examples, successful branding has helped to revive markets as diverse as shampoo, hand razors, bicycles and newspapers, all of which once seemed stuck in steady decline.

BRAND DEVELOPMENT INDEX
See BDI.

BRAND AWARENESS
The proportion of consumers who spontaneously recognise a particular brand, the extent to which the brand is well known (regardless of how highly regarded it is).

BRAND EQUITY
The value residing in a brand name. See BRAND VALUATION. If brands are really valuable, why do almost no consumer companies have a person charged with protecting and enhancing the brand equity, as opposed to exploiting it in the short term, which is what brand managers do?

BRAND EXTENSION, LINE EXTENSION
Introducing a new variant of a product in the same product category, for example, Tuna Whiskas or Pepsi Max. See also NPD.

BRAND PREMIUM
The extra price (most usefully expressed as a percentage) that a top brand can command, compared to a SECONDARY BRAND or a retailer's OWN LABEL. The maximum correct brand premium is that which is consistent with the brand keeping its market share. If the brand premium is too high, market share will be lost, and long-term value destroyed. See MARLBORO FRIDAY.

BRAND STRETCHING
The process whereby an existing well-known brand name is used on new products that compete in a different market from the brand's existing core product(s). A great deal of brand stretching is currently being undertaken. Some examples from the UK are given below:

Brand	Core Market Category	New Market Category
Bisto	Gravy	Casserole sauces
Bowyers	Meat products	Chilled salads
Flora	Margarine/spreads	Salad dressings
KP	Crisps & peanuts	Peanut butter spread
Mars	Confectionery	Ice-cream & milk drinks
Mr Kipling	Cakes	Frozen puddings
Quaker	Cereals	Bread
Ryvita	Crispbread	Cereals

Recent examples of brand stretching in the UK
Source: OC&C Strategy Consultants

The basic reason for brand stretching is the increased probability of success using an established brand. Of new product launches examined by OC&C Strategy Consultants from 1984 to 1993, only 30% of new brands survived at least four years, but brand extensions had over double the survival rate, at 65%. It is easier to get brand stretches into the trade and consumers are more likely to experiment with, and repeat purchase, the brand extensions. Moreover, the cost of launching new products is much lower using existing brands.

We appear to be moving into a new era, where brands are positioned as having emotional and life-style benefits that are transferable across several products, rather than being narrowly identified with a particular product.

The benefits of brand stretching are clear, but there are also risks, principally the danger of diluting the core brand image. These risks can, however, be contained to acceptable limits by (i) providing an excellent new product, at least comparable in quality to the current brand leader; and (ii) by *not* putting a lot of advertising support behind the stretched product, so that if consumers give it the thumbs down it can be allowed to die a decent death without contaminating the core branded product.

Brand stretching is here to stay and is an accelerating trend. It increases both the rewards and the risks for established brands, in whatever market. See NPD and LIFE-STYLE MARKETING.

BRAND SWITCHING
Moving from one brand to another. See PROMISCUITY.

BRAND VALUATION
1. The process of putting a value on a brand so that this value can be put on the balance sheet of the company owning the brand. **2.** The value of the brand thus established.

There is no doubt that brands have value: see BRAND above for the general reasons. Some particular demonstrations of value can help to make this more tangible. American Motors, a weak brand, tested a car without a strong brand, and consumers said they would pay around $10,000 for it. When the research called the car the Renault Premier, the average price went up to $13,000. Then Chrysler bought American Motors, and the car was actually sold as the Chrysler Eagle Premier for around $13,000. In this single example it can be argued that the Chrysler brand was worth $3,000 times the quantity sold.

Or take the research in consumers' preferences for cornflakes, where consumers' approval ratings went from 47% to 59% once it had been revealed that the product was actually Kellogg's Corn Flakes. Arguably the incremental profits from this extra market share are attributable to the brand.

There are a number of rival ways of valuing brands, none of which is intellectually satisfactory, but all of which produce results enabling a finance director to strengthen ostensibly his company's balance sheet. Brand valuation somewhat resembles angels dancing on the end of a pin, but most consumer goods companies have put the value of their brands on the balance sheet.

We may question whether this is really worthwhile. Brands are only one of a number of intangible assets possessed by companies, including functional skills, service competencies, franchise rights and a whole host of other 'soft assets'. Companies in knowledge industries will increasingly have a great disparity between their BOOK VALUE and their MARKET VALUE. Is it sensible to try to find artificial ways of bridging this gap or should we regard the book value as of limited relevance for these types of company?

BRAND VANDALISM
Destroying or reducing brand franchise by stretching the brand too far and/or by attaching the brand to a low-quality, new product.

BREAK-EVEN ANALYSIS
Shows when total sales turnover equals total cost thus producing a 'break-even', as well as showing the level of profit or loss at different volumes. One of the oldest, most basic, easiest-to-use and most useful tools for considering whether to go into business, launch a new product or for budgeting.

Figure 11 shows that the business has FIXED COSTS of £140,000 and VARIABLE COSTS of £400 a unit. At a production level of 200, therefore, the variable costs (shown in the gap between fixed costs and total costs) would be £80,000 and therefore the total cost would be £220,000. Revenue per item is £1,000 and therefore total revenue at 200 units would be £200,000, showing that break-even had not quite been reached. Break-even is achieved here between 233 and 234 units: at 233 there is a loss of £200 (revenue: £233,000; total cost £233,200) and at 234 a profit of £400 (revenue £234,000; total cost £233,600).

The chart can be redrawn for any given pricing decision. For example, if the managers were not confident of selling 234 units at £1,000 each, they could look at a chart showing the effect of pricing at £795 each, which would show the break-even at just under 360 units. They would then have to weigh whether there was a better chance of selling 360 units at £795 each or 234 units at £1,000 each. It might also be possible to have lower fixed cost but higher variable cost (for example by buying a cheaper production machine that was not as fast) or vice versa. The chart is useful because it shows not only the break-even but the profit or loss at any given volume and price.

One of the greatest values of break-even analysis is its simplicity. Yet this renders it of limited value when modelling large, multi-product businesses, especially when several products share costs or where there is a once-for-all

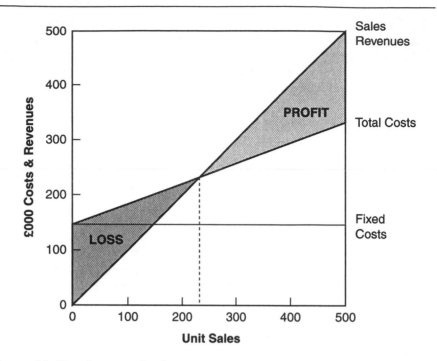

Figure 11 Break-even chart

fixed cost (such as the launch of a new product) which will not be repeated in later years. Nor can it take account of long-term strategic variables such as penetration pricing or the lowering of costs through additional volume (see the EXPERIENCE CURVE).

BREAK-UP VALUE

The value put upon a firm by a stockbroking analyst or a PREDATOR in the event that the firm is split up into its component parts and sold off piece-meal to those who would pay the highest price for each piece. If the Break-up Value exceeds the MARKET VALUE by a wide margin then the firm is a sitting duck for a BID. There is often difficulty in establishing even approximately correct break-up values, however, so the alleged total number should not always be taken very seriously, particularly if it is being touted by a stockbroker who has a vested interest in selling shares in the company. See also ASSET STRIPPER.

BRIDGING LOAN

A short-term loan to buy one asset while another is being sold. House-owners who have had bridging loans will know that this can be expensive and risky.

BROKER

Trader in financial instruments.

BROWN GOODS

TVs, CD-players and other domestic electronic goods originally sold in wooden ('brown') cabinets. Contrast WHITE GOODS. See also YELLOW GOODS.

'B' SHARES

Shares with disproportionately large voting rights.

BUBBLE CHART

A clever graphical technique for capturing three dimensions on a two-dimensional chart, by making the circle size (usually representing a business) proportional to sales, profits, capital employed, cash flow or any other important feature. Figures 5 and 10 are examples. Many business charts can be improved by turning them into bubble charts.

BUBBLE COMPANY

Fraudulent concern with no real business set up to deceive investors.

BUCKET SHOP

1. A firm of brokers or financial dealers of questionable repute or flaky backing. **2.** Travel agents selling discounted air tickets, often backed by major airlines and used to sell excess capacity to discerning and price-conscious travellers.

BUDGET

The annual plan for of sales and profits which must be met by a firm or part of a firm for satisfactory performance. Firms differ widely in their use of budgets. In some it is a stretching amount where attaining the budget is a sign of very good performance. In others the budget is deliberately set at a level which can almost definitely be attained, in order to avoid disappointing the owners, with perhaps a higher TARGET set as well for motivational purposes. In some firms failure to meet budget does not attract penalties; in others the budget is sacrosanct and failure leads to resignation or firing. Because 'budget' alone does not denote a clear enough idea of its importance or function, executives setting or monitoring budgets should think very carefully about what the budget means and ensure that everyone involved has the same understanding.

Different departments will have their own budgets which may simply be a name for the expenditure allowed (as in 'marketing budget') or may denote a more comprehensive plan, such as the PRODUCTION BUDGET. In addition the finance department will prepare a number of specialist budgets, of which the most important are the CAPITAL EXPENDITURE BUDGET and the CASH BUDGET.

BUDGETING
The process of establishing a budget.

BUFFER STOCK
A reserve supply of an important component needed for production, held to avoid delays in production occurring should the normal supply of the component be interrupted. See BOTTLENECK.

BUG
A SOFTWARE fault in a computer program.

BULL
A stock market analyst or investor who expects the market to rise. Contrast BEAR.

BULLDOG LOAN
A bond from a non-British issuer but which is denominated in sterling.

BULLET, BULLET LOAN
Repayment of principal at the end of a loan, or a loan that has this characteristic.

BULL MARKET
Period of strong stock market performance, often lasting several years, but always interrupted by falling prices (a BEAR MARKET) at some stage.

BUNDESBANK
Germany's independent central bank.

BUNNY BOND
A bond where interest can be received in the form of additional bonds (bunnies) if preferred to cash by the investor.

BURDEN RATE
Allocated overhead charge. Traditional method, now not generally helpful. See ABC.

BUREAUCRACY
Commonly used to mean a large organisation where rules and regulations are strangling entrepreneurial flair, imposing unnecessary cost and insulating managers from dealing directly and effectively with customers. In this sense bureaucracy is one of endemic weeds of business and it needs to be smashed periodically by a DELAYERING exercise or an anti-red tape crusade.

Yet 'bureaucracy' as originally invented by Max WEBER was not a pejorative term, and simply meant a rational organisation where objectives and rules could lead to efficiency and avoid the evils of personal favouritism. Because 'bureaucracy' is now irredeemably tainted, this neutral or positive sense is better conveyed by talking about an APOLLO organisation.

The advocates of BPR (Business Process Re-engineering) go further and claim that attempts to 'bust' bureaucracy are misconceived, because bureaucracy is the solution, not the problem. Bureaucracy, they argue, is a rational solution to the problem of fragmented tasks: it is the glue that holds these efforts together. The way to eliminate bureaucracy is therefore to re-engineer processes so that they are no longer fragmented.

See also the modern opposite of bureaucracy: ADHOCRACY.

BUSINESS
An organisation that can operate as a separate, stand-alone commercial entity.

BUSINESS ATTRACTIVENESS
An assessment of how attractive a business or market is, based on a number of criteria. Often a distinction is made between the attractiveness of the market, on the one hand, based on desiderata like market growth, average industry profitability, BARRIERS TO ENTRY (which should be high), BARRIERS TO EXIT (preferably low), the bargaining power of customers and suppliers (ideally low), the predictability of technological change, the protection against substitutes, and on the other hand, the strength of the individual company's business within the market, based on relative market share, brand strength, cost position, technological expertise and other such assessments. One can then produce a matrix such as that shown in Figure 12 and plot all a firm's businesses on the matrix to see where scarce corporate resources such as cash and good management should be allocated.

In Figure 12 the most obviously attractive businesses for investment would be D, followed by G, and then probably C or F. Business C could be a very good investment target, but only if the investment could drive it to a very strong position within the market (i.e. move it from the top left to the top right). If this is reckoned unlikely, it may be best to sell C for a high price. Businesses B and A are also disposal candidates if a reasonable price could be obtained.

The matrix is an alternative to the BCG MATRIX. It has the advantage that it can take into account several factors in evaluating the attractiveness of both business and market. On the other hand the lack of quantification of the axes can be a subjective trap, with management unwilling to admit that businesses are not attractive. For any overall corporate plan it is useful to position all businesses on both matrices, and see whether the prescriptions are at all different. If they are, you should carefully examine the assumptions leading to the difference.

BUSINESS CYCLE

The repetitive process whereby overall demand and investment in an economy fluctuate from depression/recession to recovery to boom and then back to recession/depression. Business cycles have been observed since the 19th century. Kondratieff divined long cycles of some 50–60 years, but nowadays attention focuses on the shorter cycle of 7–10 years (and sometimes 3–5 years) first observed by Clement Juglar in the 1860s. The variations in aggre-

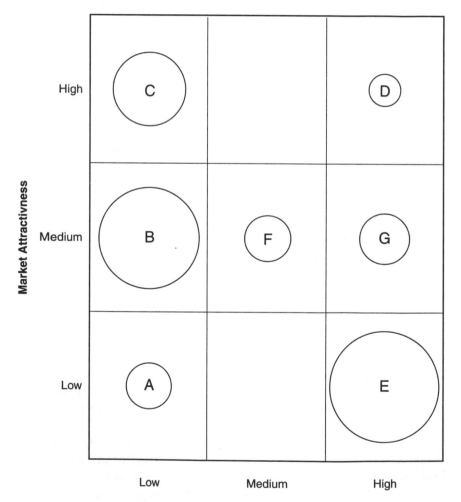

Figure 12 Business attractiveness matrix

gate demand may be relatively modest (for example, a recession may involve a growth in Gross National Product of –1% per annum and a boom may involve growth of 4% per annum) but the impact on employment, profits, real interest rates and perceptions of prosperity can be very great. Business cycles in developed countries are much less exaggerated than they were before 1945 but no-one has yet devised public policy parameters to eliminate the business cycle and no-one ever will. Investors are often curiously insouciant regarding the business cycle, yet disregarding it is a quick route to the poor house. As far as companies are concerned, it is often astute to invest during a downturn, or, if nerves are not that strong, at the very start of an upturn, in order to steal a march on competition. On the other hand, the false dawns seen in most Western economies in 1991–93 can make this a very expensive and even fatal gamble. The only sure way to be sure that your own market is recovering is to have very good market intelligence and compare demand now with equivalent demand a year earlier.

BUSINESS DEVELOPMENT

The process of gaining extra business, either by gaining market share in existing markets or by generating new business by means of NPD (New Product Development) or entering ADJACENT SEGMENTS. 'Business Development' is sometimes used to describe an allegedly holistic (but usually vague) view of how to focus firms on their customers and markets rather than their internal operations.

BUSINESS ETHICS

The principles and rules for behaviour observed by a businessman, a firm, or the business community as a whole. During the last decade a series of high profile scandals (involving marginal business characters such as Ivan Boesky, Robert Maxwell, Michael Milken and Ernest Saunders) helped to reinforce public suspicion that most business was crooked and immoral. In fact, most business behaviour in developed countries today is remarkably ethical, judged by the standards of other parts of society. The worst allegation that can be levelled at senior businessmen as a class is greed, and though this objection can be sustained, a similar condemnation could be handed down to pop stars, successful politicians, authors, sports or media personalities.

The scandals have at least had one positive effect in forcing many companies to define the standards that their people must follow. A good rule is not to do anything that an individual would be ashamed for his or her clients, friends and family to know about. More positively, firms should be making, however modestly, a positive contribution to society through their work: defining this can be very useful in re-energising staff and reinforcing common commitment. See MISSION.

BUSINESSING

Term invented by Tom PETERS in 1992 to mean the process of turning every-one in an organisation into a 'BUSINESSPERSON', responsible for external or internal customers from order to delivery of a service or product. The jargon describes a necessary process and is catching on.

BUSINESSMANSHIP

A word invented to describe the mix of attributes needed by the good busi-ness person. Businessmanship wraps up the following virtues: ability to choose a good strategy (whether through analysis or intuition); skill in understanding what particular customer SEGMENTS want and providing it; ability to put in place the necessary functional skills to deliver the product and service and ensure that all functions are co-ordinated and focused on serving customers; commercial skill in attaining a lower cost position or a better product than competitors; and the ability to inspire people in the firm and build a positive, high energy CULTURE. Businessmanship is there-fore more than entrepreneurial skill, since it also embraces managerial excellence. Good businessmen are much rarer than good managers or good entrepreneurs. Businessmanship is quite a useful concept, but it is much more often used by academics than businessmen, perhaps because it is such an ugly word.

BUSINESS PARK

A misleadingly rustic name for a business estate containing many firms, often in high technology industries, and sometimes located near a university or business school. Also known as SCIENCE PARK.

BUSINESSPERSON

Politically correct term for businessman.

BUSINESS PLAN

Simply a document describing where the business is going, usually over a 3–5 year period, containing (if at all good) at least the following:

- a description of the business itself, its history and (if a new business) the key people involved.
- a statement of the market and BUSINESS SEGMENT within which it operates.
- a definition of the main customers being targeted and how they will be persuaded to buy (a marketing and sales plan).
- the basis of COMPETITIVE ADVANTAGE for the business (i.e. why it can be successful against its competitors).
- the business's goals over the next 3–5 years, expressed in terms of market share, sales, profits, cash use or generation, product develop-ment, reputation and people development.

- a careful analysis of cash required, where it is coming from, and a DOWNSIDE CASE showing that even if sales are lower than expected, it will be possible to continue to fund the business.

Business plans are always necessary to obtain funding from a bank or venture capitalist (or from the corporate CENTRE), but few people prepare them well. This is usually because they have not thought through the key assumptions about why the business can be successful. The first requirement for a good business plan is to think first, and write only after the idea is clear. Contrary to popular belief, business plans do not need to be very long (ten pages are ample), although those who submit them should have back-up available to substantiate the key assumptions.

BUSINESS PROCESS RE-ENGINEERING
See BPR.

BUSINESS RE-DESIGN, RE-ENGINEERING
See BPR.

BUSINESS SEGMENT
A defensible competitive arena within which market leadership is valuable. Contrast MARKET SEGMENT, which is usually defined by market researchers' pre-ordained categorisations of the population into social class or psychologically defined groups, and much less useful. A business segment is an area within which a firm can specialise and gain COMPETITIVE ADVANTAGE. An example of a business segment would be high performance sports cars, which is a defensible market against mass market cars (at least for the time being). Thus Ferrari does not have to worry about its share of the overall car market, if it can be the leader in its own segment. On the other hand, companies cannot define the market in a way that gives them market leadership and *ipso facto* call that a business segment. For example, red cars are not a separate segment from black cars, because specialising in red cars would not result in either extra consumer appeal or lower cost for producing red cars, and would therefore not be a defensible segmentation. See also SEGMENTATION for a much fuller discussion.

BUSINESS SCHOOLS
Generally, places where those who are not yet confident about their ability to run companies go to be taught by those who have never run them. Business schools are clearly useful in teaching analytical techniques and in enabling people whose experience has been in just one function (say in marketing) learn about others such as finance or manufacturing. On the other hand, there is no correlation between the incidence of business school training in particular countries and their success in international market share:

Japan has had the greatest post-war success in the latter while having relatively few business graduates and no internationally renowned school, whereas the USA has expanded business schools and the highest throughput of graduates during the period when it has consistently lost global market share in many key products. Only a minority of business schools stress teamwork and the importance of culture and consensus, and even these schools cannot escape the contradiction that most of their intake are there primarily to get ahead in the competitive career stakes, rather than to become better qualified to serve their existing companies or society. See also MBA.

BUSINESS TO BUSINESS

The process of INDUSTRIAL MARKETING or providing a service to other businesses rather than to the consumer.

BUSINESS UNIT

A snappy name for a department or smaller organisational grouping within a division. Sometimes more grandly called a Strategic Business Unit (see SBU).

BUSINESS UNIT STRATEGY

Strategy for individual business units or divisions rather than for the company as a whole (the latter being described as CORPORATE STRATEGY). Typically business unit strategy is concerned with how to gain market share, customer needs, cost position relative to competitors, pricing and generally outwitting a handful of key competitors.

BUSY-WORK

Low value work to keep staff busy. An American term, the equivalent of the English MAKE-WORK.

BUY-BACK

Agreement in a deal where the seller agrees to buy back the asset for a specified price if the asset fails to perform in defined ways.

BUYER CREDIT

A loan granted to the buyer of exported goods to cover most but not all of the cost.

BUY-IN

1. See MBI (Management Buy-In). **2.** Enthusiastic acceptance of a new plan, MISSION, behaviour standard or proposition, signifying that the executives involved really believe in it and take psychological OWNERSHIP of it.

BUY-OUT

See MBO (Management Buy-Out).

BYTE

A measure of computer capacity comprising eight BITS.

C

C RATIO
The proportion of a market controlled by the top four suppliers. See also
CONCENTRATION.

C5 RATIO
The proportion of a market controlled by the top five suppliers. See
also CONCENTRATION.

CAD-CAM (Computer Aided Design & Computer Aided Manufacture)
CAD enables designers and architects to change one aspect of a design and
see on a computer screen the implications for all other aspects. CAM then
makes it possible to go straight from the design phase to production using
computers (see ROBOTICS). CAD/CAM should lower the cost and, even
more importantly, the time required for practical new product development.

CAE (Computer Aided Engineering)
Synonym for CAD.

CAFETERIA BENEFITS, CAFETERIA PERKS
See FLEXIBLE BENEFITS.

CAGR (Compound Annual Growth Rate)
The average compounded rate of growth per annum over the time period
being measured.

CALL, CASH CALL
Request or demand from a company for new money from investors, either in
a RIGHTS ISSUE or to make a further payment on PARTLY-PAID SHARES.

CALL OPTION
Right to buy a share or other asset at a fixed price at some time in the future.

CAMPBELL, ANDREW (b. 1950)
Scottish management guru, ex-MCKINSEY consultant and founder of the
Ashridge Strategic Management Centre, who is the world's leading authority on issues related to MISSION and has (with Michael GOOLD) been
a pioneer in the area of PARENTING and MANAGEMENT STYLES. In 1990
his book *A Sense of Mission* stressed that mission statements could be

unnecessary or even counter-productive: what mattered was whether a company had a driving sense of PURPOSE, a consistent set of VALUES, a commercial STRATEGY that was also aligned with the purpose and values, and a set of BEHAVIOUR STANDARDS that underpinned the value system. See MISSION, PARENTING ADVANTAGE, PURPOSE and VISION.

CANNIBALISATION

When a new product or service is introduced in the knowledge that it will eat into the market for an existing product or service already being provided by the supplier. Diet Coke, for example, cannibalised the existing market for Coke, or Turkey-flavoured Whiskas cannibalised the demand for existing Whiskas variants. Suppliers know that their goods will to some extent reduce existing product demand, but expect this to be more than compensated for by the extra demand created by the new product introduction (and in some cases higher prices too, as when Whiskas was originally introduced and cannibalised Kit-e-Kat). Moreover, if one supplier does not introduce a new product to cater for a potential new product category, the competitor might: causing loss of market share, which is always a greater evil than cannibalisation.

CAP

Ceiling on an interest rate or other payment. Often used in MBOs to limit the amount of interest on floating loans; but CAPs are often expensive to arrange in the first place.

CAPACITY

The amount of supply in an industry, or the quantity of goods that a machine or facility can produce. It is important to define the measure of capacity carefully to ensure comparability.

The addition of capacity – by whom and when – will have the most decisive impact on market share, corporate and industry profitability. No industry is ever transformed except by pre-emptive investment. On the other hand, the profitability of many industries has been almost permanently blighted by mindless, copycat capacity additions. The most effective adders of capacity are those who plonk down huge investments while persuading their competitors not to follow suit. It is a game suited to visionaries and gamblers rather than to accountants with their DCF analyses.

CAPEX

A shortened name for CAPITAL EXPENDITURE.

CAPEX BUDGET

Annual plan for spending on new fixed assets.

CAPITAL

Funding for business. Often used simply to mean EQUITY or SHARE CAPITAL, that is, the funds provided by shareholders and at risk if the business is not successful. But can also comprise loan capital, i.e. amounts provided by banks and other lenders, which has a lower degree of risk than share capital since it ranks in front of it for payment.

CAPITAL ALLOWANCE

The amount of DEPRECIATION on an asset that can be set against a firm's income taxes.

CAPITAL AND RESERVES

Also called EQUITY, SHAREHOLDERS' EQUITY and SHAREHOLDERS' FUNDS. The share of a company's assets that are due to its shareholders, comprising SHARE CAPITAL, SHARE PREMIUM, RETAINED PROFIT and any other RESERVES.

CAPITAL ASSET PRICING MODEL (CAPM)

Intellectually respected but practically useless method for comparing risk and return on shares. The theory holds that the expected rate of return on a share has two components: first, the required return from a risk-free investment like government securities (e.g. treasury bills in the USA or index-linked gilts in the UK), which sets a floor for the required rate of return; and second the risk associated with the investment. The second aspect is in turn divided into the risk of the stock market as a whole ('systematic risk') and the risk attaching to the particular company ('unsystematic', or 'a specific', or 'diversifiable' risk). The ALPHA COEFFICIENT (or simply 'alpha') measures the former and purports to explain why certain shares have a higher rate of return than others. The BETA COEFFICIENT (or 'beta') identifies the price fluctuations inherent in the market as a whole, rather than those inherent in a particular share. The CAPM helps to illustrate the divide between business schools on the one hand and managers and investors on the other. The CAPM is almost universally approbated by the former and almost never used by the latter. It may also have serious conceptual flaws, but both theory and counter-theory are best left to those who like counting angels on the end of pins.

CAPITAL EMPLOYED

The total money tied up in a business to allow it to operate, comprising FIXED ASSETS and WORKING CAPITAL. Also equals the sum of the EQUITY, DEBT and tax payable. The capital employed should be compared to the profits (returns) generated by the business: see ROCE (Return on Capital Employed). NET OPERATING ASSETS is a synonym for capital employed.

CAPITAL EXPENDITURE (CAPEX)
Spending on FIXED ASSETS.

CAPITAL FLIGHT
Also called FLIGHT CAPITAL. Money fleeing from one country, usually because its currency is weak and about to be devalued.

CAPITAL GAINS TAX (CGT)
Tax levied on the increase in value of an investment when sold by an individual or corporation. It is difficult to conceive of a worse tax. Bruce HENDERSON was right in 1974: 'The capital gains tax should be abolished. It should be eliminated even as a concept. Capital at productive work should be exempt from any taxation as long as it is fully employed as capital. Instead, the tax should fall at full personal surtax on the person who disinvests capital in order to be able to buy personal consumption.' The anomaly in many countries (including Britain) is that investing institutions are given ROLL-OVER RELIEF on investments, effectively achieving Henderson's aim, whereas private investors are taxed each time they sell an investment whether the proceeds are reinvested or spent on personal consumptions. Recent changes in the UK law have moved towards a fairer system but there is absolutely no intellectual case for discrimination against the private investor or for CGT on anyone who does not withdraw capital from productive uses.

CAPITAL GEARING
See GEARING.

CAPITAL INTENSIVE
An industry or business continually requiring large investments of cash to prosper.

CAPITALISATION, CAPITALIZATION
The MARKET VALUE of a company traded on the stock exchange, that is, the share price multiplied by the number of shares in issue.

CAPITAL PRODUCTIVITY
Sales divided by CAPITAL EMPLOYED.

CAPITAL STRUCTURE
The relative proportions of a company's funding that are provided by DEBT and EQUITY, or in a more detailed analysis taking into account the amounts comprised in ORDINARY SHARES, PREFERENCE SHARES, BONDS and LONG-TERM DEBT. The capital structure is relevant in considering what form the next tranche of capital should take, as well as in assessing risk. A company with relatively more debt than equity will have a lower COST OF CAPITAL and

therefore a competitive advantage against a firm with a more conservative capital structure, although at the expense of greater FINANCIAL RISK. Capital structure is also called FINANCIAL STRUCTURE or FUNDING STRUCTURE.

Finding the optimal capital structure is not a purely technical task, and it is too important to be left to the accountants. The optimal capital structure must support the CORPORATE STRATEGY and be designed to outwit competitors. Provided the capital structure minimises short-term liquidity problems, the greatest advantage usually derives from having as much debt and as little equity capital as possible, in order to raise the return on shareholder's funds and raise the SUSTAINABLE GROWTH RATE of the firm. The paradox is that those firms most able to run with high debt proportions of the capital structure, and thus able to make life more difficult for their hard-pressed competitors, are those who are generally most reluctant to do so. See DEBT for further exploration of this value-destroying paradox.

CAPP (Computer Aided Process Planning)

Producing process plans for products or parts. See also VARIANT PROCESS PLANNING and GENERATIVE PROCESS PLANNING, the two different types of CAPP.

CAPTIVE

A separate but wholly owned company supplying services exclusively (or largely) to its parent. Most used in insurance, insurance broking, and some other specialist financial services. Generally suitable only for very large firms.

CAPTIVE DEMAND

Demand that has no effective choice but to consume product from the supplier, because it is imprisoned within a wider business system. Thus a racetrack will have captive demand for its catering facilities, a remote hotel for its bar, an airport for all short-term consumption needs. Captive demand also arises when a product requires proprietary 'consumables' or refills, such as razor blades where razors are not interchangeable or Gucci watches that have special knobs repelling ordinary straps and requiring a small fortune to be spent on replacements. Captive demand can be high margin but if it is fleeced too flagrantly it will turn to PIRATE supplies or just stop consuming either the captive or the original product.

CAREER ANCHOR

Ed SCHEIN's term for the perceptions individuals have about themselves and their worth to and role in an organisation, that encourage them to stay in it. Can also restrict a person's ambition if the role is perceived too narrowly.

CAREER PLANNING

Planning future steps in an individual's career, either by the individual or by the firm. Few organisations have organised career planning for any but a minority of identified 'HIGH FLYERS'. For the individual, career planning should include consideration of when to move firms or even professions.

CAREER DEVELOPMENT

Includes CAREER PLANNING but is also the training and personal development of the individual, usually helped by a mentor, to equip him or her to take on additional responsibilities in the future. See MENTORING.

CAREER TEAMS

See TEAMWORK.

CAREW'S AXE

Lay-off of workers who are easiest to get rid of rather than least competent. A frequently observed sign of weak management.

CARNIVAL

Metaphor used by Tom PETERS: the company-as-carnival: fun, buzz, energy, creation and destruction, marked by constant change and unpredictability. Will the Californian view of the corporation triumph?

CARRY BACK, CARRY FORWARD

To move tax allowance or pensions payments from one year to an earlier or later one, in order to utilise them most effectively.

CARTEL

A conspiracy by producers to restrict supply of a product and/or to keep prices artificially high. Usually illegal, but not always. The most successful recent example was OPEC (the Organisation of Petroleum Exporting Countries) which sustained a dramatic rise in the international oil price in 1973. Cartels are very difficult to create or sustain if there are more than five members. The preferred name amongst many businessmen is CLUB.

CASE STUDY METHOD

Approach to teaching general management skills pioneered by the Harvard Business School that looks at the history of a company and invites small groups of students to solve the company's problems at a particular date. Reflects the legal method for which Harvard Law School was pre-eminent rather than the functional approach adopted by other schools such as Wharton (specialising in finance, and more recently management) or

Stanford (engineering). The attraction of the case study method is that it looks at the total management context and encourages the student to identify with the CEO (Chief Executive). Critics have rightly pointed out that the method is unrealistic, since the data on which the method is based are rarely clear cut or universally perceived within a firm, and the players in it each have their own agenda and are behaving in their characteristic operational way and responding to short-term stimuli rather than debating the strategy with their feet up. The case-study method is also the tool of the problem solver rather than the leader or COMPETENCE-builder. The best that can be said for the case study method is that it is an efficient way of introducing relative novices to corporate history and of stimulating debate about what the CEO should do.

CASH

The be-all and end-all of business. All that matters is compounding the cash put into a business so that it can be later extracted in as multiplied a form as possible. This simple point is neglected to an extraordinary degree in big business. Most managers and investors behave as though profit were more important than cash. In doing so they are implicitly focusing on the secondary market in businesses (the stock market and its valuation of earnings) rather than what drives wealth creation. If you ignore the 'bigger fool' theory, cash is all that counts. Anything else (for example the PROFIT & LOSS STATEMENT) is a forecast of cash to come, and usually not a very reliable forecast at that. The small, private businessman knows that cash is much more important and elusive than profit.

CASH BOOK

The set of accounts recording a firm's cash transactions.

CASH BUDGET

Annual plan showing the overall cash position and CASH FLOW expected over the year.

CASH COW

A business that is highly cash positive as a result of being a market leader in a low growth market. Such a business typically requires only moderate investment in physical assets or working capital, so that high profits result in high CASH FLOW.

Cash cows are one of the four positions on the BCG MATRIX. In the BCG theory cash from cash cows can be used to support other businesses that are leaders or potential leaders in high-growth markets and that need cash to improve or maintain their market share positions.

The BCG theory has often been misinterpreted, partly as a result of the tag 'cash cow'. Cows need to be milked, so the natural (but incorrect) inference is that the main role of cash cows is to give cash to the rest of the portfolio. Yet the original BCG theory stressed the key point that cash cows should have the first call on their own cash: whatever investment was necessary to support and reinforce the cash cows' position should come first. This common-sense prescription is often overlooked. Cash cows are not glamorous, and generally require only moderate amounts of grass, but they should still be allowed to graze on the most verdant pastures. It would have saved us all a great deal of trouble if BCG had stuck to the alternative name for cash cows, namely GOLD MINES. Nobody would dream of denying a gold mine its required share of the maintenance budget.

CASH FLOW

The change in a company's cash balance over a period. Nothing is more important than cash flow, both short and long term.

CASH TRAP

Useful jargon invented by the Boston Consulting Group to describe businesses that absorb cash but will never repay it fully or at all. BCG even went so far as to say in 1972 that 'the majority of the products in most companies are cash traps. They will absorb more money forever than they will generate. This is true even though they may show a profit in the books.' Typically QUESTION MARK businesses (poor market share positions in high growth businesses) are the worst cash traps, although some DOGS may also be. BCG crusaded against cash traps, urging managers to cut their losses in these businesses and focus cash on businesses that were or could become market leaders. The crusade has had real impact in the past two decades or so, partly through the action of managers but even more through hostile acquisitions that have led to UNBUNDLING, which is often little more than the sale or closure of cash traps. Are you sure you know what your cash traps are?

CATEGORY KILLER

Retailer that specialises in a particular type of product, like toys, baby products or furniture, and offers both the widest range and the greatest value, usually by means of very large and 'fun' out-of-town stores. See DESTINATION RETAILING.

CATS (Certificate of Accrual on Treasury Securities)

US treasury bonds that pay more interest but are redeemed at a face value much higher than the issue price. An example of ZERO COUPON BONDS.

CAUSATION

When X causes Y. Not to be confused with CORRELATION, which may not imply causation.

CAUSE

Recent pioneering work on CHANGE MANAGEMENT has stressed the need for all companies to have an overall medium-term objective that can unite everyone's efforts and focus on what the company as a whole is trying to achieve. Causes should be snappy phrases that encapsulate the company's forward momentum and help to guide individual behaviour. Examples of good Causes include 'Putting People First' (British Airways), 'Encircle Caterpillar' (Komatsu), 'Number One and Pulling Ahead' (Coca-Cola Schweppes Beverages) and 'Become larger than BCG' (Bain & Company).

CD (Certificate of deposit)

CDs are issued for large bank deposits (tens of thousands of dollars or more) and are negotiable, that is, can be traded in a secondary market.

CENTRALISATION

The process of concentrating power at the CENTRE. Out of fashion since at least 1970. See CENTRALISED.

CELLULAR MANUFACTURING

The arrangement of computer controlled equipment into groups of machines to process production. See FMS and SCHONBERGER.

CENTRALISED

One of GOOLD and CAMPBELL's minor management styles. In a centralised company the CENTRE takes the lead in developing strategies and makes all the important decisions. Business unit managers simply implement head office decisions. The control systems are more concerned with whether the CENTRE'S directions have been carried out than with results. The centralised style is very rare nowadays, with the most centralised popular style being FINANCIAL CONTROL, where the centre controls by numbers but as long as budgets are met leaves the means to the business units.

CENTRE

More positive name for headquarters, reflecting recently increased respectability of adding value from the CENTRE, and in particular the important work of CAMPBELL and GOOLD on corporate PARENTING ADVANTAGE. If the Centre does not add value, why should it exist, except for the minimalist functions of an investment holding company? If the Centre does not have a positive role, why have a highly-paid CEO or Chairman?

The Centre can have several important roles, including:

1. Setting CORPORATE STRATEGY, deciding which businesses to buy and sell, where to invest cash, and where it is possible to beat competitors by having lower costs or high prices.

2. Moulding corporate CULTURE and providing LEADERSHIP to excite people and make them believe in the company.
3. Reinforcing and creating corporate COMPETENCES in the areas which are most important to beat competitors, so that the firm has world-class skills in the critical areas.
4. Exercising financial control and ensuring that budgets are met in each business.
5. Identifying SYNERGY potential between different businesses and encouraging the appropriate parts of the group to talk to each other and collaborate effectively.
6. Recruiting, rewarding and developing business leaders within the group.

As the role of the Centre is better understood, the sterile debate and alternation between CENTRALISATION and DECENTRALISATION can be ended. The best solution is usually a very small but high powered and extremely active Centre. This solution usually requires turning the actual Centre today inside-out: sadly, most Centres destroy far more value than they add.

CEO (Chief Executive Officer)

American acronym that has triumphed in the sense that most executive company heads throughout the world now call themselves Chief Executive (rather than the more traditional Managing Director) even if they dispense with the 'Officer'. CEOs can be divided into administrators, who see their role as incremental improvement of the status quo, and radicals, who want to lead their companies to new levels and eventually leave a real stamp on the company. Most CEOs think they are the latter but their risk-averse behaviour dooms them to the former. For a view on what good Chief Executives should be doing, see CENTRE.

CHAIN OF COMMAND

Hierarchical reporting relationships as seen on an ORGANISATION CHART. Best kept short, as in the Roman Catholic Church, which has only five levels. See also SCIENTIFIC MANAGEMENT, FAYOL and SCALAR CHAIN.

CHAIRMAN

Generally the most senior person in a company, although the title itself does not convey whether the chairman is part time or full time or whether he is effectively part of the executive team or a figurehead. In the USA the chairman is clearly the boss, usually full time and usually also the CEO. In the UK combining the two roles is increasingly frowned upon (partly as a result of the Cadbury Committee on CORPORATE GOVERNANCE). The chairman is usually part time, but very important in setting strategy, liaising with the City, and making (or at least vetting) key appointments or firings, including that of the CEO. Despite Hugh Parker's well-founded adage that there should be no such thing as a non-executive chairman (even if he or she is only part time), many chairmen allow themselves to be described as such; most are eunuchs. In many Continental European countries the chairman of the executive board is the full-time boss, while there is also the chairman of the supervisory board who ensures that the interests of employees and investors are kept in some kind of balance.

CHAMPION

Influential senior executive who acts as sponsor, protector and evangelist of a specific project or projects. Important. Successful firms tend to have a number of champions who ensure that the dead weight of bureaucracy or vested interests do not kill good new ideas.

CHANDLER, ALFRED (b. 1918)

Influential American economic historian whose book *Strategy and Structure* (1962) was based on studying major US corporations between 1850 and 1920. He is important for having made three points clearly:

1. He highlighted the close relationship between strategy and structure, and said that firms should first determine their strategy, then their structure. This was more unusual for the emphasis on strategy than the sequencing, because very few writers had paid attention to strategy: it is almost completely lacking in the earlier theorists like TAYLOR and WEBER.
2. He believed that the role of the salaried manager and technician was vital, and talked about the 'visible hand' of management co-ordinating the flow of product to customers more efficiently than Adam Smith's 'invisible hand' of the market. This is an early recognition that corporations, in their internal dealings, favour a planned economy.
3. He was an advocate of DECENTRALISATION in large corporations, contributing to the DIVISIONALISATION and decentralisation trend of the 1960s and 1970s. He praised Alfred SLOAN's decentralisation of General Motors in the 1920s before Sloan published his book (in 1963), and was influential in the transformation of AT&T in the 1980s from a production-based bureaucracy to a marketing organisation.

Chandler provided much of the vocabulary for the subsequent management debate: it is still very much a live issue whether strategy should follow structure. Tom PETERS holds that Chandler 'got it exactly wrong': that structure inevitably determines strategy, and that the socialist principle of management must be broken down and subjected to market pressures. The truth is probably that Chandler was more right than wrong when he wrote, and that Peters is now.

CHANGE AGENT

Process consultant or other catalyst who helps to change the CULTURE or direction of a company. Change agents used to be outsiders, usually from an academic background (especially psychology), but now the CEO or other people at the CENTRE may see themselves as change agents. See CHANGE MANAGEMENT.

CHANGE MANAGEMENT

The process whereby companies undergo a major change in their CULTURE and performance. Fundamental change of this type is always difficult and risky: about three quarters of all serious attempts to change companies in Britain and America between 1970 and 1992 ended in failure. Yet it is apparent that many large companies will only survive and prosper as independent entities if they change their way of operating and lift performance to a new level. Many consultants offer change management services but most of them do not really understand the business realities: their skills are process related rather than strategic and operational. All successful TRANSFORMATIONS of companies have changed culture almost as a by-product of successful commercial changes: like happiness, culture change is a result of a frame of mind and taking decisive actions, not something that can be sensibly pursued as a goal in itself. And all successful transformations have depended on vigorous and visionary LEADERSHIP from one person. There is absolutely no point in paying large amounts to change management consultants unless there is an inspired leader with a sensible business strategy to start with.

CHAOS

Word increasingly used to describe the unpredictability and seeming irrationality of the modern business environment. According to the chaos theoreticians, the old rational standbys of competitive advantage like market share and low cost position may not work today. Hmmm.

CHAPTER 11

US protection for firms against creditors allowing a financial reconstruction to be put together. Similar to the UK practice of ADMINISTRATION, which is not quite as satisfactory and is not used as much.

CHARGE

First claim over an asset, usually taken as security for a loan. Also called a LIEN.

CHARGE CARD

A plastic card issued by a retailer whereby goods can be obtained and paid for in one amount monthly. Technically, charge cards are not CREDIT CARDS, in that the full amount must be paid each month. In practice, store cards that do allow credit are often referred to as charge cards.

CHARTISM

Once a mass revolutionary political creed, now a more esoteric but no less committed investment religion. Chartism is based on charts of daily share price performance and helps to inform decisions on when to buy and sell shares. It is highly technical but can be boiled down to the premise that markets for individual shares (and whole stock markets too) tend to carry on going in one particular direction (up, down or sideways) until they reach characteristic turning points. Identifying the turning points can give 'buy' or 'sell' signals which hold good until another turning point is reached.

It is easy to mock chartist analysis as a form of financial astrology, and contrast it with the virtues of FUNDAMENTAL ANALYSIS, that looks at the real economic drivers of profits and cash. Yet there is considerable evidence that chartism works: at least some of its practitioners have consistently above-average investment success that cannot be explained as mere chance. The reason it can work is that financial markets have 'herd' characteristics that usually magnify any share price momentum and lead to greater volatility than is justified by economic reality. As more astute or better informed investors decide to buck the previous trend and buy when a share has been falling, or sell after it has been rising, the results of a change in the supply/demand balance for the shares will eventually be reflected in the share price trend. When this happens and is noticed, partly because of chartist analysis, others will swing behind the new trend and magnify it.

The best judgement is that chartism is a useful supplement to fundamental analysis, particularly in advising when to buy or sell shares that one knows are worth more or less than the prevailing price.

CHECK (*US*), CHEQUE (*UK*)

Expensive way of allowing bank customers to pay for goods and services, increasingly being substituted by DEBIT CARDS.

CHERRY-PICKING

Specialising in parts of a product range that are most profitable and/or easiest to access rather than providing a full line of product. Large, full-line suppliers are often vulnerable to smaller cherry-pickers, especially if the larger player has made the mistake of AVERAGE COSTING and AVERAGE PRICING.

CHIEF OPERATING OFFICER

See COO.

CHINA MENTALITY

Kenichi OHMAE's positive expression for a firm that feels itself to be at the centre of the universe and therefore having a sense of mission to change the world and a deep, inner conviction that this is possible: being extremist, fundamentalist and being willing to propel the company to global leadership in its markets. See GLOBALISATION.

CHINESE WALLS

Inter-departmental security procedures and barriers that prevent one part of a financial institution from knowing privileged information held by another department. For example, the corporate finance advisers to a company may know that it is about to receive a takeover approach, but must be prevented by Chinese walls from any possibility that this price sensitive information could seep through to their fund management colleagues. Chinese walls are meant to be thick and unbreachable, and surprisingly enough they usually work these days: the hideous consequences of scandal make COMPLIANCE effective.

CHURN

To buy and sell shares frequently.

CIE (Computer Integrated Engineering)

See CIM.

CIM (Computer Integrated Manufacturing)

The use of information technology to integrate all the processes involved in production: design, production engineering, production planning, production control and scheduling, materials procurement and flow planning, materials handling, stock control, all manufacturing operations, distribution, and cost accounting. A CIM system controls and integrates all the sub-systems, allowing each of the processes to 'talk' to each other via computer. CIM is the ultimate refinement of CAD-CAM. It streamlines the whole process, should eliminate errors that can arise at the interfaces in a non-CIM system, increase manufacturing flexibility, lower lead times for customers and increase quality. Naturally, it is difficult to implement, but there are some notable success stories. It is important, however, to make sure that the firm has correctly thought through *what* it is doing before implementing CIM. See BPR (Business Process Re-engineering) for a discussion of how to think through the *what* from first principles.

CIRCULAR TRANSACTION

When A buys from B and B then buys from A, in order to inflate both firms' revenues.

CITY BANKS
The large Japanese commercial banks.

CLASS ACTION
When one shareholder (or member of another category or class) pursues legal action on behalf of all shareholders.

CLAW BACK
To take back money already paid, as when the buyer of a firm is entitled to a partial refund if the firm does not perform as warranted.

CLEARING BANK
UK name for RETAIL BANKS: the high street banks that take deposits from and make loans to individuals and corporations. Also called COMMERCIAL BANK.

CLEARING HOUSE
Agency handling financial paperwork on behalf of a number of institutions.

CLONE
Legal copy or near copy of an existing product, usually supplied at a significantly lower price. Most often applied to personal computers, where 'clone' manufacturers have made their products fully substitutable and compatible with IBM's products but priced them significantly below the IBM ones. Contrast COUNTERFEIT.

CLOSE COMPANY
Broadly, one controlled by five or fewer shareholders.

CLOSED-END FUND
One that has a fixed number of shares and cannot issue new shares once this limit has been reached. INVESTMENT TRUSTS in the UK are one example. Contrast OPEN-END FUND.

CLUB
Nudge-nudge name for a CARTEL.

CLUSTER
1. A group of customers or other observations that have common characteristics and that are clearly differentiated from other customers/observations that belong in other clusters. **2.** More recently, used to describe an employee grouping drawn from different functions who work together on a semi-permanent basis as a self-contained mini-firm. A cluster develops its own expertise and customers and shares accountability for action.

CLUSTER ANALYSIS

Market research technique identifying clusters by computer analysis of a large number of variables. Useful because it often throws up non-obvious linkages: for example, wealthy consumers buying behaviour may have more in common with that of the poorest consumers (because the wealthy like a bargain and the poorest must buy the cheapest) than either has with intermediate groups of customers.

CO-FINANCING

Collaborative financing involving two or more institutions, usually a commercial bank and a development institution like the World Bank.

COGNITIVE DISSONANCE

A useful concept from psychology, invented by the American psychologist Leon Festinger in 1951. The theory says that it is painful for there to be a discrepancy ('dissonance' in psycho-speak) between people's beliefs and their actions, so that they will move to bring either into line with the other. This can be exploited in marketing, for example after someone has bought a particular product. Assume someone has bought a package holiday for £500, and believes that they have bought wisely. Then they see a poster at the airport proclaiming that a direct marketing company provides exactly the same holiday for £400. The tourist either has to disbelieve the poster's claims or change her behaviour, and buy from the direct marketing company in future.

COGS

See COST OF GOODS SOLD.

COLD CALLING

Unsolicited telephone or door-to-door selling.

COLLATERAL

Technically, security for a loan that is issued by a third party rather than the borrower. In practice, often used to mean any type of security.

COLLECTIVE BARGAINING

Negotiations between TRADE UNIONS and management on pay and conditions.

COMB ANALYSIS

A very useful and simple technique for comparing customers' purchase criteria with their rating of suppliers. Let us assume that you are a textile manufacturer producing women's clothes and selling them to retailers who are fashion specialists. You want to find out what the most important reasons are for them to choose supply from one manufacturer rather than another. You also want to find out what the retailers think about you and your competitors on each of these purchase criteria.

You should then engage independent researchers to interview the retailers and ask them two questions. First, the researchers should ask the retailers to score on a 1–5 scale the importance of various purchase criteria. Let us assume that the average results are as follows:

Criterion	Importance score
Fashion appeal of garments	4.9
Strength of brand name	4.6
Service and speed of delivery	4.5
Willingness to deliver small orders	3.5
Price from manufacturer to them	3.0
Durability of garments	2.3

These results can now be displayed on the first part of the 'comb' chart (Figure 13).

The second question the researchers ask is how each of the competing suppliers rates on each of these criteria, again on a 1–5 scale. Let us start by overlaying on the previous results (the retailers' purchase criteria) their rating of the company sponsoring the research, which we will call Gertrude Textiles (Figure 14).

These results should be of great interest to Gertrude Textiles. Except on one criterion, Gertrude manages to score above the importance of the criterion to the retailer. Unfortunately, the one criterion on which Gertrude scores below market expectations is the most important one: the fashion appeal of its clothes. To increase market share, the one thing that Gertrude Textiles must focus on is improving its garments' fashion appeal. Of interest too is that on the last three criteria – willingness to deliver small quantities, price, and the durability of its clothes – Gertrude scores *above* what the market requires. No doubt this is costing Gertrude a lot of money. This comb profile suggests that Gertrude could afford to not be so accommodating on small deliveries, could raise prices, and could stop building in long life to its clothes. The money saved should be invested in doing whatever necessary to improve perceptions of its fashion appeal: perhaps by hiring away the top designer team from a rival.

This is where the rating of competitors adds to the picture. We can now overlay on the previous picture the ratings given by retailers to two of Gertrude's rivals: Fast Fashions and Sandy's Styles (Figure 15).

From this we can make three important observations:

1. The only competitor that meets the market's very high fashion requirements is Sandy's Styles. This is the team for Gertrude Textiles to poach or beat.

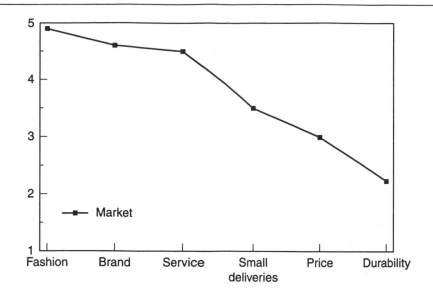

Figure 13 Comb chart: retailers' purchase criteria

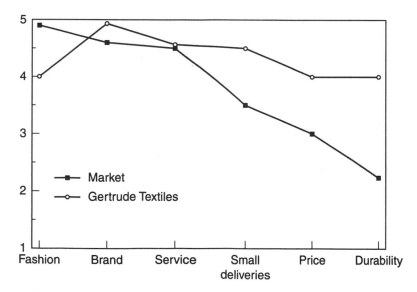

**Figure 14 Comb chart: retailers' purchase criteria and their rating of
Gertrude Textiles on these criteria**

2. Gertrude has the best brand name, according to the retailers, and can meet
   all the other purchase criteria apart from fashion. If this criterion can be
   met, Gertrude will be in a very strong position to increase market share.

3. Only Gertrude is significantly over-performing on the price requirements of retailers. This helps to confirm that some price increases to retailers may be possible for Gertrude, particularly if the fashion element improves.

COMFORT LETTER

A letter, usually written by an independent authority like a firm of accountants, providing investors with comfort that information in a PROSPECTUS or other OFFER DOCUMENT is still valid.

COMMERCIAL BANK

Retail or 'high street' bank, whose main purpose is accepting savings deposits and lending money. Contrast INVESTMENT BANK.

COMMERCIAL DUE DILIGENCE

See DUE DILIGENCE.

COMMERCIAL PAPER

Instrument issued by a creditworthy company to providers of short-term finance which may then be traded. A way of companies obtaining short-term loans.

COMMITMENT FEE

A fee paid to a bank or other potential lender in return for giving the potential borrower the right to a loan at any time. Usually a percentage (say $\frac{1}{4}$ of one per cent) of the amount committed.

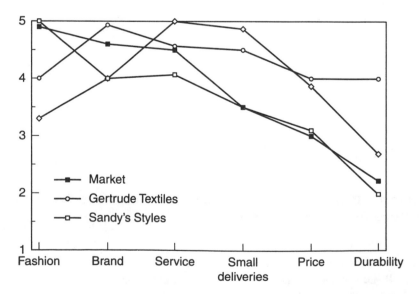

Figure 15 Comb chart: rating of three competitors against market criteria

COMMODITY

Undifferentiated product, where suppliers are doomed to compete on price, branding has no value, and the low-cost competitor will be able to earn higher returns and/or gain market share at the expense of his weaker (higher cost) brethren. Actually, commodity markets are often the result of a lack of imagination and marketing flair on the part of the participants. Almost anything can be successfully branded, and a price premium extracted. Take baked beans as an example: easy to produce and you might think a classic commodity market. Yet brilliant advertising based on brand identity – 'Beans Means Heinz' – has made it possible for Heinz to be market leader and extract a high price premium too. Or take a more recent example where a commodity market has been transformed into a branded market: flour. This is a large market where the competing products are almost indistinguishable in functional performance. Competition used, accordingly, to be based on fierce price discounting. Until, that is, RHM turned the market upside down with its branded marketing campaign for Homepride based on the bowler-hatted flour-grader and the slogan: 'Graded Grains Make Finer Flour'. RHM gained both market share and a price premium. Many industrial companies have discovered also that markets previously thought to be 'commodity' bear gardens can be turned into higher margin ones where one competitor gains an advantage based on service, technical excellence, industrial branding, or some other attribute of value to buyers.

COMMUNICOPIA

Term invented by Goldman Sachs to describe the cornucopia of new information, entertainment and communications services. Also used to describe the multimedia world, the global TELEPUTING village.

COMPANY BOARD

See BOARD and DIRECTOR.

COMPANY DOCTOR

Mr Fix-it who goes into troubled companies and runs them for a time to restore them to health (or until they die). Also called CRISIS MANAGER, INTERIM MANAGER or TROUBLESHOOTER.

COMPANYISM

Kenichi OHMAE's word for blinkered adherence to a company's traditional formulae for success, narrowing the field of vision to simply doing more better. A superior, 'non-companyist' approach is to think differently and in a consumerist way: how can the company innovate to deliver greater value to customers?

COMPANY WORKER
Term used by BELBIN to describe a team's organiser/administrator.

COMPENSATING BALANCE
An amount deposited by a customer with a bank in return for a much larger loan. Illogical practice used when there is a ceiling on the rate of interest, so that the bank can effectively make more than the maximum return, or when the bank wants an excuse to charge more than is apparent.

COMPENSATION
Very unfortunate American word for total pay. Best avoided unless you think work is injurious.

COMPETENCES
Skills that an organisation has: what it is good at. Much recent thinking has stressed that an organisation's operating skills relative to competition are at least as important to its success as the strategy it has. To be successful an organisation must be at least as good as its competition in certain CORE COMPETENCES. For example, in retailing one of the most important skills is Buying and Merchandising, that is, procuring goods that consumers will want to buy and displaying them attractively. This very obvious statement explains in large part why some retailers, like The Gap or Marks & Spencer, are consistently more successful than their market rivals. Assessing and improving competences (relative to competition) has rightly become the top priority for many managements.

COMPETENCIES
The American version of COMPETENCES.

COMPETITION, TIME-BASED
See TIME-BASED COMPETITION.

COMPETITIVE ADVANTAGE
One of the most enduring and valuable catchwords of strategy. Competitive advantage obtains when one player has identified a market or market NICHE where it is possible to have a price advantage, or a cost advantage, or both, over competitors.

Price advantage means that the product or service is thought sufficiently superior by its buyers to make a price premium (for equivalent quality and cost to produce) possible. Brand leaders usually command a price premium over secondary brands or own label products, sometimes as much as 20–40%, which far exceeds the additional cost of advertising and superior product formulation.

Cost advantage can come from superior scale (and therefore greater spreading of fixed costs), from having lower factor costs (for example, by using cheap labour), from superior technology, or simply having workers who perform their tasks more intelligently or quickly.

Competitive advantage is usually, although not invariably, related to superior market share in a defined SEGMENT. Even if not caused by competitive advantage, market leadership should be the result of competitive advantage: otherwise it is being under-exploited.

COMPETITIVE SURVEILLANCE

If business success largely revolves around beating competitors, being aware of what they are doing is clearly important. Illegal competitive surveillance, such as bugging the boardroom, is clearly both criminal and wrong. Yet many companies fail to take advantage of perfectly legal and ethical means of surveillance. These include market share intelligence, interviews with customers, machine manufacturers, suppliers and ex-employees, reading public but inaccessible data (such as local newspapers, planning applications and even in-house magazines, which sometimes go to outside public libraries). Competitive information should be gathered with a specific purpose in mind, such as thinking through what capacity expansions are planned or likely, or analysing the relative cost position of the firm against that of the competitor.

COMPLETE FINISHER

One of BELBIN's eight team roles: the person who ensures other team members follow through and meet deadlines.

COMPLIANCE

The process of firms ensuring that all their employees meet strict legal and regulatory requirements, especially those required by tax, anti-fraud and stock exchange authorities. For example, firms operating in financial markets must ensure that PRICE SENSITIVE INFORMATION is not abused by their employees, and that confidential information of clients is kept confidential. Compliance has been tightened up greatly in the last decade and all firms with access to price sensitive information have rigorous procedures enforced by line management and a Compliance Officer. Failure to comply can result in criminal penalties for both individuals and corporations in most financial centres.

COMPOUND ANNUAL GROWTH RATE

See CAGR.

COMPUTER INTEGRATED MANUFACTURING
See CIM.

CONCENTRATION
The extent to which few suppliers cover the market. The UK grocery retailing market is highly concentrated, with 75% of it being provided by five supermarket chains; the American grocery retailing market is much less concentrated. Concentration is often measured by the market share controlled by the largest four or five suppliers, known respectively as the C RATIO and the C5 RATIO. Another measure is the HERFINDAHL INDEX.

Most markets have the potential to be concentrated and a FRAGMENTED MARKET should be a challenge for suppliers to undertake the process of concentration. In the absence of misguided ANTI-TRUST constraints, it is economically logical to have up to 80% of a market controlled by three competitors, with perhaps 40%, 25% and 15% of the market for the number 1, 2 and 3 respectively.

CONCERT PARTY
A group of investors acting in league (in concert), usually to try to obtain control of a company before the target realises the danger.

CONGLOMERATE
A firm that has many different divisions making a wide variety of different and unrelated products. Examples include Mitsubishi, Raytheon, BTR and Hanson.

In the UK and many other countries the proportion of the private sector being provided by conglomerates has gone up sharply and consistently. In 1950, 75% of the largest 200 British companies derived the majority of their sales from a single business. By 1985 this proportion had more than halved to 35%. Similar changes have taken place in the USA and all the main Continental countries, although sometimes not quite to the same degree. In the UK the process of 'conglomeratisation' has been helped appreciably by relatively liberal rules allowing takeovers, including hostile bids. As other countries gradually liberalise their own acquisition rules, the incidence of conglomerates may well increase at a faster rate.

Conglomerates grow and prosper when they have a well-honed ability to add value to acquisitions (or, more rarely, to organic expansion efforts). Although they may look random, most conglomerates do in fact specialise in certain broad types of businesses: those that they can add value to. Hanson is a good example, with its focus on low technology businesses in stable markets, where its cost reduction techniques and the relentless requirement for managers to meet their budgets can squeeze a great deal out of previously under-performing firms. Similarly, Mitsubishi is in a wide range of businesses, but they are all susceptible to mid- to high-technological advance, have global economies of scale, can be branded, and respond to the quest for global market share. Unless a conglomerate has a set of skills that can be applied to new businesses (especially acquired businesses) it will simply be an INDUSTRIAL HOLDING COMPANY, a category that is declining rather than growing.

Conglomerates able to re-allocate cash in an appropriate way, and/or provide management supervision and skills capable of raising returns, will continue to grow at the expense of more focused companies with lower management skills and willpower. A conglomerate lives or dies by superior management skill. Negotiating skills – the ability to buy companies and divisions cheap and sell dear by UNBUNDLING – and the use of high financial LEVERAGE are also important tools in the conglomerate toolkit, but without superior management skills a conglomerate may make an acquisition too far and lose its edge. There are some spectacular failures of conglomerates, such as Textron, Polly Peck and Maxwell Communications, to set alongside the successes.

CONJOINT ANALYSIS

Very useful market research technique that asks consumers to make a series of choices between two alternative product/service packages. For example, would you prefer this model of car with central locking at £20,000 or without at £19,500? By iterating quickly (using a computer screen) through a long series of such trade-offs the true consumer preference can be arrived at with a high degree of reliability: conjoint analysis is able to predict market shares of new products with unusual accuracy. A specialist computer package is necessary to conduct this analysis properly.

CONSIGNMENT, GOODS ON CONSIGNMENT

Goods on a sale or return basis.

CONSOLIDATED ACCOUNTS

Accounts prepared for a parent company and its subsidiaries to summarise the total affairs of the group as though it were simply one company.

CONSOLIDATION

1. The process of rationalising an industry by acquisition in order to increase CONCENTRATION. 2. A period of digestion in a company's history following rapid change and/or expansion. 3. The process of preparing CONSOLIDATED ACCOUNTS.

CONSORTIUM

A group of companies that come together for a defined purpose, usually a one-off event relating to part of the business of each company and not implying a longer term STRATEGIC ALLIANCE. Consortia are usually formed to bid for a large contract, often a public sector one, where each party brings different expertise. Thus an INVESTMENT BANK may form a consortium with a building company for a large overseas contract to build a dam, for example, with the investment bank organising the finance and the building company overseeing the physical execution of the project.

CONSORTIUM BANK

Bank owned by a number of other banks, in order to gain exposure to new types of activity. For example, in the 1970s, consortium banks were formed to lend to Latin America or other special markets. On the wane as banks are more willing to enter new markets alone.

CONSORTIUM BID

A takeover BID where two or more parties are in alliance, as in the unsuccessful bid led by Sir James Goldsmith for ICI. Consortium bids are difficult to organise because of the different interests of the parties and the delay caused by debate between the parties.

CONSTITUENCY

Another name for STAKEHOLDER, that is, a collective group (such as customers, suppliers, employees, bankers or shareholders) to whom a firm has obligations. See STAKEHOLDER for the theory behind such language and why the theory is flawed.

CONSTRUCTIVE DISMISSAL

Where an employer forces someone to leave by making life difficult; the employee leaves apparently voluntarily, but the employer is found liable to pay compensation

CONTESTED TAKEOVER

A bid that is rejected by the board of the TARGET. See HOSTILE BID. Contrast AGREED BID.

CONTINGENCY THEORY

Theory that says there is no universally right way to organise a firm: 'it all depends' on the culture, the people, the degree of inter-dependence of activities within the firm, and the external environment. If this sounds vague and unhelpful, contingency theory goes on to say under what circumstances a MATRIX ORGANISATION is desirable (when there is a great deal of cross-functional and cross-product interaction), when it is more appropriate to centralise and de-centralise, and so on. Contingency theory at least removed many of the simplistic notions and universal prescriptions that had previously held sway. Contingency theory is held in high esteem by most academics and has been applied outside the narrowly organisational arena, for example in marketing and strategy. Managers, who still like to be told in simple, clear terms what to do on Monday morning, are not such great fans.

CONTINGENT LIABILITY

A potential liability, contingent on another event which may or may not happen. If a firm is being sued for something it confidently denies, it still has a contingent liability that must be declared to shareholders if it is potentially material.

CONTINUOUS IMPROVEMENT

A Japanese concept holding that COMPETITIVE ADVANTAGE of a company accrues from the persistent search for improvement and a series of tiny steps made continuously, rather than from great leaps forward. The latter are more consistent with Anglo-Saxon cultures, which helps to explain the popularity of BPR (Business Process Re-engineering). The evidence is that the Japanese approach works very effectively for Asian cultures, while more revolutionary techniques are both more necessary and more acceptable for Anglo-Saxons.

CONTRACT

Legal agreement, verbal or written.

CONTRACTING-OUT

Process of using outside suppliers of services to a corporation or public authority rather than using an internal department. There is a strong and increasing trend towards contracting-out in both business and government, largely to cut cost, but partly also motivated by the belief that organisations should concentrate on their CORE COMPETENCES and leave other specialists to fulfil other roles. Some astute observers, such as Charles HANDY, believe that contracting-out will eventually transform our economic landscape, leading most organisations to employ far fewer people, the CORE WORKERS, while using armies of CONTRACTORS from several smaller, specialist firms. One result will be that many people will leave larger organisations half-way through their working lives to found or join contracting organisations. See also OUTSOURCING and SHAMROCK ORGANISATION.

CONTRACTORS

Those individuals and contracting firms that provide specialist services to larger firms. Contractors may be cleaners or rocket scientists, construction workers or board-room consultants. Charles HANDY divides the labour force of the future into three groups: the CORE WORKERS, the CONTRACTUAL FRINGE (meaning the contractors who sits on the edge of the firm employing the core workers, and who may have a continuous or recurrent relationship with that firm), and the FLEXIBLE LABOUR FORCE, a pool of people available for part-time or temporary work as and when required. See CONTRACTING OUT and SHAMROCK ORGANISATION.

CONTRACTUAL FRINGE
See CONTRACTORS.

CONTRARIAN
Someone who opposes conventional wisdom, or a school of thought that does so. Often applied to investors who buy when everyone else is selling, or vice versa. Contrarians are opinionated, risk seekers, have strong nerves, and are often right.

CONTRIBUTION
Accounting term: the difference between the selling price and variable costs, or put another way, the contribution towards fixed overheads. There is often a temptation towards MARGINAL PRICING: to accept any business that makes a contribution even though it makes a FULL COST loss. If more than a small part of a firm's business makes a contribution but incurs a full cost loss there is trouble ahead.

CONTROL, COMPANY CONTROL
A firm has control if it owns over 50% of the voting shares in the relevant company.

CONTROL SAMPLE
A normal or dummy sample with which to compare the results of experiments in marketing or any other function.

CONTROL SYSTEMS
Any organised method of measuring and monitoring the attainment of objectives (such as customer quality levels or market share) or budgets, comparing actual results against plans, feeding back results and taking action to correct deviations from plan. Sensible and simple control systems are often conspicuous by their absence, since far more energy goes into deciding objectives than controlling their achievement. On the other hand, some companies such as Hanson and BTR have built their success largely on the dogged and relentless application of financial control systems. Control systems for non-financial objectives are much more difficult to enforce, because of the variability of outcomes possible and the difficulty of using a few simple measures to measure progress. Nevertheless, good control is at the heart of good management, and it is surprising how little thought is given to devising better control systems. It is at least as important to have an appropriate control system as to apply it properly. Arguably, the decline of Western industry in terms of global market share can be in part attributed to our unthinking (if often sloppy) adherence to

accounting control systems that may have been appropriate to the mid-nineteenth century joint-stock company but are totally inappropriate in the battle for global market share.

CONVENIENCE GOOD

Product bought frequently and not shopped around for (little price comparison).

CONVERTIBLE BOND/LOAN STOCK

A loan which the lender can choose to convert into shares of the company in lieu of repayment. Usually in unquoted companies.

CONVERTIBLE PREFERENCE SHARE

A long-term loan that may be converted into ORDINARY SHARES of the borrower at the option of the lender at certain times and share prices. Also called convertible shares, usually quoted on the stock market alongside the ordinary shares. Convertibles are lower risk than the ordinary shares, usually higher YIELD, have less upside potential, but more upside potential than ordinary loans. The convertibility is a bonus to the lender and enables the borrower to obtain a lower interest rate than for a straight loan. A very useful financial instrument.

CONVERTIBLE UNSECURED LOAN STOCK (CULS)

See CULS.

COO (Chief Operating Officer)

Role of US origin whereby the CEO (Chief Executive) has reporting to him the COO, who then controls the majority or all operating chiefs. It makes good sense in the USA where the CEO is usually also the CHAIRMAN. In the UK and other countries where the Chairman and CEO are separate people, the need for a COO is less obvious. Yet the COO role is increasingly popular outside the USA. It usually indicates that the CEO is tired of the day-to-day running of the firm and wants to behave more like the Chairman. This is not necessarily a bad thing, especially if the actual Chairman is not active or if the CEO is trying to transform the company and needs to act as an agent provocateur, outside the normal constraints of the hierarchy. A good CEO with a good COO can usually achieve radical change much more easily.

COOKIE CUTTER

US term for a standard methodology applied to all situations. See also UNIVERSAL PRODUCT.

CO-OP

A co-operative organisation which aims to satisfy the needs of its workers or members rather than make a profit for shareholders. Co-operatives have been important in a number of industries including retailing, wholesaling, agriculture and savings banks. Co-operatives are in tune with much modern thinking about the need for consensus in organisations, but find it difficult to have a customer focus, since most co-ops are more concerned about worker/member welfare. In most countries co-ops are consolidating and losing market share to commercial organisations.

CORE BUSINESS

During the 1980s it became fashionable for diversified firms to categorise businesses as either 'core' or 'non-core'. A core business is one which the firm intends to keep and develop. Non-core businesses are candidates for sale if a good offer arrives.

CORE COMPETENCE

What a company does especially well. See COMPETENCES.

CORE PROCESS RE-DESIGN

See CPR.

CORE SKILLS

What a business is really good at. See COMPETENCES.

CORE TIME

Under FLEXITIME, the central part of the day when all employees must be present.

CORE WORKERS

Those people who are central to an organisation's success and who need to be nurtured and rewarded accordingly. This professional core, increasingly made up of qualified professionals, technicians and managers, comprise the knowledge and skills that explain an organisation's success (or lack thereof). Core workers are precious, hard to replace, expensive and increasingly footloose. Because they are expensive, organisations are tending to be more discriminating in defining what functions and which people should be regarded as core workers, resulting both in DOWNSIZING, and also in CONTRACTING-OUT functions that used to be performed by core workers. Core workers are coming to be a privileged but hard-working elite, who in return for high pay, rewarding work and a CAUSE they can believe in, are willing to dedicate themselves to the success of their firms. See also CONTRACTORS and SHAMROCK ORGANISATION.

CORPORATE CULTURE

See CULTURE.

CORPORATE FINANCE

Department within a MERCHANT or INVESTMENT BANK that raises capital for clients and assists on major transactions such as a takeover BID or DEFENCE.

CORPORATE GOVERNANCE

The rules and procedures to ensure that a company is properly run, that the right directors are in place with their roles defined, and that directors behave appropriately and in accordance with both the law and best practice. How companies are governed varies widely from country to country and even within countries, and there is no simple, universal model that can be followed. Corporate governance was a neglected issue in most countries until the late 1980s; now it is a hot topic, both important and controversial. The debate is concerned with questions like: What is the role of the CHAIRMAN? Of the CEO? Of the outside (non-executive) directors? And even, what is the purpose and objective function of the firm itself?

Here governance issues begin to shade into the broader question of what corporations are for and to whom they should be responsible. In Britain the debate has generated consensus on only two points: that the roles of Chairman and Chief Executive should be separated, so that one person should not have both positions; and that NON-EXECUTIVE DIRECTORS should be properly independent of executive management and have more power. On the other hand there is no real consensus on whose interests the firm should put first.

Attention has recently been focused on international comparisons, and in particular the perceived value of the German model. The most important differentiators are the prevalence of large shareholders (often with 25% or more) and the interest that these shareholders (who are often suppliers or customers) take in the company, leading to a high degree of stability and commitment; and the extreme difficulty of making hostile takeovers.

Some allege that the latter makes management complacent and inclined to hang on to loss-making businesses for too long, but an opposite view is that the fear of takeover is distracting, destructive and inhibiting. German companies, like Japanese ones, do not generally place the interests of shareholders first: rather, the 'good of the company long-term' is the guiding principle. Although rather woolly, this does seem to lead to greater investment and commitment on the part of employees, suppliers and customers to the firm.

There are some indications, however, that the larger German corporations want or need to tap into the international capital markets in order to be able to finance expansion or takeovers, and, if so, the Anglo-Saxon model of management responsible to shareholders may come to the fore for these large companies (which, however, only account for a third of turnover in the German economy, owing to the predominance of the medium-sized, owner-managed firms, the *MITTELSTAND*). See FAMILY FIRM, *MITTELSTAND*, PURPOSE and STAKEHOLDERS.

CORPORATE IDENTITY

The face a firm presents to the outside world, including but not confined to its name, logo, corporate advertising, and, if it has one, corporate catch-phrase (such as Avis' 'We try harder'). Corporate identity has become big business to design firms and specialist advertising agencies and has been elevated by persuasive design gurus like Wally Olins on to the boardroom agenda. Olins and others stress that corporate identity should reflect the organisation's strategy and core values: it is not just a matter of seductive logos and pretty stationery. There is no doubt that high profile corporate identity moves can change the perception of a company, both inside and outside it, nor that corporate identity needs to reviewed from time to time, especially after major change such as a MERGER. On the other hand, when one considers that a major multinational like BT or BP may spend hundreds of millions of pounds on a corporate identity programme, one has to ask whether the corporate identity industry's tools are well enough developed to spend such money wisely.

CORPORATE LEVEL STRATEGY

Strategy for the corporate centre. See CORPORATE STRATEGY (meaning 2), CENTRE and GOOLD.

CORPORATE PLANNING

When CORPORATE STRATEGY became popular, in the 1970s, it was generally felt that every major corporate should have a large corporate planning staff to administer an annual cycle of corporate planning. This often involves operating units generating large amounts of paper, passing it to the next level up for review and consolidation with plans from other units, and so on until the corporate planning department and eventually the CEO and the Board could consider and approve the plans. Thereafter nothing much happened to change what would have happened anyway.

Fortunately corporate planning as such is on its last legs. Strategy is recognised as too important to leave to the planners. Strategy is a line function, one for all executive leaders. Strategy should involve thinking and action, not planning, with its faintly Stalinist and strongly bureaucratic taint.

CORPORATE RAIDER

Rich individual or firm that buys a STRATEGIC STAKE in an underperforming company and tries to force it to improve performance. The raider may also sell on the stake to an industrial firm interested in bidding for the underperformer, or try to force the latter to buy back his shares at a premium. The latter tactic is called GREENMAIL.

CORPORATE RAIN DANCE

When a foreign subsidiary of a multinational corporation goes through a corporate ritual to comply with head office requests, but continues to run things its own way. See also BARONS and TRANSNATIONAL CORPORATION.

CORPORATE RELIGION

The body of beliefs, CULTURE, rituals, stories, myths and symbols that characterise firms which are 'believed in' by employees. Not all firms have a sufficiently strong culture to be deemed to have a corporate religion: unscientific estimates are 10% for the UK, 20% for the USA and 50% for Japan. There is, however, increasingly robust evidence that companies with corporate religions perform better over long periods of time than their competitors. The companies themselves may fight shy of the word religion, but they have the five common attributes of: sharp corporate personality; a clear sense of direction; a PURPOSE or CAUSE to inspire people; enthusiasm, sacrifice and team work; and above-average calibre of people and strong COMPETENCES. Companies that have corporate religions include Apple, The Body Shop, British Airways, the American GE, Goldman Sachs, Hanson, Hewlett-Packard, Ikea, Marks & Spencer, Mars, Matsushita, McKinsey, Microsoft, Nike, Procter & Gamble, TI, Sony and Virgin. These firms command enthusiasm and commitment from their employees and have a degree of *esprit de corps* that makes them formidable competitors. See also CHANGE MANAGEMENT, CULTURE and TRANSFORMATION.

CORPORATE RESPONSIBILITY

The obligations a company owes to society and to its immediate environment such as the local community where it operates. Increasing attention has been focused on corporate responsibility in the past few years, and most senior businessmen are keen to stress that their companies are good citizens. Companies increasingly give not just money but the time and commitment of their employees on social responsibility programmes, and the participating companies believe they get good value in terms of greater employee commitment to the firm as a result, quite apart from any additional benefit from the way that customers, potential customers or regulators might view the company.

Some enthusiasts propose two reasons why firms should do much more: (i) the instrumental view that private enterprise is simply much better at doing anything, including social good, than government or charity; and (ii) the apocalyptic view, that unless corporations are seen to contribute much more to society (independent of their commercial function), society will increasingly restrict them and deprive them of the best people (because the most talented cadre will not want to work in business).

On the other hand, there are both like Milton Friedman who put forward a robust intellectual case that corporations are there to make profit for shareholders and that they have no business spending resources on corporate responsibility projects: that is what government and voluntary groups are for. In my view Friedman has too narrow and legalistic a view of the firm's role. No firm is an island sufficient unto itself and its customers. See PURPOSE and STAKEHOLDERS.

CORPORATE SOCIAL RESPONSIBILITY
See CORPORATE RESPONSIBILITY.

CORPORATE STRATEGY
1. The basis on which a company can beat its competitors, and the actions a company takes to strengthen its COMPETITIVE ADVANTAGE and maximise the value of the firm. Properly used, the word strategy is all about summoning up willpower and resources to beat competitors and then doing exactly that. Strategy derives from the Greek for generalship and means the marshalling and leadership of troops and weaponry in war against a particular enemy. **2.** Corporate strategy is also used to mean the strategy of the top corporate level strategy, the Centre, as opposed to the strategy for individual business units ('BUSINESS UNIT STRATEGY').Corporate strategy should include the major aspects of business unit strategy for the firm's most important businesses, but it also includes the deployment, inspiration and development of the firm's most important ammunition (in the form of people, knowledge and money) against the firm's most important competitors in order to build market share, earnings and corporate COMPETENCES and to put competitors out of business altogether or at least persuade them to withdraw from markets which are the most profitable for and important to the firm. It is often said that corporate strategy is concerned with the allocation of resources (cash and people) between different businesses, and tools such as the BCG MATRIX and BUSINESS ATTRACTIVENESS matrix have greatly helped resource allocation decisions, but more important than allocation of resources is the creation and magnification of the firm's skills, knowledge, self-confidence and fighting spirit. See also CENTRE and PARENTING ADVANTAGE.

It should be noted that corporate strategy is not a plan and it is certainly not a document, whatever the cover may say. A firm's strategy is what it does against competitors, not what it says it does or thinks it does. Every firm has a strategy, and some work better than others.

CORPORATE VENTURING
Venture capital investment by a non-venture capitalist, (i.e. by a normal commercial firm). Often done to gain experience of a new technology and market without having to staff up for it inside the venturing firm. In the USA, corporate venturing is well established and regularly accounts for

about 20% of the venture capital industry's funding. In the UK, corporate venturing cannot be hailed as a success. The proportion of venture capital funds comprised in corporate venturing peaked at 6% (£34) in 1988 and at £62m (4%) in 1989, and has headed south ever since. Further, the majority of funds come from pension funds, insurance companies and other financial institutions rather than 'real' industrial corporate venturers. It seems that large UK firms are uncomfortable with owning parts of small businesses: the view is that if the business is worthwhile, it should be wholly owned. This is short-sighted: large firms are going to have to become or behave as if they are much smaller in the future. Corporate venturing is one way of large firms observing and learning from such behaviour before it is too late.

CORPORATE VIRTUAL WORKSPACE

Non-physical work environment, comprising links between members of a firm and/or outsiders provided by modern communications and information technology. The proponents of this trend even argue that the future corporation may not need any physical space at all apart from the system hosting the corporate virtual workspace: hence the future 'cyberspace' corporation will exist entirely in CYBERSPACE. Exaggerated, but a graphic illustration of a powerful trend. See TELEWORKER and HOMEWORKING.

CORRELATION

Statistical term meaning the degree to which two variables tend to go together. Not to be confused with CAUSATION. For example, gout is highly correlated with consumption of port, but not caused by it: rich food, a third variable, is the cause.

CORRELATION COEFFICIENT

Number between -1 and $+1$ indicating the strength of correlation; -1 means a perfect negative correlation; $+1$ a perfect positive correlation, and 0 no correlation at all. In general, a positive correlation of less than 0.7 is not to be relied upon.

COST-BENEFIT ANALYSIS (CBA)

A monetary assessment of a project's worth which compares all its costs and benefits. Often used to assess public sector projects where an attempt is made to quantify social benefits. Can also be used by private sector managers to take account of 'soft' benefits of a major project.

In CBA all the benefits and costs of the project are listed and quantified. For example, the benefits of an underground rail extension will include the social benefits of lower traffic congestion and pollution above ground, as well as avoidance of unemployment pay for those whom the project will put into employment. The benefits are quantified over time and then compared to the costs, usually via a DCF (Discounted Cash Flow). The project will be approved if the benefits exceed the costs by a certain margin. Capital will be rationed by only approving the highest Cost-to-Benefit ratio projects, up until the time that capital is exhausted.

CBA is not much used by the private sector, but is finding new favour with some executives. It can be used to evaluate projects that are thought to have major but indirect value, such as a CORPORATE IDENTITY programme. Even approximate quantification of soft benefits can be useful, provided CBA is not used to justify decisions already taken.

COST CENTRE
A department within a firm that has a budget and whose performance is measured largely on minimising cost. Contrast PROFIT CENTRE.

COST DRIVERS
The most important influences on the overall and relative costs of a firm or industry. In one industry the most important cost drivers may be scale and technology, in another they may be labour cost and raw material cost. Identifying the cost drivers is key, both to understanding where the greatest improvement is possible and also understanding whether and how it is possible to build a competitive cost advantage.

COST OF CAPITAL
The cost to a firm of its capital: divided into the cost of EQUITY (share) capital and the cost of debt. The latter is nearly always much lower, so the greater the proportion of debt (that is, the greater the GEARING or LEVERAGE), the lower the weighted average cost of capital. Many market leaders serve their shareholders badly by having too conservative a CAPITAL STRUCTURE (too little debt) and thus have a higher cost of capital than is necessary: this makes life easier for managers but depresses EARNINGS PER SHARE below what they could be and may allow marginal competitors to remain in a market.

COST OF GOODS SOLD
Also called COGS and COST OF SALES. The total cost of production including raw materials cost, labour and production overhead.

COST OF SALES
See COST OF GOODS SOLD.

COST SHARING
The extent to which two products can share the same costs. If there is high cost sharing (over 50%) the two products may constitute just one SEGMENT. See ECONOMIES OF SCOPE.

COSTS OF COMPLEXITY

Very important idea that the more complex a business, the higher the costs, for any given level of scale. Complexity can mitigate the advantages of additional scale or even overturn them altogether. Complexity arises when a firm extends its product line, customers, areas of expertise and/or use of different technologies in order to expand. The wise firm seeks extra scale without extra complexity, or reduces complexity without sacrificing scale.

Complexity cannot be totally avoided, and is often market-driven. What separates the operationally skilful firm from others is very often its ability to manage customer-demanded complexity simply: providing CUSTOMISED or preferably CUSTOMERISED products with little added internal complexity.

But very often complexity is self-inflicted rather than market-driven. Customers may say they want a special product or service, but be unwilling to pay for the real extra cost: they do not want it badly enough. And in many cases complexity is nothing at all to do with the customer, but just reflects bad management, and is often against the interests of both the firm and the customer. Production systems that resemble spaghetti, poor factory layouts, unnecessary stages in the production process, quality control departments (instead of building quality in on the line), excess staff numbers and too many functional boundaries, insistence on doing everything within the firm rather than OUTSOURCING wherever possible, interfering head office functions: all of these are complexity own-goals.

Waging war on complexity can lead simultaneously to stunning cost reductions and improvements in customer value. About half of all the value-added costs in the average firm are complexity related, and half of these provide opportunities for radical cost reduction. Some clues to reducing the costs of complexity are: reducing the number of current suppliers and entering more collaborative relationships with them; buying in components and services rather than 'making' them oneself wherever possible; avoiding products or customers where added complexity is not fully compensated; eliminating complexity from product design and making product families modular; reducing the number of process steps; improving factory lay-out; creating small business units within the firm that take charge of a whole product/process from design to customer delivery; decimating head office; abolishing management hierarchy; reducing the information collected and disseminated; and generally not doing anything that is not essential to making customers happy. See BRP, AVERAGE COSTING, SPECIALS, MAKE VERSUS BUY, OUTSOURCING and VALUE CHAIN.

COST STRUCTURE

The total cost elements of a company broken down into key elements and often shown in the form of a bar, which can then be compared to the cost

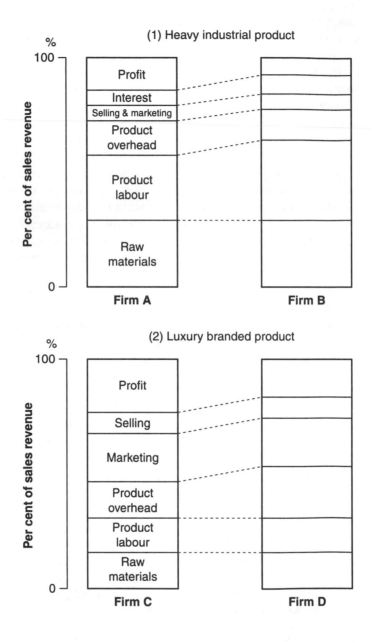

Figure 16 Competitive cost structures

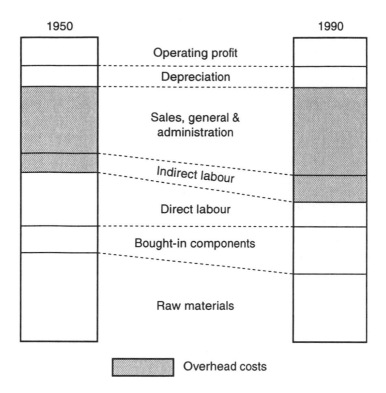

Figure 17 Typical cost structures in 1950 and 1990

structure of a competitor making the same product, or to the cost structure of other products in the same firm, as in Figure 16.

Cost structures have changed over time: as the 'typical' cost structures in Figure 17 show.

The major change has been the decrease in direct labour, due to greater automation, and the increases in indirect labour and other overhead. This makes the allocation of fixed costs to products much more important than previously. In fact, 'fixed' cost very often increases as turnover goes up, particularly if the firm is adding additional product lines or product variants, or additional customer service and after-sales support in an effort to appeal to a new customer group or just to gain more market share. Product proliferation and more demanding customers have increased the proportion of overhead costs, and the latter, if not carefully controlled, can negate or overturn the advantage of increased turnover. See AVERAGE COSTING, AVERAGE PRICING, and COSTS OF COMPLEXITY.

COTTAGE INDUSTRY

Small-scale industry where the unit of production can be one person in one home, characteristic of the time before and after the industrial revolution. See HOMEWORKING.

COST TO SWITCH, COSTS TO SWITCH

The psychological and/or financial cost to move from one supplier to another. Classical micro-economic theory held that buyers would switch from one supplier to another if there was even a very slight difference in price, provided product quality was equivalent. In practice, there are very often high costs to switch suppliers, even if they are of equal quality. A supplier may know a customer's business well and educating a new supplier may take time and effort. This is an often hidden BARRIER TO ENTRY that can make market shares STICKY and make it difficult to gain share. Consultants who know a company well can often rely on the cost to switch to keep out competitors.

COUNTERFEIT

Illegal copy of a brand or product.

COUPON

1. The interest or interest rate payable on a bond. 2. The dividend payable on a preference share.

COVENANT

Restrictions imposed on a borrower, breach of which may entitle the lender to immediate repayment.

CPR (Core Process Re-design)

An early form of BPR (Business Process Re-engineering).

CRAFTING STRATEGY

Term given by Henry MINTZBERG to the intuitive, trial-and-error process of developing strategy, both more often practised and more effective than more traditional, rational models.

CRASH

Sharp and pronounced stock market fall.

CREATIVE ACCOUNTING

The legal art of gently cooking or roasting the books in order to present a flattering picture of profits and the balance sheet. Much practised even today, despite the tightening up of accounting principles. One area particularly susceptible to such creativity is acquisition accounting, where large provisions can be made after an acquisition which may not be needed and can subsequently be released when needed to smooth profits. Some very large British, European and American companies indulge in creative accounting so that their apparently impressive record of consistent earnings per share growth needs to be taken with large doses of salt. Two recent UK examples are Polly Peck and Maxwell Communications, where the auditors and outside directors were not able to detect either creative accounting or outright fraud.

CREDIT

1. Time allowed to a customer to pay for goods. 2. In DOUBLE ENTRY BOOK-KEEPING, every entry is either a CREDIT or a DEBIT.

CREDIT CARD

A plastic card for buying goods on credit. Contrast CHARGE CARD and DEBIT CARD.

CREDIT LINE

Borrowing facility available up to a certain amount.

CREDIT NOTE

Document giving the customer the right to goods up to a certain amount often used as a refund for returned goods.

CREDITORS

Another name for ACCOUNTS PAYABLE, or for the firms to whom money is owed.

CREDIT RATING

An assessment, often in the form of a numerical or alpha-numerical score, of the creditworthiness of firms or individuals, so that firms can decide whether to trade with the firm or make a loan to the individual.

CREDIT UNION

Savings bank started by depositors with a common affiliation. In the USA credit unions have assets exceeding $100 bn.

CRISIS MANAGEMENT

Training in how to handle an emergency, like product contamination or the total failure of computer systems.

CRISIS MANAGER

Confusing term not related to CRISIS MANAGEMENT, generally used to mean the same as COMPANY DOCTOR or INTERIM MANAGER.

CRITICAL PATH ANALYSIS (CPA)

Task analysis laying out all the steps in a complex process (such as how to build a new oil refinery), how the steps relate to each other, how long each takes, and therefore the order in which they should be performed to produce the shortest overall time (the 'critical path'). Actual progress can then be monitored against this critical path, which is mapped on a chart by a series of overlapping lines.

CROSBY, PHILIP

American consultant, early pioneer of the quality movement.

CROSS-BORDER DEALS

An acquisition or merger where the two firms are domiciled in different countries. An increasing proportion, although still a minority, of all acquisitions are cross-border. Can have high synergies, but require very careful investigation and DUE DILIGENCE prior to the acquisition and very careful POST-ACQUISITION MANAGEMENT.

CROSS-RATE

Calculating a rate of exchange between two currencies by reference to a third, commonly used currency (like the US dollar).

CROSS-SUBSIDISATION

Where one profitable product subsidises an unprofitable one. Far more common than generally thought. See AVERAGE COSTING.

CROWN JEWELS

1. A company's most valuable possessions: may be a division, a particular operating company, a patent or technology, or anything most precious.
2. A takeover defence mechanism whereby the beleaguered company sells its Crown Jewels to a third party, thus removing the target's attractiveness to the hostile bidder and causing him to go away. See also DEFENCE AGAINST TAKEOVER.

CULS (Convertible Unsecured Loan Stock)

A useful type of CONVERTIBLE PREFERENCE SHARE that ranks as debt rather than equity and is subordinated to SENIOR DEBT.

CULTURE

The personality and character of a company, derived from generations of people and experience and leading people inside a firm to behave in certain characteristic ways without thinking about it. Different firms in the same country and industry may have radically different cultures, and the difference may be far more important in determining relative success than any other factor, including differences in strategy, which may themselves be partly explained by the culture. Increasing but still insufficient attention is being paid to creating and sustaining winning cultures within firms. It is impossible to succeed in a corporate TRANSFORMATION without such radical culture change, though this takes many years and single-minded determination by the leader of a firm. See also CHANGE MANAGEMENT and Charles HANDY's useful description of four GODS OF MANAGEMENT – APOLLO, ATHENA, DIONYSUS and ZEUS, which describe four broad cultural groups. Other useful dimensions of culture are:

- by class/background of senior staff;
- open and collaborative versus 'dinosaur' and backbiting culture;
- traditional/clubby versus professional;
- forgiving/low standards versus relentless/high standards;
- marketing and customer-led versus production/internal orientation;
- personal versus bureaucratic;
- intellectual versus street smart;
- 'learning' versus know-it-all;
- 'believed in' by staff versus 'not believed in'.

Such categorisations can be thought provoking but cannot fully capture the richness of each company's unique culture. Nothing is more important for management than understanding culture and how to change it. See *Wake Up & Shake Up Your Company* by Richard Koch and Andrew Campbell (1993) and *The Seven Cultures of Capitalism* by Charles Hampden-Turner and Fons Trompenaars. See also CORPORATE RELIGION.

CUM DIV
'With dividend'; a share being bought with the right to a future dividend that has been declared but not yet paid. Opposite is EX-DIV.

CUMULATIVE PREFERENCE SHARES
PREFERENCE SHARES which ensure that any backpayment of PREFERENCE DIVIDENDS due must be made before ordinary shareholders can receive a dividend.

CURRENT ASSET
An asset on a BALANCE SHEET which is expected to turn into cash within a year.

CURRENT COST ACCOUNTING (CCA)
Also called INFLATION ACCOUNTING. Adjusting a firm's traditional (HISTORICAL COST) accounts to take account of inflation, producing an additional PROFIT & LOSS STATEMENT and BALANCE SHEET. In these accounts the COST OF SALES is based on their replacement cost, while depreciation is based on the replacement cost of the assets, not their

actual historical cost. Not much used, especially now that inflation in most countries is back to moderate levels.

CURRENT LIABILITY

A liability on a BALANCE SHEET expected to be paid within a year.

CURRENT RATIO

CURRENT ASSETS divided by CURRENT LIABILITIES. Current assets should be greater than current liabilities (i.e. the ratio should be more than 1.00); if not, a liquidity crisis may loom. The problem with the current ratio is that it is not a sufficiently short-term test. Liquidity crises normally have a much shorter time horizon than one year. If you have to pay the tax authorities at the end of the month, it is little comfort that a large customer must pay you in ten weeks' time. The trend in current ratio is worth watching (especially if it is deteriorating), but a current ratio above 1.00 is not a guarantee of safety.

CUSHION BOND

Bond that an issuer can retire early.

CUSTODIAN

A bank, lawyer or other agent who looks after an investor's securities and associated paperwork.

CUSTOMER LOYALTY

The extent to which customers repeat-purchase from the same supplier. A crucial cause of high or low profits. See CUSTOMER RETENTION.

CUSTOMER PROPOSITION

A differentiating product or service of great appeal to a particular BUSINESS SEGMENT. Each important product or service offered by a firm should have a clear customer proposition.

CUSTOMER RETENTION

The extent to which customers repeat-purchase. Customers defect at average rates of 10–30%, and far more in some businesses like car dealing. Losing customers is expensive, because the marketing costs to win them over in the first place are so high. Differential customer retention can often explain a significant part of profit differences between firms. Increasing attention is being given to monitoring and increasing customer retention, since it has been discovered that a 5% shift in customer retention can result in 25–100% profit swings. Customer retention arises from CUSTOMER LOYALTY, which arises when superior value has been delivered. Loyalty in turn leads to higher market share of the chosen customer base, which is often the most value-conscious and least price-conscious part of the market, and therefore the most desirable. High share of value-conscious customers leads to lower costs, both directly through added volume, and indirectly through referrals and word-of-mouth appreciation, which lowers marketing and selling costs. The effect can carry through to employees, who are proud to be offering such good value to customers, and who in turn reinforce the value proposition by particularly good service. With turnover going up and costs going down, profits increase, which in turn allows further investment in product quality and service and in hiring and retaining the best employees: these effects further reinforce the competitive advantage of customer value and loyalty. This VIRTUOUS CIRCLE can carry on ad infinitum, until competitors with inferior value and loyalty go out of business, or are contained to unprofitable commodity segments. The most besotted adherents of customer retention claim that RELATIVE CUSTOMER RETENTION (RCR) explains differential competitor profitability much better than RELATIVE MARKET SHARE (RMS), RELATIVE COST POSITION (RCP) or any other variable. Whether this is true or not, providing customers with the best product and service is clearly one of the best ways to engender loyalty, customer retention and high relative market share, and it therefore makes sense to monitor both absolute and relative customer retention. It is clearly also true that the way to deliver SHAREHOLDER VALUE in the long term is to provide the best value to customers in the short, medium and long terms, so that the debates about whether to put customers or shareholders 'first' is largely sterile. A good starting point for creating trust between the firm and its customers, employees and shareholders alike is to provide the best possible customer value and obtain the highest relative retention rates.

CUSTOMER VALUE

The extent to which customers perceive a product or service as good value. See VFM (Value For Money) and CUSTOMER RETENTION.

CUSTOMERISED, CUSTOMERISING

Allowing customers to adapt products themselves: in Tom PETERS' words 'produced by, directed by and starring our customers'. The customer, not the firm, is the initiator. Why does Peters have a penchant for coining useful but ugly words?

CUSTOMISED, CUSTOMISING

Process of giving consumers a wide choice of product options or variants and letting them choose from the menu.

CV (Curriculum Vitae)

English for resumé.

CYBERNETICS

Study of regulatory mechanisms that have influenced computer systems and ROBOTICS and which stressed the role of FEEDBACK.

CYBERSPACE

What the corporation of the future will inhabit, rather than real physical space, according to certain business futurologists. To some extent it is already happening. See CORPORATE VIRTUAL WORKSPACE.

D

DATA

A much abused plural noun (incorrectly used by most managers as though it were singular) indicating the objective numerical and factual basis of analyses and conclusions. Roughly equivalent to 'facts' but implying a body of supporting figures and/or documents. Data are often not what they claim or seem to be: they could frequently better be described as 'capta', that is, data selected or even created to lead to the desired conclusion. When someone claims that 'the data say(s) X', it is best to remember Disraeli's comment on statistics.

DATABANK

Collection of DATA, usually stored on computer.

DATABASE

Often used as synonym for DATABANK but more correctly a computer SOFT-WARE package for storing data. See DATABASE MANAGEMENT SYSTEMS (DBMS).

DATABASE MANAGEMENT SYSTEMS (DBMS)

Interrelated software which makes multiple use of the same data in different applications possible. Comprises data description, data entry, data access, file creation and management applications generation. Most such systems are 'hier-archical', (i.e. follow a vertical logic), but in the last ten years RELATIONAL DATABASES have become popular because they relate all the data to all the other data, enabling quicker and easier access from any starting-point.

DATA HIGHWAY

The new electronic infrastructure vital to a nation's international competitiveness in the next century. In the USA, Congress has been debating the establishment of a National Research and Education Network, while a consortium of IBM, MCI and the State of Michigan is working on a private-sector version called Advanced Network Services.

DATA PROCESSING

Computing.

DAVID'S DICTUM

People in a firm are never where they should be.

DAWN RAID

1. Sudden early morning swoop on a company's shares shortly after the market opens when a RAIDER or bidder will offer to buy shares at above the prevailing price for a few minutes, and hope thereby to secure a sizeable stake without building it up patiently over weeks. Similar raids can also happen towards the end of a trading session, when they are called TEA TIME RAIDS. **2.** In the UK, the Inland Revenue also has a penchant for dawn raids, which in this case are when a large number of tax officials and police arrive at the premises of a business suspected of tax fraud, as with the swoop on Nissan UK in 1991. The UK Serious Fraud Office also conducts the occasional high-profile dawn raid.

DAY BOOK

Also called JOURNAL. **1.** Accounting book of original entries of documents and vouchers. **2.** Bound notebook in which notes are taken of all meetings in chronological order, often favoured by corporate financiers who want a near-verbatim record of what happened when.

DCF (Discounted Cash Flow)

Calculation used in valuation and investment appraisal which involves listing all the cashflows from a particular business or investment, applies a discount rate to each of them to equalise their effective value today (on the grounds that £100 cash this year is worth more than £100 cash next year), and then adds them up to provide a total value or DCF, which can then be compared either with the value today, or the amount of investment required, or with the value of other businesses or investments.

As a simple example, assume that you could invest £1,000 today, and that you would receive back £200 in each of the years 1 to 5, and then an additional (and final) £500 in year 6. Is this a good investment? On the face of it, yes, since you would receive in total £1,500 for your £1,000. But nearly everyone prefers cash now to cash later, both because spending is more pleasurable (for most people) than saving, and because inflation eats away at the value of money over time. Let us assume that you require money to increase at 15% per annum for you to be happy to make the investment. This 15% becomes your DISCOUNT RATE or HURDLE RATE. (15% is pretty much in line with average discount rates prevailing today, although arguably this is too high during times of low inflation.) You can now calculate the discounted value of the cash to come in over the next six years (Figure 18).

The cash flow from years 1–6 is only £817 instead of £1,500 on an undiscounted basis, so that the discounted cash flow including the £1,000 initial investment is negative (minus £183).

Another way of saying the same thing is that the PRESENT VALUE (PV) of the investment of £1,000 is only £817, and the NET PRESENT VALUE (NPV),

now	– £1,000	1.00	– £1,000
end year 1	+ £200	0.85	+ £170
end year 2	+ £200	0.72 (0.85 x 0.85)	+ £145
end year 3	+ £200	0.61 (0.72 x 0.85)	+ £122
end year 4	+ £200	0.52 (0.61 x 0.85)	+ £104
end year 5	+ £200	0.44 (0.52 x 0.85)	+ £88
end year 6	+ £500	0.38 (0.44 x 0.85)	+ £188
Discounted cash flow			– £183

Figure18 Illustration of a DCF calculation

that is, net of the original investment, is minus £183. Having done this calculation you would not invest.

DEAD CAT BOUNCE
Temporary stock-market up-tick after a crash.

DEBENTURE, DEBENTURE STOCK
Fixed-interest SECURITY issued by companies in return for long-term (usually 10–40 years) loans, secured either against specific company assets or by a FLOATING CHARGE on them.

DEBIT
1. An accounting entry in DOUBLE ENTRY BOOK-KEEPING of goods or services supplied by the company, thus either increasing its ASSETS or decreasing its LIABILITIES. **2.** To enter the value of goods supplied to a customer in his account with the supplier.

DEBIT CARD
A plastic CHEQUE used at stores instead of cash; it automatically debits the holder's account.

DEBT SERVICE RATIO
The value of a country's hard currency exports divided by its annual debt (interest and repayment) payments, and hence a crude way of assessing a country's credit-worthiness.

DEBIT NOTE

A note charging a customer for additional products supplied for which payment has not yet been received.

DE BONO, EDWARD (b. 1933)

Inventor and apostle of LATERAL THINKING. One big idea that has spawned 38 books and world-wide fame. Lateral thinking is not sequential, vertical or rational: it is discontinuous, turning ideas on their head or creating them 'from left field'. Uses analogy and random word association to break the tyranny of established ways of thinking. But is it lateral or vertical thinking that has developed this one theme into so many books?

DEBT

1. Funding that has a right to a known rate of interest and repayment terms and a first call on assets (ahead of the other form of funding, EQUITY) in the event of liquidation. Debt should be, but rarely is, used as a strategic weapon by profitable market leaders. Because these do not require high levels of debt in the CAPITAL STRUCTURE they do without it; but with more debt, they could be more aggressive, invest more, lower prices, provide better customer service, and still meet the required rate of return of shareholders while making life very difficult for marginal competitors. **2.** Money, goods or services owed.

DEBT SERVICE RATIO

The value of a country's hard currency exports divided by its annual debt (interest and repayment) payments, and hence a crude way of assessing a country's credit-worthiness.

DEBT TO EQUITY RATIO

DEBT divided by EQUITY. A measure of GEARING. High gearing can mean high risk (or, more rarely, an aggressive and well thought strategy). Bruce HENDERSON held that there was an optimal debt/equity ratio for every business, and that it was generally much higher than the actual debt/equity ratio: 'it is rarely less than the principal competitor's debt/equity ratio if there is real competition. It is usually much higher for the low cost market leader.' Another unheeded Hendersonism, but right.

DEBTOR

Someone who owes money, goods or services.

DEBT TO TOTAL FUNDING RATIO

DEBT divided by the sum of debt and EQUITY. An alternative ratio to DEBT TO EQUITY, also mostly used to assess risk.

DEBUG

Taking software faults out of a computer program.

DE-BUREAUCRATISATION

Turning an organisation from a BUREAUCRACY into an ADHOCRACY by means of DELAYERING and other techniques to wake up and shake up the firm.

DECENTRALISATION

Process of giving power to decentralised divisions or operating units. Popular trend from 1921 to 1993, but now the virtues of a small but powerful Centre are being rediscovered. See DIVISIONALISATION and CENTRE.

DECISION TREE

A flow chart that sets out possible future events and highlights the effects of decisions or chance occurrences in a sequential order. Can be very useful in estimating the probability that any event may happen, or simply in pinpointing the critical decisions that have to be made. For some peculiar reason decision trees are nearly always drawn from left to right, although I much prefer to draw them from top to bottom. Two examples are given. In Figure 19 a manufacturer is trying to decide whether to open a new factory, in the face of uncertainty about whether his main rival will decide to do the same thing and whether the economy will move into recession or boom. The decision tree helps him to lay out the possibilities and calculate the returns under all eight possible outcomes (Figure 19).

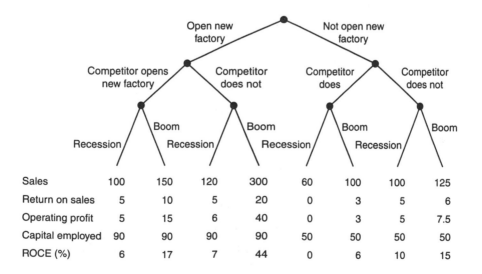

Sales	100	150	120	300	60	100	100	125
Return on sales	5	10	5	20	0	3	5	6
Operating profit	5	15	6	40	0	3	5	7.5
Capital employed	90	90	90	90	50	50	50	50
ROCE (%)	6	17	7	44	0	6	10	15

Figure19 Decision tree for Superior Sproggetts Limited

So far the decision tree has helped by laying out the possibilities, although it does not yet tell Superior Sproggetts Limited (SSL) what to do. For this we need to overlay on the decision tree the *probabilities* of each of the four possible outcomes arising from (a) an investment by SSL; and (b) a decision by SSL not to invest. Figure 20 overlays these probabilities and therefore allows a calculation of the EXPECTED VALUE (the weighted average value) in terms of ROCE (Return on Capital Employed) under both (a) and (b).

From Figure 20 it can be seen that investment has a much higher expected return on capital, at 22%, than the decision not to invest, which has an expected value of 8%. One important reason for this is that the competitor is much less likely to invest if SSL does so first. Adding the probabilities helps to highlight the importance of this judgement.

Decision trees can be used for a wide variety of purposes and are a great help in clarifying what should be done when events are uncertain and outcomes depend to some degree on earlier uncertain events.

DECLINING INDUSTRY

One where demand is falling and expected to continue to do so. Two comments can be made about declining industries. One is that there is no inevitability about secular decline in many cases. An industry may continue

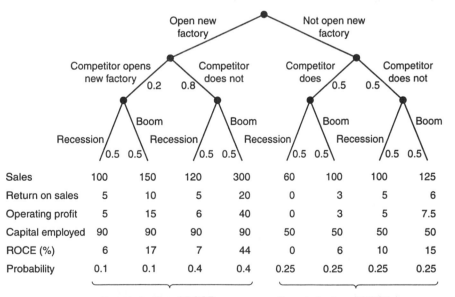

Figure 20 Decision tree with probabilities and expected values

declining solely because of lack of investment and imagination. Railroads in the USA are an example, where poor service, lack of investment and industry fatalism wrecked the industry, and more recent initiatives reversed the decline. Similarly, newspapers declined in most countries as TV gained ground, but the growth of segmented titles and freesheets have turned declining into growing markets. Cider in the UK is another example, as is 'real ale'. An example from Japan is the way that Yamaha has revived the piano industry by creating a PC-based retrofit and a new digital electronic piano, turning a market declining at 10% annually into an explosive growth market.

The second comment is that even if a market continues to decline, the last one or two players in the market can end up with a very profitable, extremely cash positive business. Often there is a greater payoff to gaining market share in declining than in growing markets, particularly if a position of DOMINANCE can be attained. Decline is often a mirage or an opportunity.

DEED

Legal document sometimes required to make a contract binding, as with transfers of shares or property.

DEFEASANCE

When bond issuers put liquid assets into trust so that they can then be used to pay interest and repay the principal.

DEFENCE AGAINST TAKEOVER

In the UK and particularly in the USA activity by management, aided by often very expensive advisers, to repulse unwanted bids has created a whole new set of tactics. These include: CROWN JEWELS DEFENCE, POISON PILL DEFENCE, SCORCHED EARTH DEFENCE, SHARK REPELLENT DEFENCE. Some of these, more often practised in the USA than the UK, are plainly against the interests of most shareholders. Defence activity is only justified if it is to gain the best possible price for all shareholders, rather than to serve the interests of incumbent management.

DEFERRED REVENUE OR INCOME

Revenue (usually in the form of cash) already received but which cannot yet pass through the books (cannot be recognised) because the goods or services have not yet been provided.

DEFERRED SHARES

Shares that do not yet have a right to a dividend (until and unless certain conditions, such as future profit targets, have been met).

DEFERRED TAXATION

Tax that will not have to be paid in the next year (but which may be paid thereafter and for which provision has been made).

DEFLATED MONEY

Money expressed in real terms, usually in today's currency. See REAL MONEY.

DEFAULT

Failing to pay interest or principal of a loan on time. Default may give the lender rights to intervene in a business to obtain repayment.

DE-INDUSTRIALISATION

Trend towards manufacturing comprising a smaller and smaller part of GNP. This tends to happen in all prosperous countries as the service sector becomes more important, but the extent of de-industrialisation varies dramatically from country to country, with the UK showing a much higher degree than Germany or Japan. See DUTCH DISEASE and NATIONAL INDUSTRIAL DECLINE.

DELAYERING

Removing whole layers of management, resulting in a more FLAT STRUCTURE, lower costs, less BUREAUCRACY, and greater ACCOUNTABILITY of executives. Very often, a high proportion (often in the range of 30–50%, sometimes even 90%) of overhead and head office staff can be removed by delayering. A typical example is removing two whole tiers of management from a firm that starts with five. This is not just cost reduction in response to crisis or recession, but a secular trend.

DELEGATION

Passing down responsibility for a task to a cheaper or less experienced executive. Rarely practised as much as it should be. Contrast its opposite, UPLEGATION.

DELIVERY SYSTEM

The activities a firm performs in delivering a product and/or service to the customer. The concept of the delivery system far transcends physical distribution and can be used to think about new ways of delivering value to the customer. A good example is IKEA, the Swedish furniture and home furnishing company that has grabbed global leadership in an industry previously characterised by local suppliers. IKEA did this by developing a totally new delivery system by rethinking the structure, processes and skills across the entire SUPPLY CHAIN from timber to customer. IKEA offers customers a new division of labour: in return for high design and low prices the customer takes on key tasks previously performed by manufacturers or retailers, such as assembly of products and delivery to the home. Every aspect of the IKEA business system facilitates customers taking on this new role, from the time that customers at the front door are given catalogues, tape measures, pens and paper, to the time that they leave with a loaned roof rack.

DELPHI TECHNIQUE

Forecasting technique using a number of experts (or managers) who each make estimates in round one, then receive everyone else's estimates and re-estimate in round two, and so on until consensus is reached.

DE-MERGE

See DE-MERGER

DE-MERGER

Split of one company into two (or very rarely, more than two) separately quoted companies, each with a clear and distinct product and market identity. Most common where a company already has two divisions engaged in different businesses. Generally involves shareholders in the original company being given shares in both the new companies, with the new shares being quoted separately. An alternative is where a company demerges one division by selling it and pays out a one-time dividend to shareholders.

Demergers are increasingly common but not common enough. Where two businesses have different CULTURES and little SYNERGY they should be separated, both to allow management in each business to focus and have full control, and to enable investors to have a 'purer play'.

DEMING, W EDWARDS (b. 1900)

American originator of the quality revolution: consulted by many major Japanese firms in the late 1940s and 1950s and was the single greatest external influence on Japanese industry. Until Deming, Japanese goods were inferior. Became known in America only in the 1980s, when he helped to stem the tide of superior Japanese imports into the West that he had earlier contributed towards. He was a statistician who emphasised the importance of the consumer ('the consumer is the most important part of the production line') and that reducing variation was the key to superior profitability. See also Joseph DURAN, a contemporary and compatriot who also influenced Japan.

DEMOGRAPHICS

The study of changing population mix according to age especially (but also sex, nationality, etc.). Knowing the proportion of babies in the population is important, for example, for baby-food suppliers.

DENATIONALISATION

For international companies, this means deliberately throwing out vestiges of nationalism derived from the country of origin/domicile, and creating a system of values shared by executives in all countries. See MULTILOCALS.

DEPOSIT PROTECTION, DEPOSITOR PROTECTION

When bank deposits are protected (usually only up to certain limits, and not for the full amount) by an insurance scheme or protection fund.

DEPRECIATION

The amount by which an asset's BOOK VALUE is deemed to have fallen each year. Depreciation is then charged as an EXPENSE for that year, that is, it decreases profits. Since depreciation has no cash cost (the cash went in one fell swoop when the asset was bought), however depreciation does not affect CASH FLOW. One way of calculating cash flow is to add back the depreciation to the profit.

DERECOGNITION

Process of removing a trade union's negotiating rights, going from a 'union shop' to a 'non-union shop'.

DEREGULATION

Removal of government controls which may open up new fields (e.g. bus services) to private companies.

DERIVATIVES

Hugely important financial instruments which are derived from other, simpler financial instruments such as shares or bonds. OPTIONS, WARRANTS and FUTURES are examples of derivatives: they could not exist without the underlying shares, but they are becoming increasingly important in driving share prices. Derivatives are the financial instruments and investments of the future: volatile, increasingly technical, increasingly powerful. It is likely that within a decade or two more money will be traded in the USA via derivatives than via shares or bonds.

DESIGN

Manufacturers and retailers are putting increasing muscle behind design as a way of differentiating their product offerings. Design is an under-rated dimension of BRANDING but will become a much more important part of it.

DESIGNER CAPITALISM

Cute term indicating practice in certain countries (notably Japan and Singapore but also at times France and Spain) of fashioning capitalism to particular national designs of political elites in order to gain world trade advantage. Often referred to as INDUSTRIAL POLICY although this term can include wider and anti-capitalist policies. Designer capitalism realises the importance of global market share in certain key industries and technologies and gives them a higher priority by means of tax concessions or by persuading and cajoling the industrial elite to invest in them. These attempts may or may not succeed, but are interesting in that they recognise that the principles of competitive strategy are not totally consistent with those of laissez-faire.

DESKTOP PUBLISHING

Using a PC and appropriate graphics packages to create professional quality reports without using outside suppliers.

DESTINATION, DESTINATION RETAILING

The practice of running large, out-of-town or edge-of-town superstores that are themselves a 'destination' rather than just part of the high street or a shopping mall. The retailer therefore needs to offer a sense of excitement, fun and facilities for the whole family in order to attract people to the destination. IKEA, the Swedish furniture retailer, is a classic example (see DELIVERY SYSTEM); so too is Toys R Us. Increasingly, retailing is polarising between the high street, which is still economic for frequent and generally low ticket items, and destination retailers out of town, for infrequent and high ticket items. Destination retailing is increasing its share of total retailing in the UK and many other countries, particularly when associated with CATEGORY KILLERS, that is, specialists in a particular product range like toys, baby products, CDs or furniture.

DEVALUATION

When a currency's value is allowed to drop dramatically.

DEVELOPMENT CAPITAL

Most so-called VENTURE CAPITAL is in fact Development Capital – financing the expansion of small firms (rather than financing start-ups). See VENTURE CAPITAL.

DIFFERENTIATION

Giving a product competitive edge by making it different, or making it appear so. See BRAND.

DILEMMAS

Management issues where there is a clear choice or TRADE-OFF between alternatives. Charles HAMPDEN-TURNER has shown that managers of different nationalities resolve such dilemmas in different ways, reflecting the influence of their national cultures.

DILUTION

Event whereby a shareholder's share of a company is decreased (he is 'diluted') if new money is required in a RIGHTS ISSUE and he cannot or does not want to provide his share of the new money. Does not necessarily imply that the shareholder is worse off afterwards, but he will have less control over the company.

DILUTION OUT OF SIGHT

Mass swamping of shareholders' rights to profits and votes in a company, usually because the company has run into trouble and needs to placate lenders by agreeing to swap EQUITY for DEBT. Very bad news for existing shareholders, who may end up with shares of very little value.

DINKIE (Double Income, No Kids)

Affluent two-worker family with no children.

DINOSAUR

Company that ignores what customers are demanding and competitors are doing, and that is likely to suffer self-inflicted death or takeover, not because it is inherently in a bad position, but because of myopic management. A useful term, although unfair to dinosaurs.

DIONYSUS

In Charles HANDY's GODS OF MANAGEMENT, Dionysus is the god of EXISTENTIAL CULTURE, and Dionysians are the most individualistic and anarchic of those found in organisations. The Dionysian culture is found in universities, research institutions, some professions, and some 'way out' professional service firms, especially small ones, as well as in many self-employed businesses, the arts, and crafts. Dionysians often comprise outposts within large firms, notably in R&D or any other rarefied, highly qualified technical post. Dionysians are difficult to manage and often impossible to motivate: they are self-motivated, inner-directed, self-contained, and concerned about the quality of their work, not what anyone else thinks about it or them. It is difficult to make Dionysians behave as team players, unless they have strong personal bonds with the rest of the team. They are most effective in very small firms or as one-person units.

DIRECT COST

The cost of labour and materials in a product, but not including any overhead costs.

DIRECT LABOUR

Production workers (or their cost) excluding 'indirect' support functions and overhead.

DIRECT MAIL

An attempt to sell through the mail, usually targeted via a MAILING LIST at individuals thought most susceptible to respond. Direct mail is a cheap marketing method but whether it pays off depends on the RESPONSE RATE. Depending on the type of product or service marketed a low response rate may still be viable: for example, in one case 1% may be good enough but in another 5% is required to cover the cost of the mailing. From the uninterested consumer's viewpoint direct mail is simply JUNK MAIL.

DIRECT MARKETING

An attempt to sell direct to the customer without a salesforce calling on prospects. Includes DIRECT MAIL, TELESALES and ELECTRONIC SHOPPING.

DIRECT TAX

A tax on income or wealth, rather than on spending.

DIRECTOR

1. Member of the BOARD of directors, the people legally responsible to shareholders and government for ensuring that a firm is run competently and that its obligations are fulfilled honestly. In most countries, including the USA and the UK, the law makes no distinction between the duties and obligations of the inside (EXECUTIVE) and the outside (NON-EXECUTIVE) directors, thus requiring the latter to exercise effective control despite often having little knowledge of the details of the business and limited time to spend on the corporation's affairs. The law is right to insist on all directors' individual and several responsibility, but the role of the outside directors is unsatisfactorily ambiguous and extremely difficult to discharge well in practice. 2. Particularly in the USA, 'director' is often used to designate a senior executive, even if not a member of the board.

DIRECT PRODUCT PROFITABILITY

See DPP.

DIRECTIONAL POLICY MATRIX

An early version of the BUSINESS ATTRACTIVENESS MATRIX developed by Royal Dutch/Shell.

DISCLOSURE REQUIREMENTS

What must by law be revealed to shareholders or other interested parties (such as trade unions) by companies.

DISCOUNT

1. In a management or marketing context, reduction given from list price. See also OVERRIDERS. The word also has a number of more narrowly financial meanings. 2. The amount by which an invoice or BILL OF EXCHANGE is valued below its face value, or the action of buying or selling such a claim at a discount. 3. The amount by which the future value of a currency is less than its current, SPOT, value. 4. The amount by which a share is valued below its issue price. 5. The amount by which an OPTION is valued below its intrinsic value.

DISCOUNTED CASH FLOW

See DCF.

DISCOUNTERS

Retailers whose formula relies largely on low price. Discounters can offer rock-bottom prices by having a narrower product range and less (or no) service provided, by arranging their business systems to have the lowest possible cost. Discounters are particularly active and gaining market share in grocery retailing in most European countries. Some of them (called 'HARD DISCOUNTERS') such as Aldi provide no in-store service and simply stack the goods instead of putting them on shelves. Very much flavour of the decade in retailing.

DISCOUNT RATE

1. The percentage rate by which the FUTURE VALUE of an investment stream is discounted, to reflect a required premium for risk and inflation. Effectively therefore a HURDLE RATE that investments must promise to reach before the investment can be made. 2. Rate of interest at which central banks will lend to commercial banks short-term.

DISCOUNT STORE

See DISCOUNTERS.

DISCRETIONARY ACCOUNT

An investor's account where the broker can choose which securities to buy or sell (at the broker's discretion).

DISECONOMIES OF SCALE

Literally when larger scale in one product line leads to higher unit costs. This almost never happens. The term is generally used when a company grows too big, or enters too many product lines or markets, to make it possible to control and co-ordinate without adding another layer of overhead cost, which can make the firm higher cost than smaller and simpler competitors; and/or when bigness makes the firm less flexible or responsive to customers. A better term for both of these frequent events would be 'diseconomies of scope', since the real problem is not scale in one product line but having too many products. See ECONOMIES OF SCALE, ECONOMIES OF SCOPE, and COSTS OF COMPLEXITY.

DISINTERMEDIATION

A fearful word for a very simple and beneficial process: having fewer middlemen. Originated and most often used in banking, disintermediation occurs, for example, when a company lends to another company, so that a bank is not used in the process.

DISJOINTED INCREMENTALISM

A glorification of the 'wait and see as events unfold' view of organisational decision-making (or not making). Term invented by Charles

Lindblom (b. 1917). Sounds better than prevarication. To be fair, it may also be nearer the real world than the OPERATIONS RESEARCH models such as DECISION TREES.

DISK DRIVE
Computer mechanical device for storing and retrieving data.

DISTANCE LEARNING
Studying (especially MBA courses) away from the teaching institution (i.e. at home and/or work) by using specially prepared and often interactive material.

DISTINCTIVE COMPETENCES
In 1957, Philip Selznick first suggested that a key role of the centre in an organisation was to identify the distinctive competences of an organisation and build on them. See COMPETENCES, CENTRE and PARENTING.

DISTRIBUTED LOGIC
A computer system that supplements a main system with smaller machines or terminals 'distributed' throughout the firm.

DISTRIBUTED PROCESSING
See DISTRIBUTED LOGIC.

DISTRIBUTION
1. Act of getting product to market. **2.** Accounting term meaning payment of profits to shareholders by way of a DIVIDEND.

DISTRIBUTION CHANNEL
Way of getting product from supplier to customer. Many firms will have several channels of distribution, including DIRECT MARKETING, own direct salesforce to retailers, selling to wholesalers who then sell to retailers, and so on. For example, a publisher may distribute via its own salesforce to bookshops, also use wholesalers to do the same thing outside main cities, also sell directly to readers via catalogues, also sell to book clubs, and finally have overseas distributors as well. The efficiency and relative bargaining power of different distribution channels will differ and so therefore will the supplier's profitability in selling through each of them. It is important to understand distribution channel profitability, and try to maximise share of the most profitable channels, and nudge competitors towards having their highest shares in the least profitable channels. It is always dangerous to rely on a few powerful distributors as these are likely to have too much bargaining power.

DIVERSIFIABLE RISK
See CAPITAL ASSET PRICING MODEL.

DIVERSIFICATION

1. Being in or moving towards being a group of companies engaged in several different products and markets. Diversification is usually driven by the wish (or financial ability) to expand beyond the apparent limits of existing markets, and/or by the wish to reduce business risk by developing new 'legs'.

Many forests have been destroyed by writers praising and damning diversification. The balance of recent opinion has been against diversification (as in 'stick to the knitting'), although this has not stopped CONGLOMERATES (diversified companies) gaining a larger and larger share of corporate activity throughout the world, and especially in Britain.

The main justifications behind diversification are:

(i) Financial: the BCG MATRIX developed a theory in the late 1960s/early 1970s that central management of successful firms can and should shovel cash around the corporation in order to move it away from businesses that would always consume cash and into those few businesses that have the potential for market leadership and thus for long term cash generation. This was a rather selective theory of diversification, but Bruce HENDERSON became an apostle of conglomerates, convinced that the strategically directed conglomerate could continually compound its cash generation capability and expand the scope of its operations. Modern financial theorists counter that shareholders, not managers, should diversify their holdings and that it is better for shareholders to be offered a selection of 'pure plays' of non-diversified companies.

(ii) Management skills: several diversified companies such as Hanson and BTR are highly skilled at identifying under-performing companies and at changing management structures and behaviour in order to improve performance. Diversification of this type involves buying, fixing, and at the right time selling, such companies.

(iii) CORE SKILLS or COMPETENCES: a company's expertise may not really reside in knowing a particular market, but in certain skills that are applicable across several markets. This is well illustrated in Figure 21, a list of examples of successful diversification compiled by Charles Coates.

Companies must not fool themselves about whether they have competences that are applicable in new areas. But a moment's thought is usually all that is necessary to dismiss many instances of clear wishful thinking. The most notorious instances of unsuccessful diversification could not have been justified by the principle of core skills. Had this principle been the touchstone, Cummins, the world leader in diesel engines, would not have gone into ski resort development; Letraset, the world specialist in dry transfers, would not have bought stamp dealer Stanley Gibbons; General Mills would not have ventured from its core area of food manufacturing into toys; Coca-Cola would not have gone into the film industry by buying Columbia Pictures; and Lex Service, the car dealer and importer, would not have gone into the specialist world of electronic distribution.

Company	Country of origin	Original Core Business	Key Skills	Growth Path
Honda	Japan	Motorcycles	Piston engine design and development	Cars, lawnmowers, small generators
Gillette	USA	Shaving products	Advertising effectiveness	Other toiletries, e.g. deodorants
Hanson	UK		Financial control; acquisition evaluation	Post-acquisition cash maximisation in low technology businesses
McDonalds	USA	Hamburger restaurants	Site selection; quality standardisation	Extension of opening hours to include breakfast; products innovation (fish, pizza, salads)
Marks & Spencer	UK	Clothes retailing	Supplier management; value-for-money branding	Diversification into food, furniture, flowers
Sony	Japan	Transistor radios	Production innovation; evaluation of future customer desires	Broad consumer electronics; TV cameras; computer components
NEC	Japan	PABX; Semiconductors	Semiconductor technology	Telecommunications products (mobile phones, faxes, etc). Lap-top computers; office automation
Toyota	Japan	Cars	Flexible manufacturing; quality control	Geographical expansion

Figure 21 Diversification using core competences
Source: Coates, Charles (1994) The Total Manager

All good diversification builds on competitive advantage in core businesses and reinforces rather than detracts from that by strengthening still further the competences that drive success in the existing businesses. This is true even though the product areas may seem only tangentially related, as in Marks & Spencer's inspired move from clothes retailing to selling a narrow line of up-market foods. The core competences of buying and merchandising, branding, stock management and customer care were reinforced by the diversification, even though at the time it seemed to many observers an odd move. See also ANSOFF MATRIX.

2. Investment diversification is the process of spreading risk by buying a number of different assets. Analysis of share diversification suggests that this sort of risk reduction can be achieved by buying as few as 15 shares (provided they have a reasonably low BETA COEFFICIENT).

DIVERSIFIED COMPANY

1. One that has a large number of unrelated operations. 2. Some writers, such as Kenichi OHMAE, distinguish between a diversified company and a CONGLOMERATE. For them, the diversified company actively tries to add value to its different divisions by (a) exploiting COMPETENCES and functional synergies across several businesses; and (b) using specific knowledge about customers and competitors and the KEY FACTORS FOR SUCCESS in each business to beat conglomerate competitors. See also CENTRE.

DIVESTMENT

Selling or in extreme circumstances closing one of a firm's business units.

DIVIDEND

Payment to shareholders out of a firm's after-tax profits (earnings). If current earnings do not exist or are insufficient to meet a dividend, one may still be paid if the firm has adequate reserves and the management is optimistic about future prospects: this is an UNCOVERED DIVIDEND. Dividends are generally not increased in direct line with the progress of earnings: most managements try to 'smooth' dividend growth to avoid the possibility of having to cut the dividend from one year to the next.

DIVIDEND COVER

The number of times a dividend is 'covered' by the after-tax earnings: i.e., profit after tax for the year divided by the dividend payable. If dividend cover is less than 2, investors may get nervous about the possibility of a future dividend cut; if the dividend cover is less than 1, the dividend is 'uncovered' and very vulnerable unless profits rise sharply.

DIVIDEND YIELD

A firm's gross (pre-tax) dividend per share divided by the share price. Alternatively, the total gross dividends of the firm for the year divided by the MARKET VALUE of firm. The number will be the same, and will reflect the 'interest' being earned on the share at its current share price. If the dividend yield is less than elsewhere (on other shares, or bank interest) the rational investor must be expecting a compensating capital gain to justify continuing to hold the shares. And in practice, companies that are growing their earnings at above-average rates do tend to have below-average dividend yields.

DIVISIONALISATION

The process of reorganising a company into separate product divisions, usually away from a centralised or functionally controlled structure. The most famous example is Alfred P. SLOAN who revived General Motors in 1921 by 'FEDERAL DECENTRALISATION' into eight autonomous operating divisions. See CENTRE and DECENTRALISATION.

DOG

1. Bad business, candidate for disposal. **2.** Term invented by BCG to describe a company's LOW RELATIVE MARKET SHARE businesses (i.e. those that are not market leaders) in low-growth markets (those growing at less than 10% per annum). BCG originally said that dogs (which it called PETS in the early days) were unlikely to be very cash positive or to be capable of being driven to market leadership; dogs should therefore be sold or closed. Since a majority of nearly all firms' businesses are dogs, this advice is draconian indeed, and was later soft-pedalled by BCG. Dogs are in fact often quite cash positive, especially if they are STRONG FOLLOWERS (i.e. not very much smaller than the market leader). It is also untrue that dogs cannot be driven to market leadership (i.e. become CASH COWS), though this is less usual than for followers in high growth markets (QUESTION-MARKS). See BCG MATRIX and STRONG FOLLOWERS.

DOMINANCE

1. When a market leader is so much larger, lower cost or more profitable than its rivals that it dominates the market. As a rule of thumb this may happen once it is at least four times larger than its nearest rival. **2.** When one decision is better than another under any conceivable scenario, as in 'opening a new factory in Korea dominates opening one in Italy, whatever the level of market demand'.

DOMINANT FIRM

One that has a RELATIVE MARKET SHARE well above that of competitors in a particular market. There is no accepted definition of how much larger a firm should be to be considered dominant, but it should be at least double the size of the next largest competitor (i.e. have a relative market share of at least 2), and probably be at least four times as large. A dominant firm should be highly profitable.

DOOM LOOP

Consultantese for VICIOUS CIRCLE. A doom loop is a self-reinforcing downward spiral that follows from inadequate response to competitor initiatives. Figure 22 shows a typical doom loop. Doom loops are easier to describe than to correct, so the first priority must be to avoid getting in one in the first place, which requires continual effort to upgrade the customer product proposition and service and to improve the efficiency of the DELIVERY SYSTEM. Once in a doom loop, the only way out is to do something quite radical, usually involving a major re-focus of the firm on a smaller number of businesses and a fundamental change in the firm's CULTURE and way of conducting itself. Existing top management can almost never escape from a doom loop if it affects the firm's most important business.

DO'NUT, INVERTED AMERICAN

A way of looking at jobs, based on the analogy of the American do'nut, which has a hole in the middle and a tasty rim. Charles HANDY then inverts this do'nut, so the core is filled in and the outside rim is the space. The core

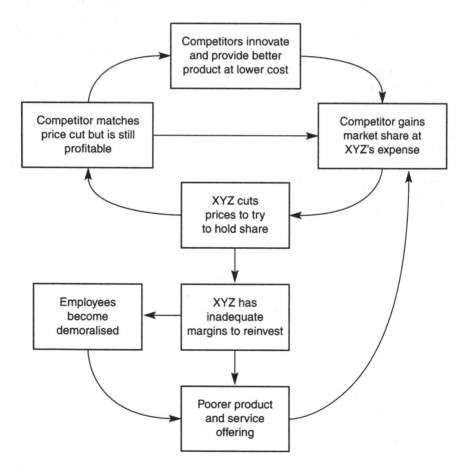

Figure 22 Example of Doom Loop for firm XYZ

is what someone's JOB DESCRIPTION or accepted role is; the space is the extra that the individual must take on to be effective, even though it is not defined and difficult to pin down. Traditionally, jobs were all core and no rim. Now, jobs are increasingly the space on the outside, where it is difficult to specify and measure what is being done. This way of viewing management, although clearly correct, is unsettling, and challenges the view of the traditional hierarchy. It is a metaphor for the uncomfortable process of liberation.

DOTTED LINE RELATIONSHIP

Where an executive reports to a second boss in addition to his 'main' line reporting relationship. For example, the R&D director of a division may have a dotted line relationship to the group R&D director, though his day-to-day boss is the head of the division. Dotted lines are sometimes more important in practice than solid lines. Dotted lines are also much more prevalent in practice than on organisation charts. See MATRIX ORGANISATION.

DOUBLE-ENTRY BOOKKEEPING

The fundamental principle of accounting, whereby each transaction is recorded twice, as a debit and a credit.

DOUBLE TAXATION

The unfortunate event where a firm (or individual) is taxed twice, in two countries. Should be capable of being avoided by good tax planning.

DOUBTFUL DEBTS

Money due to a company which it cannot be reasonably sure of receiving.

DOUGHNUT

See DO'NUT.

DOWNGRADE

When an analyst, broker or independent assessor reduces the rating of a company, in respect of its credit rating, the quality of its debt or the desirability of buying its shares. Opposite is UPGRADE.

DOWNSIDE

1. Risk of losses from a business or project. 2. Extent of such losses. 3. More generally, used to indicate what could go wrong with a decision, as in 'the downside of moving the head office is that we lose some of our best people'. 4. A scenario that estimates the returns if a number of things go wrong. Contrast UPSIDE.

DOWNSIZING

Radical reduction in the size of an organisation, usually by DELAYERING. May also imply a refocus on certain CORE BUSINESSES and disposal of peripheral ones.

DOWNSTREAM

Operations that are towards the market/consumer end of the VALUE CHAIN, as opposed to towards the start ('UPSTREAM') like production. Companies can be classified as to whether the majority of their VALUE ADDED ('their centre of gravity') is downstream or upstream. Interestingly, Shell in London has had an 'Upstream' and a 'Downstream' building since the South Bank was constructed, although this predated the use of the word in the sense above and just indicated which building it was by the Thames. Neither building is that close to exploration and production or to customers.

DOWNTIME

1. When a machine is out of action because of a fault or for maintenance, or (more rarely used in this sense) because of lack of demand. **2.** Wasted time ('there is a terrific amount of downtime in that department because they have endless meetings').

DPP (Direct Product Profitability)

System that has revolutionised many retail businesses by making it possible to calculate the profit from any given product in any given position within a store (in terms of money amount per facing per week) and even the effect that putting one product next to another will have on the sales and profitability of each product. Typically retailers make the best returns on leading brands and on their own label products, but poor returns on secondary brands, many of which are being squeezed out as a result of DPP.

DRAW DOWN, DRAWDOWN

To make use of funds committed but not previously provided.

PETER DRUCKER (b. 1909)

The most original and prolific management guru of the twentieth century. A string of firsts: first to establish the primacy of the customer; first to preach decentralisation; first to say that structure had to follow strategy; inventor of MbO (Management by Objectives); first proponent of privatisation; first to call profit a cost rather than the objective of business. Hugely influential and well worth reading his many books, despite their sometimes tortured English.

DUE DILIGENCE

Investigation by or on behalf of an intended buyer of a business to check that it has the desired assets, turnover, profits, market share positions, technology, customer franchise, patents and brand rights, contracts and other attributes required by the buyer or claimed by the seller. Due diligence requires the co-operation of the seller in making available information that is commercially sensitive and not normally disclosed, and so is not usually undertaken until the terms of a deal have been agreed, subject only to due diligence. There are two types of due diligence: that related to the accounts, undertaken by accountants; and that related to wider commercial matters (sometimes called COMMERCIAL DUE DILIGENCE) such as customer relationships and competitors. The latter are important and should be fully investigated; this is better done by a firm of strategy consultants than by accountants.

DUMPING

Foreign competition alleged to be unfair because it is selling below cost. Usually though, the costs really are lower than the domestic competitor can believe.

DUTCH DISEASE

Referred originally to the DE-INDUSTRIALISATION of Holland as a result of the discovery of North Sea gas, the consequent appreciation of the guilder, and the loss of primary manufacture competitiveness. Applied to any country which has a strong currency and is losing world market share in manufacturing. Now also the British disease and the American disease. See also NATIONAL INDUSTRIAL DECLINE.

DYSFUNCTIONAL

Counter-productive.

E

EARNINGS

Profit of a company for the year. In the UK, earnings generally implies after-tax earnings. In the USA, earnings is just a synonym for profit and may well mean pre-tax profits. Make sure you know what is meant!

EARNINGS BEFORE INTEREST AND TAX (EBIT)

Self-explanatory. Also known as OPERATING PROFIT, TRADING PROFIT and PROFIT BEFORE INTEREST AND TAX (PBIT). The best guide to underlying performance of a company, undistorted by differences in interest earned or paid or by variations in the tax rate.

EARNINGS DILUTION

Reduction in EARNINGS PER SHARE as a result of the company issuing new shares. See DILUTION.

EARNINGS PER SHARE (EPS)

After-tax profits divided by the number of shares.

EARNINGS YIELD

After tax earnings expressed as a percentage of the share price. Thus if the earnings are 10p per share and the share price is 200p, the earnings yield is 10 divided by 200 times 100% = 5%. Note that this is the reciprocal of the PE RATIO: in this case the PE ratio would be 200 divided by 10 = 20. In the UK, people generally refer to the PE ratio rather than the earnings yield: they both capture (with different but corresponding numbers) the same phenomenon: the extent to which the company is valued relative to its earnings. The earnings yield is not to be confused with the DIVIDEND YIELD, which will generally be lower. The dividend yield is what is actually paid out to shareholders; the earnings yield is what could be paid out, if there were no retention of earnings or resort to raiding reserves.

EARNOUT

Future payment to be made for buying a business based on its future profits. In this way a modest initial payment can be made for buying a business, to be followed by a short series of earnout payments. The earnout is complete after these payments have been made.

ECONOMETRICS

The study and analysis of economic data using advanced statistical techniques, especially to forecast demand.

ECONOMIC ORDER QUANTITY

A formula used in production in order to minimise stock holding costs.

ECONOMIC SEGMENTATION

The segmentation based on competitors' cost structures. See SEGMENTATION.

ECONOMIC VALUE-ADDED (EVA)

Method of cost and profit analysis that can be used to calculate the RETURN ON NET ASSETS (RONA) of any product line, by imputing a capital cost to it. EVA is calculated as the normal operating profit on a product minus the imputed cost of capital; or put another way, it is Price minus all Operating Costs and Raw Materials minus the cost of capital. The cost of capital can be the firm's average capital cost but it is much better if calculations can be made of the capital tied up in producing various different product lines. EVA is usually not too difficult to calculate and it has the great value that it focuses managers on the efficient use of capital. EVA is a relatively old technique that is now enjoying a well deserved comeback.

ECONOMIES OF SCALE

Reduction in unit costs through having greater scale. One of the main reasons why the high market share competitor has lower costs than the smaller player. Economies of scale can cease to operate (or more precisely, are thought incorrectly to exist) when additional revenue is not exactly of the same type, that is, requires additional cost. See COSTS OF COMPLEXITY.

ECONOMIES OF SCOPE

Economies that come from having a broad product line that can utilise the same skills or cost infrastructure. Relies upon COST SHARING between two different lines of business. Even if such sharing is not perfect, that is, only part of the costs can be shared, the importance of economies of scope may outweigh economies of scale. For example, the supplier of product A may have 100 units and an average cost of $10, and a smaller supplier of product A may have only 50 units and an average cost of $12. This means that the larger supplier has economies of scale, the smaller supplier suffers DISECONOMIES OF SCALE. But assume that the smaller supplier now enters two other markets, producing 100 units of product B and 100 units of product C. Assume also that products B and C each manage to share half of their costs with product A. The smaller supplier of product A now has economies of scope, and his unit costs for producing A will effectively be based on 150 units equivalent of A (the 50 actual units of A, and half of the 200 units of B and C, giving a total scale for cost sharing purposes equivalent to 150 units of A). The economies of scope mean that the smaller player in the A market can have lower costs even in that market: in the example above, the economies of scope may reduce the unit cost from $12 to $9.

Economies of scope only exist if there is genuine cost sharing and if there are no additional, hidden costs (such as additional supervision or overhead) required by having a broader product line. See COSTS OF COMPLEXITY.

ECR

See EFFICIENT CONSUMER RESPONSE.

ECU (EUROPEAN CURRENCY UNIT)

Currency based on a basket of currencies from the European Community's member states. Any future European single currency would probably be called the ecu.

EEO

See EQUAL EMPLOYMENT OPPORTUNITIES.

EFFICIENT CONSUMER RESPONSE (ECR)

The increasingly fierce battle between retailers and grocery retailers can be constructively defused by ECR, which is when the grocery industry supply chain (involving manufacturers, distributors and retailers) collaborates to produce the most efficient solution. ECR involves reduction in cost for all parts of the supply chain by sharing information, using EPOS systems, and reducing infrastructure costs, by reducing stocks kept by manufacturers, wholesalers and retailers, and using their assets as efficiently as possible. ECR is most well developed in the USA but is spreading quite fast everywhere.

EFFICIENT MARKET HYPOTHESIS

Highly respected but demonstrably wrong theory that the stock market adjusts prices to all available information efficiently, and that therefore it is impossible for shares to be significantly over-valued or under-valued. This hypothesis cannot explain why it is that certain individuals are able to consistently beat average stock market performance through identifying under-valued shares. In the case of Warren Buffett, America's richest man, who built up his fortune solely through investment performance, the out-performance has been consistent over 40 years. The probability of this being due to luck is statistically negligible. It is extraordinary how this foolish theory is able to command the allegiance of distinguished business school professors, despite all the evidence to the contrary. Perhaps the idea that the stock market may be wrong is just too unsettling to contemplate.

EIGHTY/TWENTY RULE, 80/20 RULE

See PARETO RULE.

ELASTICITY OF DEMAND

Concept loved by economists and only very rarely referred to by flesh and blood business people. The elasticity is the degree of responsiveness of demand to a change in price and is: the per cent change in demand divided by the per cent change in price. Demand is said to be inelastic if price changes have little effect on demand, as is the case with cigarettes and other drugs. One of the problems of the concept is that it assumes that products are homogeneous and that competitors all have the same products, costs and prices. The key thing for most firms is not the elasticity of demand, but what competitors are likely to do, the relative appeal of competing products, and the relative cost positions.

ELECTRONIC MAIL

Also called E-mail. Sending letters or documents via computer.

ELECTRONIC SHOPPING

Shopping by computer. A form of DIRECT MARKETING where a computer catalogue displays catalogues and the shopper can order by responding on the screen. Slow to take off because shopping is often viewed as a leisure activity and because product descriptions have been inadequately interactive. As the latter fault is corrected, electronic shopping may become much larger.

E-MAIL

See ELECTRONIC MAIL.

EMOLUMENTS

Total pay or COMPENSATION: salary plus the money value of all PERKS.

EMPIRICAL SEGMENTTION

Defining BUSINESS SEGMENTS according to competitor presence and RELATIVE MARKET SHARES. Useful technique. See SEGMENTATION.

EMERGING MARKETS

Term given to fast growth economies of the world such as China, Latin America, Africa and Eastern Europe, and to the increasingly popular invest-ment in shares and bonds of these countries. Over the past ten years most of these investments have performed very well, and are expected to do so again after a shakeout in 1994.

EMPIRICAL SEGMENTATION

The SEGMENTATION defined by looking at whether there are different com-petitors, or different RELATIVE MARKET SHARES, in different product lines. See SEGMENTATION.

EMPLOYEE STOCK OPTION PLAN

See ESOP.

EMPOWERMENT

Giving individuals in a firm the power to act on their own initiative but in the interests of the team as a whole. One of the great management buzz-words of recent years, empowerment is meant to release latent energy of individuals and encourage them to use their talents to the full within flatter management structures and autonomous work groups.

Empowerment as a concept and proselytising force is largely the creation of Rosabeth Moss KANTER, a US sociologist who is currently editor of the *Harvard Business Review*. 'By empowering others', she urges, 'a leader does not decrease his power; instead he may increase it – especially if the whole organisation performs better'. Every individual in a firm should feel 'powerful' in what he or she does: effective, in control of events, working constructively for the good of the whole firm. If not, those who feel powerless may exercise what power they have to frustrate top management's intentions.

Empowerment is a concept and a way of life rather than a set of management tools. Kanter's influence is difficult to measure, but it has been considerable. Her three main books are all stimulating and go well beyond the empowerment concept itself.

ENABLING TECHNOLOGIES

Those that facilitated breakthroughs in a number of areas, being applicable to many different industries. Examples include fibre optics and BIOTECHNOLOGY.

ENCOUNTER GROUP

Technique used by organisational psychologists and management developers whereby members of a work group say what they think of each other and come to terms with suppressed emotions. Intended to increase sensitivity and teamwork. Can be effective but requires openness on the part of participants, and without this may be more harm than good.

ENCOUNTER POINTS

The critical points at which a customer comes into contact with a service provider. For example, for an airline one of the key encounter points is the check-in. Jan Carlsson of SAS (Scandinavian airlines) called such occasions, especially when the customer needs a high level of service, 'moments of truth'.

END-GAME STRATEGY

Strategy for dealing with a declining industry, particularly when few competitors are left. See DECLINING INDUSTRY.

ENDOWMENT MORTGAGE

UK mortgage linked with a life assurance policy, as security for unpaid principal.

ENGINEERING PSYCHOLOGY
American for ERGONOMICS.

ENTREPRENEUR
Risk-taker who starts and runs a new business. More loosely used to describe any small businessman. Many entrepreneurs are brilliant at starting businesses but less good at managing them once they reach a certain size. A critical break-point appears to be at around £20m turnover, when more professional management may be required.

ENTRY BARRIERS
See BARRIERS TO ENTRY.

ENVIRONMENTAL AUDIT
A firm's systematic review of its impact on the environment, to ensure that green values are being observed.

ENVIRONMENTAL SCANNING
Rather grand title for SWOT ANALYSIS, but with particular emphasis on customers and competitors.

EPOS (Electronic Point of Sale)
Advanced cash tills that scan purchases and automatically adjust stock levels.

EQUAL EMPLOYMENT OPPORTUNITIES (EEO)
The concept and practice of giving employees equal opportunities for advancement, regardless of sex (and sometimes sexual orientation) or race or (in the USA) age. EEO related to social background or education is curiously (and expensively) neglected.

EQUITY
Also known as 'capital and reserves', 'shareholders' equity' and 'shareholders' funds'. Funding by shareholders in the form of shares (in contrast to funding by bankers in the form of DEBT), in return for which shareholders are entitled to part of the company's assets: the latter is the technical meaning of equity.

EQUITY METHOD
Method of accounting for associated companies where the investment is shown on the investor's balance sheet as a share of the NET ASSETS of the associate.

ERGONOMICS
The study of people and technology ('human engineering') to produce a better fit between man and machine.

ESCROW, ESCROW ACCOUNT

Account holding funds in dispute between two parties; the escrow account is held by a neutral party until it is agreed to whom the funds should go.

ESOP (Employee Stock Ownership Plan)

American device which has now spread to other countries (including the UK) whereby employees gradually buy a company and assume ownership of it by making a series of stage payments. A very useful method but inhibited outside the USA to a large degree by more complex and less favourable tax treatment.

ESTATE PLANNING

Working out how to hand on wealth to the next generation or to other beneficiaries in the most tax-efficient way.

ETHICS

See CORPORATE RESPONSIBILITY.

ETHICAL INVESTMENT

The practice of investing only in the shares of 'ethical' companies, which is usually defined by exclusion: not investing in companies making harmful goods (cigarettes, armaments, etc.) or having harmful effects on the environment (e.g. toxic chemicals). There are a number of ethical investment funds that ensure investors' money is not put to unethical purposes. It would be nice to see a 'positive ethical fund' that only invested in companies advancing the cause of humanity in a direct way.

ETZIONI MODEL

American sociologist Amitai Etzioni categorised organisations according to the kind of power they used *vis-à-vis* their members: (i) coercive power, as in prisons; (ii) utilitarian power, based for example on 'a fair day's pay for a fair day's work', as in most business firms he studied; (iii) normative power, based largely on common commitment to values, as in universities or churches; and (iv) a mixed category.

Etzioni is more respected by academics than businessmen, but he was one of the first outside Japan to stress that organisations, including business firms, will be most effective if their members share commitment to common values and are enthusiastic in propagating them.

EUROBOND

A BOND issued in a Eurocurrency, that is different from the currency of the company issuing the bond. The eurobond market is now very large and still growing. Contrast YANKEE BOND.

EURODOLLARS
Dollars put into financial institutions outside the USA (not necessarily in Europe).

EUROMARKET
Confusingly, a market, not necessarily in Europe, in securities in a country other than the one issuing the security. This includes the market for Eurodollars (anywhere but in the USA), but also the market for sterling-denominated bonds in the USA.

EUROPEAN CURRENCY UNIT
See ECU.

EVA
See ECONOMIC VALUE-ADDED.

EXCEPTIONAL ITEM
An unusual item of income or expense that is part of a firm's normal activities, but is very large and cannot be relied upon to recur.

EXCEPTION REPORTING
Practice within a system of management ACCOUNTABILITY whereby executives get on with fulfilling their objectives and only report back to their bosses when something unusual occurs. Avoids wasting time and can increase sense of EMPOWERMENT but based on a rather mechanical view of the world and ignores bosses' roles as supporter, confidante, technical resource and second opinion.

EXCHANGE CONTROL
Nasty government restrictions on the free flow of capital between countries. Abolished by market-oriented governments in the UK and France.

EXCHANGE GAIN OR LOSS
Profit or loss made solely because exchange rates have changed and not because of the firm's operations. For companies with extensive international trade the distinction between exchange gains/losses and normal fluctuations in prices and costs can become blurred.

EXCHANGE RATE EXPOSURE
Same as TRANSLATION EXPOSURE, a firm's potential loss if exchange rates change.

EX DIV
Shares sold without entitlement to a future dividend (already declared but not paid). Opposite is CUM DIV.

EXECUTIVE BOARD

The board of DIRECTORS composed of top managers, rather than the SUPER-VISORY BOARD composed entirely or largely of non-executive directors. When the phrase 'executive board' is used, it generally implies the existence of a supervisory board. If (as with most companies) there is not a supervisory board, there is generally one BOARD OF DIRECTORS, comprising both inside (executive) and outside (non-executive) directors.

EXECUTIVE PROGRAMME

Business school course for middle or senior executives. Shorter than MBA PROGRAMMES, usually lasting between a week and three months. Much more difficult to teach than MBA courses, but more rewarding for the teachers and extremely profitable for the business schools.

EXECUTIVE SEARCH

The polite name for HEADHUNTING.

EXECUTIVE SHARE OPTIONS

See SHARE OPTIONS.

EXERCISING AN OPTION

Activating an OPTION to buy or sell the shares to which the option relates.

EXERCISE PRICE

The price paid or received when EXERCISING AN OPTION. See BASIS PRICE.

EXISTENTIAL CULTURE

See DIONYSUS.

EXIT

1. To leave a market or close down a business. **2.** To leave a firm. **3.** To sell a firm and take the proceeds: in this last sense see EXIT ROUTE.

EXIT BARRIERS

See BARRIERS TO EXIT.

EXIT INTERVIEW

Interviewing someone who is about to leave an organisation to find out why.

EXIT ROUTE

The way in which venture capitalists and the managers in an MBO sell a business and realise the return on their investment and work. The two main exit routes are FLOTATION (going public on the stock exchange) or a TRADE SALE (selling to a larger firm in the same business). Consideration of the exit route usually also involves thinking about when to exit and how much the business might be worth at the time of exit. The exit is thought about before a decision is made about whether to fund the business: this is entirely reasonable, since an MBO is by definition a transitional mechanism and most venture capitalists want to turn around their money within a defined period, often three years. Everything the management does will be geared towards realising the exit along the lines envisaged, although the preferred exit route may change with circumstances, for example if there is a stock market crash or if a particular trade buyer expresses interest.

EXPAT, EXPATRIATE

Executive working abroad, and often living (existing?) in a closed, company-obsessed compound.

EXPECTED VALUE

The weighted average expectation as to what an investment will be worth or what any other outcome (revenues, profits, etc.) will be. Usually calculated by constructing various scenarios and weighting them according to probability. For example, if I think there is a 10% chance of selling an asset (usually at a specified future date) for £3m, a 50% chance of selling it for £4m, and a 40% chance of selling it for £5m, its expected value is £4.3m (0.1 × £3m + 0.5 × £4m + 0.4 × £5m). The expected value is not necessarily or even normally the most probable outcome (£4m in this case) but is the weighted average expectation. Expected value is sometimes guestimated without resorting to a formal calculation. For a further example, see DCF.

EXPENSE

An operating cost (as opposed to CAPITAL EXPENDITURE or PREPAYMENTS) that relates to a particular accounting period.

EXPERIENCE CURVE

Along with the BCG MATRIX, the greatest discovery of Bruce HENDERSON, although it started life in 1926 as the 'learning curve'. Briefly it states that when the accumulated production of any good or service doubles, unit costs in real terms (i.e adjusted for inflation) have the potential to fall by 20%. Accumulated production is not a concept much used, nor is it usually very easy to calculate: it is the total number of units of a product that have ever been made by a firm, or the total number of units of a product ever made by all participants in the market. It is not related to time, because accumulated production can double within one year for a new or very fast growth product, or take centuries for a very old or slow growth one.

BCG found and documented many exciting instances in the late 1960s and 1970s where accumulated production had increased rapidly and deflated (inflation adjusted) costs had fallen to 70–80% of their previous level each time this happened. One of the most important examples is the decline in the

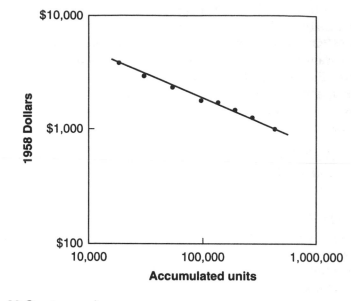

Figure 23 Cost experience curve
Source: Automobile Manufacturer's Association, BCG Analysis

cost of integrated circuits (ICs), which explains why the cost of calculators was able to plummet so dramatically. A typical example of a cost experience curve is shown in Figure 23.

BCG used the experience tool both to identify cost reduction opportunities and as a dynamic tool for describing and influencing the battle between competitors in a particular product. If a particular firm was found *not* to have cut costs in line with the experience curve, this was held to be a cost reduction opportunity. The beauty of the method was that it described precisely the point that costs should have reached (although not how to get there), and therefore set a firm and seemingly objective target for management to meet. A great deal of cost reduction was actually achieved this way.

In terms of competitive strategy, BCG invented a second type of experience curve: related not to costs but to prices. For any market as a whole, but particularly for an individual firm, BCG would chart how real prices (after adjusting for inflation) had behaved in relation to accumulated production of the product. The price experience curve might or might not follow the shape of the cost experience curve. In Figure 24 we show a cost experience curve of 80% (that is, costs behaved as they should, reducing by 20% each time accumulated production doubled), but different cost behaviour in three phases. In the first phase, prices did not come down at all: in other words, the deflated price experience curve was 100% (prices were increased in line with inflation). In the second phase, prices come down very sharply, to compensate for the earlier failure to match cost reductions. In the third phase, prices fall in parallel with costs, that is, the price experience curve is also 80%.

BCG explained the first phase as one of complacency and excess profits, where consumers are willing to continue paying a high price and where competitors all enjoy higher margins by not passing cost savings on to customers. Eventually, however, these high profits encourage new players into the market-place, and at least one of these new players cuts costs to try to gain market share. The other players have to respond, and prices are therefore reduced until 'normal' margins obtain again.

BCG preached that it was doubly foolish to have a flatter price experience curve than cost experience curve (i.e. to widen margins in the first phase): first, because it would lead to loss of market share initially, and second because the player with the greater market share himself would have lower costs, so that a market leader who held market share (by having competitive prices, so that his price might be below new entrants' cost) would continually compound his competitive advantage of low cost and make it impossible for new players to enter unless they were willing to lose money initially. Prices should therefore be reduced by the market leader at least as fast as costs, in order to keep competitors out or unprofitable, and thus consolidate market leadership and compound the low cost position.

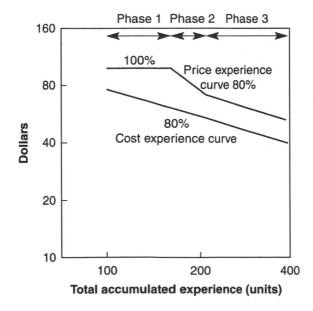

Figure 24 Price experience curve in three phases compared to cost experience curve

BCG was able to explain the success of Japanese companies such as Honda in motorcycles by reference to 'experience curve cost reduction' and 'experience curve pricing'. Ultimately the experience curve effect was used to explain the incidence of SHORT-TERMISM in Western industry and the consequent loss of global market share.

The concepts behind the experience curve are wholly correct. It must be admitted that calculating accumulated volume was often a black art, and that BCG sometimes exaggerated the scientific and empirical nature of the experience curve. Since the late 1970s the experience curve as a practical management tool has fallen into disuse, though lone adherents still persist (and use it effectively). Experience curve thinking, even if no experience curves are drawn (and one suspects that very few Japanese executives ever drew such curves), should be an integral part of good management. The mysterious disappearance of the experience curve from Western boardrooms is much to be deplored, even though experience curve thinking is in part embedded in the Quality Revolution of the 1980s and the BPR Revolution of the 1990s.

EXPERIENTIAL LEARNING
Learning by doing.

EXPERT SYSTEMS
A computer program that summarises the opinions of experts and allows non-experts to make decisions that are likely to be correct. See AI (Artificial Intelligence).

EXPONENTIAL SMOOTHING
Forecasting technique which weights recent data more heavily than less recent. Useful way of extrapolating.

EXPORT FINANCE
Generally refers to government-sponsored insurance support for exporters.

EXTERNAL FUNDS
Funds for a firm that come from the outside, from shareholders and banks, rather than INTERNAL FUNDS generated by the firm's operations.

EXTERNAL GROWTH
The opposite of ORGANIC GROWTH, although not used as much: it means relying on acquisitions and joint-ventures as the main source of growth. See ACQUISITIVES.

EXTERNALITY
A negative or positive by-product that is not paid for by an individual, a firm, or society. If a new firm sets up alongside a restaurant, and the

restaurant's lunch trade zooms up, that is an externality for the restaurant: it has not paid the firm, but benefits from an event 'external' to itself. Similarly, if a manufacturer pollutes the environment, that is a negative externality for society.

EXTRAORDINARY ITEM

Income or expense that is not part of a firm's ordinary activities and not expected to recur.

F

FACTOR ANALYSIS

Statistical technique for analysing customers or competitors (or any diverse group of people or firms) into clusters of variables ('factors') that sub-sets have in common. See CLUSTER ANALYSIS.

FACTORING

Providing finance to a firm by buying its debtors (i.e. taking on unpaid invoices and collecting the money from clients). Factoring firms (called 'factors') initially provide up to 85% of the value of the invoices up-front. Useful as a way of getting immediate cash but usually an expensive form of finance. Not quite a last resort, but often approaching this. See also INVOICE DISCOUNTING.

FAILURE RATE

The rate at which a component or machine fails.

FAILURE RATE CURVE

A graph of failure rate over time. Sometimes called a 'bath tub curve' because it is a gently sloping 'U' curve, where failure is relatively high at the beginning ('burn-in period') and the end ('wear-out period') and low in-between.

FAMILY FIRM

There is perhaps a PhD thesis available (if it has been completed I am not aware of it) looking at the proportion of economic enterprise comprised in the family firm over time and in different countries. At what precise date did the majority of economic activity cease to be family controlled in the main industrial countries and the world as a whole? Almost certainly not until this century. But the decline since then has been remarkable, and even more so for being largely unremarked. It has been calculated that some 70% of all businesses world-wide are family controlled, but the proportion of turnover, profit or MARKET VALUE of family businesses must now be well under 10%. This change, perhaps more than any other, has changed our whole view of management from a personal to a bureaucratic, and now post-bureaucratic view. The family firm is still irrevocably in decline, nor perhaps could it ever have been different: but if it could have been, it would have been better. Mars and Toyota are glorious exceptions to a near universal rule for big business: gone is the family control of such landmarks as Guinness, Martell, Cadbury, Rowntree, Ford, Hanson and Gestetner. Too many families have been unequal to the challenge; yet the very few who have shows that it might conceivably have gone the other way. Ultimately the decline of the family firm has led to ownership by absentee landlords (institutions and individuals owning shares) and control by footloose and often greedy top managers who feel responsibility towards the long-term future of a firm only by accident (if they have a noble disposition) and by exception. See GODS OF MANAGEMENT and especially ZEUS, and *MITTELSTAND*.

FASHION

Increasingly all business is related to fashion: with frequent and rapid new product introductions, the need to CUSTOMISE and CUSTOMERISE, to gamble, display flair and create a sense of fun for customers and employees alike. Most managers are uncomfortable with fashion.

FASHIONISE

To pursue a 'fashionising' strategy, launching many new products and getting them to market quickly, segmenting the customer base repeatedly, and moulding the organisation so that it can respond quickly to customers, by DELAYERING, using TASKFORCES, partnering with outside firms, and pushing down decision-making to small, entrepreneurial units positioned as close to the customer as possible.

FAST MOVING CONSUMER GOODS

See FMCG.

FAST MOVING LINE

A product with high stock-turn.

FAST TRACK

1. Special system for expediting orders where delivery times need to be short.
2. Accelerated career path for HIGH FLYERS.

FAX

Universal word for fascimile machine. When high quality, plain paper faxes are cheap they will render business post obsolete for everyone except lawyers.

FAYOL, HENRI (1841-1925)

French mining engineer who invented a version of Taylorism long before TAYLOR. He distilled 14 general principles of management: division of work by specialisation; authority with matching responsibility; discipline; unity of command (one man, one boss); unity of direction via a common plan for the business; subordination of individuals to the general interest; meritocratic pay; an explicit decision on centralisation or decentralisation according to circumstances; the SCALAR CHAIN of hierarchy; order; fairness in treating employees; stability of tenure; initiative; and *esprit de corps*. Many of these describe the classic BUREAUCRACY or APOLLO organisation, but some look forward to more advanced cultural models. Well ahead of his time, although arguably the model he proposed has had pernicious side-effects.

FEASIBILITY STUDY

Work to determine whether, rather than how, a project or investment should be initiated or a new product launched.

FED, THE FED

The Federal Reserve Bank, the US Central Bank.

FEDERALISM, ORGANISATIONAL FEDERALISM

A potentially useful but confusing word that is given a different slant by its opponents and proponents. The root meaning is that a federal organisation is decentralised into separate units (SBUs, countries, functions or divisions) that largely control their own destiny, but retaining an overall sense of identity and purpose. The proponents of federalism talk of TOP-LESS FEDERALISM and the co-operation it can engender. One example is the international postal service, where letters posted in Peru can be delivered in Delhi: the International Postal Authority is a federal organisation, even though it does not have a headquarters. But the detractors of federalism claim that most commercial firms that like to be called federal are really more feudal, with powerful BARONS obstructing central purposes and causing wasteful duplication, solely to maintain their own personal power. See FEUDALISM and GLOCALISATION.

FEEDBACK

Technical term from systems design now used widely to mean informal responses to people or what they have done. Feedback should come from all levels of an organisation; without it people will be less effective.

FEUDALISM, ORGANISATIONAL FEUDALISM

Organisations are feudal when they have powerful BARONS (heads of divisions, countries or functions) who insist on doing things their way and keep the flow of information to the rest of the firm at a minimum. European organisations are particularly prone to this debilitating and expensive luxury. See BARONS, FEDERALISM and GLOCALISATION.

FIELD THEORY

Psychologist Kurt Lewin made a breakthrough (obvious in retrospect) when he hypothesised that people do not carry around a set of invariable traits that lead to consistent behaviour as individuals whatever the social context. Rather, a 'field' (like a magnetic field) of forces operates around a person, giving rise to quite different behaviour according to how they are treated, who is around them, and the CULTURE of an organisation. The insight is no less great for being merely an extension of Christ's Golden Rule.

FIFO (First In, First Out)

Method of accounting for STOCK whereby the oldest is assumed to have been used first. The distinction between FIFO and its opposite, LIFO, is only relevant where the stock has different input costs.

FILOFAX

Personal organiser or similar paper-based management organiser, the registered TRADEMARK of Filofax Group plc.

FINAL DIVIDEND

Not the last ever to be paid, but rather the DIVIDEND declared at the end of each financial year.

FINANCE HOUSE

UK financial institution, often specialising in HIRE PURCHASE.

FINANCE LEASE

Where the lessee effectively owns the asset and has nearly all the risks and rewards thereof. For accounting purposes finance leases are treated as if the lessee had actually bought the asset with a loan from the lessee, thus reflecting the economic reality.

FINANCIAL CONTROL COMPANY

One of the three prevalent MANAGEMENT STYLES identified by GOOLD and CAMPBELL (the others being STRATEGIC CONTROL and STRATEGIC PLANNING). In Financial Control companies the Centre's main role is in agreeing budgets and capital expenditure, ensuring that the operating managers understand that they must meet the budgets, and in replacing the managers if they fail, as well as in buying and selling companies. Financial Control companies have little time for planning or strategy and do not seek to exercise non-financial control over subsidiaries; the watchwords are simplicity, ACCOUNTABILITY and DECENTRALISATION. Little or no attempt is made to realise SYNERGY between different parts of the group. The Financial Control companies examined by Goold and Campbell were BTR, Ferranti, GEC, Hanson and Tarmac.

Financial Control companies generally perform very well in terms of EARNINGS PER SHARE growth, best of all the management styles examined by Goold and Campbell. Much of this comes from acquisitions; organic growth tends to be less important. Financial Control companies are often accused, sometimes fairly, of SHORT-TERMISM. The Financial Control style is suited to groups that have a wide variety of different businesses that have few linkages in common, where technology is relatively stable and where the CEOs are able to create relentless pressure for results. See PARENTING ADVANTAGE.

FINANCIAL ENGINEERING

Clever use of financial instruments to facilitate transactions such as takeovers or to increase the MARKET VALUE of a firm without changing the underlying industrial performance: that is, financial rather than strategic or operational engineering. Examples include use of off-balance sheet financing, sale and leaseback of property, valuation of brands, greatly increased GEARING, and DEMERGER. The 1980s saw an explosion of financial engineering driven by the large (especially American) investment banks. Although financial engineering has waned slightly in the early 1990s (largely as a result of lower incidence of takeovers), it is set for a huge comeback later this decade. The use of DERIVATIVES and STRATEGIC HEDGING could transform our view of how large industrial firms create extra SHAREHOLDER VALUE.

FINANCIAL STRUCTURE

See CAPITAL STRUCTURE.

FIRST IN, FIRST OUT

1. Method of valuing stock: see FIFO. **2.** (Very rarely) method of deciding who leaves when a firm's head count is being cut: much more common (because thought to be more equitable) is the opposite: LAST IN, FIRST OUT (LIFO).

FIRE

To dismiss, to sack.

FIRST MOVER ADVANTAGE

The (usually correct) idea that the first into a market, the innovator, has an opportunity to stay ahead of competition, provided that the first mover builds in as much customer value as possible, lowers costs aggressively, and pursues a low-price policy rather than maximising short-term profits. See PRICE UMBRELLA for an explanation of how the opposite often happens, and INNOVATION.

FISCAL YEAR

Another name for the firm's financial year (which may not be a calendar year, e.g. may run from April to March each year) for tax and reporting purposes.

FISHBONE CHART

A production flow chart with arrows and angles resembling (for the imaginative) a fishbone.

FIXED ASSET

An asset used on a long-term continuous basis, as opposed to assets bought to sell on to customers or assets that will be consumed soon.

FIXED ASSET PRODUCTIVITY

Sales divided by the NET BOOK VALUE of FIXED ASSETS.

FIXED CHARGE

Same as MORTGAGE: a legal agreement giving a lender conditional ownership of an asset until the loan is fully repaid.

FIXED COSTS

Costs that do not go up or down with volume. Typically overhead costs such as rent, depreciation and central services. In practice fixed costs have a tendency to go up in steps when volume increases beyond a certain point, as when larger premises are required. Increasingly, business people are asking whether the division of costs into fixed and variable is all that helpful.

FLAT ORGANISATION

One with relatively few levels, like the Roman Catholic Church (only five levels). Work by HAMPDEN-TURNER and TROMPENAARS has shown that managers from different countries describe their organisations with different degrees of flatness, as shown in Figure 25.

This display should make one pause before asserting that flatter is better: it may be in many Western countries, but Japan, Hong Kong and Singapore have hierarchical structures that work well. Hampden-Turner and Trompenaars explain the paradox by these countries having 'Organic Ordering' mechanisms: they are hierarchical, but they are also 'integrating', where knowledge flows *up* the hierarchy and where each level is harmonised effectively with the layer immediately above and immediately below. Western hierarchies operate in reverse, where orders and initiatives flow from top to bottom. Organic ordering allows the organisation to be close to the customer and may actually speed up the process of operating effectively in knowledge-intensive industries such as electronics. Flatter may only be better, therefore, in the Western paradigm, where knowledge has difficulty percolating up a steep structure. See *The Seven Cultures of Capitalism* by the two authors referred to: a brilliantly original and thought-provoking work. See also DELAYERING and DE-BUREAUCRATISATION.

FLEXIBLE BENEFITS

Also known as CAFETERIA PERKS (British) and PACKAGED COMPENSATION (Australian), but originated in the USA. Very sensible personnel policy that allows employees a very wide degree of choice in the fringe benefits that they take up to a certain monetary value, so that they only take the benefits they

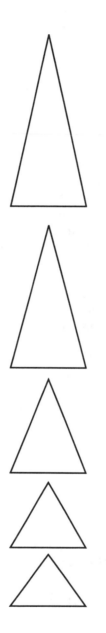

Turkey
Pakistan
Venezuela
China
Hong Kong
Singapore
India
Austria
Ethiopia
Malaysia
Mexico
Brazil
Nigeria
Spain
Bulgaria
Belgium
Thailand
France
Greece
Argentina
Indonesia
Philippines
East Germany
Japan
Portugal
Italy
Finland
Ireland
UK
South Korea
Germany
Switzerland
Netherlands
Australia
Sweden
Norway
Denmark
Canada
USA

Figure 25 Company triangles
Source: Riding the Waves of Culture, Fons Trompenaars, (1993)

really value and they realise the full cost of the benefits to the employer. For example, one person may want the maximum possible insurance packages for herself and her family, whereas a young man without dependants may only want to take the maximum holiday entitlement. In some cases flexible benefits also allows employees to take cash in lieu of benefits, or to forego some salary in exchange for extra benefits. Such schemes are very popular with employees, and cost employers no more than inflexible systems.

FLEXIBLE MANUFACTURING SYSTEMS
See FMS.

FLEXILIFE
Charles HANDY's term meaning 'flexible career', with a number of different careers and, before long, a 'portfolio' of work rather than a single job. See PORTFOLIO, definition 3.

FLEXITIME
System allowing employees to choose, within certain limits, hours of work provided they are always present during CORE TIME (the middle of the day) and work a total number of hours a week. Limits the frustrations and costs of commuting.

FLIGHT CAPITAL
See CAPITAL FLIGHT.

FLIP-FLOP BOND
One where the bond can easily be converted into another type of debt instrument, and back again, when the investor wants.

FLOATING CHARGE
1. Correctly, a charge that 'floats' above named assets and that can descend on them (that is, the lender can gain access to the assets) only when a predefined event occurs, such as receivership 2. Sometimes used to mean a charge over all the assets of a firm, rather than over any specific asset.

FLOATING RATE
Same as VARIABLE RATE; not mixed; varies according to current benchmark rate.

FLOPPY DISK
Vinyl disk for storing and retrieving computer data and records.

FLOTATION
Introduction of a company on to the stock exchange. Equivalent US term is IPO (Initial Public Offering).

FLOATING-RATE NOTE (FRN)
A debt instrument where the interest rate is not fixed, but varies according to prevailing rates: usually according to LIBOR. Very common in EUROBONDS.

FLOWCHART
Chart showing the direction of operations or how goods are processed.

FLOW STATEMENT
See FUNDS FLOW ANALYSIS.

FMCG (Fast Moving Consumer Goods)
Consumer products (usually branded) that are bought frequently, including all grocery products, confectionery, cosmetics, toiletries, newspapers and magazines, and even petrol, but excluding infrequent purchases such as WHITE and BROWN GOODS. FMCG are known as RED GOODS. They seem to obey certain general rules for marketing that are less appropriate for less fast-moving goods ('ORANGE GOODS'), even ones that are not particularly expensive. Marketing personal organisers (which may cost as little as £10), for example, requires different techniques from marketing equally expensive cosmetics. See BRANDS.

FMS (Flexible Manufacturing System)
Modular manufacturing process using computers to produce a wide range of components and products and able to switch at short notice to making other products; involves being able to make any one product on several different machines, so that demand can be satisfied quickly despite large fluctuations. In many ways also a way of thinking about production just as much as a set of computers, procedures and multi-purpose machines. While mass, production line manufacturing is the result of thinking in a series of sequential steps, flexible manufacturing means thinking in a 'synchronised' way: doing many things at the same time. See SEQUENTIAL MANAGEMENT and SYNCHRONISING MANAGEMENT.

FOCUS
One of the fundamental principles of strategy: preached with passion by Bruce HENDERSON since 1964, no less relevant today, and only a little less neglected. Smaller firms in particular must focus on a small number of BUSINESS SEGMENTS where they can be the largest. Even most large companies could raise their profits and market value by a tighter focus on the things they do best and most profitably. A good example of focus and tenacity is provided by Sharp, who stuck to exploiting liquid crystal technology in electronic calculators and concentrated all its efforts on making them as slim as possible. In 1975 there were 45 competitors; today Sharp is one of two dominant producers, largely as a result of superior focus.

FOCUS GROUP

Useful technique in market or employee research, using a group (usually of 6–10 people) to discuss a semi-structured topic. The participants lead each other on and talk more naturally about what is important to them than is usually possible in a one-to-one researcher-respondent interview, which is a more artificial event.

FOLLETT, MARY PARKER (1868–1933)

American political scientist, active at the turn of this century, who was the first to extol management as the most important element in industry, above bankers and shareholders. Stressed the role of management in encouraging TEAMWORK in reaction to TAYLOR's mechanistic and hierarchical principles. Largely neglected in the West, but like her later compatriots DEMING and JURAN honoured in Japan, where there is a Follett Society.

FOLLOWER

Opposite of market leader, that is, someone who is smaller than a competitor in a particular BUSINESS SEGMENT. If the latter has been correctly defined, the follower will usually have lower profits and a less advantageous strategic position. See DOG and QUESTION-MARK.

FOOD CHAIN

Products are increasingly building blocks for another, and this quality is captured in this very apt Japanese phrase (our own 'PRODUCT GENERATIONS' being a less felicitous description). In a food chain, product A leads to product B, which in turn begets products C and D; C then begets E, and D begets F; and then C and F begat G, and so on. For example, black and white television evolves into colour television, which evolves into multimedia devices and video recorders, which in turn migrate into camcorders. Many amazingly successful new products such as the Sony Walkman built on the technology of other products that had been around for some time but gave them an imaginative new twist and a new application. Thinking up new products by extending food chains of the present is a rich vein of discovery. Fertile food chains often flourish in very local regions, like California's Silicon Valley, stimulating mutually dependent innovation through person contact, as with links between different levels of electronics firms, from circuit-board assemblers through to the most sophisticated system providers.

FORCES OF LOYALTY

See CUSTOMER RETENTION and CUSTOMER LOYALTY.

FORDISM

Phrase first coined by Aldous Huxley in *Brave New World* to describe the religion of mass production via specialisation and assembly line, which in turn was first extolled by Adam Smith in 1776 and celebrated by F W TAYLOR in 1911. Tremendously powerful in its day, but that day has now well and truly passed.

FORECAST
1. Estimate of future profits or EARNINGS PER SHARE **2.** More widely, any prediction.

FOREIGN BOND
Any bond denominated in a foreign currency.

FOREIGN EXCHANGE GAIN OR LOSS
See FOREX.

FOREX (Foreign Exchange) GAIN OR LOSS
Gain or loss resulting from change in exchange rates between different countries. Also abbreviated to FX.

FORFAIT
See FORFAITING.

FORFAITING
Trade finance: technically, the discounting of financial instruments used for big-ticket exports like capital goods.

FORTRAN
Human-friendly computer language.

FORTRESS EUROPE
A view of the European Community from America or Japan: far from encouraging free trade, perhaps it is a club of Europeans where internal free trade is the precursor to co-ordinated DESIGNER CAPITALISM, where the design is to advance the global market share of European companies, in part by erecting Japanese-style barriers to imports. Would that it were true!

FORWARD CONTRACT
An agreement to a future purchase, with price and time specified.

FORWARD COVER
Buying foreign exchange now in the FUTURES market to cover the cost of a future payment.

FORWARD INTEGRATION
Moving into the next stage of the VALUE CHAIN, as when a manufacturer buys a wholesaler, or a wholesaler buys a retailer. Contrast and see BACKWARD INTEGRATION.

FORWARD PE
See PROSPECTIVE PE.

FOUR Os OF PURCHASING
(1) Objects: what uses will the products, when supplied to customers, have?
(2) Objectives: why will product be bought: what do customers want it to do?
(3) Organisation: who within an organisation is the actual buyer?
(4) Operations: how do they actually buy, what procedures do they follow?

FOUR Ps OF MARKETING
(1) Product: which product line variants to supply, how to brand them, how to design and package them?
(2) Price.
(3) Promotion.
(4) Place: how to get the product to the customer. See DELIVERY SYSTEM for a more holistic and better way of thinking about the CUSTOMER PROPOSITION.

FRAGMENTATION
The process (unusual today) whereby a market is served by an increasing number of small suppliers. Opposite of CONSOLIDATION.

FRAGMENTED MARKET
A market where there are many competitors and none has a large market share. See also CONCENTRATION.

FRANCHISE
The right to sell branded products or services in an approved format and under tight rules designed to ensure consistency of product/service offering to the consumer. Examples of organisations whose growth has been largely or partly driven by franchising include Benetton clothes, Café Rouge restaurants, Kentucky Fried Chicken, McDonalds, Mrs Field's cookies, and Tie Rack. Typically, the franchisee pays most of the capital cost of setting up the new outlet, and then pays a proportion of revenue; in return, the franchiser provides a detailed formula for how to conduct business, approved supplies of products and consumables, marketing and branding. Where a firm has a proven formula, franchising is a quick and cheap way of growing, but to be really successful the formula must be strong and universal, the business system low cost and efficient, and the franchisees have to be monitored and quality carefully controlled to ensure consistency. If the latter condition is not fulfilled, the integrity of the brand may suffer irretrievable damage.

FREQUENCY DISTRIBUTION
Grouping numerical data into categories (0–99, 100–199, 200–299, etc.) and then counting the frequency of the data in each category (30% in the first one, 24% in the second, and so on).

FRN
See FLOATING RATE NOTE.

FULL COST, FULL COST PRICING
1. Pricing goods based on the full rather than marginal cost of production.
2. Looser term indicating that a fat profit has been taken.

FULLY DILUTED EPS (Earnings Per Share)
EPS calculated after taking into account unissued shares which may have to be issued in future as a result of outstanding options or other obligations. The most reliable, and certainly the safest, way of thinking about EPS.

FUNCTION
Usually means an area of organisational skill specialisation such as Production, Finance, Marketing, Personnel, Research and Development, and so forth.

FUNCTIONAL ORGANISATIONS
Those with a FUNCTIONAL STRUCTURE.

FUNCTIONAL STRUCTURE
Organisation of a firm where the main hierarchy is drawn on functional lines. Once popular for large firms, now largely discredited. Even the existence of functions as powerful internal clusters of expertise is now being attacked, and will change over the next 25 years. One palliative is to encourage crossfunctional co-operation by such mechanisms as TASKFORCES, but the real answer is to abolish functions and organise by job task or business process, centred around the DELIVERY SYSTEM to the customer. See BPR (Business Process Re-engineering).

FUNDAMENTAL ANALYSIS
Analysing companies from the bottom up and first principles, usually for investment purposes. An alternative (or supplement) to CHARTISM, which is investment by following market trends rather than worrying about underlying industrial reality.

FUNDAMENTAL PRINCIPLE OF ACCOUNTING
That the ASSETS of a firm must always exactly equal the CLAIMS over those assets. See DOUBLE ENTRY BOOK-KEEPING.

FUNDING
The process of procuring or providing money for business, in the form of DEBT and EQUITY. Funding can take place at any stage in a company's history: either initially to start it, or later on to provide money for expansion or to replace earlier funding.

FUNDING STRUCTURE

The relative proportions of DEBT and EQUITY in the money provided for a firm. Also known as CAPITAL STRUCTURE and FINANCIAL STRUCTURE. See CAPITAL STRUCTURE.

FUND MANAGEMENT

Taking and investing other people's money for a fee.

FUND MANAGER

Either an individual or a firm engaged in FUND MANAGEMENT.

FUNDS FLOW ANALYSIS

Comparison of two successive BALANCE SHEETS to see where funds have come from and where they have gone. See SOURCES AND USES OF FUNDS STATEMENT.

FUNGIBLE

Able to be exchanged and move around, accepted as a means of exchange (e.g. gold coins when the Gold Standard existed, US dollars today), versatile.

FUTURES

Contracts to buy or sell shares, bonds, currencies or commodities at some future date at a price now specified. Can be used by commercial firms to lower or hedge risk, but increasingly used to speculate on the future direction of markets. The direction of the world's largest stock markets is increasingly influenced, and very often driven, by activity in the futures markets. A very important type of DERIVATIVES.

FUTURE VALUE (FV)

Value that an investment is expected to have in the future. See DCF (Discounted Cash Flow).

FUZZY WORK ROLES

Where it is unclear who is accountable for what. Can be very unproductive, but can work extremely well in small groups which are tackling a new opportunity and where role definition is premature.

FX

Along with FOREX, an abbreviation for FOREIGN EXCHANGE.

G

GALBRAITH, JAY

For business people, much more important than his famous namesake J K Galbraith. American professor who has written the best guide to organisational structuring, and developed the CONTINGENCY THEORY thereof.

GAMBARE

Japanese term roughly meaning persistence: refusing to accept defeat.

GAMEPLAN

1. Precisely, an action plan developed through GAME THEORY. **2.** More loosely and commonly, a plan of attack for increasing sales and profits and outwitting competitors.

GAME THEORY

OPERATIONS RESEARCH technique developed in 1944 by J von Neumann (1903–57) and O Morgenstern (b. 1902) for analysing and predicting competitors' reactions under different scenarios, and for developing a particular GAMEPLAN.

GANTT CHART

Chart used in production scheduling, showing work steps or customers on the left and weeks on the right.

GAP ANALYSIS

1. Marketing technique for identifying 'empty niches': product or service opportunities not yet exploited by any competitor. **2.** Identification of gaps in a firm's own product line where competing products do exist. **3.** Analysis of where precisely and why budgets or plans have not been met.

GARAGE-SHOP COMPETITOR

A low overhead competitor offering a limited line of high volume product (that he has CHERRY-PICKED as easiest to produce), often at prices 20–30% below those offered by traditional industry leaders. DISCOUNTERS (discount retailers) are a good example today. It is always worth asking: is there room for a garage-shop competitor in this particular business?

GARBAGE IN, GARBAGE OUT

Idea that analysis or decisions based on false data will be flawed even if the analysis has been correct.

GATEKEEPER

1. Someone who is the route into an organisation, especially for a firm trying to sell into another. **2.** An executive with the power to decide what information will flow into or out of an organisation.

GAUSSIAN CURVE

Normal bell-shaped FREQUENCY DISTRIBUTION.

GAZUMPING

When a seller who has agreed a sale (usually of a house) at a certain price sells it later to another buyer at a higher price.

GAZUNDERING

When a buyer refuses to complete unless the price is reduced from that originally agreed. Venture capital companies are sometimes notorious as gazunderers, leaving sellers of private companies to accept a lower price or go through an expensive and uncertain process of finding another buyer.

GEARING

1. Use of debt to increase return for equity shareholders (although at added risk). **2.** Used more specifically to describe the extent of debt usage relative to equity: see DEBT TO EQUITY RATIO. Gearing is the English for the American term LEVERAGE.

GENBA

Japanese for the SHARP END, where the action is.

GENERATIVE PROCESS PLANNING

The more complex of the two forms of CAPP (Computer Aided Process Planning), in which a description of the parts, process and tooling are put into the computer system, which then devises the process plan. The simpler form is VARIANT PROCESS PLANNING.

GENERIC STRATEGY

Term used by Michael PORTER who said there were three generic strategies: differentiated, undifferentiated, and concentrated.

GESTALT

German word used in management to mean the overall mood, feel, CULTURE or way of thinking of an organisation.

GIFFEN GOOD

Product where it is alleged that demand rises as price does. Potatoes during the Irish Famine of 1845–6 and Rolls Royces have been alleged to be examples. May be a mythical beast.

GILTS, GILT EDGED SECURITIES

Stocks and bonds issued by the UK government and quoted on the stock exchange.

GLASS CEILING

Invisible barrier preventing women (or blacks, or low social status groups) from reaching the top in business.

GLOBAL BRAND

American-originated term for a brand like Coca-Cola, Levis, Walt Disney or McDonalds that aims to be within arm's reach of consumers anywhere. The idea of a UNIVERSAL PRODUCT is also generally implied: it is the same anywhere. Could anywhere but America have spawned this concept, or made it a reality?

GLOBALISATION, GLOBALIZATION

1. The process whereby global tastes and product offerings converge and are increasingly satisfied by GLOBAL PRODUCTS rather than local ones. **2.** Also used to indicate something much more significant and far reaching. Few real GLOBAL PRODUCTS exist, but globalisation is a reality for most of the world's largest companies, in the sense that they think and operate with a global perspective on customers, technology, costs, sourcing, strategic alliances and competitors. The market for these firms' products is wherever there are affluent consumers or significant industrial customers; the firms must appeal to their customers wherever they are, regardless of borders, the firm's nationality (an increasingly tenuous concept) or where its factories are. Globalisation is driven by hard economics: to compete effectively firms have to incur high fixed costs (for R&D, development of technology, sales and distribution networks, brand building and so on), forcing executives to spread these costs over higher volumes, which means trying to gain market share in all important world economies. New technologies also get dispersed globally very quickly, so that innovators must exploit their property on a global scale, if necessary by means of strategic alliances, or see it adopted and adapted by competitors. Global competition has accelerated sharply. Between 1987 and 1992, US direct investment outside the USA rose 35% to $776 billion, while the value of foreign direct investment into the USA more than doubled, to $692 billion.

These trends do not require product universalism: product localisation is necessary for global success in most businesses. Some observers, such as Kenichi OHMAE, believe that the economic thrust of globalisation is irresistible and will cast aside conventional views of national politics, macro-economics, trade and citizenship. See also GLOBAL LOCALISATION,

GLOCALISATION, MULTILOCALS and ILE.

3. Ability to carry out financial transactions on an international basis (in London, New York, Tokyo etc) around the clock.

GLOBAL LOCALISATION

Sony catch-phrase where a GLOBAL PRODUCT is adapted to local tastes by low cost customisation. Has the advantages of low cost but somewhat differentiated product. May also involve use or creation of a local distribution network peculiar to one country or region. For example, Coca-Cola's success in Japan was due both to setting up its own route sales forces and to the rapid introduction of many products sold only in Japan. For most markets, the quest for the holy grail of a global product will fail; global localisation is a much surer route to success.

GLOBAL PRODUCT

The product behind the GLOBAL BRAND, often used as a synonym. See also UNIVERSAL PRODUCT.

GLOBAL VILLAGE

The idea that the world has shrunk as a result of the telephone, the aeroplane, the computer and the satellite, not to mention the GLOBAL PRODUCT.

GLOCALISATION OF ORGANISATIONS

Contraction of 'global localisation' and a very useful word, describing an escalating process. Glocalisation aims at making the organisation everywhere responsive to customers, who may themselves be global, and insists that the organisation be structured in the way that makes it as easy as possible for the global customer to deal with. An important by-product of this approach is elimination of operational duplication and often dramatic reductions in management numbers and cost. The opportunity for organisational standardisation worldwide in large organisations is enormous. Standardisation alone usually reduces overhead by 20% by eliminating administrative confusion on an international scale. Chief executives need to insist on the standardisation of organisations and roles worldwide in order to remove the heavy, hidden costs of complexity and confusion. European companies find this both harder to achieve, and more rewarding when accomplished, than US or Japanese companies, because the European firms are more likely to exhibit corporate FEDERALISM and FEUDALISM and therefore huge local autonomy and diversity.

GMAT (Graduate Management Admission Test)

Test widely used by business schools to help assess applicants for MBA COURSES. Also known as the PRINCETON TEST (whence it came).

GODFATHER OFFER

Takeover bid pitched so high that it is impossible to refuse.

GODS OF MANAGEMENT

Four cultural types defined by Charles HANDY in the book of the same name. Strikingly original formulation of truths immediately recognisable by those who have worked in organisations. For a description of each god, see ATHENA (task culture), APOLLO (role culture), DIONYSUS (professional culture) and ZEUS (patron culture).

GOFER

An office junior, whose job is to 'go for' whatever errands are required by more senior staff.

GOING CONCERN

Firm that is solvent and not about to go bankrupt.

GOING CONCERN CONCEPT

Basic accounting principle: when preparing a BALANCE SHEET, assume that the company will continue in business indefinitely.

GOLDEN HANDCUFFS

Employment contract locking management in and dissuading them from leaving, for example by having a profit sharing scheme where money earned is only paid out over several years. Sensible.

GOLDEN HANDSHAKE

Generous final payment to an employee when retiring or losing his job.

GOLDEN HELLO

Generous lump-sum incentive for valued new recruit.

GOLDEN PARACHUTE

Generous severance terms for directors or senior directors that come into operation if they are fired, particularly after a takeover.

GOLDEN SHARE

A share in a privatised company that allows the government to stop the company being taken over by a firm it deems undesirable.

GOLDEN TRIANGLE

Prosperous industrial area bounded by London, Paris and Amsterdam.

GOLD MINE

BCG's original name for a CASH COW. Much misunderstanding would have been prevented if this name had been retained. See BCG MATRIX.

GOODWILL

Accounting term that arises when a firm buys another for more than its NET BOOK VALUE: the excess amount is goodwill. There can also be negative goodwill, when the reverse applies. Goodwill is an INTANGIBLE FIXED ASSET that can be carried as an asset in the BALANCE SHEET; alternatively, it may be charged against profits and fully or partly written off in any year.

GOOLD, MICHAEL (b. 1945)

British management writer and founding director of the Ashridge Strategic Management Centre after a career with BCG. Made his name with the excellent book, *Strategies & Styles* (1987) which looked at the way in which the Centre of large, diversified firms managed their businesses: see MANAGEMENT STYLES and the three main categories of firms: FINANCIAL CONTROL, STRATEGIC CONTROL and STRATEGIC PLANNING. More recently he has developed a framework for CORPORATE LEVEL STRATEGY built round the concept of PARENTING ADVANTAGE described in another landmark book, *Corporate Level Strategy: Creating Value in the Multibusiness Company* (1994). It looks at the justification for multi-business companies and concludes that sound corporate strategies are based on the advantage created by the PARENT organisation. Goold's work is always original, incisive and important.

GOVERNANCE

See CORPORATE GOVERNANCE.

GRACE PERIOD

Period during which principal repayments do not have to be made.

GRADUATE MANAGEMENT ADMISSION TEST

See GMAT, its common name.

GRAPEVINE

Informal office or plant network that transmits information and rumour.

GRAPHOLOGY

Study of handwriting, increasingly used in industry to help make recruiting decisions and to improve team dynamics.

GRAVEYARD SHIFT

Night shift.

GREENBACK

The US dollar.

GREEN CONSUMERS

Consumers who are predisposed to buy GREEN PRODUCTS, such as cosmetics from The Body Shop that are not tested on animals and do not harm the environment.

GREENFIELD INVESTMENT

A new plant or office in a new site, rather than an addition to an existing site or the purchase of an existing facility.

GREENMAIL

US 1980s technique whereby a speculator acquires a STRATEGIC STAKE in a target company and then threatens to sell it on to a potential bidder unless it is bought back by the company at a higher price. Not allowed in many countries and now taxed in the USA.

GREEN PRODUCT

Environmentally-friendly product, for example, deodorant sticks rather than aerosols.

GREEN SHOOTS

The early indicators of recovery from a recession. Often used ironically to indicate deceptive and unfulfilled assertions, after the phrase used prematurely by the UK's former chancellor of the exchequer, Norman Lamont.

GRESHAM'S LAW

Bad money drives out good.

GREY KNIGHT

Confusingly, two different meanings in the same context. 1. Firm that appears in the guise of a WHITE KNIGHT to save a target from an unwanted bid, but afterwards does much the same things to the acquired company as were feared from the original bidder. The treatment of Distillers by Guinness (when run by Ernest Saunders) is a good example: Saunders did almost exactly what Argyll (or the original unwanted bidder) had planned to do. 2. A counter bidder whose intentions are unclear and whose involvement may be unwelcome to everyone else.

GREY MARKET

Unofficial market in shares before they are officially traded.

GROSS ASSETS

The total assets of a company before deducting liabilities.

GROSS DIVIDEND
DIVIDENDS before deduction of tax.

GROSS MARGIN
Gross profit as a percentage of revenues.

GROSS PROFIT
Revenues minus COST OF GOODS SOLD.

GROUP ACCOUNTS
Consolidated accounts for a group of companies, eliminating intra-group trading effects.

GROUPTHINK
Term from George Orwell's *1984* to describe collective delusion or corporate myth.

GROUP TRAINING
See ENCOUNTER GROUP.

GROWTH/GROWTH MATRIX
Useful two by two chart (invented by BCG) which compares the growth of a firm's business in one product or BUSINESS SEGMENT to the growth of the market as a whole, thus enabling one to see whether market share was being won or lost and by whom (Figure 26).

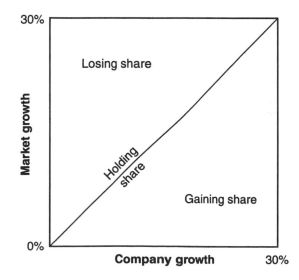

Figure 26 Growth/Growth Matrix

Figure 27 shows an example, using imaginary data, of three competitors in a particular market at a particular time (three, five or ten years are generally used). According to the (made up) data, the largest competitor is McKinsey, which is growing slower than the market as a whole (and therefore losing share); the next largest in BCG, which is growing at the same rate as the market); and the smallest but fastest growing competitor is Bain & Company. Note that companies on a growth/growth chart are always at the same vertical height, since this represents the overall market growth and must by definition be common for all.

Growth/growth charts are not much used nowadays but are very useful, especially if used in conjunction with the main BCG MATRIX (the GROWTH/SHARE MATRIX).

GROWTH SHARE, GROWTH STOCK
A share expected to grow its earnings quickly (or one that already has and is expected to continue doing so) and is therefore on an above average PE RATIO.

GROWTH SHARE MATRIX
Two-by-two matrix that encapsulates what are probably the most important insights into business since the Second World War. See BCG MATRIX.

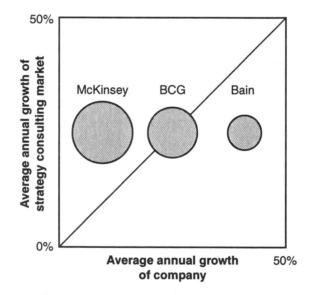

Figure 27 Examples of Growth/Growth Matrix with competitors arrayed

H

HALO EFFECT
Rating of an individual or firm higher than deserved on a specific piece of work or product because of a predisposition to think well of him, her or it. Perhaps we should not be at all concerned about the halo, however, because evidence suggests that if someone is held in high esteem he or she will try hard to live up to the expectation.

HAMMERING
1. Technically, when a stock exchange broker fails. **2.** Heavy selling in a stock market. **3.** Heavy adverse pressure ('Sproggets Inc. took a hammering in the Brazilian sprogget market last week').

HAMPDEN-TURNER, CHARLES
British academic and consultant, one of the leading international experience authorities on CULTURE, both at the corporate and at the national level. He has an holistic understanding of management processes and combines a refreshing, high-level view of the world with nitty-gritty examples of how to make the most out of each firm's unique culture.

He has written several highly acclaimed books, but in my opinion the two best are *Corporate Culture* (1990) and *The Seven Cultures of Capitalism* (1993, written with Fons TROMPENAARS). The first of these starts with some insights about corporate culture: cultures provide firm members with continuity and identity ('without a shared culture Volvo would not be recognisably Volvo'); cultures are patterns, where behaviour at one level (bosses to subordinates) are repeated, for good or ill, in relation to customers; cultures facilitate the sharing of experience and information; cultures are the mechanism through which organisations can learn (there is no other way); and changing culture is increasingly the only way that a leader can achieve anything; culture is a stronger and cheaper way to motivate than money; cultures are deeply rooted, but can be changed by intervention by managers and consultants, provided this is skilful and does not attack the culture head-on.

Hampden-Turner believes that the key issues facing companies are *dilemmas*: safety and productivity, the need to cut staff and demonstrate a new caring view of employees; the need to exercise personal initiative and the need to maintain group solidarity; the need to raise profits and also spend money to improve infrastructure; and so on. The culture of a firm will respond to a new leader if he or she can find constructive ways of resolving these dilemmas, in a way that satisfies both its horns. Culture can be negative or positive, and the change process is seen as subtly turning what is negative (and a strong cultural belief or trait of the organisation) into something that is positive (and equally strong, using the same cultural substrate). At times Hampden-Turner comes close to making 'culture' almost the 'General Will' of an organisation, which must warm to a new task or way of doing things for it to be effective. He presents organisational dynamics as a series of either VICIOUS CIRCLES or VIRTUOUS CIRCLES, and shows how new initiatives can use the same cultural attributes to turn a downward spiral into an upward one.

Seven detailed examples are given. One of the greatest challenges quoted was the attempt of a new Swedish manager in 1982–6 to turn Volvo's unsucessful and loss-making business in France into a success. The French team and Volvo dealers in the country had convinced themselves that failure was inevitable: the French people would never warm to Swedish cars, which, like the Swedes, were seen as melancholic, cold and dull. The French subsidiary talked down to the dealers, attempting to motivate them by threatening to replace them if they failed to sell more. The dealers passed this indifference on to the customers, and, having a pessimistic view of their task, failed to invest in their showrooms, resulting in a depressing sales picture which in turn reinforced the view that the 'hot' French would never buy 'cold' Volvos. Instead of hitting the dealers over the head, the new manager held a series of meetings with them, listening, breaking down the hierarchy, inviting the entire French dealer network to visit Sweden, giving them pride in the company and their role, encouraging them to invest in their showrooms and treat customers differently – and doubling sales within two years.

The case examples all stress the importance of positive 'rituals', corporate events that build on the existing culture but help to stress the desired values.

See also: CULTURE, CORPORATE RELIGION, FLAT ORGANISATION, NATIONAL COMPETITIVE ADVANTAGE, SYNCHRONISATION, SYNCHRONISING MANAGEMENT.

HANDY, CHARLES (b. 1932)

My favourite management thinker, and certainly the most fun to read, because both style and content are original, provocative and engaging. British, but the son of an Irish vicar, and only just being properly appreciated in America.

As an introduction to Handy, read both *The Age of Unreason* (1989), and *The Empty Raincoat* (1994), and then if you are interested (as you should be) in CULTURE, read *Gods of Management* (1978). Handy believes that the nature of work and the type of organisation needed today is changing profoundly: that the number of CORE WORKERS in firms will continue to fall sharply and that the future firm will be a SHAMROCK comprising core workers, a network of qualified CONTRACTORS, and the hired help. Many talented people will increasingly not think in terms of a career, but a succession of roles and after a time a PORTFOLIO of part-time activities: soon, he says, there won't be any promotions after 30. Handy is a radical humanist who believes that both government and business organisations in the West need to transform the way they think and act: he both prefers the Eastern model of company-as-community to the Western model of company-as-property, and thinks it is more effective. Ultimately the market will clear: those who have knowledge will insist on being treated as partners, and the role and rights of shareholders will be reduced.

The Empty Raincoat develops the themes contained in *The Age of Unreason*, but puts a much more pessimistic gloss on them. The famous Handy formula of $\frac{1}{2} \times 2 \times 3$ – firms employing half as many people, paying them twice as much, and getting three times the output – is still here, but rather than emphasising the increase in incomes and productivity implied, Handy dwells more on the adverse personal and social implications. Longer hours and a flawed lifestyle for the core workers, the difficulty for young people to find their first conventional job, and the ever increasing problem of unemployment ('governments seem surprised when each recovery soaks up fewer unemployed . . . organisations belatedly have realised that it is possible to grow without growing the labour force') are put into stark relief. The liberated ex-core workers with their portfolio of part-time activities beloved of the earlier book turn into 'reluctant independents. They may be the way of the future but few wanted to be the pathfinders.' *The Empty Raincoat*'s final words are characteristic of a much less gung-ho Handy: 'It is up to us to light our own small fires in the darkness'.

I much preferred the upbeat message of *The Age of Unreason*, and I believe its tone will seem more appropriate to those looking back from the twenty-first century. But whether you are an optimist or a pessimist, read at least one of Handy's books. A boiled-down version of his views is no substitute for the instructive pleasure of reading them first-hand.

HARD CURRENCY
One currency which is strong and appreciating. Contrast SOFT CURRENCY.

HARD DISCOUNTERS
No-frills retailer selling purely on price. See DISCOUNTERS.

HARD DISK
Storage device inside a computer. Contrast FLOPPY DISK.

HARVESTING

Deliberate or unintentional running down of a business and its market share position in order to extract short term profit: 'selling' market share. Harvesting can result from a number of policies: holding or raising prices higher than competitors, not reinvesting in marketing and selling effort or in new equipment, or by stopping advertising. Such steps could result in a short-term increase in profits but the competitive position of the business will be weakened and with loss of market share it will end up as a smaller business which may not even be viable in the medium term. Harvesting may happen without management being aware of it: reinvestment does not occur because it 'cannot be afforded', and market share is gradually lost without management realising, or, if they do realise, without them connecting it to the failure to invest as much as competitors.

Harvesting as a deliberate strategy is not much practised, and for good reason: you cannot tell how fast market share will be lost, and the business can disappear into an irreversible DOOM LOOP much faster than expected. Harvesting can be a very rewarding tactic, however, if it is intended to sell a business within a year or so. The final year's profits can be significantly boosted, and the buyer may apply a normal PE RATIO to buy the business without realising that it is losing market share and that the current profits are not sustainable.

Harvesting, like so many other concepts, was the invention of the Boston Consulting Group. See BCG MATRIX.

HAWTHORNE EFFECT

Term derived from the HAWTHORNE STUDIES where output improved simply because experiments were taking place that persuaded workers that management cared about them. The term can imply either that output is improving because of higher morale, or that an experiment is not to be trusted because the very fact of the experiment is influencing the results.

HAWTHORNE STUDIES

Early experiments into workers' attitudes and behaviour conducted in the late 1920s and early 1930s at the Western Electric Plant at Hawthorne, Chicago. Path-breaking research that showed the importance of workers' perceptions of management and of informal work groups and norms.

HAY-MSL JOB EVALUATION

The most famous and prevalent form of JOB EVALUATION, criticised because it can easily reward and stimulate empire-building.

HEAD AND SHOULDERS

Not a shampoo, but rather a share price pattern that gives a sell signal to CHARTISTS. A plot of a share price that shows it moving up (from the left arm), levelling off (the left shoulder), moving up again before peaking and moving down again (the head), flattening again (the right shoulder), then plummeting (the right arm). By the time the right shoulder is discernible (if not before) you should sell. Oddly enough, it often works.

HEADHUNTER

Person or firm that finds executives for senior positions by means of a 'search', rather than by advertising ('advertised recruitment'). Headhunting at a senior level is very lucrative, because convention sets the fee at a proportion (up to a third) of the annual pay of the person placed, and because reputation is so important there is a small number of top-notch firms who all refuse to break ranks on price. Headhunters are a very useful intermediary between an organisation and potential recruits: skilled headhunters know what type of person is needed better than their clients. Headhunters are increasingly searching for suitable NON-EXECUTIVE (outside) DIRECTORS: this business is a LOSS LEADER that is useful for building a network. Contrary to popular belief, headhunters do not resent the title.

HEAD OFFICE

What do you call the CENTRE of an organisation? Head office is better than HQ or headquarters, with its faint military connotations, but it still suggests a degree of overlording that is inappropriate. Many firms simply refer to the head office by its location, thus avoiding the term altogether. See PARENTING ADVANTAGE.

HEAD OFFICE, DEMISE OF

A modern school of thought, including Tom PETERS, argues that head office represents one of the last, but doomed, bastions of central planning, which is now crumbling under the impact of market forces. Head offices do not have to compete in providing their services to subsidiaries and are often woefully inefficient and unresponsive. Hence the virtues of OUTSOURCING, not to mention radical DOWNSIZING. This school of thought makes an excellent point, but neglects the opportunities for small central teams to add real value. See CENTRE.

HEARTLAND

A firm's core area of expertise and/or main customer base where LOYALTY is greatest.

HEAVY USER

The 80/20 RULE applies to consumers too; very often 20% of consumers will account for 80% of a product's sales, and 10% for 65%. The frequent buyers are called heavy users in marketing-speak.

HEDGING CURRENCY EXPOSURE

Currency transactions intended to cancel out the effect of any future change in interest rates to which a firm is exposed.

HELICOPTER QUALITY

Ability to escape from the minutiae of daily business and see what is really happening at a higher level, before descending to practical management the next moment. Very rare. Most people of vision are bad at management; most excellent managers are poor at the 'vision thing'. This is why a team of two or three people is usually best in achieving major change. See Hal LEAVITT'S ONE-TWO-THREE CONCEPT.

HENDERSON, BRUCE (1915–92)

Founder of the Boston Consulting Group (BCG) and one of the most original and far sighted American business thinkers of all time. He and a handful of colleagues invented the GROWTH SHARE MATRIX (BCG MATRIX), the EXPERIENCE CURVE, and PORTFOLIO MANAGEMENT, as well as developing the best view of BUSINESS SEGMENTATION that yet exists. Bruce weaved it all together in a coherent philosophy of business that highlighted more clearly than ever before the compelling importance of market leadership, a low cost position, selectivity in business, and look at cash flows. He was ahead of his time in seeing the threat to American business posed both by Japan and by America's (and Britain's) obsession with RETURN ON INVESTMENT, which he roundly condemned. Although a capitalist, red in tooth and claw, he understood the importance of corporate CULTURE long before it became fashionable: he was a weird but ultimately consistent mix of right wing economist and revolutionary critic of standard American corporate practice. His love of paradox, and unique style, which alternates short and shocking sentences with Gibbonesque long ones, are all of a piece with his revolutionary mind.

Bruce changed the way we think about STRATEGY and through BCG has had a major impact on many Western companies. Yet perhaps he achieved much less than a man of his energy and vision should have. He was always a loner, and did not stamp his personali/ty on BCG in the same way that Marvin BOWER had on MCKINSEY. Consultants in BCG were always apprehensive about encounters with Bruce, which were always challenging and often disturbing. BCG has continued his heritage of providing new ideas for management, but no-one after Bruce has had his single-minded crusading drive, and after being a tremendous hothouse of ideas in the late 1960s and early 1970s, BCG soon became (even when Bruce was still active in it) an only slightly unconventional commercial consultancy, which would often undertake work where it had little chance, and often no desire, to change the client's thinking and behaviour fundamentally. In short, BCG became domesticated, more concerned to do good professional work and to make money for its vice presidents than to change the world. Bruce realised that this was happening, but lacked the practical management skills or close colleagues to stop it.

Even in terms of ideas, Bruce and BCG never fully exploited the force of the original insights, which even today are not evangelised to the extent that they should be. America continued to lose global market share for the same reasons Bruce had pinpointed so well. One is tempted to conclude that, if BCG had had an organising genius interested in implementation but deeply committed to Bruce's vision, history could have been different. Bruce never developed around him a school of thought that took root in academia either: he could have done with his own Michael PORTER to develop and codify the ideas and help market them to business schools.

Bruce Henderson was a genius. That his achievements fell well short of his insights is much to be regretted.

HERFINDAHL INDEX

A clever measure of the degree of CONCENTRATION in a market. The nearer the index is to 1, the greater the concentration. To calculate the index, express the market share of the participants in a market so that they add up to 1 (so a 50% market share becomes 0.5, and so on), take the square of each number, and add them (the squares) together. For example, if there is only one competitor in the market with 100% market share, you take 1, square it (also 1), and there is your answer: 1, or perfect concentration. If there are two players, each with 50% market share, you square 0.5, giving 0.25, and then take another 0.5 squared (0.25), then add these together to give the answer: 0.5. If there are four players each with 25% market share, the answer is (0.25 × 0.25)4 = 0.25. The beauty of the index is that it is logarithmic: intuitively a market with two equal players is half as concentrated as one with one monopolist: hence 0.5 versus 1, and similarly, four equal players is half as concentrated as two equal players, hence 0.25 versus 0.5. The index can be calculated whatever the market shares and however many the players: cunning indeed! The index is sometimes used by ANTI-TRUST regulators as a better measure than just taking the market share of the top one, two or three players. It can also be used by business people to see how concentrated or fragmented markets really are and as a basis for AIMING for CONSOLIDATION of a market with a low Herfindahl index.

HERITAGE

An organisation's collective skills, values and prejudices. See CULTURE.

HERZBERG, FREDERICK (b. 1923)

American clinical psychologist and perhaps the most influential of the HUMAN RELATIONS SCHOOL: the *Harvard Business Review* sold well over a million reprints of his 1968 article, 'One More Time: How Do You Motivate Employees?', by far their biggest hit. He held that business organisations could be an enormous force for good, provided they liberated both themselves and their people from the thrall of numbers, and got on with creative expansion of individuals' roles within them. He invented JOB ENRICHMENT, which he believed would make supervision unnecessary, as well as his famous HIERARCHY OF NEEDS. There can be no doubt that Herzberg has done an enormous amount of good, and that he is both passionate and powerful as a writer. The quality of his thinking has, however, none of the intellectual depth or imaginative range of Charles HANDY or Hal LEAVITT: I always come away from reading Herzberg feeling slightly disappointed, as though I had gone to a two-star Michelin restaurant and had a very good, but not great, meal. The whole concept of 'motivating' employees and 'enriching' jobs also has a dated feel: too mechanistic, too individualistic and still trapped within the Anglo-American 'programme' mentality.

HIDDEN AGENDA
An executive's undeclared objectives, obscured behind the declared agenda.

HIERARCHY OF NEEDS
Motivational construct invented by Abraham MASLOW (1908-1970) that postulated an ascending series of human needs, starting with warmth, shelter and food and ending with 'self-actualisation': achievement of personal potential. Once one need had been satisfied, it no longer motivated. See HERZBERG.

HIGH FLYERS
Junior staff with high potential.

HIGH NET WORTH INDIVIDUAL (HNWI)
Banking jargon for rich person.

HIGH-TECH
Business like BIOTECHNOLOGY or INFORMATION TECHNOLOGY where technology is crucial to COMPETITIVE ADVANTAGE and also rapidly changing.

HIGH TICKET GOODS, HIGH TICKET ITEMS
Expensive products like consumer electronics.

HIRE PURCHASE
Buying goods on credit. They are not owned by the consumer until the final payment has been made. Compare with INSTALMENT CREDIT.

HISTOGRAM
A bar chart representing a FREQUENCY DISTRIBUTION.

HISTORIC COST

The price paid for an asset (and not necessarily its current market value).

HISTORIC COST CONVENTION

The normal method of accounting whereby assets are recorded in a firm's books at their cost and not at replacement (current market) value.

HISTORIC EARNINGS

Profits (usually after tax) most recently reported, that is, those of the last year for which data are available. Contrast with PROSPECTIVE EARNINGS, which are the estimated earnings for the current year or a designated future year.

HISTORIC PE

Also known as historic P/E, historic PER, or historic Price Earnings Ratio. The PRICE EARNINGS RATIO calculated using HISTORIC EARNINGS.

HITO-KANE-MONO

Japanese business phrase meaning 'people, money and things (fixed assets)', management's key resources that must be deployed on the most important products, markets and operations.

HIVE OFF

See SPIN-OFF.

HOCKEY STICK

A forecast that shows a short-term continuation of a downward trend (in revenues, profits or market share) and then a sudden reversal of the trend in the longer term forecast, so that the right things go up rather than down. The shape of the graph thus resembles a hockey stick or a tick. Hockey stick is used to designate and denigrate any over-optimistic forecast which contradicts current trends.

HOLDING COMPANY

1. A company controlling another company or (more normally) several other companies. 2. A management style, where a company simply buys, sells and holds other companies without trying to add any value to them. In this sense, most CONGLOMERATES are not holding companies (because most conglomerates do seek to add value in one way or another to their holdings), although technically they are.

HOLLOW CORPORATION

Firm that splits its brains and hands, perhaps having product development, design and head office in Los Angeles, and its factories in Taiwan and Brazil. The hollow corporation has gone offshore to reduce production costs, but is likely to suffer from the split of roles: the triumph of analysis and specialisation over coherence and integration. Many doubt that hollow corporations can be successful long term. See also GLOBALISATION and GLOBAL LOCALISATION.

HOME BANKING

Electronic banking at home.

HOMEWORKING

Work done at home for a firm. Important in the early stages of the Industrial Revolution. Now increasingly important again, as phone, fax and computer links are more powerful and cheaper. More and more professionals will choose to work from home and thus become a modern and highly paid cadre of homeworkers.

HORIZONTAL INTEGRATION

Specialisation of a firm in one stage of the VALUE CHAIN, and growth by undertaking more activities of the same type. If a supplier of personal organisers moves into selling 'time managers' or pens, this is horizontal integration; if he moves into retailing organisers (as opposed to supplying them to retailers) this is VERTICAL INTEGRATION. Horizontal integration can imply either ORGANIC or acquisitive growth. The term is perhaps not very helpful as a description, and not used much by managers themselves. A more apt and instructive metaphor is entering ADJACENT SEGMENTS, since this concept can indicate when such expansion is suitable.

HORIZONTAL TECHNOLOGIES

Those that are perhaps most valuable to a nation, since they cut across the whole economy, like BIOTECHNOLOGY, materials science, and microelectronics. See also ENABLING TECHNOLOGIES.

HORIZONTAL TRACKING

The idea that the career of individuals within an organisation can progress and be tracked horizontally as well as vertically: that is, significant development can be marked by horizontal moves into a different area of the firm rather than just by 'vertical' moves (promotion). This will be increasingly necessary as the FLAT ORGANISATION becomes more prevalent.

HORSE RACE

See SUCCESSION PLANNING.

HORSE TRADING

Mutual hard bargaining with something being given up on both sides.

HOST COUNTRY
A country receiving inward foreign investment from a MULTINATIONAL ENTERPRISE.

HOSTILE BID
One resisted by management. Contrast AGREED BID, which hostile bids often become by paying more. A hostile bid is not usually hostile to share-holders! The idea of a hostile bid was invented by Charles Clore, founder of Sears. It is still very much a technique highly concentrated in, if not totally confined to, English-speaking countries.

HOT DESKING
When an executive (as in IBM) does not have a personal office, but uses any available desk in a general office to plug in his computer terminal, log on to the telephone system, and start working.

HOT MONEY
Volatile money crossing borders to find the best interest rate now.

HUB AND SPOKE SYSTEM, HUB AND SPOKE
Distribution system whereby one or several central depots has a number of other delivery points. The hub delivers to each delivery point, but they do not trans-ship between each other.

HUMAN ASSET ACCOUNTING
Attempt which has never really taken off to look at people in an organisa-tion as assets (as well as costs) in which the firm invests via training and management development. Well meant but rather chilling: would you want your value to a firm to be precisely measured in monetary terms?

HUMAN RELATIONS SCHOOL
Humanist industrial psychology that originated with Elton MAYO (1880–1949) and included ARGYRIS, HERZBERG, LIKERT, McGREGOR, and MASLOW. Most influential between about 1930 and 1970. Now a new gener-ation of industrial catalysts stressing the importance of the human side to corporate performance and the need to change CULTURE to change perfor-mance has grown up, incorporating most of the new thinkers of the last 20 years. The new generation, which includes Rosabeth Moss KANTER, Ed SCHEIN, Robert WATERMAN, Charles HAMPDEN-TURNER, Charles HANDY, Andrew CAMPBELL, and, on good days, Tom PETERS, is rather less starry-eyed and rather more hard-hitting, having realised the cultural influences behind the success of Japanese and Korean industry and the weakness in most Anglo-Saxon ways of doing business. There is as yet no accepted name for this new group of cultural revolutionaries, though it is clearly descended to a substantial degree from the human relations school.

HUMAN RESOURCE ACCOUNTING
See HUMAN ASSET ACCOUNTING.

HUMAN RESOURCES
American-originated description for an organisation's people and/or for its personnel function. Often adopted in order to sound more modern, but deeply unsatisfactory: puts people on the same level as machinery or money, as in the phrase, 'human and financial resources'. It is much better to refer to 'people', 'members' or 'associates' if that is what is meant; the problem is that there is not an attractive alternative way of describing the personnel function.

HUMAN RESOURCES AUDIT
Internal or external inspection of a firm's personnel policies and procedures to ensure that they comply with the law and represent corporate BEST PRACTICE.

HURDLE RATE
The required rate of return that an investment must meet in order to be approved: a way of rationing capital. Very widely used, but not a good way of allocating investment funds. In a period of low inflation, hurdle rates in the West have remained unrealistically high (typically 15–25%), well above the WEIGHTED AVERAGE COST OF CAPITAL. This is partly because finance departments do not believe the projections being made by those requesting investment funds, and the only way they can easily build in slack is by having a high rate, rather than confronting the fact that they don't believe the numbers. The whole concept of a hurdle rate is dubious. It is much better to make whatever investments are necessary to hold and increase market leadership positions (or, rarely, to build them) and to provide the best products and service in a particular BUSINESS SEGMENT, and let the numbers take care of themselves. Nor should the CENTRE be passively receiving (and resisting) investment requests: it would be far better in most companies if the Centre took the lead in encouraging appropriate investment rather than stifling it. The hurdle rate is an Anglo-American donation to management that has probably done much to help both countries lose global market share.

HYBRID
Mixed. Used in a wide variety of contexts, the most interesting of which are given below.

HYBRID MANAGER
Executive who combines technical and managerial skill. Simply called managers in Germany.

HYBRID ORGANISATION

One that does not follow any simple model, but is a mixture of several dimensions, such as both centralisation and decentralisation. For example, an organisation may have a high level of expertise in the business of one division, and a close working relationship, but add very little to another division which could be almost totally autonomous.

HYBRID TECHNOLOGIES

Interesting concept that came from Japan, where a product development team draws on several different technologies, and mixes and matches existing technology to produce a product breakthrough. Hence for example the development of a Total Home Media System drawn from audio, TV, computing, telephone and video technologies, but integrating them in a new way. See also ENABLING (or basic) TECHNOLOGIES.

HYGIENE FACTORS

Also called 'maintenance factors'. HERZBERG's name for basic economic needs, which he contrasted to MOTIVATION FACTORS meeting deeper aspirations. The basic idea is that good hygiene is necessary but not enough. Herzberg was right but definitely underplayed the influence of economic motivation, which, in a consumer society, is also a badge of achievement, status and self-esteem, quite beyond the point at which money is really 'needed'.

I

IC
See INTEGRATED CIRCUIT.

ICON
Small picture on the screen of a PC to depict a particular program or facility.

IDLE TIME
See DOWNTIME.

ILE (Inter-Linked Economy)
Kenichi OHMAE's phrase for the 'borderless' economy comprising the USA, Europe and Japan (the TRIAD), and increasingly taking in aggressive, outward-looking economies such as Korea, Taiwan, Hong Kong and Singapore. The economy embraces much more than trade, being a complex network of corporate inter-dependencies led by the world's largest companies (which used to be called multinationals but are now more accurately described as multilocals). The ILE comprises a billion people, mainly affluent consumers, and most of the world's wealth is created and consumed in the ILE. See GLOBALISATION, GLOBAL LOCALISATION and MULTILOCALS.

IMAGE
A firm's perception by outsiders and its members. Perhaps more closely related to its CULTURE and way of doing business than to the quality of its PR.

INCREMENTAL ANALYSIS
Developing a new product or service based largely on existing resources: the result is an INCREMENTAL PRODUCT. See COST SHARING, ECONOMIES OF SCOPE and COSTS OF COMPLEXITY.

INCREMENTAL PRODUCT, INCREMENTAL SERVICE
One that has high COST SHARING with existing products or services.

INDEMNITY
Agreement to cover any loss incurred.

INDEPENDENT DIRECTOR
See OUTSIDE DIRECTOR.

INDEPENDENT PROFIT CENTRE
Used by ABB (Asea Brown Boveri) to describe 50-person autonomous units, a sort of mini-SBU. There is something magical about 50: organisations of this size (and smaller) seem to function much better than larger ones. Organisations of 40 to 200 are often described as independent profit centres. See NUMEROLOGY.

INDEXATION
Linking pay or payments to inflation.

INDEX FUND
A very useful investment fund that invests in all stocks in a stock market index and whose performance will therefore approximate that of the index. Most index funds do better than other funds, demonstrating that most FUND MANAGERS have negative value.

INDEX-LINKED
Automatic adjustment in line with inflation, average earnings, or some other index.

INDIRECT LABOUR
Support or overhead labour. Opposite of DIRECT LABOUR.

INDIRECT MATERIALS
Any materials required by production but not incorporated in the product: part of production overheads.

INDIRECT TAX
Tax on spending, rather than on income or wealth.

INDUCTION
Being introduced into a firm and trained as a new recruit.

INDUSTRIAL ACTION
Would have been better called industrial inaction: a strike, go slow, restrictive practice or 'work to rule' pursued by individuals or trade unions.

INDUSTRIAL DEMOCRACY
Power sharing within industry between management and workers, which may take the form of worker-directors and boards elected by workers.

INDUSTRIAL ENGINEERING
Application of science and technology to production and office management in order to increase efficiency. Tainted by the association with WORK STUDY and the stop watch.

INDUSTRIAL HOLDING COMPANY

Company that buys and sells businesses, treating them simply as investments, and not trying to add value to them. See also CONGLOMERATE, the more active and growing variant.

INDUSTRIAL MARKETING

Marketing to other business firms rather than the consumer. Industrial marketing is an important activity where BRANDS can be as important as with consumer goods. The importance of service and other non-price related purchase criteria should not be under-estimated. Sometimes known as BUSINESS TO BUSINESS activity.

INDUSTRIAL POLICY

Government policy designed to help or regulate industry, but usually indicates a form of 'indicative planning' whereby the government aims to stimulate international competitive advantage. There is absolutely no consensus on how far the economic success of Japan is due to its industrial policy: probably not as much as has been claimed, but the effective barriers to imports have allowed a large home market base from which to capture global market share. Small differences can have important results. Germany and Japan have shortened or abolished most forms of patent protection, making it easier to imitate and roll out new technology in a variety of applications. It is likely that cultural differences are both more important than, and themselves largely produce, differences in countries' industrial policies. See DESIGNER CAPITALISM, NATIONAL COMPETITIVE ADVANTAGE and NATIONAL INDUSTRIAL DECLINE.

INDUSTRIAL RELATIONS

The handling of negotiations between management and trade unions or other representatives of employees.

INERTIA SELLING

1. Sending unsolicited goods by mail in the hope that they will be appreciated and paid for, as with charity Christmas cards. **2.** More broadly, putting the onus on someone else to reject your solution, as when a memo is sent saying 'I will assume everyone agrees unless I hear to the contrary within the next week'.

INFLATED PAPER

Over-valued shares.

INFLATION ACCOUNTING

See CURRENT COST ACCOUNTING.

INFORMAL ORGANISATION

The way that an organisation really works, as opposed to its formal organisation structure. Ask anyone inside an organisation to put themselves or their boss at the centre of a piece of blank paper and then draw who they interact with. The result will normally be quite different from looking at the department's ORGANISATION CHART. The informal organisation may support or subvert the formal one, but it is always there, and always greatly different from the formal organisation. Sometimes also known as the SHADOW ORGANISATION.

INFORMATED INDIVIDUALS

A one-person organisation within an organisation, the entrepreneur in a big firm who has access to the firm's data and can behave as though a real business, able to make his or her own customer-related decisions and fulfil them. See also NUMEROLOGY.

INFORMATING

The process by which IT informs (rather than automates) and changes the way an organisation is run, providing information to lower level employees and removing much of the need for middle management. This rather rosy view of IT derives from Shoshana Zuboff of Harvard Business School, who holds that IT is the first technological innovation not to automate but to change the character of work. This may be one reason why IT so often does not produce its promised benefits: informating requires behavioural as well as technical change.

INFORMATION

DATA collected and disseminated in an organisation There is far too much information slopping around most firms. It is expensive to collect, analyse and communicate. Too much information is often worse than too little: it obfuscates, focuses attention on trivial issues, and makes it difficult to see the big issues in stark simplicity. In most firms between a third and a half of all information adds more cost than value.

Charles Coates of OC&C Strategy Consultants has identified three simple rules to use when deciding what information should be generated (or no longer collected):

1. Identify and generate only information required by customers or internal suppliers as an essential part of the actions they take.
2. Communicate information in the simplest way possible: if possible, visibly; if short and simple, verbally; electronically only if repetitive; and on paper only as a last resort and if nothing else is simpler.

3. Sort information needs into different categories (even if the information in different categories is part of the same task) and treat it differently, both in terms of how it is transmitted and the priority given to it. For example, you do not need the same amount of information on low-value parts as on high-value parts or on ones that frequently interrupt production.

Large stacks of computer print-out should only be generated in extreme circumstances and after ensuring that there is no simpler method of achieving the objective.

INFORMATION TECHNOLOGY
See IT.

INITIAL PUBLIC OFFERING
See IPO.

INJECTION, INJECTION OF ASSETS
When an entrepreneur puts a live BUSINESS into a SHELL COMPANY. See SHELL.

INNOVATION
The commercialisation of an invention: bringing a new product or service to market. Innovation, if successful, can for a time give a firm 100% of a new BUSINESS SEGMENT: the key thing is to keep most of that market share thereafter. If that is not done, the whole innovation process may just have consumer cash, never to give it back. Innovation can confer a FIRST MOVER ADVANTAGE which if wisely nurtured can be permanent, as in the case of the Sony Walkman or Coca-Cola. On the other hand, innovation can yield technical success but commercial failure, as in the case of the British computer industry (see *Innovating For Failure*, by John Hendry). There are three steps in successful creation of a new business segment: INVENTION, innovation, and market share retention. Britain and America are very good at invention, not so good at innovation, and generally poor at market share retention.

IN PLAY
Indicates that a firm is expected to be bid for, perhaps because an arbitrageur has taken a strategic stake. Once the perception has developed that a firm is in play, it tends to become self-fulfilling and an 'open season' on the target develops, as firms that might have an interest in bidding feel that they must act before someone else pre-empts them. It is not true, however, that firms that are in play always get taken over: Cadbury Schweppes was in play for a long time because of a strategic stake taken by General Cinema, but is still independent. See ARBITRAGEUR, and DEFENCE AGAINST TAKEOVER for how a firm might react when in play.

INPUT

1. Data going into a computer or to assist a decision. **2.** In accounting, raw material, equipment or services bought in by a company to help it produce OUTPUTS.

INSIDE INFORMATION, INSIDER INFORMATION

See INSIDER DEALING.

INSIDER DEALING

Buying or selling shares (or other traded assets) on the basis of INSIDE INFORMATION, that is, privileged access to data not yet released to the public domain, such as knowledge of a takeover bid. Illegal in the USA since 1934 and the UK since 1980. Despite being difficult to prove, the incidence of insider dealing has almost certainly fallen sharply in recent years.

INSIDERISATION, INSIDERIZATION

1. Kenichi OHMAE's term for the process of replicating or recreating a home-country business system in a new national market, adapting the system to the new market's unique characteristics. The classic example is Coca-Cola's innovation in Japan when confronted with the multi-layered distribution system for soft drinks. Coke organised local bottlers to create a national network of Coke vans distributing bottles and collecting empties, driven by a new Coke national salesforce. The company thus became a fully paid-up 'insider', and was able to use its distribution network to sell a variety of soft drinks as well as Coke. Insiderisation means taking the trouble to understand and develop a local market rather than imposing a model based on 'home' market characteristics; it is an important method of GLOBAL LOCALISATION.

2. The process of making outsiders to an organisation in some sense insiders, by sharing information with them and encouraging them to identify with the firm. See CONTRACTORS.

INSIDER TRADING

See INSIDER DEALING.

INSOLVENCY

Another word for bankruptcy: when a person or firm cannot meet their LIABILITIES.

INSPECTION

Quality examination. Not the best way of ensuring high standards: see QUALITY.

INSTALMENT CREDIT

Often used as a synonym for HIRE PURCHASE. Technically, people using instalment credit own the goods at once, whereas goods on hire purchase are 'hired' and are not owned until the final payment has been made.

INSTITUTIONS, INSTITUTIONAL INVESTORS

Financial investment firms that take money from the public and manage it by investing in shares, bonds, or other assets. Broad category including mutual funds, insurance companies, pension funds, UNIT TRUSTS, INVEST-MENT TRUSTS, and venture capitalists. In most countries institutional investors own a majority of the value of the stock market, with a small and receding share being held directly by private individuals. This has occurred despite the average performance of institutions being shown time and time again to be inferior to the performance of the stock market indices. The under-performance is not because funds pick losers but because of the charges imposed by the funds, amounting to around 2% of assets each year. It has now been realised that these are not necessary: INDEX FUNDS (also called TRACKER FUNDS) simply invest in shares in a stock market index and have very low expenses (about 0.3% per annum). How long it will take for most investors to switch to such funds (or do it themselves) remains to be seen, but theoretically most of the people employed in fund management worldwide could be removed and the performance of funds improved significantly. Professional fund management has, broadly, proved a failure for investors: it would be good to see individuals managing their own money again, with appropriate objective advice from fee-based advisers. More broadly, the existence of faceless institutions as absentee owners of industry has been unsatisfactory.

INSTRUMENT

Generic term of any type of EQUITY or DEBT mechanism. Also called a SECURITY.

INTANGIBLE ASSET, INTANGIBLE FIXED ASSET, INTANGBLES

A fixed asset which is 'non-physical' (literally, cannot be touched), such as patents, brand names or GOODWILL.

Intangibles are increasingly the dominant part of many firms' balance sheets, and many intangibles that are at the heart of a firm's value, like the knowledge of its technicians and managers, do not even appear on the balance sheet at all. For a discussion of this important trend, see TOBIN'S Q and SERVICE-COMPETENCY VALUES.

INTEGRATED CIRCUIT (IC)

Electronic circuit built on a semiconductor chip. The invention of ICs and their stunning cost reduction in the late 1960s and the 1970s has revolutionised industry.

INTELLECTUAL PROPERTY, INTELLECTUAL PROPERTY RIGHTS (IPR)

Legal ownership of a patent, brand, design or copyright.

INTERACTIVE

1. A computer system that the user can communicate with and that can prompt the user. **2.** A training programme, presentation or other event where there is no fixed agenda or outcome but where the interests and inputs of the participants determine how time is spent.

INTERBANK MARKET

Market between banks.

INTERDEPENDENCE

The degree to which two functions, departments, SBUs or divisions depend on each other to do their job effectively. For example, R&D may need close contact with Marketing (and customers) to know where to focus effort, but may not need to have much to do with the Commercial function. Organisation design specialists have developed tools to measure interdependence precisely, but a rough cut can be made by asking each executive whom they have most contact with. The principle to be applied is that where there is a great deal of interdependence, the organisation structure and other mechanisms (such as TASKFORCES and other bridges) should facilitate communication. It is surprising how often an organisation structure cuts across this simple principle. Where there is a great deal of interdependence a MATRIX ORGANISATION may be required.

INTEREST COVER

The number of times that OPERATING PROFIT covers interest due: that is, operating profit divided by interest.

INTERIM DIVIDEND

A dividend declared at the half-year, or at any other point in the year other than at its end (when a FINAL DIVIDEND may be paid).

INTERIM REPORT

A short annual report and accounts during the course of a financial year, usually covering the first six months.

INTER-LINKED ECONOMY

See ILE.

INTERMEDIATE TECHNOLOGY

Term invented by E F SCHUMACHER to mean small-scale production units for developing countries using modern technology but avoiding the expense and alienation inherent in large Western industrial units.

INTERNAL AUDIT

Inspection of a firm's accounts and operations by a small, high-level team of internal accountants to ensure that the accounts give a true record of its affairs and that operations have been carried out honestly and to required standards.

INTERNAL FUNDS

Cash generated by a company's own operations; contrast EXTERNAL FUNDS from banks and shareholders.

INTERNAL RATE OF RETURN

See IRR.

INTERPERSONAL SKILLS, INTERPERSONAL RELATIONSHIPS

The theory and practice of effective interaction between people in organisations. Studies have shown that 95% of people believe that they are above average in their interpersonal skills. Whether the area deserves its own sub-branch of business academia may be questioned.

IN THE MONEY

CALL or PUT OPTION that has some intrinsic value, that is, where the current market price of the share is respectively above or below the STRIKE PRICE.

INTRAPRENEURIAL GROUP

A group set up within a firm to act like entrepreneurs in selling goods or services within the corporation and sometimes outside it too.

INTRODUCTION

Introducing a firm to a stock market by selling existing shares to a wider number of shareholders.

INVENTION

Generating an idea for a new product or service, to the stage where a patent can be obtained. Usually the work of one person. In contrast, INNOVATION, which follows it, usually requires a team. Polaroid estimates that less than 10% of its patented inventions reach the next stage of innovation. Different skills are required for the two stages and different countries are relatively better at each.

INVENTORY

American for STOCK: raw materials, WORK IN PROGRESS, and finished goods.

INVERSE YIELD CURVE

See YIELD GAP and REVERSE YIELD GAP.

INVERTED DO'NUT

See DO'NUT.

INVESTMENT

1. Adding to fixed capital assets. 2. Buying a financial asset. 3. Any activity (including training, advertising and other 'soft' investments in knowledge and reputation) that has a long term payback and may depress short profits and/or cash flow. 4. In accounting, any asset that is not directly used in a firm's operations.

INVESTMENT BANK

American name for a MERCHANT BANK, a bank that raises capital, trades, assists in M&A, fund manages and seeks to benefit from financial market imperfections rather than one whose main role is accepting deposits and lending (the latter being a COMMERCIAL BANK).

INVESTOR RELATIONS (IR)

The serious branch of PR concerned with informing and capturing INSTITU-TIONAL INVESTORS: attracting them to and keeping them on the share register of particular quoted companies. A firm can and should influence the sort of investors it has: rather than shareholders selecting companies, the procedure can be inverted. Investor relations used to mean ex-journalists planting favourable stories and deflecting unfavourable ones with financial journalists; now the skills and practitioners have been upgraded, and good IR professionals will have an excellent understanding of the company and its value.

INVISIBLES

Internationally traded services that cannot be seen at the docks: like financial services and tourism.

INVOICE DISCOUNTING

A form of FACTORING where a proportion of the value of outstanding invoices is advanced by the factoring firm, but the client continues to collect the money itself rather than having the factor do so. This avoids customers knowing that factoring is involved, which itself can lead to the assumption that it is in trouble. Still an expensive way of obtaining finance.

IPO (Initial Public Offering)

US term for a new issue on the stock exchange.

IPR

See INTELLECTUAL PROPERTY RIGHTS.

IR

See INDUSTRIAL RELATIONS or INVESTOR RELATIONS.

IRR (Internal Rate of Return)

The profitability of an investment measured by the compounded interest rate it implies after projecting a FUTURE VALUE. Assume that an investment of $1,000 today will return $20,000 in ten years' time. What is the implied CAGR (Compound Annual Growth Rate) (another way in this case of saying the IRR)? The answer is very close to 35%, which happens to be the IRR rate required by VENTURE CAPITAL. IRRs are difficult to calculate by hand, but can be calculated in seconds using an advanced pocket calculator like the HP 12C. The requirement for high IRRs (see HURDLE RATE) is one reason why there is less investment in Anglo-Saxon countries than in most other advanced economies.

ISSUED SHARE CAPITAL
Also called ALLOTTED SHARE CAPITAL the amount of the authorised share capital that has actually been allotted to investors.

ISSUE PRICE
The price at which a new share or bond is first sold to investors.

IT (Information Technology)
Collection, processing and dissemination of data via computers to provide an organisation with information. Also means both the department that does this, and the associated hardware and software. In many organisations, sophisticated and expensive IT has not greatly improved the quality or speed of decision-making. This is not wholly the fault of IT or its providers, but more that careful thought has not been given to what information should be collected and how it should be used. Very often IT has been used to 'pave over the cow paths' rather than think about how to do things better. It is not helpful that many IT departments report to someone (such as the Finance Director) who does not understand IT, who is scared of it and who treats it as a 'black box', instead of persisting in asking simple questions about what it is meant to do and insisting on receiving simple answers. BPR (Business Process Re-engineering) offers some hope here: it unleashes computer and IT power while making it the servant of 'clean sheet' thinking. Recent use of IT, both with and independent of BPR, has finally begun to expose the administrative nature of most management tasks. Put simply, most of them can be eliminated by good, simple IT. The result in some cases has been a 500% increase in productivity, or, put another way, a stunning 80% reduction in management staff. IT is about to enter its golden age, freed from the tunnel vision of IT professionals. See also BPR, AI (artificial intelligence) and INFORMATION.

J

JACQUES, ELLIOTT (b. 1917)

Path-breaking Canadian psychologist and doctor who was a founder of the TAVISTOCK INSTITUTE OF HUMAN RELATIONS in London. Conducted a very long series of studies on the factory floor of the Glacier Metal Company between 1948 and 1965. Difficult to categorise because always eclectic and, some would say, at times confused. He is most famous for having developed a theory of the value of work based on the TIME SPAN OF DISCRETION, which basically said that different levels of management should be based on how long it was before their decisions could be checked, and that people should be paid accordingly. The theory is developed at great length with a huge amount of supporting data and analysis. It encapsulates one important truth: that leaders of businesses should be concerned with the very long term. Apart from that, in my opinion, it is bizarre and unhelpful.

On the other hand, Jacques was well ahead of his time in many respects. He was one of the first to stress that ORGANISATION CHARTS do not tell the true story of who reports to whom, and that wise executives knew who their real managers and subordinates were, and acted accordingly. He quotes from the example of war and military hierarchies: in the field the latter are irrelevant and must be ignored, or else 'they would all be killed while trying to sort out who was giving orders to whom'. He was also one of the first to realise the importance of changing company CULTURE and of employees feeling that the firm was run fairly ('equity' is a word he constantly uses in this context). A real one-off.

JAPAN

Country spawning global competitors that are much feared and little understood. It used to be said that the way to innovate successfully in financial services was to bring what was being done in the USA to the UK and the rest of Europe. Now business trends come from Japan to the USA. The irony is that many of these techniques, whether relating to quality or self-managed groups, were originally inventions of Americans that were ignored by US business, enthusiastically adopted in Japan, and could only then take off back in America. One explanation for this is that many of the approaches were slightly 'collectivist' or 'communitarian' and were offensive to American individualism and only legitimised when it was proved that they worked and that America was losing the global competitive battle as a result.

Japanese ways of working have been successfully introduced to their factories outside Japan, particularly in Korea and Britain (e.g. Toshiba UK). Yet it is very much to be doubted that English-speaking economies (or those of other countries with strong individualistic traditions, like the Dutch) can ever be reorganised to support individual front-line global competitors in the way that Japanese society and the Japanese economic infrastructure do. A prerequisite would be a transformation in the general view of what companies are for, and a downgrading of the short-term expectations of bankers and shareholders, together with much greater collaborative behaviour between suppliers and the front-line firms. Cultural and legal change of a sort never yet seen except after a calamity would be necessary first. See KEIRETSU and JAPANESE OVERSEAS MANUFACTURING INVESTMENT.

Some far-sighted observers argue that Japan's future potential weakness lies in the difficulty with which it can change the size and shape of the organisation, particularly support and overhead functions outside the factory. Japanese organisations are large and generally bureaucratic: the best sort of bureaucracy, in many cases, but bureaucracy nonetheless in all cases. Some US corporations have shown the ability to use BPR and other radical techniques to DELAYER and DOWNSIZE their companies dramatically, leading to a new level of customer service (as senior management are redeployed to work mainly on external relationships, and as all the firm's systems are geared to work back from the customer) and to very much lower costs. Although a few Japanese companies like Honda have made tentative steps towards new reward systems, it will be very difficult for Japanese firms to renege on their style and values and downsize and delayer in the same way. There is the prospect, therefore, that if Western firms can be as efficient in their factories as the Japanese, they may attain a lower cost position overall (through less management and overheads) than their Japanese counterparts. We are far from that point now; by the end of the century things may be different. See GLOCALISATION.

JAPANESE OVERSEAS MANUFACTURING INVESTMENT

In 1878 Mitsui kicked off Japanese investment in Europe by opening its Paris office. Only in the past 15 years, however, has direct investment by Japanese firms in European and US plants become significant. The factories have been set up in the pursuit of global market share in order to get round import restrictions. Such investment helps the economies of the host countries but at the expense of digging in the dominance of the particular Japanese firm. The latter have two advantages denied to Western competitors: first, almost no corresponding large-scale manufacturing investment is made by Western firms in the Japanese market, so that market shares will always be lop-sided in the 'home' country; and second, Japanese firms, both in their home market and where they invest abroad, use a high proportion of bought-in components (see OUTSOURCING), so that the investment in the West acts to some degree as a Trojan horse for Japanese components, whose scale and quality in turn comprise a large part of the Japanese competitive advantage. Western countries should only encourage inbound investment by Japanese firms if they have already conceded the competitive battle in the relevant product area.

JAPANISATION

The adoption of Japanese work practices outside Japan. See JAPAN, KANBAN, KJ METHOD, QUALITY.

J-CURVE

Term from economics, not much used by managers, indicating a small decrease in some variable (e.g. revenues, profits) followed by a large, rapid increase. Like a HOCKEY STICK that works.

JIT

See JUST-IN-TIME.

JOB ANALYSIS

Breakdown of a job's responsibilities in order to compile a JOB DESCRIPTION.

JOBBER, JOBBING BROKER

Market-making in shares and bonds.

JOB DESCRIPTION

It is now almost universally accepted that each job should have a description of duties, roles and reporting relationships, or at least a JOB SPECIFICATION (a summary thereof), against which potential recruits can be assessed to see if they fit the job description. This idea of 'slots' into which people can be 'fitted' rests upon assumptions about the nature of work that are often not realised or made explicit. In fact there is no universal and self-evident truth that says everyone should have a job description, and in practice what many executives actually do bears little resemblance to what the job description says he or she should be doing. In practice, people often report to 'non-bosses' far more than they do to their formal boss, and in turn supervise and help many people who do not report to them.

The whole idea of job descriptions, and all associated paraphernalia like JOBS, JOB ANALYSIS, JOB EVALUATION, JOB DESIGN, JOB ENLARGEMENT, JOB SATISFACTION, JOB TITLE, RATE FOR THE JOB, MANAGEMENT BY OBJECTIVES (MbO), and even JOB ENRICHMENT, rests upon the assumption that the firm is a role-oriented hierarchy, a BUREAUCRACY in the technical sense. This assumption is only one way, and not usually the best, to run a firm, and only suitable for firms in stable and predictable industries: see APOLLO, and GODS OF MANAGEMENT for the other ways. Yet we persist in thinking about jobs and describing them, in most cases basing our pay systems wholly or partly upon them. Why?

JOB DESIGN

Deciding which tasks should be in which job, or what a job should do. See JOB DESCRIPTION.

JOB ENLARGEMENT

Redesigning a job to give it more to do. See JOB DESCRIPTION.

JOB ENRICHMENT

Term invented by Frederick HERZBERG to upgrade the creativity and scope of a job. Well intentioned, but missed the point. See JOB DESCRIPTION.

JOB EVALUATION

A method of measuring the importance of jobs relative to one another, based on a JOB DESCRIPTION and the skills required by the job. The job is then assigned a score, and the score in turn leads to a grading level (usually using letters and/or numbers, like Category 'A' or E8). In turn the grading level determines a SALARY BAND for base pay (and maybe total pay). Job evaluation is meant to be a systematic (though not scientific) basis for a 'rational' pay structure.

The most widely used job evaluation system in the world is the Hay-MSL system, invented by Edwin Hay, and the basis of a large consulting practice based in Philadelphia. The Hay system claims to be universally applicable to middle and senior jobs, whatever the industry or circumstances of the firm, and is supported by a large historical database. It has, however, been justly criticised because it awards higher scores to jobs that control higher revenues: it is insufficiently related to earnings or EARNINGS PER SHARE progression. Recently new US systems have developed which do not share this fault.

More radically, the whole concept of basing people's pay on an artefact like a job description, rather than on what they do as people, is deeply flawed because it is so mechanistic. See JOB DESCRIPTION.

JOB ROTATION

When employees swap jobs within a department or firm on a regular, organised basis, on the grounds that (1) greater variety gives higher JOB SATISFACTION, and (2) that it will encourage greater co-operation.

JOB SATISFACTION

When an individual is happy with his job's role: a round peg in a round hole. See JOB DESCRIPTION.

JOB TITLE
Usually descriptions of rank as well as function: being a 'Manager' or 'Vice President' or 'Executive Director' can be a coveted badge. But should we run business like a public school? See JOB DESCRIPTION.

JOINT VENTURE
Term that can mean, precisely, a firm that is owned in some proportion (50%–50%, or 49%–51%, or any other mix) by two parent firms; or more loosely, collaboration between two or more firms for specific purposes. The latter sense is sometimes called a STRATEGIC ALLIANCE. Joint ventures in both senses, but especially the second, are becoming more frequent, larger, and more important. When more than two firms are involved (particularly if there are many), a joint venture is usually called a CONSORTIUM.

A joint venture happens because the participating companies each have skills that the other does not, or because they want to share high development costs. For example, a manufacturer wishing to export to Japan may form a joint venture with a Japanese distributor; or firms in similar businesses, who may even be competitors, come together to help develop a new and very expensive technology like High Definition TV. Thus Toshiba has a joint venture with IBM, or, until recently, Honda with Rover. Long-term strategic alliances are the wave of the future, and Western firms must learn how to make them work, which means un-learning some of our traditional views about competition. See also KEIRETSU.

JOURNAL
See DAY BOOK.

JUNK BOND
Loan stock carrying a high coupon used to finance small American companies and later large LBOs (Leveraged Buy Outs). Originated in the USA and made into a major business force by Drexel Burnham (now liquidated) and the now disgraced Michael Milken. Milken proved that most junk bonds had historically not been high risk, and that the returns outweighed the risks. He created a market for smaller, less highly rated companies that was genuinely helpful, because the cost of issuing junk bonds was lower than the cost of raising equity (which many private firms did not want to do anyway). It was unfortunate that Milken engaged in sleazy and illegal behaviour that discredited, for a time, the concept of junk bonds. Due for a revival under more respectable auspices.

JUNK MAIL
Unsolicited and unwanted DIRECT MAIL material.

JURAN, JOSEPH M (b. 1904)

Romanian-born American electrical engineer and quality guru, who was jointly responsible (with W Edwards DEMING) for the quality revolution in Japan after 1950. He published his Quality Control Handbook in 1951 and began work in Tokyo in 1953. He developed Company-Wide Quality Management (CWQM), a systematic methodology for spreading the gospel of quality throughout a firm. He insisted that quality could not be delegated and was an early exponent of what has come to be known as EMPOWERMENT: for him quality had to be the goal of each employee, individually and in teams, through self-supervision. He was less mechanistic than Deming and placed greater stress on human relations. In 1988 he published Juran on Planning for Quality which included his QUALITY TRILOGY of quality planning, quality management and quality improvement. A firm and all its people must commit to and be obsessive about quality: it must become a way of life built into the firm's CULTURE. Well worth reading, though not the lightest of reads.

JUST-IN-TIME (JIT)

Valuable system developed first in Japan for production management aimed at minimising stock by having materials and WORK-IN-PROGRESS delivered to the right place at the right time. As well as lowering costs, JIT can have other major benefits: the systematic identification of operational problems and their resolution by technology-based tools; higher levels of customer service and speeding up the TIME TO MARKET; higher quality standards by being 'RIGHT FIRST TIME'; and higher standards of COMPETENCE in the production function generally. To be most effective, JIT should be introduced as part of TQM (Total Quality Management), and it should be recognised at the outset that JIT is not just a technique, but a way of changing behaviour. A full JIT programme such as introduced by Toyota or Matsushita may take years to complete. But companies without JIT who compete against those with JIT will have a major handicap.

Properly conceived, JIT should be seen as a SYNCHRONISING way of life: jobs must be completed quickly, but even more important is that they be completed just in time to fit in with the next step in the dance. This is a radically different concept from traditional assembly line thinking, which is sequential rather than synchronising. Charles HAMPDEN-TURNER and Fons TROMPENAARS point out that culturally, the USA, UK, Sweden and Holland are disposed towards trying to speed things up sequentially, whereas Japan, Germany and France are more geared towards synchronisation. This means that when installing JIT and other synchronising techniques in 'Anglo-Saxon' and similar countries, it should be realised that JIT can go against the cultural grain: people need to be retrained to think and act in a synchronised way. See SYNCHRONISATION and SYNCHRONISING MANAGEMENT.

K

KAFFIR

Shares in South African mines.

KAISHA

Second half of KK, meaning corporation. See *Kaisha, the Japanese Corporation* by Jim Abegglen and George Stalk, which stresses that there is a range of performance in Japanese companies, from the truly excellent like Canon, Honda, Matsushita, Toyota and Toshiba, through to the truly dreadful.

KANBAN

Literally card or label. Japanese system by which every part or component in a factory has a card attached to it describing what exactly it is and what place it has in the total production process. Originated as part of Toyota's JUST-IN-TIME system. Some observers see this as a symbol of the holistic nature of Japanese thought: every part carries attached to it a picture of the whole and the part is seen as a microcosm of the whole. See also KJ METHOD.

KANTER, ROSABETH MOSS (b. 1943)

US sociologist, Harvard Business School professor and editor of the *Harvard Business Review* and the driving force behind EMPOWERMENT as a CHANGE MANAGEMENT crusade. Three of her books are important.

Men and Women of the Corporation (1977) criticised the way that human talent was cramped within bureaucratic structures, hurting both the corporation and the individuals. She proposed CAREER DEVELOPMENT mechanisms to move more women (and some other 'powerless' groups) into more senior jobs, and also urged empowering strategies leading to flatter structures and autonomous work groups.

The Change Masters (1983) profiled companies that were good at INNOVATION and identified their underlying characteristics. The most significant finding was that such firms have an 'integrative' view of the world and were iconoclastic; firms poor at innovation were analytical, compartmentalised, 'segmentalist' and conservative. The book developed the theme that individuals should be made more powerful, but within a framework of common corporate purpose.

When Giants Learn to Dance (1989) stresses the need for even giant corporations to become 'post-entrepreneurial': demonstrating all the attributes of an entrepreneur such as flexibility, responsiveness and personal initiative, but combining this with the discipline of a large firm and the realisation of SYNERGIES between different parts of the firm by having a vision of the firm overall and where it can go. In a striking metaphor, she talks about the dancing elephant: 'the power of an elephant with the agility of a dancer'. Another useful phrase is 'the corporation as a SWITCHBOARD', where a small CENTRE helps to direct other parts of the organisation to realise synergies. She also invents PAL, not a type of dog food but rather '*pool* resources with others, *ally* to exploit an opportunity, or *link* systems in a partnership'. The wise corporation becomes PALs with customers, suppliers, JOINT VENTURE partners and outside CONTRACTORS. The company of the future will be lean but not mean, able to do more with less (fewer layers), but operating within a framework of SHARED VALUES.

Kanter is right about all of this, though to me she misses (or chooses not to stress) the key role that an individual LEADER has in transforming a corporation. See also EMPOWERMENT, JOINT VENTURES, STRATEGIC ALLIANCES, SYNERGIES, and KEIRETSU.

KEIRETSU

Literally, a 'headless combine', and one of the most important secret weapons of Japanese industry. An economic grouping of many firms organised around trading companies and/or banks. These groups originated from the ZAIBATSU, the large and in many cases centuries-old groups of industrial and financial holding companies. Keiretsu are their descendants, and involve intricate cross-holdings of shares, where a bank will hold shares in all commercial companies, and the latter will own shares in each other. Examples include Dai Ichi Kangyo, Fuyo, Mitsui, Mitsubishi, Sanwa and the Sumitomo group.

Keiretsu are organised on the basis of common loyalty, reciprocity and complementarity. They collaborate to help members maximise their market shares, particularly in the case of 'front line' companies competing on a global scale. They help procure cheap raw materials, share technology, raise and enforce quality standards, share market intelligence, and provide mutual financial support. They can pool resources to help the front line company win: Chrysler competes not with Mazda, but with the combined might of the Sumitomo group, which is willing to forego short term profit for market share gain. Technology sharing is perhaps the most important single benefit.

Not all Japanese firms belong to keiretsu: Canon, Sony and Toyota do not, for example. Even in these cases, however, the mentality of the keiretsu is evident: they collaborate with partners inside and outside Japan to develop new technologies and improve quality standards.

KERB TRADING

Trading in shares outside official hours.

KEY FACTORS FOR SUCCESS (KFS)

The reasons why some firms are more successful than others in particular products or industries. Should be based on an in-depth understanding of why consumers buy the products concerned, as a spur to RE-SEGMENTATION and/or INNOVATION. See SEGMENTATION.

KFS

See KEY FACTORS FOR SUCCESS.

KICKBACK

Bribe or illegal payment for commercial favours.

KJ METHOD

Originally a form of anthropological investigation which gathered together a mass of facts about a tribe and then asked the natives to make meaningful wholes from the facts. Japanese business has adapted the technique so that employees put down on scraps of paper suggestions about what the group should do or improvements they would like to happen. These scraps are then organised into larger patterns to create an integrated view of what the group and firm should do. Note the integrative rather than analytical nature of the method.

KK (KABUSHIKI KAISHA)

Japanese for PLC, Inc, SA etc.

KNOW-HOW

A firm's proprietary knowledge and/or COMPETENCES. See COMPETENCES.

KNOWLEDGE INDUSTRY

One where KNOW-HOW and expertise rather than low factor costs are the key to COMPETITIVE ADVANTAGE. Most of the world's wealth is created in knowledge industries today.

KNOWLEDGE LADDER

Something that is climbed by producing goods and services of greater added value and complexity, away from standardised products and services.

KNOWLEDGE MANAGEMENT STRUCTURE (KMS)

Concept put forward by Tom PETERS as a development of the LEARNING ORGANISATION. The 'new' firm must destroy bureaucracy but needs to nurture knowledge and skill, building expertise in ways that enhance the power of market-scale units, and that encourage those units to contribute knowledge for the benefit of the firm as a whole. This is a matter of shared values, feeling part of a family, and big travel budgets! MCKINSEY and Goldman Sachs are examples of firms operating KMSs, but the concept is applicable to all corporations, not just professional service firms.

KNOWLEDGE WORKER

The worker of the future, by brain and not brawn. Implies a redistribution of power away from owners towards employees of firms.

KNOWN VALUE ITEM (KVI)

Term used by grocery manufacturers and retailers to indicate those items which shoppers know the price of and use as a benchmark of value, like baked beans or Coca-Cola. Prices and profit margins on these items are usually kept very low in order to give the impression of excellent value, while margins on other products that are not KVIs (especially fresh produce, the deli, meat and fish) may be quite high.

KRUGERRAND

South African gold coin.

L

LABOUR TURNOVER
The rate at which employees leave an organisation: the number leaving in a year, divided by the average number employed in the year, time 100%.

LAME DUCK
A firm making losses, that is not viable and should not be supported by public money.

LAN
See LOCAL AREA NETWORK.

LAPTOP
Small portable computer that competes with the cat at home and can be used on aeroplanes; a lightweight PC.

LAST IN FIRST OUT
See LIFO.

LATERAL THINKING
The process of discontinuous thinking, not vertical or linear, but by provocative leaps in unpredicted directions, in order to generate a new idea. Invented by Edward DE BONO, for whom it has been an excellent CASH COW since 1967.

LAUNDERING
1. Passing of money obtained from crime through enough bank accounts to make it appear legitimate. **2.** Manipulation of accounts to present a false picture.

LBO (Leveraged Buy Out)
American 1980s piece of FINANCIAL ENGINEERING, whereby takeover bids are put together using a small amount of EQUITY and a large amount of DEBT (hence: a high degree of LEVERAGE). Because debt (even expensive debt using JUNK BONDS) is cheaper than equity, such deals could be constructed and bids made for large companies without the expectation of or requirement for hugely improved operational performance after the bid had succeeded: the increased leverage was at least half the battle in making the takeover viable. The problem with many late 1980s LBOs was that when the

recession started, and demand and profits fell, they were unable to service the debt, resulting in many cases in failure. LBOs differed from their British cousin, MBOs (Management Buy Outs) in two ways: the degree of gearing was much higher in LBOs, often ten to one as against one to one in the UK; and the LBOs did not always include managers as the main players, sometimes involving outside promoters as the principals. LBOs are difficult to finance currently because the banks are (rightly) more conservative in their lending.

LEADER

1. Head of a firm or unit. **2.** Person who points the way for a group or firm, irrespective of rank. **3.** Firm that is the market leader (i.e. has the greatest market share).

LEADERSHIP

1. Ability to point the way forward; quality of vision, team-building and creation that is as rare in business as elsewhere. Leadership has the unfashionable characteristic that it generally has to be exercised by one person (though even this is now disputed: see LEADERSHIP NETWORK). Modern management writers are extremely leery of praising leadership or elevating 'heroes' onto pedestals, or of helping develop our thinking on how to find, develop or nurture leaders. Too much stress on one individual is felt to be anti-democratic, anti-group, anti-EMPOWERMENT, and generally a bad thing. This view is both wrong and highly unfortunate. Good leadership is none of the above: good leaders exercise a great deal of power and influence, but they manufacture it too; there is not a fixed supply of power in an organisation so that it is a ZERO SUM GAME. Good leaders create more power for everyone who will subscribe to the vision and share it. It is a clear but widely ignored fact that every major corporate TRANSFORMATION – where the firm has been raised to a new and higher level of market and financial success – has had an inspired and inspiring leader who was crucial to the process. Only ideological blinkers stop us from realising that we would be a great deal more successful if we spent more time finding leaders or making it possible for people with leadership potential to come to the top of organisations. Very often, leaders are there, but not in power. But for freak circumstances, neither Winston Churchill nor Margaret Thatcher would have been able to demonstrate their leadership qualities. Great leaders are often unconventional, offbeat and ignored. Industrial psychologists should provide tools to assess leadership potential in firms and to ensure that it rises to the top wherever possible. We should also pay much more attention to the cultivation (as well as identification) of leadership qualities. Little serious work has been done on this since John ADAIR, and useful as his work is it could certainly be improved upon. See also: MANAGERIAL GRID.
2. Market leadership, meaning the largest company is a market.

3. Market or industrial leadership, a code name in the bad old days of American business of colluding to keep prices artificially high.

LEADERSHIP NETWORK

Term used by John Kotter, one of the few US business school professors to take leadership seriously, to mean collective leadership or leadership distributed around a corporation. Leadership is not just the preserve of the chief executive, but something that everyone in a firm should be encouraged to exercise.

LEADING INDICATOR

Early signal that something is about to happen. Noah's dove was a leading indicator that the flood was over. Market share gains can be a leading indicator of higher profits, even if these are currently depressed by the investments to gain market share.

LEAD MANAGER

Banks' management of the liabilities side of their balance sheet.

LEAD TIME

Time between placing an order and its delivery. Minimising lead times is often the key to competitive advantage

LEAKAGES

Customers or customer SEGMENTS that leak away from particular suppliers because the right product or service is not being provided; loss of revenue as a result. Very often a firm tries to find new customers without applying the same energy to the even more important task of retaining existing customers. See CUSTOMER RETENTION.

LEAN ENTERPRISE

Catch-phrase describing re-engineered companies that have five attributes: (1) they embrace a cluster of cross-functional processes; (2) they include close relationships with suppliers, distributors and customers to enhance value continually – the 'extended enterprise'; (3) they have a core of defined expertise; (4) functional areas like design, engineering, marketing, procurement, personnel and accounting should still exist, but be schools of learning and skill-bases that different teams in the firm can draw on; (5) careers should alternate between membership of multi-functional teams and time spent building up skill within particular functions or departments. Honda has used this alternating approach successfully both in Japan and the USA.

LEAN PRODUCTION

Techniques used to help companies attain low cost status (e.g. JUST-IN-TIME and TQM). The lean production system was pioneered by Toyota and involves three main points: (1) redesigning each process step so that it is part of a continuous flow; (2) setting up multi-functional teams; and (3) continually striving for improvement, both in terms of quality and cost reduction. See also WORK FLOWS, BPR and LEAN ENTERPRISE (which goes beyond lean production and applies similar principles to the whole firm).

LEARNING CURVE

The father of the EXPERIENCE CURVE.

LEARNING ORGANISATION

Term first used by Chris ARGYRIS to mean a firm that learns as it goes along, adjusting its way of doing business very responsively. The organisation retains knowledge independently of its employees. All organisations are in fact learning organisations – they all have a CULTURE based in one way or another on their experience – but some are better than others in taking the rights lessons from experience and in changing accordingly. See also Tom PETERS' preferred concept of the KNOWLEDGE MANAGEMENT STRUCTURE.

LEASE

Agreement between the owner of an asset (the LESSOR) to allow someone else (the LESSEE) to use the asset.

LEAVITT, HAROLD J

American management psychologist who is one of the most stimulating and original thinkers in the field. His 1978 book, *Managerial Psychology*, is one of the best texts on the subject, and in particular on the interactions and communication patterns of groups, and the distortions that arise from links in a chain. But his most interesting, landmark, work is his recent *Corporate Pathfinders*, which examines the characteristic personalities of leaders. In particular, he has a very useful typology into TYPE 1, TYPE 2 and TYPE 3 EXECUTIVES. See these entries and also HUMAN RELATIONS SCHOOL and TEAMWORK.

LEDGER

Accounting record of transactions, or book for keeping such records. The main ledger accounts are: Sales ledger (for each customer); Purchases ledger (for each supplier); Asset ledger; Cash Account or CASH BOOK (record of all cash incomings and outgoings); NOMINAL LEDGER (for each income or expense); and Payroll Ledger (for each employee).

LEFT BRAIN PROCESSES

Linear thinking: analytical and rational, rather than intuitive, pattern-recognising, and synthesising (RIGHT BRAIN PROCESSES). Management thinking has been dominated by the left brain since it started (TAYLOR etc.), but most managers use both parts of the brain and there is some evidence that the most successful managers are right brain specialists. The value of right brain thinking is increasingly being realised by the new school of HANDY, PETERS and especially Henry MINTZBERG.

LESSEE
User of an asset owned by someone else under the terms of a LEASE.

LESSOR
Owner of an asset who grants a LEASE for its use by someone else.

LETTER OF CREDIT
Document used to pay for foreign goods.

LETTER OF INTENT
Letter from one firm to another stating its intention to form a relationship or buy an asset or company subject to certain conditions and DUE DILIGENCE. Not legally binding.

LEVEL PLAYING FIELD
US businessmen often demand a level playing field, by which they mean an equal opportunity for all firms to compete on the same, fair terms. The same principle is applied within firms: individuals are given the opportunity to achieve and it is up to them to make what they can of it. This egalitarian elitism is very different from the practice in France or Japan, where students compete fiercely but once they are accepted into a firm the hierarchy will assume responsibility for developing their potential.

LEVERAGE
1. American word, increasingly used, for what the British call GEARING. **2.** bargaining power. **3.** OPERATING LEVERAGE: the same as OPERATIONAL GEARING, that is, the extent to which profits can be increased when revenues and capacity utilisation rise.

LEVERAGED BID
See LBO.

LEVERAGED BUY OUT
See LBO.

LEVITT, THEODORE (b. 1925)
German-born American marketing guru, professor at Harvard Business School. Wrote the legendary HBR article on MARKETING MYOPIA in 1960: it has since sold half a million reprints. The article said that firms and industries should be 'customer-satisfying' rather than 'goods-producing' in their

orientation: marketing-led not production-led. He said that it was not good enough to meet customer demand with a new product, and then believe that the key to continued success was low-cost production. He criticised 'FORDISM' for giving the customer what was thought to be good for him, rather than continually being alert to what the customer wanted. Hence Ford's decline in the face of General Motors' policy of offering cars in any colour and later in the face of the compact car from Japan and Europe. He also castigated the myopia of the US railroad industry in thinking that they were in the railroad business (a production-led view) rather than consumer transport: if they had had the latter view they would have diversified into airlines and not seen their business wither.

Levitt was wholly right and partly wrong. He was well ahead of his time in telling firms to be customer-obsessed. But his railroads example and the other he gave (such as buggywhips) were simplistic and possibly wrong. What possible expertise or cost sharing did the railroads have for entering the airline business? Perhaps they should have been experts at marketing transport to passengers, expertise that would have been transferable. But they weren't, and if Penn Central had bought an airline it would have gone bust much quicker than it did. The criticism was right, the remedy wrong.

More recently, Levitt has become a prophet of GLOBAL BRANDS. Levitt is fun to read, stimulating and bursting with ideas. We should not complain if some of them are flawed.

LEWIN, KURT

German-born Jewish professor of psychology who fled to America from the Nazis in 1932. He originated the model of change that says that behaviour patterns need to be 'unfrozen' before they can be changed and then 'refrozen'. To help such change he designed the T-GROUP (see ENCOUNTER GROUP). He also contrasted the different kinds of 'life space' in the American ('U-type') and German ('G-type') personalities. The American personality has a small 'private space' but a large and accessible 'public space'. The German personality, he said, has a cavernous private space but a small and inaccessible outer public space. But once an individual admits another into his private space, the bond created is life-long and very strong. If we accept this distinction, it is actually very important for thinking about senior executive team building. In American companies this will appear to be relatively quick and easy, but the quality of the bond may be low. In German companies it may be slow and difficult (and in many cases impossible) to build a real senior team, but if and when that happens the quality of the bond will be very high. There is a lot of evidence that corporate TRANSFORMATION requires, inter alia, a small team of top managers who are really committed to each other. Any adviser who is trying to make this happen should, if Lewin is right, be cautious about easy successes when dealing with Americans, and not give up too early when helping Germans. It is interesting to note that German business is highly atypical, in that it has a very large number of small- and medium-sized successful private companies in industries (such as engineering) that do not have a similar structure in other countries. Often these firms are still run by the family of the founder and are well run and export-focused, although with little ambition to grow larger. Are these facts related to Lewin's G-type personality? See also FAMILY FIRM.

LIABILITY
Money, goods or services owed by a company.

LIABILITY MANAGEMENT
Banks' management of the liabilities side of their balance sheet.

LIBOR (London Interbank Offered Rate)
Pronounced 'lie-bore': the main benchmark interest rate used in the EURO-MARKET. Many floating rates are linked to LIBOR.

LICENSING
Assigning the right to another firm to use proprietary technology, product/service formulation or other INTELLECTUAL KNOWLEDGE. Generally, those who pay for licences do better than those who take the licence. The solid state transistor was invented in the USA in 1947. In 1953 Sony obtained a licence from Western Electric for the princely sum of $25,000. Similarly, the US colour TV industry's downfall can be traced to RCA's decision to grant licences to several Japanese firms to make colour TVs. See INVENTION and INNOVATION.

LIEN
A CHARGE, or first claim over an ASSET, usually taken as SECURITY for a loan.

LIFE CYCLE
See PRODUCT LIFE CYCLE.

LIFO (Last In First Out)
1. Accounting method for valuing stock, where if identical stock bought or produced at different times cost different amounts, the newest stock is assumed to be used first, and costed accordingly. **2.** Basis for deciding who is cut first when a firm DOWN-SIZES: the most recent recruits get chopped first, as this is considered fairest.

LIKERT, RENSIS (1903-81)
American psychologist and researcher, who was a pioneer in studying LEADERSHIP and MANAGEMENT STYLES, and a great exponent of PARTICIPATION. He identified four types of management style, which he called System 1 through System 4:

1. Exploitative authoritarian: management by fear.
2. Benevolent autocracy: carrot more than stick, but top-down.
3. Consultative: communication is up and down, but decisions are still largely top-down.
4. Participative: decision-making in working groups which communicate with each other via individuals who are LINKING PINS, team leaders or others who are also members of one or more other groups.

Likert asserted that System 4 was better and more profitable. He also postulated a future System 5 in which all formal authority disappears.

LIMITED COMPANY

A company with limited liability, where the most that shareholders can lose is what they have already put into the company. Contrasts with PARTNERSHIPS where liability can be unlimited (in Anglo-Saxon countries).

LIMITED PARTNERSHIP

Useful legal form, originally from Germany, where some partners (the limited partners) may have limited liability, while other partners (the general partners) still have unlimited liability. The general partners run the business, while the limited partners supply cash or assets or technology to the partnership, and can do so without suffering unlimited liability for something they cannot control.

LINEAR PROGRAMMING

Mathematical technique in OPERATIONS RESEARCH for helping to decide how to optimise sales, profits or some other desired objective, where the resource limits are expressed as constraints.

LINE EXTENSION

Introducing a new variant of the same product, for example Pepsi Light or Sainsbury's Gold Decaffeinated coffee. Also called BRAND EXTENSION. See also NPD.

LINE MANAGER

Normal term for manager with subordinates. Generally implies that the manager is part of the 'line', that is, operational personnel, rather than 'STAFF', which implies support or overhead functions. Confusingly, though, managers in staff functions can have 'line management responsibility' for their own subordinates. In practice the distinction between 'line' and 'staff' is blurred; and perhaps it was never a very useful distinction in the first place. All managers should be trying to meet customer needs and beat competitors; there is no simple distinction between people who do things and those who support them. Talk of 'line' and 'staff' can help to set up mental barriers to teamwork.

LINE OF CREDIT
Borrowing facility available.

LINKING PINS
See LIKERT.

LIQUID ASSETS
Cash assets or those that can easily and quickly be turned into cash.

LIQUIDATE
To end a company's life by selling off all its assets, pay off liabilities and distribute any remaining cash to shareholders.

LIQUIDATION
The process of WINDING UP a company. See LIQUIDATE.

LIQUIDATOR
Accountant who oversees LIQUIDATION.

LIQUIDITY
1. A firm's ability to pay its short-term liabilities. **2.** The existence of cash available for investment and expenditure. **3.** The amount of room to trade in a financial market: a liquid market is one able to absorb large sales or purchases because there is a good two-way market.

LISTED COMPANY
A company quoted on the stock exchange. Also called a QUOTED COMPANY.

LIST PRICE
The full asked price before DISCOUNTS.

LOANSTOCK
A loan issued by a company with a defined rate of interest and a fixed term. Loanstock is the same as BONDS or NOTES. Loanstock can usually be traded. There are many different types of loanstock, so it is very important to understand the conditions and rights of each issue. Loanstock is often UNSECURED, so that if a company goes bust the loanstock holders will have no more rights than ordinary creditors. Unsecured loanstock commands a higher interest rate because of this risk. It is really a hybrid between DEBT and EQUITY, although more the former. There is also SUBORDINATED LOANSTOCK, which means that in a LIQUIDATION, the subordinated lenders receive nothing until all other creditors have been paid in full. Such loans are even riskier than unsecured loans and carry an even higher interest rate.

LOCAL AREA NETWORK (LAN)
Linking several PCs together so they can communicate with each other.

LOCK-OUT
1. Way of excluding (or the process of excluding) competitors from a given market. **2.** (Archaic) employers excluding workers from the workplace: thus the opposite of a strike.

LOGISTICS
Very important process of moving goods and people to deliver product to customers by co-ordinating the whole DELIVERY SYSTEM. Includes raw material, work-in-progress and stock movement and scheduling, stock control, warehousing, packaging and physical distribution. See JUST-IN-TIME.

LOG ON
To start a computer and gain access to its programs.

LONDON INTERBANK OFFERED RATE
See LIBOR.

LONG POSITION
When a market maker in shares or other instruments is selling less than he is buying: that is, he is choosing (or being forced) to hold or accumulate stock. If the price goes up, he will make a non-trading profit; if the price goes down, he will lose. The opposite is a SHORT POSITION. Traders typically hold both short and long positions according to their view of which way the market is going. Holding neither short nor long positions is called a BALANCED BOOK or a SQUARE BOOK.

LONG-TERM CAPITAL EMPLOYED, LONG-TERM NET WORTH
See CAPITAL EMPLOYED.

LONG-TERM LOAN/LOANSTOCK/BOND
A loan that is not due to be repaid in the next 12 months: so not necessarily all that long-term!

LONG-TERM LIABILITY
One that does not have to be settled within the next 12 months.

LOSS LEADER
Selling something at below cost to attract other business. The term is often used more loosely to include goods sold at below average profitability, even if not sold at a loss.

LOW-TECH
Business using basic, stable technology (e.g. quarrying, brick manufacture).

LOYALTY

The extent to which customers repurchase, and a major determinant of relative profitability. See CUSTOMER LOYALTY and especially CUSTOMER RETENTION.

LSI CIRCUITS

Large-scale integrated circuits, the design of which is critical to the success of consumer electronic products.

M

M&A

Universal abbreviation for 'mergers and acquisitions'. Can describe the process of acquisition, but more normally the department of a merchant or investment bank that tries to stimulate acquisitions, or the whole concept of acquisition. 'M&A' it will always be, but a far more apt description would be 'A&D', Acquisitions and Disposals, since: (a) mergers are almost unheard of today; and (b) a great deal of corporate finance activity is to help companies sell NON-CORE BUSINESSES, that is, disposals (what the cognoscenti call 'the sell side').

MACAULAY'S TRANSFER

The great nineteenth-century British historian commented in respect of the East India Company that because it was difficult to exchange information, the managers had to act on their own initiative; when communication improved, the individuals thought less for themselves. Thus communication is the enemy of initiative. There is something in this, which helps to explain why the IT revolution has proved so disappointing to many firms. EMPOWER-MENT is an attempt to combine information with initiative: but in the absence of major effort, the cultural bias in Western firms is away from front-line initiative, and the phone, the fax and the computer tend to reinforce dependence on others.

MCGREGOR, DOUGLAS (1906-64)

American social psychologist and central figure in the HUMAN RELATIONS SCHOOL. He stressed the role of belief in management: everything stems from the mental models and beliefs held by managers. He pioneered two ways of describing managers' thinking: THEORY X and THEORY Y. Theory X was traditional carrot and stick thinking: workers were inherently lazy, needed to supervised and motivated, and work was a necessary evil to provide money. Theory Y, on the other hand, posited that people wanted and needed to work, and what should be sought was the individual's commitment to the firm's objectives, and then the liberation of his or her abilities on behalf of those objectives. McGregor had great faith in what people could do if their potential was tapped.

Nowadays, Theory X and Theory Y are generally regarded as old hat. But what is EMPOWERMENT, if not repackaged Theory Y? And, if we are honest, do not many of our attitudes to work still reflect Theory X? What proportion of employees in a company really believe in the company and what it is trying to do?

McGregor's disciple, Abraham MASLOW, was honest enough to admit that Theory Y management was often difficult, because it demanded initiative from everyone, and many people needed the structure of being told what to do by others. But the criticism, though valid, somewhat misses the point. Theory Y is most useful not as a statement of what works best now, but what should work in the future. A generation on, Theory Y looks more attainable: and a version of it is already in operation in many Japanese firms and a few elsewhere. IKEA, SAS, Sony, Toshiba, Toyota, Hewlett-Packard, Apple, Microsoft, The Body Shop: these are all firms that embody Theory Y characteristics. McGregor was ahead of his time, and is still well worth reading. See MISSION.

MACHINE LOADING
1. The utilisation rate of a machine in a factory. **2.** Allocating tasks to machines.

MACHINE TOOLS
Electronically controlled machines for cutting metal, creating other tools, controlling materials or making parts. Now so reliable that they can be left unattended to cut metal all night if necessary, and can maintain themselves.

MCKINSEY
Probably the most prestigious management consultancy in the world. It has a presence wherever business is done, and has a huge 'installed base' of chief executives who used to work with the Firm. The nominal founder was James O McKinsey, an American accounting professor and industrialist, but the real founder was Marvin BOWER, who made McKinsey in the 1930s into the first really professional firm of management consultants, based on the (relatively high) ethical standards of law firms. McKinsey has consistently aimed to be 'boardroom' consultants, concerned with whatever issues concern the chief executive and the rest of the board. McKinsey arrived in Europe in the 1960s and expanded internationally during the 1970s. McKinsey were the original sponsors of the 'excellence project' of the early 1980s: Tom PETERS and Robert WATERMAN were consultants with the Firm then. Kenichi OHMAE is still a McKinsey man, heading the Japanese practice. The Firm has resisted the lure of GOING PUBLIC, still watched by the steely eye of Marvin BOWER, guardian of its conscience. McKinsey's critics accuse the Firm of being self-satisfied, conventional, Establishment-oriented and sometimes pedestrian; but it is still the consultancy all others take as the industry standard.

MAGAZINER, IRA C
Important American writer and consultant who has written on industrial policy in Japan, Sweden and Ireland and whose 1982 book, *Minding*

America's Business (co-authored with Robert B Reich) is still the best account of how and why the USA has lost market share to Japan. It stresses the need for the US government and industrialists to focus on competitive productivity and to develop industrial policy for specific industries in a discrete and precise way. Magaziner swims against the American tide of *laissez-faire* but is totally correct. He is now one of many advisers to President Clinton; it is important to America's industrial future that he is heeded in areas outside his immediate healthcare brief.

MAIL ORDER

Catalogue shopping. Traditional mail order in the UK has been 'agency' mail order, whereby an army of agents distributes catalogues to friends and collects their orders together, receiving commission on the sales. This form is declining, as the competition for good agents has hotted up and their loyalty been weakened, so that the expense of recruiting new agents is escalating. Single customer direct mail order is growing, particularly in special interest segments, where the mail order firms issue 'specialogues' to buyers.

MAINFRAME

The largest type of computer. Traditionally any large business had to have a mainframe, but with the increased power of PCs and LOCAL AREA NETWORKS (LANs) this is no longer true.

MAKE OR BUY DECISION

1. The decision on whether to make components or any other part of the product or service in-house, or whether to use outside suppliers (the latter being called OUTSOURCING). 'Make or buy' has long been a topic of debate, but it is becoming increasingly important. It can now determine relative profitability in an industry, as in computers.

2. Igor ANSOFF used 'make or buy' to mean organic expansion versus expansion by acquisition.

Charles Coates, an expert on manufacturing strategy, believes that a key condition of competitive advantage is that firms focus only on those activities that are critical to its proposition and where it has distinctive COMPETENCES, and outsource all other components and activities. In practice this means a great deal more outsourcing than most firms currently use. The reason outsourcing is so valuable is that the COSTS OF COMPLEXITY are crippling for a firm engaged in many activities. In some cases this complexity is not avoidable, but in most it is, via outsourcing.

Coates says that make/buy policy should follow three rules:

1. Divide all components into 'critical' and 'non-critical'. Critical components are those that are key to the firm's competitive advantage, where it can undertake them to a quality standard and cost that is second to none. 'Critical components are those upon which delivery of the key attributes of

the firm's proposition depend. They may include components which incur a high proportion of total cost, those that require specialised skills, high-quality levels or quick response that outside suppliers could not match, or those that have proprietary technology that the firm must protect.' All critical components must be made in-house. It does not follow, however, that all non-critical components should be outsourced: a further rule is required.

2. Outsource all non-critical components where suppliers have an advantage through greater focus and lower cost.

3. For non-critical components where suppliers do not have an advantage, make them but manage the production of critical and non-critical components separately, and be ready to switch to outsourcing the latter if a low cost specialist emerges.

In the computer industry, make/buy decisions are now the most important in determining success. Coates showed that in 1991 there was a clear correlation between higher profits and higher outsourcing (Figure 28).

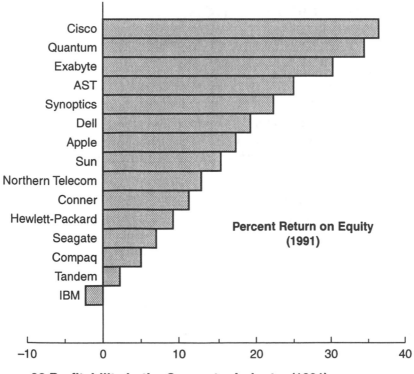

Figure 28 Profitability in the Computer Industry (1991)
Source: Charles Coates, *The Total Manager, Financial Times/Pitman 1994*

Major established suppliers like IBM make many of their parts, including disk drives and processors. Recent entrants like Dell assemble products in leased factories and outsource all their parts. IBM's investment went into production, Dell's into an effective purchasing network and into sales and service training, focusing particularly on the quality and productivity of its TELESALES people.

MAKE-WORK

Low value work to keep staff busy. English equivalent of the American term BUSY-WORK.

MANAGEMENT

From an Italian word meaning to handle horses, horsemanship. Generally held now to be achieving business objectives by mobilising other people. But how, and with what mental model? For an eloquent contrast between Western and Japanese views of management, see Konosuke MATSUSHITA.

MANAGEMENT ACCOUNTING

The process of providing accounting information to management, as opposed to preparing accounts for external reporting purposes.

MANAGEMENT BY EXCEPTION

See EXCEPTION REPORTING.

MANAGEMENT BY WANDERING AROUND (MBWA)

Open and participative style invented by Hewlett-Packard of face-to-face management that works well for them. The idea is to be aware of what is happening throughout the firm and in particular at lower levels: 'managers must move around to find out how people feel about their jobs – what they think will make their work more productive and meaningful.' Not so much a technique as a value system, which embodied the insights of EMPOWERMENT long before it was invented.

MANAGEMENT CONSULTING

Covers a huge range of services and has an interesting industrial structure, with a few very large firms (the accounting consultancies, a few generalists like Booz Allen and PA, a few specialists like Proudfoot and Hay-MSL, and the leading strategy houses), many medium to small firms, and a massive tail of one-man-and-a-dog suppliers. Brand is crucially important in consulting, both to attract clients and also the best consultants. Most consultancies are specialised by both what they do (with the main divisions being: strategy, IT, manufacturing strategy including quality, logistics, and organisational effectiveness and change management) and by the industries they serve (financial services, heavy manufacturing, utilities, engineering, consumer goods, retailing, services). The largest and most expensive consultancies are international, although having most of their sales in Europe and the USA, which are by far the largest markets. Management consultants are thin on the ground in Japan, but very few Western organisations do not use consultants from time to time, or in some cases almost continuously. The relationship between consultants and the organisations they serve varies enormously, but the best results are nearly always obtained for both sides in long and close relationships where the consultants help to make change happen. One social problem that has been identified is that many of the best, most committed and most creative people available to business prefer to work as consultants rather than in large organisations: but perhaps this is more an issue for the latter to address, by changing the way they work. See also BCG and MCKINSEY.

MANAGEMENT DEVELOPMENT

Improving the skills, both technical and managerial, of managers. Hugely important, but there is no magic formula for doing it well. See HUMAN RELATIONS SCHOOL, ADAIR, ARGYRIS, BENNIS, HANDY, KANTER, LEAVITT, PETERS, and WATERMAN.

MANAGEMENT INFORMATION SYSTEM

See MIS.

MANAGEMENT RATIO

The ratio of managers to non-managers. But who is a manager?

MANAGEMENT SCIENCE

Old name for management studies, reflecting an engineering and operations research bias.

MANAGEMENT STYLES

A useful categorisation of styles of managing diversified firms has been provided by Goold and Campbell in their book *Strategies and Styles* (1987). They define three prevalent styles: FINANCIAL CONTROL, STRATEGIC CONTROL and STRATEGIC PLANNING, as well as five other less frequent styles: CENTRALISED, FINANCIAL PROGRAMMING, HOLDING COMPANY, STRATEGIC PROGRAMMING and STRATEGIC VENTURING. See these entries for definitions and comments on each.

MANAGEMENT SYNERGY

See SYNERGY.

MANAGERIAL GRID

Figure 29 shows the grid developed by Blake and Moulton measuring managers by both their 'Concern for People' and their 'Concern for Production'.

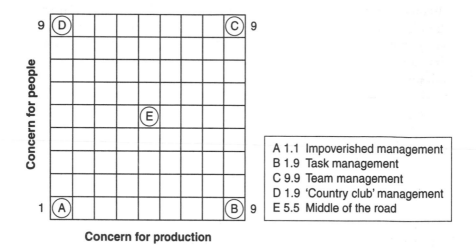

Figure 29 The managerial grid

There are 81 possible positions on the grid, the best being 9.9: the highest on both dimensions, which Robert Blake (b. 1918) and Jane Mouton (b. 1930) called team management. They claimed that this led to best performance.

MANAGERIALISM, THE MANAGEMENT THEORY OF THE FIRM, THE MANAGERIAL HERESY

Very important view that given absentee landlords in the form of INSTITU-TIONAL INVESTORS, power in corporations falls to the senior managers, who may advance their own interests rather than those of the owners. Evidence that the managerial theory has a strong element of truth can be seen in any or all of the following: valuing turnover growth even without profit growth; reluctance to sell non-core companies or DE-MERGE, leaving a smaller company; reluctance to OUTSOURCE to the proper extent; a preference for acquisition rather than disposal, or than being acquired; large perquisites for executives, so that you would need a massive income to have an equivalent lifestyle if outside the firm and paying tax; executive jets, chartered planes, or, if times are hard and you have to slum it by flying on a commercial airline, first class travel, which almost nobody can afford if required to pay for oneself; retreats in expensive hotels; hospitality trips (at which the British excel) to Ascot, Wimbledon, Henley, Cheltenham, Glynbourne, Covent Garden, and all the other delights of the season; paying top executives a very high multiple of average employee or lowest employee pay; increasing top executive pay above the rate of inflation, or when profits fall; granting oneself large share options, which give a free ride when the stock market goes up, regardless of the performance of the company itself; and generally ensuring that one has a pleasant lifestyle and interesting work, regardless of what the corporate priorities are. None of these activities advances the interest of shareholders, or of the firm as a whole. Who says that the managerial heresy is dead?

MANPOWER PLANNING

Technique popular in the 1960s and 1970s for planning how many people are required for an organisation and for ensuring that recruitment and training produce the right employee profile. Only a few, very large, companies still practise manpower planning as a separate discipline: prediction is too difficult, and the world is changing with many fewer CORE WORKERS and more use of CONTRACTORS and flexible labour forces.

MANUFACTURING REQUIREMENTS PLANNING

See MRP.

MARGIN

Usually means 'profit margin', the difference between price and cost. See OPERATING MARGIN.

MARGIN ACCOUNT

Brokerage account, popular in the USA, for buying shares on credit, with the shares themselves as security. Dangerous.

MARGINAL COMPETITOR, MARGINAL SUPPLIER, MARGINAL PRODUCER

The weakest player in a market, who might go bust if prices fell. Generally, there is no point in a marginal competitor staying in business; it would be best for everyone if he left. The leading competitor has a duty to try to force him out of business, by lowering costs and improving service in a way the marginal competitor cannot match.

MARGINAL COST

The cost of producing one more unit.

MARGINAL COSTING

1. Costing that does not include overheads. 2. The practice of pricing some product at above marginal cost but below full cost, in order to produce a contribution. More properly called MARGINAL-COST PRICING or MARGINAL PRICING, but usually referred to as marginal costing. Dangerous if a significant proportion of revenues come from this practice.

MARGINAL-COST PRICING, MARGINAL PRICING

See MARGINAL COSTING (definition 2).

MARKETABLE

When a share or other asset can be sold readily and without affecting the market price of other similar shares or assets.

MARKET CAPITALISATION

The total value of all the ordinary shares of a company. Sometimes also called MARKET VALUE.

MARKET CHALLENGER

STRONG FOLLOWER in market share terms: companies that are not far behind the market leader in a particular product or service. The term is not wholly satisfactory, because it implies that the second or third player is gaining relative market share on the leader and challenging him. The term Strong Follower does not carry this implication, and is reserved for a RELATIVE MARKET SHARE of at least 0.7x, that is, at least 70% the size of the leader. Neither term is widely used, hence the neglect of DOGS that may have potential. See BCG MATRIX.

MARKET CHANNEL

See DISTRIBUTION CHANNEL.

MARKET CONCENTRATION

See CONCENTRATION and HERFINDAHL INDEX.

MARKET DEVELOPMENT PROCESS (MDP)

An integrated approach to NPD and increasing sales, based on pooling efforts and understanding between sales, marketing, and other functions that have contact with customers.

MARKET ENTRY

A decision to enter a new market and the implementation thereof.

MARKET EXIT

One supplier leaving a market. See BARRIERS TO EXIT.

MARKET FOLLOWER

See MARKET CHALLENGER and STRONG FOLLOWER.

MARKET IMPERFECTIONS

The absence of perfect competition, that enables firms to enjoy above-average returns on capital. In a sense all business is the pursuit of market imperfections. The rule rather than the exception.

MARKETING

Planning and carrying out all customer related activities except selling.

MARKETING-LED

Until the late 1950s most Western firms were production-led. The focus was on making the product, expanding volume and driving down costs. In the early 1960s Theodore LEVITT and others told managers to be marketing-led. The emphasis was now on winning the hearts and minds of customers and working out what new products to sell them. Marketing executives replaced those with production backgrounds as chief executives. More recently, in the 1980s and 1990s, customer obsession has become the watchword of the wise.

The focus is absolutely right, but can have a dangerous side effect if the product line is extended too far into new areas. With additional product range, overhead costs rise sharply, as the costs of complexity proliferate. Overhead costs are the new battleground that will determine the winners and losers in the late 1990s and the next century. The message is therefore simple: be obsessed with customers, but focus your product range and on the part of the VALUE-ADDED CHAIN where you have the greatest competitive advantage, and abolish all unnecessary overheads. See MARKETING MYOPIA and COSTS OF COMPLEXITY.

MARKETING MIX

The FOUR PS: Product (quality, branding, features, packaging); Pricing; Promotion; and Place (where sold and use of distributors). It is often instructive to compare the marketing mix used by your company compared with competitors, or to compare your marketing mix across different products.

MARKETING MYOPIA

Taking too narrow a view of one's market: see Theodore LEVITT, who invented the term in 1960.

MARKET INTELLIGENCE

Useful information about customer needs, perception of different competitors, and about what competitors are doing.

MARKETISING

The process of turning cost centres into profit centres, making them respond to an internal or external market.

MARKET LEADER

The firm with the greatest market share in a BUSINESS SEGMENT. Leadership is usually very valuable. See BCG MATRIX.

MARKET MAKER

JOBBER or STOCKBROKER who makes a market in shares, bonds, currencies, commodities (i.e. who buys and sells these instruments).

MARKET NICHE

A small BUSINESS SEGMENT where leadership is valuable and attainable for small firms, where they are protected from competition from their larger brethren.

MARKET PENETRATION

1. The percentage of all potential customers (in a defined market) who have bought a company's product: thus Filofax may have a penetration of 10% in the UK (meaning 10% of the population has bought a personal organiser from Filofax) but only 1% in the USA. Where a product has differential market penetration in different countries there is often an opportunity to improve distribution and raise penetration. **2.** A similar meaning can be applied to the penetration of a product, from all competitors, in a market. Thus the penetration of colour TVs in the USA may be 99%, regardless of which companies supply them.

MARKET PENETRATION PRICING

Pricing in order to gain market share rapidly or establish a new product in the market place, that is, pricing lower than normal profit margins or even pricing at a loss. The EXPERIENCE CURVE suggests that this is generally a wise strategy, providing market leadership can be attained and defended.

MARKET PERFORMANCE

How good suppliers are at meeting requirements of a market.

MARKET POSITIONING

The relative position that a product has in a market, or the process of trying to attain a certain position. There can be a large number of market positioning dimensions, but obvious ones are upmarket versus downmarket and 'high service' versus 'no frills'. Often displayed on PERCEPTUAL MAPS which are two-dimensional charts showing where a product falls (e.g. fashion appeal versus durability on one axis and youth oriented versus mature market appeal on the other axis). See MARKET SEGMENT.

MARKET POTENTIAL

How large a market might become with appropriate supply side actions.

MARKET POWER

The ability to dictate terms to a market (e.g. on pricing) as a result of market DOMINANCE (being much the largest supplier).

MARKET RESEARCH

Data collection and analysis to provide information about customers and competitors. Market research is essential, but rarely used well. The keys to good use are: thinking extremely carefully about the questions before commissioning or conducting research; asking customers and potential customers open-ended as well as close-ended questions; listening well and shifting the discussion on to what the customer wants to talk about rather than what you originally intended to ask; ensuring that you know how customers rate you on their purchase criteria relative to competition; and finding out what competitors are doing and why it is successful. It should be apparent that the best sources of market research are not professional researchers (though they have a role), but your firm's own front line: any employees who are in touch with customers, for whatever purpose. See COMB ANALYSIS for an example of simple but valuable market research.

MARKET RISK

Also known as NON-DIVERSIFIABLE RISK. Risk in holding shares that is not peculiar to the particular company or companies' share price performance, but that relates to fluctuations in the stock market as a whole. See CAPITAL ASSET PRICING MODEL (CAPM).

MARKET SATURATION

When a product has reached as many new buyers as it is likely ever to reach, and is reduced to a lower level of replacement demand. For example, if it is believed that only 70% of households will ever buy a video recorder, and the MARKET PENETRATION has already reached 65%, that market may be approaching saturation. Suppliers will have to wait until the product wears out before seeing a new surge in demand. The concept of saturation is, however, too passive and defeatist. When a product is approaching saturation it should still be possible to find ways of boosting demand by innovative product development or finding new markets.

MARKET SEGMENT

Part of a market where buyers have similar purchase criteria. Market segmentation has historically been done by marketeers, who have focused on socio-economic variables (like the dreaded and discredited income groups of A, B, C1, C2, D, and E) or, if slightly more enlightened, psychologically-categorised groups, like innovators. This type of market segmentation ignores the importance of competition in defining segments. Better than market segmentation, therefore, is BUSINESS SEGMENTATION, sometimes known simply as SEGMENTATION, which defines competitive arenas within which it is possible to gain competitive advantage. Traditional market segmentation occasionally corresponds to business segmentation, but much more often is concerned with tactical implementation of business segmentation. There may be several market segments within a business segment; business segmentation should be done before market segmentation, which in any case should be given lower priority. See LIFE-STYLE MARKETING, BUSINESS SEGMENTATION and SEGMENTATION.

MARKET SHARE

A supplier's sales (measured by money or volume) divided by the size of the total market. Market share is very much less useful (although easier to ascertain) than RELATIVE MARKET SHARE. If you have a market share of 10%, you could either be the market leader (if the next largest competitor has 5%), or you could be much smaller than the market leader (if he had 50%). Correctly defined market share (that is, share of a business segment), or more precisely high relative market share, is at the heart of competitive advantage: do not let anyone persuade you that this view is dated!

MARKET SKIMMING, MARKET SKIMMING PRICING

Charging a high price for a new product so as to skim off what the first tranche of buyers are willing to pay, and then reducing the price after a time to capture the next tranche. A good example is books, where a high priced hardback will skim off the price-insensitive or impatient demand, before a paperback comes out a year later at half the price. Market skimming can be sensible, but there are only a few markets where it is generally a good idea. Too often, if competitors do not skim, the innovator obtains high initial profits but loses the longer term battle: the result can be that the new product is cash negative over its total life.

MARKET STRUCTURE

The characteristics of a market that will influence its profitability, including: the degree of CONCENTRATION in the market, the behaviour of competitors in it; the bargaining power of suppliers; and the bargaining power of buyers. See PORTER.

MARKET TARGETING

Usually refers to tactical MARKET SEGMENTATION: trying to reach and raise market share of a particular type of buyer. Can also refer, more usefully, to BUSINESS SEGMENTATION, that is, trying to increase share and obtain or reinforce leadership in a particular business segment.

MARKET TO BOOK RATIO

MARKET VALUE of shares divided by their BOOK VALUE. A ratio of more than one shows a PREMIUM OF MARKET TO BOOK, indicating that the shares are highly rated; conversely, a market to book ratio of under one shows a DISCOUNT TO NET ASSETS and indicates a poor rating. Comparisons can only be made with confidence, however, in the same industry, and even there differences in accounting practices (such as how quickly goodwill is written off after acquisitions) can make simplistic interpretation of the market to book ratio misleading. See INTANGIBLE ASSET, TOBIN'S Q and SERVICE-COMPETENCY VALUES.

MARKET VALUE

1. Generally used as a synonym for MARKET CAPITALISATION, that is, the value of 100% of a firm's shares on the stock market. 2. The BREAK-UP VALUE of a firm, often thought to be higher than its current market capitalisation. 3. The liquidation value of a firm, that is, what you would be left with for the shareholders after selling all assets and paying off all liabilities. Market value is most often used in the first sense.

MARK TO MARKET

When an investment is revalued to the current market price, rather than the more usual (and prudent) practice of taking the lower of cost or market value.

MARK UP

The profit MARGIN on a product expressed as a percentage of its total cost.

PHILIP MORRIS, THE MARLBORO FRIDAY (April 2, 1993)

When this US tobacco company slashed the price of its branded cigarettes by 25% in order to reverse the long-term loss of market share to generic (unbranded) cigarettes, which had claimed almost 40% of the US market.

The move sent shockwaves around the boardrooms of all branded goods manufacturers around the world, and ended the stockmarket's long love affair with branded company shares. In the 1980s and early 1990s many branded manufacturers had grown earnings year after year, largely on the back of real price increases, sometimes up to 15% per annum. Overdoing the price increases had led to growth in market share of retailers' OWN LABEL products and in TERTIARY BRANDS, but short-term market share loss had been more than compensated, in short-run earnings terms, by the price increases. The fight back by brands has undermined their short-term earnings, but also raised fears that the magical qualities of brands have been grossly exaggerated.

Philip Morris' move led to a savaging of its shares: they dropped 23% in one day. Since then the shares have largely recovered and Philip Morris has grown its total share of the US tobacco market from 42% to 46%, with Marlboro alone growing from 22% to 27%. It was a courageous move, even if it smelt of panic. Brands do have value, but so too does market share, and in the long run it is unwise to sell market share to impress stockmarket analysts. A brand premium should never be so high that it leads to market share loss. See also OWN LABEL and BRAND PREMIUM.

MARZIPAN LAYER

Rich expression for employees, especially in professional firms, who are just below the top (the icing), but differentiated from the bulk of employees (the cake). Taking care of the marzipan layer is crucial; its members must be treated as partners, or else they will take their expertise to a shop where it is better appreciated. There is often more energy and know-how in the marzipan layer than in the icing.

MASLOW, ABRAHAM (1908-1970)

Inventor of the HIERARCHY OF NEEDS which stressed the progressive upgrading of needs as earlier needs were satisfied, culminating in 'self-actualisation'. Not wholly correct as an observation of what was, or is, industrial reality; the theory under-estimates the propensity of people to want money and more money and continuously upgrade their standard of living. An honest man and a good researcher in the Californian electronics industry. See McGREGOR, and HUMAN RELATIONS SCHOOL.

MASS MANUFACTURE, MASS MARKETING

Selling a standard product in high volume around the world. America's special forte. See UNIVERSAL PRODUCT. Now no longer enough for success, as niche markets, CUSTOMISING and CUSTOMERISING come to the fore.

MATCHING

Accounting process under the ACCRUALS CONCEPT whereby all expenses incurred in a period are recognised in the accounts for that period, that is, the books match the operational reality.

MATCHING

Banks' policy of balancing risk characteristics of its assets and liabilities.

MATERIALITY

Accounting concept that takes account of how important ('material') a fact or calculation is. It would not be material to value a nuclear power plant down to the last cent.

MATERIALS REQUIREMENTS PLANNING

See MRP.

MATRIX, MATRIX MANAGEMENT, MATRIX ORGANISATION

An organisation structure which is not based on a simple CHAIN OF COMMAND, but where individuals may report to two (or more) bosses. This can imply either a primary reporting relationship to one boss and a DOTTED LINE RELATIONSHIP to another boss, or equal reporting relationships. Royal Dutch/Shell and Philips pioneered matrix structures, either to give weight to functions as well as products, or to balance product divisions and national selling organisations. Matrix management is necessary when functions are closely inter-dependent, even if there is not a formal matrix structure. Matrix organisations reached their peak of popularity around 1980, and today many people claim that they don't work well. The problem may lie in trying to define on paper very complex reporting relationships: these can often exist and work well without being defined. The underlying concept of matrix management is a lot closer to reality than the pretence that there can be a simple chain of command. See also JACQUES for a discussion of this point.

MATRIX PRICING
Strategy of harming a competitor by pricing low in a segment where your own firm has few sales but the competitor has high sales. The idea is that the competitor will have to match your low price and that this will so harm his profitability that he will not have the resources to attack you in your own high profit segments. The strategy is not much used in practice, but often succeeds when it is.

MATSUSHITA, KONOSUKE
Visionary leader of the company of the same name and one of the first to recognise the importance of creating a corporate religion in order to inspire people in a firm and galvanise all the brainpower within it for the commercial battle. In 1932 he developed his philosophy:

people need a way of linking their productive lives to society . . . a business should . . . stand . . . on the service it provides society. Profits should not be a reflection of corporate greed, but a vote of confidence from society that what is offered by the firm is valued . . . . Human unity and harmony are indispensable for job achievement. Always show clear objectives and perform business as a united whole, uniting everyone. The foundation for unity and harmony is sincerity.

More recently, Matsushita has given the West a frank warning. The Japanese are usually very polite in public, especially to foreigners, but he broke ranks in 1985 with a brutal and accurate analysis of the weakness of Western management:

We [the Japanese] are going to win and the industrial West is going to lose. There is nothing much you can do about it, because the reasons for your failure are within yourselves. Your firms are built on the TAYLOR model; even worse, so are your heads . . . for you, the essence of management is getting the ideas out of the heads of the bosses and into the hands of labour. For us the art of management is mobilising and pulling together the intellectual resources of all the employees in the service of the firm . . . . Only by drawing on the combined brainpower of all its employees can a firm face up to . . . today's environment.

MATURE INDUSTRY
Fallacious idea that industries generally go through a life cycle, ending with maturity or a DECLINING INDUSTRY. It is fair enough to describe an industry as 'mature' if it has very low or negative market growth, but mature industries can often be rejuvenated by imagination and energy on the part of suppliers. See DECLINING INDUSTRY.

MAUGHAM'S MUFFLER

Information from the base of an organisation can become 'muffled', that is, distorted as it passes up. Ensuring this does not happen is essential if a firm is to be customer centred.

MAVERICK

An unconventional competitor, often a newcomer to the market, who does not respect the rules of the game, but writes his own rules. Excellent examples are Apple (revolutionising the computer business by developing very powerful PCs) and IKEA (the Swedish furniture retailer that made this a business susceptible to international scale and a new division of labour between customer and supplier: see DELIVERY SYSTEM for more on IKEA). It is very difficult for established competitors to cope with mavericks: all the familiar levers for dealing with competitors do no good. When considering market entry, a good question is: is there scope for being a maverick here? If not, enter another market, unless there is very high sharing of cost or know-how in the new market.

MAYO, ELTON (1880-1949)

Australian founder of the HUMAN RELATIONS SCHOOL and propagandist of the HAWTHORNE STUDIES at Western Electric in 1927–32. Realised the importance of self-esteem and group consensus. Also one of the first to realise the importance of the INFORMAL ORGANISATION and how it could be either destructive or harnessed. He pioneered proper communications between management and workforce, that helped ultimately to corrode the negative power of trade unions. Prophet of teamwork and securing the commitment of the individual and the group to corporate objectives. See EMPOWERMENT, of which he was (though he never used the term) probably the first exponent.

MBA (Master's degree in Business Administration)

A curiously legalistic title, reflecting the legal origins of Harvard Business School, for the standard business qualification in English-speaking countries. MBA is also used to designate a person who has the qualification, as well as the course itself.

What can usefully be said about MBAs? It is difficult to be against management education, but the proliferation of MBA courses and the growth of the MBA industry (which grew relentlessly until 1991 in both the USA and the UK, and is now suffering its first recession) coincided with the decline of the West in global market share. A spurious correlation? Then consider that countries with the best economic performance, notably Japan, tend not to have business schools or regard the MBA as an important qualification. A distortion is entered in the debate because nearly everyone active in management education and responsible for framing business opinion in the Anglo-Saxon world has some sort of vested interest in the MBA, both because they are likely to have one themselves but more particularly because they are likely to be part of an institution that manufactures huge quantities of MBAs. Most enlightened observers say the problem is not the MBA itself, but how it is taught: in a competitive context within the school; with the emphasis on analysis rather than synthesis; on learning rather than personal development; on technical rather than managerial skills. The solution, then, is not to abolish the MBA but to reform it. Do you find this wholly convincing?

In any case the coinage of the MBA has been devalued by the large number of second- and third-rate institutions offering it. There are only about a dozen schools in the world whose MBAs are rated by the cognoscenti, and an MBA from elsewhere may repel rather than attract the top recruiters.

MBI (Management Buy-In)

A takeover where a group of outside managers, backed by venture capitalists and banks, buys a firm, generally an under-performing QUOTED COMPANY. Only developed on a serious scale in the UK in the mid- to late 1980s. An MBI is thus different from the more common MBO, in that the managers buying the company and running it after the deal come from outside rather than inside. Although less common, MBIs are more logical than MBOs, in that the injection of fresh and proven management should be able to raise performance better than existing managers who have already had their chance. I am not aware of good data regarding the relative performance of MBIs versus MBOs, but it does not appear empirically that MBIs are actually more successful than MBOs. The latter may succeed because the team already know what can be done with the firm once the shackles of the previous PARENT are thrown off, whereas MBIs may be riskier because less is known by the incomers about the state of the firm and because the way that they will interact with existing management adds another dimension of uncertainty. Certainly there have been some spectacular failures of MBIs, such as the Lowndes Queensway takeover of Harris Queensway, as well as some notable successes. Many US LBOs (Leveraged Buy-Outs) were really LBIS (Leveraged Buy-Ins), because the promoters and one or two top managers came from outside, although in general Americans use the term LBO to cover both classes. See also MBO.

MBO (Management Buy-Out)

A bid by the top managers of a firm to buy it, backed by providers of EQUITY (VENTURE CAPITALISTS) and DEBT (commercial bankers). MBOs became common in the UK in the 1980s and are still popular, although on a smaller scale than during the wave of large MBOs at the end that decade. For a firm wishing to sell a NON-CORE BUSINESS it can make sense to sell to the management, as there is much less disruption than when selling to a

TRADE BUYER. For the managers there is the opportunity to work fanatically for a period of three years and then, if successful, make very high returns. Typically in an MBO the venture capitalists will look for an IRR (Internal Rate of Return) of 35–40% (compounded per annum), and once this is satisfied will be willing to hand over most of any excess profit to the managers. This can lead to very high personal returns, as when Paul Judge, the leader of the very successful Premier Brands MBO, received £45m on the sale of the company to Hillsdown Holdings.

MBOs can be small scale events in private companies as well as takeovers of large listed companies. They are a permanent and useful addition to the world's stock of financial engineering. Note that they are by definition transitional mechanisms, taking a company from one state (under-performance) to another (high performance) within a relatively short space of time. It is necessary therefore to plan for the EXIT right from the start, and to gear the company to the post-MBO outcome envisaged. It is also important to change the CULTURE of a firm experiencing an MBO in order to raise it to new levels of market and financial success. Explicit recognition of this dimension will speed up the improvement process and may be a prerequisite for success. Recent research shows that of MBOs that failed, most of them were not successful in changing the culture, and this was at least a contributory cause of failure (although too high leverage was often the most obvious culprit).

MbO (Management by Objectives)

Venerable Anglo-Saxon management tool originally conceived by Peter DRUCKER in the 1950s and introduced into the UK by John Humble, who defined it as 'the attempt to clarify the goals of management objectively, so that the responsibility for achieving the goals was reasonably distributed round the management team'. Basically MbO invites all managers to sit down and compile a list of objectives for which they were willing to be held accountable, and agree with their boss these objectives, together with how to measure them and the timetable involved.

MbO as an organised management tool was popular in Britain and America in the 1960s and 1970s, but is now little practised in the grand, all-embracing way urged by Drucker and Humble. One difficulty was that objectives tended to be set either too high or too low, and it was impossible to make everyone's objectives equally challenging. A second reason why MbO fell from grace was that it came to be viewed as manipulative, with objectives being imposed on managers. A third criticism was that MbO did not encourage teamwork, but rather a chain of achieving individuals. MbO even of the best type also does not travel well outside Anglo-Saxon cultures, since it requires a perception of equality between boss and executive: in effect, they negotiate with each other. MbO also embodies the view of the firm as a large, rational structure: the APOLLO cultural model. MbO becomes cumbersome when circumstances change quickly and new responses are required. Nevertheless, MbO still has its adherents for whom it seems to work well.

MBWA

See MANAGEMENT BY WANDERING AROUND.

MEAN

Arithmetic average.

MECHANISTIC ORGANISATION

Term invented by Burns and Stalker to describe a rigid BUREAUCRACY. Contrast their term ORGANISMIC ORGANISATION, a very ugly phrase for fast moving ones, close to what are now called ADHOCRACIES.

MEDIAN

Middle value in a series: not necessarily even close to the MEAN. For example, the median of 10, 12, 13, 50, 88 is 13, whereas the mean is 34.6. If there are two middle values (that is, the series has an equal number of observations as opposed to an odd number), the median is the mean of these two (in the series 2, 5, 6, 8, the median is 5.5).

MEDIATION

A third party helps deadlocked negotiations, although without the power to decide the outcome.

MEMBERS

1. Shareholders (are members of the firm). **2.** Sometimes used to describe employees: well intentioned but slightly precious. 'ASSOCIATES' is better.

MEMORANDUM OF ASSOCIATION

Legal document setting out a company's rules and who can do what.

MEMORY

Computer data storage that can be recalled.

MENTORING

Acting as the mentor of someone in an organisation: someone to help with management development and advice on the individual's career development. The mentor is usually not the individual's boss, although usually is more senior or more experienced. Very useful if done well.

MERCHANDISING

In-store promotion.

MERCHANT BANK

British term for an INVESTMENT BANK.

MERGER

Mutual decision of two firms to join together to become one firm. Rare. Usually a euphemism for a takeover. The 'M' in 'M&A'.

MERGER MANIA

Period (e.g. 1986–90 in USA and UK) when there was a high incidence of acquisitions, often using INFLATED PAPER (over-valued shares rather than cash).

MERIT PAY

Bonus based on personal performance, rather than the base pay for the job or a firm-wide bonus. Also called PERSONAL BONUS.

METHOD STUDY

The 'M' in 'O&M'. Work study. Somewhat more than TIME & MOTION, but not much more. Little used today.

ME-TOO PRODUCT

Product with no distinguishing features. Not necessarily bad, if lower cost and lower price: for instance, Compaq PCs, that were indistinguishable from IBM PCs but much cheaper.

METRIC, METRICS

Means of measurement. Very important: 'what gets measured gets done'. But what gets measured may not be what should be.

MEZZANINE, MEZZANINE DEBT

Debt that carries a high rate of interest, that is the 'mezzanine floor', half-way between normal debt and equity. Usually used in the context of an MBO, MBI or LBO. Holders of mezzanine rank below the SENIOR DEBT, which has earlier rights of repayment and the first rights in a LIQUIDATION, but ahead of the ordinary shareholders (providers of equity). As an illustration, in an MBO, the senior debt might carry an interest rate of 10%, the mezzanine 18%, and the equity an expectation (but no guarantee) of a 35% IRR (annual return). A very useful financial instrument, but one that can bear disproportionate risk relative to the upside. To compensate for this, providers of mezzanine are sometimes given EQUITY KICKERS, which give a right to a share of the equity, which may ratchet up if the buy-out does especially well. Mezzanine is sometimes confused (by those who should know better) with JUNK BONDS, which are instruments issued by a promoter or firm (often in the context of an LBO) rather than a form of bank debt.

M-FORM ORGANISATION

Originally used by Oliver Williamson in *Markets and Hierarchies* (1975) to mean a multidivisional enterprise. More recently a book by Bill Ouchi called

The M-form Society described Japanese corporations as forming multidivisional companies around a common central core of technology. M-form companies include Fujitsu, Honda, Hitachi, Matsushita, Mitsubishi, Nippon Electric, Toshiba, Sharp, and Sony. For example, Matsushita has a common technological 'learning core' that feeds into seven different divisions (consumer electronics, home appliances, lighting equipment, system/media products, business machines and electronic components). There are examples of M-forms in the West, including IBM, ICI, Apple, DEC and Philips, but in general there is a greater proportion of technology located in the divisions than in the Japanese M-form, and technological know-how tends to ooze around the divisions rather less luxuriantly. The West also has far more pure CONGLOMERATES, where there is common ownership but few or no operating links between the divisions or companies. The M-form is clearly superior at utilising technology.

MICROCHIPS
Integrated circuits that comprise on one chip all that is needed to direct and control a computer process. Called by the Japanese 'the rice of industry'.

MICROCOMPUTER
Before PCs (personal computers), there were MAINFRAMES (the largest), MINICOMPUTERS (the middle class) and microcomputers (the smallest). Now both of the latter are usually called PCs.

MICRO-ENTERPRISE
Self-contained business of 2–4 people. See NUMEROLOGY.

MICROPROCESSOR
See MICROCHIPS.

MIDDLE MANAGER
One between top management and the shop floor. Imprecise but still useful term. The death of the middle manager has been predicted by many management futurologists, including Tom PETERS and Rosabeth Moss KANTER, who claim that successful firms will have almost no middle managers. Middle management has had a run of almost 150 years: can the game really be up? Maybe.

MIDDLE PRICE, MIDDLE MARKET PRICE
The price for shares or bonds shown in the papers, but actually rarely paid: half way between the price for sellers (OFFER) and buyers (BID).

MIDDLE-UP-DOWN MANAGEMENT
Japanese term for the role of middle management. In the West middle management is often seen as a mechanism for conveying orders or direction

down the organisation, and may be vulnerable if IT can replace this role. In Japan middle management integrates top and bottom by passing information both ways and helping to form consensus on what to do for both the short and long term.

MID-TECH

Business like engineering where technology is important but not as volatile and fast-moving as in HIGH-TECH industries like BIOTECHNOLOGY.

MIGRATION STRATEGY

How to take a business from an unhealthy to a healthy state: a detailed plan (the 'migration route') for implementation in a specified, short time horizon.

MINICOMPUTER

See MICROCOMPUTER.

MINI-ENTERPRISE

Tom PETERS' term for a business with 12–20 people. See NUMEROLOGY.

MINIMUM STOCK LEVEL

The level below which stock should not go. Can be precisely calculated.

MINORITY INTEREST, MINORITY

1. Holding held by one firm in another, where there is a majority holding by another firm. There are laws protecting the rights of minority holders ('minorities'), but the holders of minority interests in private (unquoted) companies are very exposed to what the holders of the majority interest do. Unlike such holders in quoted companies, they cannot easily sell if they do not like what is happening. This has led some observers to claim (with not ungrounded hyperbole) that a minority interest in a private company is worthless.

MINTZBERG, HENRY (b. 1939)

Canadian strategy and management guru. Refreshing, original, fun to read, iconoclastic, and moralistic in the best sense. In 1973 he published a study of how managers work, *The Nature of Managerial Work*, that debunked the idea of the manager as a cerebral planner and long-term thinker. Pointed out that managers on average only spent an uninterrupted half hour on any subject once every two days. Good managers lived by responding to events as they occurred, responding to the stimuli of the minute, juggling people around them, absorbing information first-hand, relying on gossip and hearsay rather than reports. He concluded that 'the executives I was studying – all very competent by any standard – were fundamentally indistinguishable from their counterparts of 100 . . . or even 1,000 years ago. The information they need differs, but they seek it in the same way: by word of mouth. Their

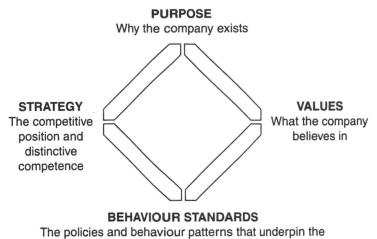

PURPOSE
Why the company exists

STRATEGY
The competitive
position and
distinctive
competence

VALUES
What the company
believes in

BEHAVIOUR STANDARDS
The policies and behaviour patterns that underpin the
distinctive competence and the value system

Figure 30 The Ashridge Mission Model
Source: Campbell, Andrew, Devine, Marion and Young, David (1990) *A Sense of Mission*,
Economist

decisions concern modern technology, but the procedures they use are still
the same as [for] . . . the nineteenth-century manager.' He praises 'soft' as
opposed to 'hard' information and the ability of managers to respond constructively to disturbances. He is critical of business schools for their focus
on 'cognitive learning' rather than management skill training: 'cognitive
learning no more makes a manager than it does a swimmer'. Stern critic of
industrial BUREAUCRACY and advocate of ADHOCRACY. Also advocates
'crafting strategy', that is, developing it and adapting it in the heat of experience rather than devising it from immutable first principles. Finally, an
eloquent exponent of chief executives using the 'right' (creative) rather than
'left' (analytical) parts of their brains: intuition is worth more than data and
analysis. The best introduction to Mintzberg is the rather pretentiously titled
Mintzberg on Management (1989): but a super read. His latest book *The Rise
and Fall of Strategic Planning* (1994) also provides a useful, if somewhat
muted, summary of his philosophy.

MISSION

What a company is for; why it exists; its role in the world. This is an enormously important issue. A majority of US and UK companies now have
formal MISSION STATEMENTS; but a big distinction must be made between
such documents and the company having a real mission, or 'sense of mission'.
Most companies that have mission statements do not have a sense of mission:
the document is propaganda, or at best well intended pablum, but not what

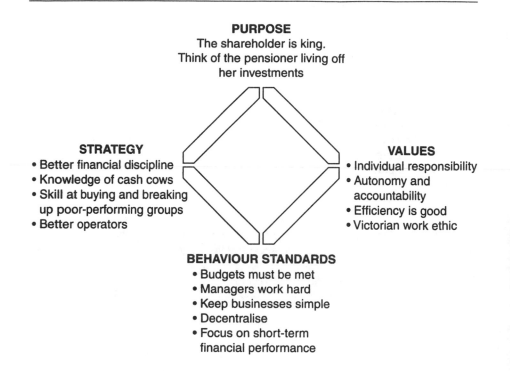

Figure 31 A Summary of Hanson's Mission
Source: *A Sense of Mission*, op.cit.

most people in the organisation believe. Yet some firms like Marks & Spencer that clearly have a sense of mission, do not have mission statements.

A sense of mission is essential if employees are to believe in their company. They have to think that the company is there to achieve something.

The concept of mission and 'sense of mission' covers all aspects of the firm's sense of direction and the way in which its members behave: there must be a consistent pattern that runs through all aspects of the firm's personality. The most useful way of thinking about this is the Ashridge Mission Model, which describes four parameters of mission: PURPOSE, VALUES, STRATEGY and BEHAVIOUR STANDARDS, as shown in Figure 30.

The model can be illustrated by two examples of very different companies and mission. First Hanson, which is highly unusual in actually believing in shareholder value, rather than just making MOTHERHOOD statements about it (Figure 31).

The second example is Hewlett-Packard, a decentralised corporation with very different values to Hanson, but a similarly consistent sense of mission (Figure 32).

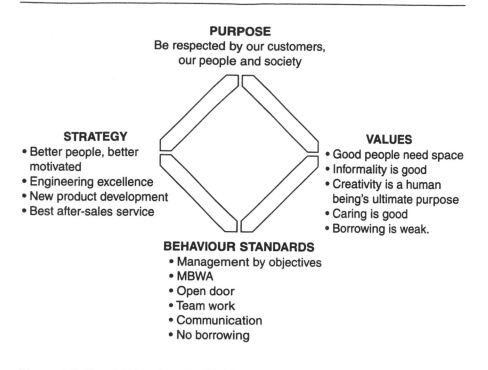

PURPOSE
Be respected by our customers,
our people and society

STRATEGY
• Better people, better
  motivated
• Engineering excellence
• New product development
• Best after-sales service

VALUES
• Good people need space
• Informality is good
• Creativity is a human
  being's ultimate purpose
• Caring is good
• Borrowing is weak.

BEHAVIOUR STANDARDS
• Management by objectives
• MBWA
• Open door
• Team work
• Communication
• No borrowing

Figure 32 Hewlett-Packard's Mission
Source: A Sense of Mission, op.cit.

Why does it matter that employees believe in their company? Well, most would rather work for a company they can believe in. A company that can be believed in will attract the best available recruits, and keep them. It will get the most out of its people, both as individuals and in teams. It will be respected by customers and investors. It will learn, renew itself, and become more powerful, while still having the ethic of service to others. It will gain market share, and have the best long term profitability, and the highest market rating.

All in all, it is quite important. Unfortunately, though most Western firms have mission statements, few have a sense of mission. Though precise data are not available, the best estimates are that 10% of large UK firms, 20% of US, but 50% of Japanese, have a sense of mission. Clearly there is a great deal of need for TRANSFORMATION.

MISSION STATEMENT

A document that often pays lip service to the idea that a company should have a flesh-and-blood purpose, but occasionally reflects what a company believes in. See MISSION.

MITTELSTAND

Germany's owner-managed, medium-sized firms, usually of a few hundred employees (up to a maximum of about 3,000). Provide generally high value added products, focused on a narrow market NICHE, customer- and export-oriented, non-bureaucratic and long-termist. Living proof that the FAMILY FIRM did not have to die.

MLC

See MULTILOCALS (Multi-Local Corporation).

MNC (Multinational Corporation)

See its synonym, MULTINATIONAL ENTERPRISE (MNE).

MNE

See MULTINATIONAL ENTERPRISE.

MODE

The most popular number in a series: not necessarily close to the average.

MODELLING

Developing a computer model to describe and analyse a market, a firm's financial results, or anything else of interest. Because modelling can now be done cheaply and quickly, too much is done without thinking about the underlying assumptions. Yet another example of how IT generates too much INFORMATION.

MODEM

Device connecting a computer to the telephone.

MODULE

Building block allowing several products to share costs.

MONEY MARKET

Wholesale market for funds and marketable securities, dominated by banks, large corporations' liquid funds, and those of rich individuals.

MONEY MARKET FUND

Fund taking in small amounts from individuals and investing in the MONEY MARKET.

MONEY VALUE

The value before adjusting for inflation (before calculating the REAL VALUE).

MONITOR-EVALUATOR

The ANALYST or TYPE TWO EXECUTIVE whose role in BELBIN's ideal team is to keep the score, crunch the numbers, dissect the data and spot logical flaws in others' arguments.

MONOPOLY

High RELATIVE MARKET SHARE, or even 100% supply of a market. Monopolies are unpopular with public policy setters, largely for bad reasons.

MONTE CARLO TECHNIQUE

Mathematical simulation technique called by the boffins 'stochastic digital simulation'. Early operations researchers had fun with this because they used roulette wheels to generate chance numbers. The role of chance can then be input, based on past experience, to indicate the range of outcomes possible. The technique is widely taught in business schools but I have never met anyone in an organisation who uses it: perhaps I have led a sheltered life.

MOONLIGHTING

Having two jobs, especially if evading tax.

MOP UP STRATEGY

Consolidating an industry by gaining market share at the expense of smaller competitors and/or buying them up, usually in a so-called DECLINING INDUSTRY. Almost always a good strategy.

MORATORIUM

Period during which interest payments or debt repayments do not have to be made.

MORTGAGE

Any CHARGE over a specific asset.

MOTHBALLING

Putting manufacturing (or other) capacity into cold storage.

MOTHERHOOD

Bland statements of corporate intentions or values that mean very little in practice and do not differentiate the firm from others. For example, IBM says it has three core values: respect for the individual, devotion to customers and insistence on excellence. This statement could come from or be an aspiration of 95% of corporations, and is therefore motherhood. A good test of whether something is more than motherhood is to ask whether the opposite could be sensibly pursued by another firm: would it make sense for any firm to show contempt for the individual, ignore its customers, and exalt mediocrity? On the other hand, a decision to focus on large firms as customers, to go for high volume, low margin business, and to aim to serve multinational customers would not be motherhood: the opposite could be sensible for another firm. Avoiding motherhood is particularly important when defining MISSION.

MOTIVATION

Why people work; or the stimulation of workers' energy. See ARGYRIS, BENNIS, HERZBERG, HUMAN RELATIONS SCHOOL, KANTER, LIKERT, McGREGOR, MASLOW, MAYO, and SCHEIN.

MOUSE

Small device for moving a pointer around a computer screen. Intimidating until one has the knack. And yes, the plural is mice.

MOVING AVERAGE

Sales revenue (or some other variable like market share or profit) tracked on a continuous basis, usually by month or quarter, to produce a seasonably-adjusted result. For example, in a monthly moving average, a new month's revenue is added and the corresponding month's revenue from a year ago is dropped, to produce a new figure that can be compared to the previous month's. Extremely useful in detecting underlying trends. It is amazing how few businesses use this simple and very revealing technique. See Z-CURVE.

MOVING THE GOALPOSTS

When the centre or the boss shifts objectives in midstream, usually in response to an external crisis. A common corporate lament.

MRP (Manufacturing Resource Planning, Materials Requirements Planning)

A good computer-based planning system, with the current version designated at the end by a Roman numeral.

MULTI-BUSINESS COMPANY

A commercial organisation which contains businesses that could be successful as independent companies.

MULTILOCALS, MULTILOCAL ENTERPRISE, MULTI-LOCAL CORPORATION (MLC)

New term for companies that used to be known as WORLD ENTERRPISES or MNCs (Multinational Corporations). Successful global firms are to a large degree a collection of successful local operations, though with common core values and sometimes similar (though rarely identical) core GLOBAL PRODUCTS. See also Kenichi OHMAE.

MULTIMEDIA

Computer software that allows production/editing of text, graphics, sound, and 'moving pictures' on the screen.

MULTINATIONAL ENTERPRISE (MNE)

Firm that operates in many countries. In fact, all MNEs are domiciled in one (or two) countries, and their CULTURE usually reflects this to a significant degree. Both fears and hopes about the universality of MNEs are exaggerated. One day a real MNE will evolve; but not yet. See also MULTILOCALS, GLOBALISATION and LOCAL GLOBALISATION.

MULTIPLE SCENARIO, MULTIPLE SCENARIO PLANNING
See SCENARIO and SCENARIO PLANNING.

MUTUAL FUND
American name for what the British call a unit trust.

MUTUAL SAVINGS BANK
US bank for small savers, owned by their depositors, similar to old-style British building society.

MYTH, MYTHOLOGY, CORPORATE MYTHOLOGY
Two different meanings. 1. The body of assumptions in a firm that blinds it to what customers want and what competitors are really doing. 2. Useful legends within a firm about its past and present leaders and their eccentricities, or about critical times in the history of the firm. Myths help to articulate and pass on the firm's CULTURE.

N

NARROW MARKET
Same as THIN MARKET.

NATIONAL COMPETITIVE ADVANTAGE
The modern pioneers in this field are Ira MAGAZINER and Michael PORTER, although work on the different national cultures by Charles HAMPDEN-TURNER and Fons TROMPENAARS is also important. From their work it is clear that:

1. The key unit of account in explaining national competitive advantage is neither the firm nor the overall economy, but particular industries;
2. It is nevertheless true that the driving ambition of individual firms (often individual leaders of firms) to dominate a particular product or industry is very often the starting-point;
3. Intense domestic rivalry to provide better and cheaper products is key;
4. Global industries are often dominated by a few competitors based in the same country and in the same region, where the knowledge infrastructure is key;
5. Further, a key role is played by related and supporting industries: localised, mutually reinforcing innovation through the FOOD CHAIN;
6. Demanding customers and heavy domestic demand are important, as with the Japanese demand for motorcycles or the American demand for health-care;
7. University research is often key in sophisticated areas like electronics and pharmaceuticals, as is the ability of firms to tap into such research efficiently and seamlessly;
8. A cultural commitment to the firm, of almost religious intensity, using consensus and shared values as the main control mechanism, is essential for firms to establish global leadership: this can happen anywhere, but is much more likely to occur in certain countries (e.g. Japan and Sweden) than in others;
9. Excluding competitors from setting up manufacturing in your own country, while investing abroad in factories which nonetheless import a high proportion of components from your home country, helps to tilt the balance in favour of certain nations, notably Japan;
10. Investors and banks willing to accept low initial returns and to look for long-term capital gains rather than high dividends are also important;

11. A general commitment to continual improvements in productivity and customer value is also essential.

The role of government is limited to encouraging unrestricted competition and helping to put the knowledge and communications infrastructure in place, plus if possible helping to exclude investment from competing countries. In particular, attempts to encourage national firms in the same business to collaborate rather than compete (as with some French industrial policy) are self-defeating.

NATIONAL INDUSTRIAL DECLINE
The progressive loss of global market share, especially in manufacturing. There is a fierce and unresolved debate about whether it matters that manufacturing share is lost, if the difference is made up in services. Perhaps the debate misses the point: the best way for Britain or America to reverse their national industrial declines is to pursue both goals, in particular industries. See MAGAZINER and INDUSTRIAL POLICY.

NATURAL LANGUAGE PROCESSING
When computers use natural, that is, human, language. See also AI (artificial intelligence).

NATURAL WASTAGE
Reduction in the number of people in an organisation through resignation, retirement or death rather than because of enforced job cuts. Natural wastage typically runs at 3–5% per annum.

NEEDS
1. Marketing often focuses on 'needs' of consumers, what they must have, rather than 'WANTS', that are optional. An increasingly blurred and unhelpful distinction. 2. Employee needs: see HIERARCHY OF NEEDS.

NEGOTIABLE INSTRUMENTS
Anything that can be readily traded, like shares, bonds and commercial paper.

NEGOTIATING THEORY
Taught at business school, though teaching and practising poker would be more useful. One useful rule is that if you have a weak case, it is better to negotiate face-to-face; if you have a strong case, use the telephone, which permits you to be harder and more unyielding, since you do not respond to the human appeals for compromise that are better communicated in person. Another useful hint is that negotiating in a coldly rational way is unwise. The rational negotiator can afford to compromise until there is no advantage left. The irrational and emotional negotiator's response cannot be predicted and he will usually end up with the balance of advantage.

NEO-HUMAN RELATIONS SCHOOL
See HUMAN RELATIONS SCHOOL.

NERD
US-originated colloquialism for a spotty, intense student, often one obsessed by computers and/or business. Do not despise the nerds, Tom PETERS counsels, or you will end up working for one.

NET ASSETS
The NET WORTH of a business, that is, total assets minus liabilities. Also called NAV (Net Asset Value).

NET ASSETS PER SHARE
The total NET ASSETS divided by the number of ordinary shares. See also MARKET TO BOOK RATIO.

NET ASSET VALUE (NAV)
See NET ASSETS.

NET BOOK VALUE
The value of an ASSET recorded in the company's books, after deducting (that is, net of) ACCUMULATED AMORTISATION and DEPRECIATION.

NET OPERATING ASSETS
Synonym for capital employed. The total money tied up in a business in FIXED ASSETS and WORKING CAPITAL. Also equal to the sum of the firm's EQUITY, DEBT and any CORPORATION TAX payable.

NET PRESENT VALUE
See NPV.

NEW HIGH, NEW LOW
When an individual share reaches a price higher or lower than it has so far reached in a given period, usually a year.

NEW PRODUCT DEVELOPMENT
See NPD.

NET REALISABLE VALUE
What an asset (usually stock) could be sold for after all expenses of selling.

NETTING, NETTING OFF
Calculation of a net number (e.g. after deduction of tax) from a gross number.

NETWORK ANALYSIS
Also called PERT (Programme Evaluation and Review Techniques). Drawing charts for major engineering projects to plan the work. Similar to CRITICAL PATH ANALYSIS.

NETWORKER

See SHAMROCK ORGANISATION.

NETWORKING

1. Linking of computers so they can communicate with each other. **2.** Using a network of professional contacts to sell worth or exchange favours. **3.** Part of Charles HANDY'S SHAMROCK ORGANISATION. **4.** Linking a firm to others that can help it by a series of informal, mutually reinforcing contacts and contracts. See NETWORKS.

NETWORKS

To be successful, firms need to bring knowledge to bear quickly and effectively and compound that knowledge over time. Part of this must be done in-house, but the depth and breadth of network that a firm possesses with other firms will also be key. Organisations to network with include suppliers, distributors, customers, consultancies, universities, firms in parallel industries needing similar technology, franchisees, and customers' customers. Networks must include real commitments, however informal, from one organisation to another, so that the benefit from their knowledge goes to your firm rather than one of your competitors. See also OUTSOURCING.

NET WORTH

See NET ASSETS.

NEW ISSUES

Shares that are newly introduced on to the stock market. In many countries, including the USA and the UK, new issues tend to be launched at a significant discount (usually 5–15%) to their intrinsic value, in order to ensure a good AFTER-MARKET, and also lower risk for the UNDERWRITERS, who are often also the SPONSORS setting the price. This means that it is generally a good investment strategy to subscribe to new issues: this is even more the case when the seller is the government. Many non-PRIVATISATION new issues, unfortunately, are in the form of PLACINGS, where it is more difficult for individual investors to obtain the shares than it is for INVESTMENT INSTITUTIONS.

NICHE

Protected market where small companies can be market leader. See BUSINESS SEGMENT and MARKET NICHE.

NICHE MARKETING, NICHE STRATEGY

See MARKET NICHE.

NIH (Not Invented Here) SYNDROME

Tendency to reject ideas related to product development or ways of doing business because they do not fit with the company's existing approach; unwillingness to examine or apply good ideas that originated elsewhere (in other markets, from consumers or from competitors); being conservative, smug, defensive and emu-like.

NODES

1. Circles in NETWORK ANALYSIS and planning charts that depict an event, such as the start or completion of a task. **2.** More generally, times and places where events come together.

NOISE

Confusing data that obscure what is really happening.

NOMINAL ACCOUNT

An account that is eventually consolidated to arrive at the BALANCE SHEET. Firms usually have hundreds of nominal accounts for different transactions.

NOMINAL LEDGER

Book or computer file recording the details of each NOMINAL ACCOUNT.

NOMINAL VALUE

The face value of a company's shares (usually set very low and much lower than the ISSUE PRICE). When new shares are issued they cannot be for less than the nominal value. Also called PAR VALUE. Of little or no economic significance. nominee, company holding shares on behalf of the owner. Often done to disguise the ultimate owner's identity.

NON-CORE BUSINESS

One not central to a group's future and liable to be sold if a good offer materialises.

NON-DIVERSIFIABLE RISK

MARKET RISK that cannot be diversified away by investors holding a portfolio of shares. See CAPITAL ASSET PRICING MODEL (CAPM).

NON-EXECUTIVE DIRECTOR, NON-EXEC

British name for OUTSIDE DIRECTOR. Non-executives have been posited as the solution to many problems of CORPORATE GOVERNANCE, and the Cadbury Report in the UK recommended that there be more, more highly qualified, more independent, more powerful and better paid non-executives. The idea is that qualified outsiders can give an additional perspective and exercise control over the executives, when this is important, and so protect shareholders and society against abuses of managerial power. But are non-execs not more part of the problem than the solution? Experienced and well-respected non-execs have failed to spot and stop many recent corporate abuses, and seem better at closing stable doors after horses have bolted than keeping them inside. It is not the want of will or independence, or the rules of corporate governance, either, that usually limit the effectiveness of non-execs. The job of non-exec corporate policeman is simply too difficult and demanding to be done with a few days a year, or even a few days a month. Also, the responsibilities of non-execs (who have equal responsibility as directors with the executives) deters many of the best from going on to new boards, especially of small and developing companies that most need their help. If someone is to take on responsibility as a director, he or she needs to be very well paid, and this means that they should contribute much more than most non-execs can do today. We probably need a new cadre of experienced 'semi-execs' who get involved with a company and provide material assistance to its business (not just being a policeman), while still being independent of the executive and having the time to nurture the firm's long-term development.

NON-PERFORMING LOAN
One not paying interest (or at least 90 days overdue).

NON-TERRITORIAL OFFICE
One where managers do not have a designated office or desk, but use common space. Increasingly firms like IBM, Digital, Apple and GE (USA) are realising the importance of SPACE MANAGEMENT and are installing comfortable non-territorial furniture (like sofas, reclining seats and bar-like areas) to encourage informal interaction. Some firms like Mars realised all this long ago.

NON-VERBAL COMMUNICATION
Body language: 'listen' (i.e. watch) for it.

NON-VOTING SHARES
See 'A' SHARES.

NO PAR VALUE SHARES
American share that has no face value. Sensible.

NORM
1. In statistics, a representative value (such as the MEAN). **2.** A social norm, that is, accepted behaviour or value within a group.

NORMAL CURVE
A GAUSSIAN CURVE, normal FREQUENCY DISTRIBUTION or bell-shaped curve: the most frequent values occur in the middle.

NORMATIVE
Prescriptive (suggesting how something should be done) rather than descriptive.

NORMATIVE CURVE
See OPPORTUNITY/VULNERABILITY MATRIX.

NOTEBOOK COMPUTER
The smallest type of LAPTOP computer.

NOT-FOR-PROFIT ORGANISATIONS
A more fitting, though clumsier, US version of the British 'non profit' organisation.

NOT INVENTED HERE SYNDROME
See NIH.

NOTIONAL INTEREST
Interest income that a company would have earned had option holders paid money to the firm to exercise their options. Used in calculating FULLY DILUTED EARNINGS PER SHARE.

NPD (New Product Development)
The branch of marketing, or department within a firm, that develops new products, test-markets them, and introduces them to the market as a whole; or the process of developing new products. There are really four different types of NPD, as shown in Figure 33.

The risks of failure increase as we go down the list. Note that BRAND STRETCHING involves an established brand name in a new product area, whereas LINE EXTENSION or BRAND EXTENSION is simply new variant of the existing product. See also BRAND STRETCHING for a detailed discussion of this growing trend.

NPD is more an art than a science: some firms consistently do better than others.

	Type of NPD	Examples
1	Product improvements	'New improved' Persil; new year's car model
2	Line extension	Diet Coke; Rabbit and Chicken Whiskas
3	Brand stretching	Flora salad dressings; Mars ice cream
4	New brands	Diamond White; Neurofen

Figure 33 The four types of New Product Development

NPV (Net Present Value)

The sum of all future cash flows from an investment or project minus all out-flows. The NPV is discounted to take account of inflation and/or the DISCOUNT RATE (investment return rate) required by the investor. See DCF (Discounted Cash Flow).

NUMERICAL CONTROL

Using numbers to control machines, machine tools and other equipment, usually involving computers. First developed in 1952 as basic numerical control (NC), it has progressed to Computer Numerical Control (CNC) and now Direct Numerical Control (DNC), where several machines are controlled by one computer. DNC is an integral part of any CAD/CAM system.

NUMEROLOGY, TOM PETERS' NEW

PETERS has provided a useful list of corporate definitions to correspond to different numbers of employees. He stresses that 50 is a magic number, with firms being at their most creative and effective below this number. His list is as follows:

1. 1 person: the INFORMATED INDIVIDUAL.
2. 2–4 people: the MICRO-ENTERPRISE.
3. 7–10 people: the SELF-CONTAINED WORK GROUP.
4. 3–12 people: the PROJECT TEAM.
5. 12–20 people: the MINI-ENTERPRISE.
6. 40–200 people: the INDEPENDENT PROFIT CENTRE.

NV

Dutch version of PLC, Inc, etc. Full name is Naamloze Vennootschap. The Dutch also have BVs, which are private limited companies.

O

O&M (Organisation & Methods)
Work study applied to offices. Popular in the 1960s and 1970s.

OBJECTIVES
Things an individual executive or a firm is trying to achieve, usually with a 1–3 year time horizon. See MbO (Management by Objectives).

OCCUPATIONAL TESTING
Psychological and psychometric tests used in the world of work intended to gain an objective assessment of personal attributes, such as aptitudes, interests or personality, and to provide information which is difficult to glean from interview impressions or past performance.

OCR (Optical Character Recognition)
Important technology enabling computers to read typescript directly.

OD (Organisation Development)
School of thought and practice of developing management groups in order to improve interpersonal and organisational effectiveness. Uses psychological techniques such as T-GROUPS or their more modern equivalent, ENCOUNTER GROUPS. Closely related to the HUMAN RELATIONS MOVEMENT.

OEM (Original Equipment Manufacturer)
Providing unbranded product to suppliers who then badge it with their own brand.

OFF-BALANCE SHEET FINANCING
Using financial engineering to avoid having to put assets on the balance sheet; any form of finance that does require a liability to appear on a firm's balance sheet. Examples include leasing computers rather than buying them, or doing business through associates, where the associate may have a very high level of debt but none of it appears on the first company's balance sheet. Off-balance sheet financing is a way of lowering perceived debt levels for a company that is in trouble. Investors or those doing business with a firm need to scrutinise any off-balance sheet financing very carefully.

OFFER DOCUMENT
A PROSPECTUS offering the public shares in a company being floated or issuing new shares.

OFFER FOR SALE

A FLOTATION of a new company on the stock exchange, where the shares are offered to the public and investing institutions. See NEW ISSUES.

OFFER PRICE

The price at which a MARKET MAKER will sell shares, or a unit trust sell units to the public. Contrast BID PRICE and see MID-MARKET PRICE.

OFFICE AUTOMATION

Data processing and analysis in offices, using computers. Uses IT in various ways including INTEGRATED WORK STATIONS, ELECTRONIC MAIL, VIDEO-TEXT SYSTEMS, VOICECOM and VIDEOCONFERENCING. Can lead to too much INFORMATION, and somehow doesn't cut costs as one would expect. Can the electronic Luddites be right?

OFFICER

American term for a DIRECTOR or other senior corporate executive.

OFF-LINE

1. When computer equipment is not on-line, that is, under the control of a CPU (Central Processing Unit). **2.** Outside a meeting, or outside formal channels, usually meaning that two executives sort something out privately and informally, without taking up the time of a larger group.

OFFSHORE FUND

Money and financial instruments held in a tax haven.

OFFSHORE PRODUCTION

Production of components (or, more loosely, a total product) in a low labour cost country, not the country where the corporation is domiciled. See HOLLOW CORPORATION.

OFF-THE-SHELF

Standard product.

OHMAE, KENICHI (b. 1943)

Brilliant, un-Japanese, Japanese, whose book *The Mind of the Strategist* (published in Japan in 1975, but not in the USA until 1982) is one of the best books on strategy, and who contributed towards the development of Toyota's JUST-IN-TIME system. An analyst who gives a higher place to intuition and insight, Ohmae was amongst the first to drive everything outward from the customer, and place the customer at the heart of the firm's value system: 'customer-based strategies are the basis of all strategy'. *The Mind of the Strategist* is an eloquent plea for creative, customer-based strategies, while giving a large number of hints and prompts in the form of analytical diagnoses and examples of unconventional strategies successfully pursued by Japanese companies. See also KEY FACTORS FOR SUCCESS (KFS) and STRATEGIC DEGREES OF FREEDOM (SDF).

In recent years, notably in his landmark 1990 book, *The Borderless World*, Ohmae has turned his attention to the way that the world's largest companies are creating what he calls the ILE (Inter-Linked Economy) of the USA, Europe and Japan/Asia, based largely on the need to meet the requirements of demanding consumers in all important economies. He argues persuasively the case for inevitable and beneficient GLOBALISATION, albeit based on LOCAL GLOBALISATION rather than UNIVERSAL PRODUCTS, a process being slowed down but not stopped by the rearguard actions of protectionists, bureaucrats and governments around the world. The companies forcing the change are becoming MULTILOCALS rather than multinationals. According to Ohmae, 'nothing is "overseas" any longer'; the word is banned from Honda's vocabulary, for example, 'because [Honda] sees itself as equidistant from all customers'. Multilocals must become 'insiders' to each important market (a process he describes usefully as INSIDERISATION) and be driven by a determination to serve customers better wherever they are: 'Global players must have the engine and knowledge to propel themselves. They must be directly familiar with the key markets. That knowledge is the secret of success in the borderless world.' See GLOBALISATION (definition 2), GLOBAL LOCALISATION, and STRATEGIC TRIANGLE.

OLIGOPOLY
Economists' term for a market with five or fewer suppliers controlling 75% or more of the market. Oligopolies may be profitable for the suppliers but it does not follow that they are bad for consumers. Markets generally become oligopolies because the first two or three players are efficient and provide what most customers want.

OMNIBUS RESEARCH
For everyone rather than for bus lines. Multi-client market research, often based on a panel, where individual questions of interest to a single firm can be inserted.

ONE-STOP SHOPPING
Service industry strategy for providing clients with a wide range of professional services. Best exemplified by Saatchi & Saatchi in its heyday: advertising agencies, marketing, consulting of many types. Also followed by some banks, diversifying into estate agency and insurance. But brand extension of this type is difficult, and Lenin's comment that 'a chain is as strong as its weakest link' is relevant. The case for one-stop shopping in professional services is at best unproven.

ON-LINE
Computer equipment that is being controlled by a CPU.

OPEN DOOR POLICY
A key part of the 'HP Way' practised by Hewlett-Packard and since embraced by many companies including Shell. The symbolism of managers not shutting the doors to their offices is only part of the policy; the basic idea is free speech for employees, so that they can express their feelings to any executive, however senior. 'Any effort,' declares the HP Way, 'to prevent an employee from going up the line is absolutely contrary to company policy'. See also MISSION.

OPEN-END FUND
Investment fund or UNIT TRUST that has no limit to the number of new shares that can be issued. Contrast CLOSED-END FUND.

OPEN POSITION
When a trader has an unhedged position rather than a BALANCED BOOK.

OPERATING CASH FLOW
Cash that comes in (during an accounting period) as a result of the company's operations, not including any cash flows of a non-operational nature (such as payments of interest, tax or dividends, or cash received from issuing more equity or taking on more debt).

OPERATING EXPENSE
Expense incurred by a firm's underlying operations, not including financial items such as interest or tax.

OPERATING LEASE
A normal lease where the LESSEE does not take over the risks and rewards of owning the asset. The opposite, where he does, is a FINANCE LEASE.

OPERATING LEVERAGE
A firm's fixed costs over its total costs. When this is high, it means that there is great benefit from increasing capacity utilisation. If there is a recession and demand takes off again, or the firm can gain market share without cutting prices too much, high operating leverage should lead to a rapid recovery in profits. Also called operating gearing or operational gearing.

OPERATING PROFIT
Profit from a firm's underlying operations, before taking account of interest paid or received, or taxes. Also called EARNINGS BEFORE INTEREST AND TAX (EBIT) and PROFIT BEFORE TAX (PBT).

OPERATIONAL RESEARCH
See OR.

OPERATIONS MANAGEMENT
The management of production. Should be closely integrated with all other functions, especially those related to serving customers. See DELIVERY SYSTEM.

OPERATIONS RESEARCH
See OR.

OPINION LEADERS
Term in marketing where approval from certain consumers (the opinion leaders) will lead to others joining the bandwagon.

OPPORTUNITY COST
The cost of not doing something else: if I spend a day writing a book, my opportunity cost is a day's worth of consulting revenue foregone and therefore that monetary amount (should anyone want my services). If money or people are being used on one project, there is always an opportunity cost (the highest value alternative) against which to judge the project. Very often the opportunity cost cannot be known with any certainty or precision, yet people always like asking, 'But what is the opportunity cost?'

OPPORTUNITY/VULNERABILITY INDEX
An interesting outgrowth from the BCG MATRIX, although not developed until the late 1970s/early 1980s (mainly by Bain & Company) and refined later that decade by The LEK Partnership, another strategy boutique. BCG had posited that high RELATIVE MARKET SHARE (RMS) businesses (leaders) should be highly profitable, and the logic of the EXPERIENCE CURVE certainly suggested that the higher the market share, the higher the profitability (unless the firm was not using its potential advantages, or pricing to penetrate the market still further). It followed that it should be possible to construct a 'NORMATIVE CURVE' to describe the profitability of the average BUSINESS SEGMENT in a particular industry, or, with a wider band, all industries, according to a normal expectation given the segment's relative market share. This normative band is shown on the matrix in Figure 34.

The parallel area between the two curved lines represents the normative curve: depending on the exact data used, perhaps 80% of observations would fall between these broad limits, and it would be unusual (only 20% of business segment positions) for businesses to fall outside the bands. (The normative band can be constructed based on actual data of business segment positions and profitability, but only after correct segmentation: in practice such data can only be obtained with any degree of confidence after working within a client organisation, and building up an anonymous database of the relationships.)

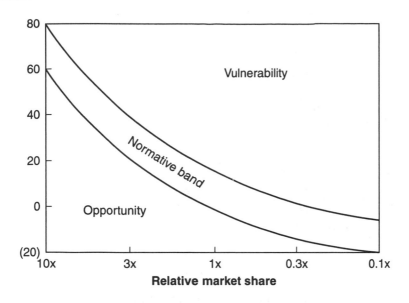

Figure 34 Opportunity Vulnerability Matrix

In fact empirical data did enable the normative band to be built up in this way. The band used to be shown coloured in yellow, hence the chart became known in some circles as a BANANAGRAM.

So what? Well, one implication is that high relative market share positions, correctly segmented, are as valuable as BCG said, whatever reservations one has about the experience curve. Managers should therefore strive to be in such businesses and cannot expect to have profitability above the required rate of return of investors unless a majority of their sales are in leaders or STRONG FOLLOWERS (at least 0.7x Relative Market Share, that is, at least 70% as the leader in the segment). Another implication, not really made clearly by BCG, and in some ways obscured by the doctrine of the BCG matrix about DOGS, was that it was useful to improve relative market share in a business segment *whatever the starting position*: useful to take a 0.3x RMS business and move it to a 0.6x RMS position, to take a 0.5x position and take it to 1.0x, to take a 2x position and move it to 4x, and so on.

The chart enables one to calculate roughly what equilibrium profitability can be expected from any particular position, so that it is possible to state roughly the benefit of moving any particular segment position in this way and compare it to the expected short term cost of doing so (by extra marketing or service, product development or lower prices). In this way it can be seen (a) whether it is worth trying to raise RMS, and (b) which segments give the biggest bang for the buck.

255

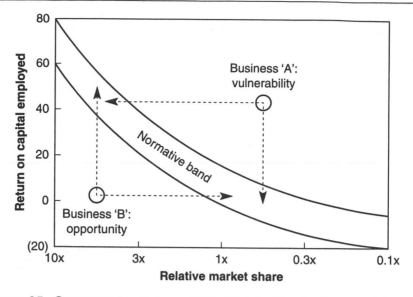

Figure 35 Opportunity Vulnerability Matrix Illustrative positions of business outside the Banana

But the most valuable use of the matrix lies not in the 80% of positions that fall within the banana (normative curve), but rather in the 20% that fall outside. Two examples of possible such positions are given in Figure 35.

Business A is earning (say) 20% RETURN ON CAPITAL EMPLOYED, a good return, but is in a weak Relative Market Share position (say 0.3x, or only 30% the size of the segment leader). The theory and empirical data from the matrix suggest that the combination of these two positions is at best anomalous, and probably unsustainable. Business A is therefore in the 'VULNERABILITY' part of the matrix. The expectation must be that in the medium term, either the business must improve its Relative Market Share position to sustain its profitability (the dotted arrow moving left), or that it will decline in profitability (to about break even). Why should this happen? Well, the banana indicates that the market leader in this business may well be earning 40% or even more ROCE in the segment (the beauty of the method is that this can be investigated empirically). What may be happening is that the leader is holding a PRICE UMBRELLA over the market: that is, is pricing unsustainably high, so that even the competitors with weak market share are protected from normal competitive rainfall. What happens if the market leader suddenly cuts prices by 20%? He will still earn a good return, but the weaker competitors will not. (The leader may not cut prices, but instead provide extra product benefits or service or other features, but the effect would still be a margin cut). It is well to know that business A is vulnerable. If relative market share cannot be improved, it is sensible to sell it before the profitability degrades.

Now let's look at Business B. This is a business in a strong relative market share position: the leader in its segment, four times larger than its nearest rival. It is earning 8% ROCE. This is a wonderful business to find. The theory and practical data suggest that such a business should be making 40% ROCE, not 8%. Nine times out of ten when such businesses are found, it is possible to make them *very* much more profitable, usually by radical cost reduction (often involving BPR), but sometimes through radical improvement of the service and product offering to the customer at low extra cost to the supplier, but enabling a large price hike to be made. Managements of particular businesses very often become complacent with historical returns and think it is impossible to raise profits in a step function to three, four or five times their current level. The bananagram challenges that thinking for leadership segment positions, and usually the bananagram is proved right. After all, high relative market share implies huge potential advantages: but these must be earned and exploited, as they do not automatically disgorge huge profits.

OPTICAL CHARACTER RECOGNITION
See OCR.

OPTIMISATION
Literally, arriving at the best solution. A phrase much beloved by analysts, and in particular by OR people. But optimisation means knowing what is best mathematically, and who can say how to weight the objectives?

OPTIMISED PRODUCTION TECHNOLOGY (OPT)
Proprietary shop floor scheduling system.

OPTIMUM ORDER QUANTITY
See ORDER QUANTITY.

OPTION
The right to buy or sell shares (or other financial instruments) at a certain price (the EXERCISE PRICE) within a defined period. Some options in major corporations are TRADED OPTIONS, that is, they can be bought or sold readily: traded options are more volatile than the underlying shares to which they relate, and therefore can make or lose large amounts of money quickly.

OR (Operations Research)
Also called Operational Research in the UK. OR began in the USA and boomed during the 1960s and 1970s. It involves applying mathematics and statistics to management issues, principally those related to production, logistics and forecasting. Subsets include QUEUING THEORY, DECISION

THEORY, MODELLING, SIMULATION, ABC ANALYSIS, LINEAR PROGRAMMING, SENSITIVITY ANALYSIS, GAME THEORY, PROBABILITY THEORY and NETWORK ANALYSIS. DECISION TREES are also owed to OR. OR is unquestionably useful but no longer exciting or of central importance.

ORDER INTERVAL
The time between placings of orders for new STOCK.

ORDER QUANTITY
The amount of an item to be reordered to replace STOCK. The OPTIMUM ORDER QUANTITY may be calculated using a formula.

ORDINARY DIVIDEND
DIVIDEND paid to holders of ORDINARY SHARES.

ORDINARY SHARES
Most shares are ordinary shares, entitling the owners to a proportion of DIVIDENDS and NET ASSETS, and to vote.

ORGANIC GROWTH
Growth from expanding market share, being in growth markets, and entering new markets from existing resources; not growth by acquisition, merger or joint venture. Also called INTERNAL GROWTH. See ACQUISITIVES.

ORGANICS
Firms that grow wholly or largely from internal growth, without acquisitions. See ACQUISITIVES (the opposite group).

ORGANISMIC ORGANISATION
Early description of what is now called an ADHOCRACY. See its opposite, MECHANISTIC ORGANISATION, and ADHOCRACY.

ORGANISATIONAL ANALYSIS
Using ORGANISATION THEORY to define or restructure reporting relationships in an organisation. Also called ORGANISATION DESIGN.

ORGANISATION AND METHODS
See O&M.

ORGANISATIONAL BEHAVIOUR
General term for academic work on organisational effectiveness, drawing on the disciplines of psychology and sociology. Again, closely associated with the HUMAN RELATIONS SCHOOL, many of whom were professors of organisational behaviour.

ORGANISATIONAL CULTURE
See CULTURE.

ORGANISATIONAL FEDERALISM
See FEDERALISM.

ORGANISATIONAL FEUDALISM
See FEUDALISM.

ORGANISATIONAL GLOCALISATION
See GLOCALISATION and GLOBAL LOCALISATION.

ORGANISATIONAL SLACK
Very useful concept invented by Cyert & March, who said that organisations tended to build up surplus resources that could be eliminated when there was a downturn. They saw organisational slack as a natural part of an organisation's growth and as 'functional', because if there wasn't anything to cut in hard times, how could an organisation survive? Another way of looking at it is to say that except in the depths of a recession, most organisations are inefficient, and that costs can nearly always be cut intelligently without harming operations.

ORGANISATION CHART
Also grandly called an ORGANOGRAM. Diagrammatic representation of the CHAIN OF COMMAND, showing who reports to whom and hierarchical levels in an organisation. A fundamental principle of SCIENTIFIC MANAGEMENT, but not always helpful, and rarely accurate in terms of working relationships. See also MATRIX ORGANISATION and DOTTED-LINE RELATIONSHIPS.

ORGANISATION DESIGN
See ORGANISATION ANALYSIS.

ORGANISATION DEVELOPMENT, ORGANISATIONAL DEVELOPMENT
See OD.

ORGANOGRAM
See ORGANISATION CHART.

OTC (Over The Counter) MARKET
US expression for a junior stock market, where shares can be traded retail. Similar to the UK's USM (Unlisted Securities Market).

OUT-PLACEMENT

Helping employees who are being made redundant to find jobs elsewhere: assistance provided internally or via a specialist employment agency.

OUTPUTS

1. Data or analysis from a computer program. 2. A firm's production or the services it sells.

OUTSIDE DIRECTOR

NON-EXECUTIVE DIRECTOR independent of the executive directors. Common term in the USA, where a majority of the directors are normally from outside. Also called INDEPENDENT DIRECTOR. See also DIRECTOR and CORPORATE GOVERNANCE.

OUTSOURCING

Buying components, goods or services from outside. Terrifically important trend that could transform companies and their profitability. In manufacturing, the best companies are only making those components where they have real and provable competitive advantage, thus greatly reducing the COSTS OF COMPLEXITY and attaining cost and performance advantage. Many companies have also virtually abolished their HEAD OFFICES by outsourcing most of the functions. Outsourcing is the wave of the future. See MAKE OR BUY DECISION.

OUTWORKER

See HOMEWORKER.

OVA (Overhead Value Analysis)

Form of cost analysis used by MCKINSEY and other consultants to help reduce overhead and especially head office costs. Precursor to some extent of BPR (Business Process Re-engineering).

OVERCAPACITY

When industry supply exceeds industry demand. Can persist for long periods. See BARRIERS TO EXIT.

OVERDRAFT

European banking credit facility.

OVERHEADS

Costs (like top management, administration, finance, IT and personnel departments, R&D and distribution) that are not allocated directly to particular products. The term is somewhat imprecise, because PRODUCT LINE PROFITABILITY exercises often do allocate such costs, though they are still generally called overheads. Increasing product complexity and the increased factory efficiency (resulting in a decrease in non-overhead costs) has raised the importance of overheads. Firms that can organise themselves effectively around customers and their needs, and therefore have lower overhead costs than competitors, will be the winners in the future. See COSTS OF COMPLEXITY, COST STRUCTURE and BPR.

OVERRIDER, OVERRIDING DISCOUNT

A discount given by a supplier to a wholesaler, distributor or retailer, whereby the latter is given a special discount (usually annually) on the total value of his purchases. An inducement to channel as much business as possible to the particular manufacturer. Wholesalers are often very dependent on such overriders; can be a very effective way of increasing market share for the manufacturer. Sometimes also called AGGREGATED REBATE.

OVERSEAS MANUFACTURING INVESTMENT

Often a key part of the battle for global market share in a particular product. See JAPANESE OVERSEAS MANUFACTURING INVESTMENT.

OVERSOLD

1. A stock market or other market which has fallen too far too fast and may therefore be expected to rebound. 2. When a firm has sold more than it can produce.

OVERSUBSCRIPTION

When demand for a NEW ISSUE of shares exceeds the offer.

OVER THE COUNTER MARKET (OTC)

See OTC.

OVERTRADING

When a firm expands too fast and does not have enough cash to cover the additional WORKING CAPITAL required by sales increases.

OVERWEIGHT

Fund managers' term for being more heavily invested in a particular sector than its actual weighting as a proportion of the total stock-market value. Indicates that the fund managers expect the sector to perform relatively well. Contrast UNDERWEIGHT.

OWN BRAND

See OWN LABEL.

OWNERSHIP

Enthusiastic acceptance of an idea by a firm's employees (or a subgroup thereof, or an individual employee). Ownership thus mean psychological

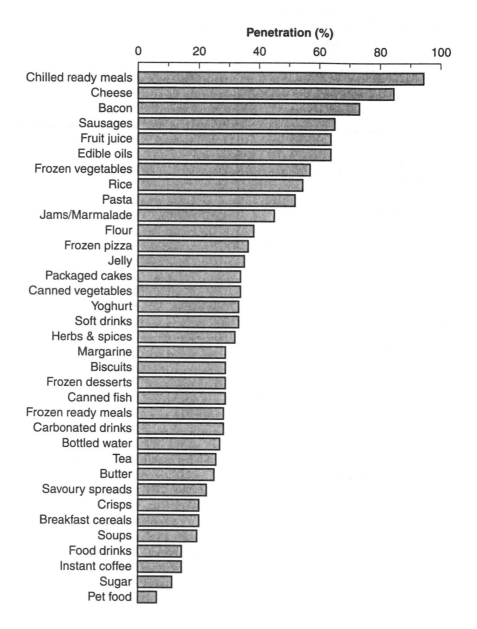

Figure 36 UK penetration of own label by product category, 1992
Source: OC&C Strategy Consultants

ownership: not just acquiescence, because the employee or group believes in it and 'owns' it. The same idea as when employees 'BUY IN' to an idea.

OWN LABEL

Product bearing a retailer's brand rather than that of a manufacturer. Own label has been a huge success story in many markets, for example the UK supermarket industry, where retailers have greatly increased their proportion of own label sales and make more money from these than from PROPRIETARY BRANDS (i.e. those of manufacturers). Own label today does not necessarily mean 'cheap and cheerful'. Some retailers' brands, such as St Michael (Marks & Spencer) and Sainsbury, connote high quality. Own label has helped to shift the balance of power away from manufacturers and towards the retailers. Yet it is interesting that the incidence of own label varies so much between product categories, as shown in Figure 36, for the UK in 1993. Where a leading branded manufacturer, who is also low cost, like Pedigree Petfoods or Kellogg's, stands up against private label it can be contained to low levels.

On the other hand, the low penetration areas are being increasingly targeted by retailers like Sainsbury and Tesco who want to beat the branded suppliers. What will happen next?

P

PACKAGED COMPENSATION

Australian term for FLEXIBLE BENEFITS (American) or CAFETERIA PERKS (English). See FLEXIBLE BENEFITS for a full discussion.

PACKAGING

Packaging and its design can be a crucial dimension of branding. Who can say whether Coca-Cola would have taken off without its beautiful bottle, or Perrier would have been able to charge the earth for mineral water without its design quality? Packaging can also be functional and a spur to genuine innovation, as in pump dispenser toothpaste, which is a brilliant example of how to enlarge a mature market by packaging innovation.

PAC-MAN DEFENCE

A tactic against takeover where the target bites back, as in the video game of the same name. The defence can take the form of taking a STRATEGIC STAKE in the bidder (with the implied threat of passing it on to a predator), or of making a bid oneself. In some ways it is difficult to defend against, because if the original bidder has argued that there is economic logic in the deal, why should there not be as much logic if the target takes over the bidder as there would be vice versa? If the industrial logic is common to both sides, it comes down to a judgement on which is the stronger management team. The pac-man defence is therefore most suitable for a firm that has at least as good a track record in growing EARNINGS PER SHARE and market share as the original bidder. If the original defendant's track record is weak (as is often the case), the pac-man defence is only likely to work via the strategic stake route of introducing a third party into the battle.

PAID-UP CAPITAL

Issued capital that shareholders have paid for.

PAL (Pool, Ally and Link).

See KANTER.

P&L ACCOUNT, P&L, PROFIT AND LOSS ACCOUNT

The second most important accounting statement, after the BALANCE SHEET. Explains how the RETAINED PROFIT as shown on the balance sheet got there: how and why it changed over the period, by starting with revenues and then deducting all costs including taxes.

PAPER
Shares or another SECURITY (rather than cash).

PARADIGMS OF MANAGEMENT
The set of assumptions one has about management. One of the most deeply rooted paradigms of management is that of the traditional CHAIN OF COMMAND. The new paradigm that puts customers at the centre of the universe implicitly challenges this view of management.

PARALLEL IMPORTING
A distributor supplying a branded product which he buys in countries where it is cheap and sells into countries where the manufacturer of the brand has high prices. Not liked by manufacturers for obvious reasons, so they may try to stop supplying the distributor, but it is often difficult to eliminate because there may be many distributors in the chain and finding out the source of supply can be difficult. Advocates of free trade claim that the best way to deal with parallel importing is to have roughly similar prices in all countries.

PARALLEL LOAN
The same as a BACK-TO-BACK LOAN.

PARALLEL PROCESSING
One of the secrets of getting products to market quickly and efficiently: the elimination of sequential processing of work steps wherever possible, so that work can proceed in parallel. See BPR (Business Process Re-engineering).

PARENT COMPANY, PARENT
A company with two or more SUBSIDIARIES. The role of the CENTRE has been the subject of interesting work, see PARENTING ADVANTAGE. A good parent does not try to stunt the independence and development of its 'children', but rather seeks to add value to bring out their true potential, enhancing their strengths, encouraging cooperation where appropriate and setting standards for them.

PARENTING ADVANTAGE
A new term essential to the management of MULTI-BUSINESS COMPANIES. These companies are being challenged because they are often worth more broken up or slimmed down than their current market capitalisation. In a landmark book, *Corporate-Level Strategy: Creating Value in the Multibusiness Company* (1994), Michael Goold, Andrew Campbell and Marcus Alexander of the Ashridge Strategic Management Centre have explained when multi-business companies should exist, when they should be broken up and how managers can develop better corporate level strategies.

The search for parenting advantage is the key to success as a multi-business company. Unless the PARENT COMPANY is creating value from owning the businesses, it should be eliminated. Yet creating value is not sufficient. To succeed, parent companies must create more value than rivals: they must have parenting advantage. If they do not, they may fall prey to a hostile takeover.

Parenting advantage is similar to COMPETITIVE ADVANTAGE but refers to the activities of the parent company rather than the business.

PARETO RULE

The 80/20 RULE, that 80% of sales or profits or any other variable may come from 20% of the products. Can clearly be looked at empirically in any case, and usually one of the most valuable simple steps to understanding any business. Invented by Alfredo Pareto, the 19th-century economist. Looked at in retrospect, many of the major insights of business in the last half century are derived from the Pareto principle, including BCG's focus on those few high relative market share businesses that generate most of the cash for a company, the insight that COSTS OF COMPLEXITY derive from too extensive a product range, and that therefore maximum use should be made of OUT-SOURCING, as well as the movement to rationalise stock-holding, restrict the numbers of SKUs (Stock Keeping Units), and conduct ABC ANALYSIS of true profitability. The 80/20 rule applies to individuals as well: 80% of the value you provide in your job may come from 20% of your time, so if you delegated the activities that take the remaining 80% of your time to a lower cost or less experienced person (or stopped doing them altogether), you could multiply your impact up to five times. For both firms and individuals, some of the low-value 80% may actually have negative value. Perhaps firms should legislate that all of their people spend at least 15 minutes a week contemplating the 80/20 rule.

PARKINSON'S LAW

C Northcote Parkinson's dictum that 'work expands to fill the time available for its completion'. As with the PARETO RULE, many recent management techniques like the whole TIME TO MARKET school and JIT (Just-in-Time) can be seen as belated and valuable attempts to overcome Parkinson's law.

PARTICIPATING PREFERENCE SHARE

A PREFERENCE SHARE where the DIVIDEND is increased if the company meets certain financial targets.

PARTICIPATION

The attempt to involve employees in the 'big picture' and give them control over decisions and their destiny. Can, however, be seen as manipulative if senior management retains control over important decisions. See HUMAN RELATIONS SCHOOL and EMPOWERMENT, the latter being today's version and extension of participation.

PARTLY-PAID SHARES,

See CALL.

PARTNERSHIP

Legal structure which has many advantages in most countries but one major disadvantage: in nearly all cases it consigns the working partners to UNLIMITED LIABILITY, that is, creditors can pursue the partners for all their personal assets in the event of default. In the UK, partnership law was heavily influenced by the lobbying of the large firms of lawyers and accountants, with the result that the tax treatment of partnerships can be extremely liberal (though you need to be or hire a tax lawyer to exploit the best advantages). The problem of unlimited liability can be circumvented for non-working, financial partners by the device of LIMITED PARTNERSHIP, though even here the working partners retain unlimited liability.

Aside from unlimited liability, there can be three main drawbacks to partnership as the legal structure: (1) paradoxically, the favourable tax treatment can also be a disadvantage, because it becomes very difficult to estimate future tax liabilities, and who they belong to (when the composition of the partnership changes over time), so that partnerships have been known to under-provide for tax, even when they thought they were being conservative; (2) for an international firm, it is very difficult to construct a global partnership, because the law differs markedly from country to country; and (3) in large partnerships, such as the world's major accounting firms, it is difficult to reconcile the ethos of partnership with the reality of hierarchy and bureaucracy, so that many junior partners come to feel partners in name only, while also making it difficult to run such firms in a fully commercial way. Partnerships in their current form may not survive much into the next century.

PART-TIME WORK

A clear trend and a useful one. See Charles HANDY.

PAR VALUE

The face value of a company's shares. Same as NOMINAL VALUE. See also NO PAR VALUE.

PASSION

The missing ingredient in most large businesses. Without passion, there cannot be will; and without will there cannot be unusual achievement. From TAYLOR onwards, most management theorists, and most managers, have denied the place of passion, along with intuition, and worshipped the gods of rationality, order, roles, hierarchy, analysis and specialisation. Passion cuts across these essentially conservative values; it shakes things up, inspires people, builds teams, and changes the world. Passion comes from leaders: it cannot come from anywhere else? Firms that (at certain times in their history) have been made great by passion (and passionate leaders) include Matsushita, Apple, MCKINSEY, BCG, Mars, LL Bean, McDonalds, GE (US), Sony, Honda, SAS and British Airways. Does your firm have passion? See also MISSION, CAUSE, CORPORATE RELIGION, MINTZBERG, PETERS and CAMPBELL.

PATENT

INTELLECTUAL PROPERTY RIGHTS (IPR) granted to inventors of new products, processes etc. Rules are highly complex and differ from country to country. Some observers believe that patent protection, while encouraging INVENTION, discourages the far more important process of INNOVATION, and that patent protection should therefore be abolished. Both Germany and Japan have very much more restricted patent rights and so there may be something in this view. It is difficult, however, to imagine patent rights being restricted significantly in the USA or the UK, given their highly individualistic cultures.

PATERNALISM

Management style much practised in France, and popular in 19th-century Britain, whereby top management takes all the decisions but pays genuine attention to the personal circumstances and development of 'his people' (by analogy, his children). Out of fashion except in small firms and France. Paternalism is not to be confused with AUTHORITARIANISM, which is manipulative and has no real interest in the welfare of the employees.

PATHFINDER, PATHFINDER PROSPECTUS

Initial rough prospectus to generate investor interest.

PAYBACK, PAYBACK PERIOD

The time it takes for an investment to return its original capital: if a restaurant takes £450,000 to start, and it pays back cash (after all costs and taxes) of £150,000 per year, it has a payback period of three years. The payback period is disliked and held in contempt by many sophisticated analysts, because it takes no account of inflation, and because cashflow is almost never a matter of a large lump out now and a series of discrete annual amounts later. The payback period cannot take account of when the cash flow alternates between negative and positive either. The preferred method is generally DISCOUNTED CASH FLOW (DCF), though this has the major disadvantage that it is time consuming and sometimes difficult to calculate. For small businesses, or as a very rough first cut, the payback period is not a bad method. Incidentally, a payback within three years is generally very good.

PAY DIFFERENTIAL

The difference between one grade of workers' pay and that of the next grade up or down. Studies have shown that people are often much more concerned about differentials than absolute levels. This has a number of implications, amongst them that giving a large pay rise to one group of workers will almost always lead to large pay rises being given to everybody, and that it is better to operate in a low wage area and pay close attention to internal equity (the distribution of pay within a firm so that it is felt to be fair), than it is to operate in a high wage area and do the same. Many people in firms that pay above the going rate still have in them people who are dissatisfied with their pay, not because they could earn more (or even the same amount) outside the firm, but because they see other people of less value to the firm who are paid more than them. This helps to indicate that perhaps HERZBERG McGREGOR and MASLOW were right after all: trying to use pay as a motivator is a losing battle.

PAYOUT RATIO

DIVIDENDS as a percentage of annual profits (usually after tax).

PAY SYSTEMS

Also called in the US 'COMPENSATION' systems. Methods of determining who should be paid what in an organisation, by means of a systematic structure. The most prevalent, although pernicious, is some form of JOB EVALUATION, where the basis of pay is what the job 'is worth', that may then be topped up with a PERSONAL BONUS and/or a firm-wide bonus. A much better alternative is a simple system of PERFORMANCE-RELATED PAY, where the salary is largely determined by the individual and his or her performance, rather than by a rigid job specification.

PBIT (Profit Before Interest & Tax)

Also called EBIT and OPERATING PROFIT.

PBT (Profit Before Tax)

Profit after all expenses including interest but before corporation tax.

PC (Personal Computer)

The arrival and increasing ubiquity of the PC has probably changed work habits more than any other aspect of the IT revolution. A PC is one that is 'personal' to one individual and not shared: because PCs are so much cheaper than their predecessors this is an economic policy, and one that saves a huge amount of toing and froing. PCs are continually becoming cheaper and more powerful, and because an individual can organise his or her files for very easy recall, PCs are probably also the only IT tool to have led to a decrease in the amount of paper generated. PCs can also be linked to other PCs via LANs (Local Area Networks). PCs have changed and will increasingly change work habits, and make it much easier for people to do without a centralised office and work effectively from home, while still being in touch with colleagues. Moreover, PCs are friendly and fun, with beautiful graphics and cute ICONS. In short, PCs are one of the best changes to have happened to business in the past 20 years, and more, and better, are still to come. See HOMEWORKING.

PCB (Printed Circuit Board)

Electronic printed circuitry used as component in manufacture of electronic products. Many specialist sorts of PCB now exist for particular industries.

PD, P/D RATIO, PDR (Price Dividend Ratio)

The current price of a share divided by the total dividends per share in the previous financial year.

PE, P/E, PER (Price Earnings Ratio)

The number of times that the stock market multiplies the after-tax earnings of a company in order to place a total value (the MARKET CAPITALISATION or MARKET VALUE) on the company's shares. A high PE therefore means that a company is valued more highly, relative to its earnings, than a company with a low PE. The PE is both: share price divided by EARNINGS PER SHARE; and market capitalisation divided by total earnings.

The PE is the fundamental way that stock markets and their analysts around the world value shares, and can serve as the basis for comparing any shares. In order to increase shareholder wealth, therefore, companies should be trying to gain a high PE as well as high earnings.

Quite how the PE came to have its commanding position is unclear: in theory there could be 1,001 ways to value a company. It is fascinating to see the complexity of all companies in all industries in all countries reduced to this single measure of performance. It is a good and useful measure, but one that has its quirks and uncertainties, that astute investors can exploit to their advantage.

The idea of valuing a company by taking a multiple of its earnings makes intuitive sense. If you assume that earnings eventually translate into cash, you could imagine someone being willing to pay several times the earnings now in a lump sum in exchange for enjoying the stream of future earnings for ever. If an investor was willing to pay ten years' worth of today's earnings now in exchange for the earnings of the company (whatever they actually are) for ever, the company would be on a PE of 10.

PEs vary from time to time and country to country depending on whether there is a BULL or BEAR market. In normal market conditions, the following rules of thumb apply to PEs:

1. A PE of 5 or less means that the stock market expects the company's earnings to decline severely, possibly even for the company to go bust.
2. A PE of 5–10 means that the stock market expects the company to grow its earnings slower than inflation, if at all.
3. A PE of 10–12 means that earnings are expected to move roughly in line with inflation.
4. A PE of 12–15 means that earnings are expected to rise somewhat more than inflation.
5. A PE of 15–20 means that earnings are expected to rise well ahead of inflation.
6. A PE over 20 means that major earnings growth is expected.

The multiplicative way of deriving the MARKET CAPITALISATION of a firm can lead to some interesting quirks for a company that suddenly starts to increase its earnings. Suppose a firm with moderate growth is on a PE of 10 and has earnings per share of 10p. The shares will therefore be 10 × 10p = £1. But suppose now that earnings go up by 30% a year for two years. What would you expect the share price increase to be? Most people might first guess that the share price would go up over the two years by 69% (30% compounded for two years). But the chances are that the PE would go up, to reflect the expectation of continued earnings growth. The PE might very well go up to 20, so that the share price would now be 20 × 16.9p (the new earnings) = 338p, an increase over the two years of 238%!

This means that it is well worth trying to spot companies whose earnings are about to accelerate, or even to buy shares in such companies after earnings have started to surge, but before the PE has fully adjusted.

An under-researched area which is of special interest to investors is high PE companies, especially those on very high PEs. In the early 1970s a group of American shares, dubbed the 'nifty fifty' zoomed up to PEs never seen before; they included Xerox, McDonalds and IBM. At the time many observers claimed that the share ratings were far too high: they 'discounted not only the future, but also the hereafter'. The observers were right in many cases: Professor Jeremy Siegel of The Wharton School has calculated that IBM, sitting on a 35 PE in the early 1970s, was really only worth 6.1 times earnings, based on subsequent performance; Xerox, also on a very high PE, was only worth 6.8. But Philip Morris, that sat on a PE of 21 times earnings in 1972, should have been on a PE of 89, and McDonalds, that sat on the stratospheric multiple of almost 60, which most observers ridiculed for nothing more than a drive-in hamburger chain, should actually have been on a PE of 120!

So high PEs can be merited, though it is clearly safest as well as most lucrative to find companies on lowish PEs that are starting to grow earnings and could be the Philip Morris or McDonalds of tomorrow.

PEG (Price Earnings Growth factor)

Very useful ratio invented by Jim Slater to highlight undervalued growth companies. The PEG is the PROSPECTIVE PE ratio divided by the expected growth in earnings in the current year. For example, if a company is on a forward PE of 20, based on analysts' estimates of the prospective earnings, and the implied growth rate in EPS (Earnings Per Share) is 20%, then the PEG is 1.0. If the prospective PE is 25, and the company is expected to grow earnings by 40%, then the PEG is 25/40 or 0.625. The lower the PEG, the better; anything below 0.75 (and especially 0.66) is a possible buy signal. There are, however, two possible problems with the PEG: (1) the earnings growth predicted by analysts may not occur; and (2) even if it does, it may not be sustained. Still, a quick and easy means of screening potential growth companies for anyone with access to analysts' forecasts.

PENETRATION PRICING

Pricing in order to hold or gain market share by accepting low (or even negative) margins in the introductory period. See MARKET PENETRATION PRICING and EXPERIENCE CURVE.

PENNY SHARES

Shares that are of low price. Nowadays, penny shares are reckoned to be those priced below 30p, although some include shares up to £1. A low price in itself does not mean anything (if there were a very high number of shares, the total MARKET CAPITALISATION might be quite high), but most penny shares have a market cap. of well under £25m. Penny shares may be in small companies or in companies that were once great but are now en route to the knacker's yard: they nearly all have low profits or none at all. The value is in the hope that the future will be better than the present. There were some fantastic gains from penny shares in the 1980s, but mostly they rested on hype. Penny shares tend to be low quality, illiquid, expensive to buy or sell, and highly speculative. Many are run by persons of dubious repute. They are best avoided.

PENSION FUND

One example of an INSTITUTIONAL INVESTOR.

PER

See PE.

PERCENTILES

In a FREQUENCY DISTRIBUTION, the observations that fall in each one per cent of the total number of observations. See also DECILES.

PERCEPTUAL MAPS, PERCEPTUAL MAPPING

Drawing a chart or map of consumers' perceptions of a brand, usually along a series of two-by-two matrices which embody different dimensions of quality or performance. Usually based on extensive research and computer analysis of responses. See also MARKET POSITIONING.

PERFECT COMPETITION

The classical economists' mirage, where all information is instantly available to all, there are no BARRIERS TO ENTRY or BARRIERS TO EXIT, and, incidentally, where long run equilibrium profit (after taking into account interest payments) is zero. Shareholders should be glad that perfect competition does not exist anywhere, and probably never has done. All good strategy is building barriers to make competition as imperfect as possible, and, contrary to popular thought, this is what serves consumers best too.

PERFORMANCE-RELATED PAY (PRP)

Popular in some countries (such as the UK currently) because of pay breaks, but in any case a better way than basing pay on a JOB EVALUATION system. See PAY SYSTEMS.

PERIPHERAL

Separate part of a computer network but controlled by it.

PERK, PERQUISITE

Generally described as a fringe benefit, which may be tax efficient for employees; but perks can also include benefits not normally called fringe benefits, such as a large and luxurious office, a PA (personal assistant), a driver, a flat in town, and any number of comfortable devices for screening out reality. British and French industrialists tend to have more perks than their American or German counterparts. In general, a very bad thing for companies, their ordinary employees, shareholders, consumers, the balance of payments, and society as a whole.

PERSONAL COMPUTER

See PC.

PERSONAL BONUS

Payment (usually once or twice a year) to reflect the contribution an individual has made to his or her organisation.

PERSONALITY INVENTORY

Method used in RECRUITMENT and SELECTION to assess candidates: a (usually not very good) form of PSYCHOLOGICAL TEST.

PERSONAL SELLING
Usually means face-to-face selling.

PERSONNEL
1. The department or function concerned with RECRUITMENT, SELECTION, INDUCTION, TRAINING, MANAGEMENT DEVELOPMENT, MANPOWER PLANNING, APPRAISAL, PAY SYSTEMS, and other matters related to people in an organisation, and also dealing with INDUSTRIAL RELATIONS, particularly when the workforce is unionised. Sometimes chillingly called HUMAN RESOURCES. Personnel departments are often resented because they are thought by LINE MANAGERS to have too much power, and the modern theory is that it is best to have a very small Personnel department and devolve as much responsibility as possible for all people-related matters to the line managers. Personnel departments can certainly be responsible for bureaucratising a firm, but it is a job that is extremely difficult to do well. **2.** Employees.

PERT (Programme Evaluation and Review Technique)
See NETWORK ANALYSIS. PERT was the very early (1958) forerunner of JUST-IN-TIME (JIT).

PETER PRINCIPLE
Laurence Peter (b. 1919) said that people in an organisation would rise to their level of incompetence, through being promoted until they failed to do well in their current job. Perverse, logical, generally untrue.

PETERS, TOM (b. 1942)
Probably the world's foremost management guru and the one who has made most money out of the profession. His achievements are real: a MCKINSEY consultant until after he and Bob WATERMAN wrote *In Search of Excellence* (1982), which now has sales approaching six million (absolutely unprecedented for a business book), Peters left MCKINSEY shortly after to publish, lecture and evangelise for passionate management. He has built up a massive and highly profitable business in merchandising himself and his artefacts: books, videos, cassettes, TV series, consultancy, and personal appearances. He is the Billy Graham of management, though in his case the profits go back to The Tom Peters Group.

The Excellence project had prosaic origins in a MCKINSEY business development exercise that started in 1977. The simple and relatively uninspired idea was to isolate the best performing US companies over the previous 20 years, looking at the top *decile* of the Fortune 500. In the end, Peters & Waterman chose 43 companies and tried to describe what common characteristics had led to their success.

The methodology was sensible, if rather loose; the conclusions questionable; and the glorification of some of the companies naïve, the product of hindsight and corporate propaganda as much as a real understanding of what had gone on. Within five years after publication, two thirds of the 'excellent' companies celebrated had hit trouble, and one, People Express, had gone bust. Yet the success of the book was well deserved. It was an inspiring read, quite unlike any previous book on management: it made readers want to go out there and do great deeds, like those celebrated in the book. It put PASSION, LEADERSHIP, VALUES, and the CUSTOMER at the centre of excellence, and in these respects it was 100% correct, even if the particulars it used to celebrate excellence were often flawed. The gospels and other great religious writings do not depend for their meaning on literal truth. Simply because people can respond to them, and achieve subsequent miracles, is testimony enough. So it was, and is, with Excellence.

Peters wrote a sequel (with Nancy Austin), *A Passion for Excellence* (1985), then changed tack significantly by writing *Thriving on Chaos* (1987), demonstrating enormous chutzpah by starting with the sentence, 'There are no excellent companies'. Clearly true, but not many opinion formers would have demonstrated such bravado, and fewer still would have emerged with their reputations enhanced rather than tarnished by such a U-turn two years after another book celebrating more excellent companies. *Thriving on Chaos* is about change and whether it is possible to manage it, and if so, how. In the book Peters took a relatively optimistic view about change management, broadly advocating a move from hierarchical BUREAUCRACIES to customer-centred ADHOCRACIES. In classic Anglo-Saxon style he provided a checklist of 45 precepts for managers, of which the most important are:

- Specialise/create NICHES/differentiate.
- Provide top quality.
- Become a SERVICE addict.
- Make MANUFACTURING the prime marketing tool.
- Over-invest in people, front line sales, service, distribution (make these the company heroes).
- Become customer-obsessed.
- Support failures by publicly rewarding well thought-out mistakes.
- Make innovation a way of life for everyone.
- Guarantee continuous employment for the core workforce.
- Radically reduce layers of management.
- Become a compulsive listener.
- Demand total integrity in all dealings, both inside and outside the firm.

Not many of these are original, but the synthesis is good and the way in which they are urged is, well, excellent.

Since then Peters has moved on, and become much more 'pessimistic about *planned* change'. It is true that 75% of such efforts at TRANSFORMATION fail, but should he not say that the cup is a quarter full rather than three quarters empty. Concentrating on the 25% and trying to move that to, say, 50%, might be a better use of Peters' talents than defeatism. His latest book *Liberation Management* (1992) is important but difficult to handle: long, rambling, poorly organised, easy to put down and full of American jargon. It reads more like *Bonfire of the Vanities* than *In Search of Excellence*, though without the plot of either. There are five main points being made in *Liberation Management*:

1. All business is becoming FASHION.
2. Create mini-SBUs everywhere.
3. Organise everything and everyone around projects.
4. Destroy functional departments.
5. Use partners outside the formal organisation.

The book is very concerned with structure, because Peters believes that without changing the structure of organisations very little can be achieved. He is probably right, but the message in *Liberation Management* is not put across as eloquently as in his previous books. See CHANGE MANAGEMENT, WATERMAN, PASSION, LEADERSHIP.

PETS

Up to 1970, pets was the name BCG used for low relative market share positions in low growth markets. BCG initially took an extremely hard line with pets, worthy of the most old-fashioned landlady: 'pets are not necessary', BCG intoned. Later, pets became DOGS, and were treated slightly more tolerantly. See DOGS and BCG MATRIX.

PETRODOLLARS

Ordinary dollars, derived from the sale of oil by producing countries. See RECYCLING PETRODOLLARS.

PETTY CASH

Small fund for incidental expenses.

PHANTOM OPTION SCHEME

A tax-efficient device for simulating the effect of EXECUTIVE SHARE OPTIONS. Under a phantom scheme, options are not actually granted, but payments are made as if they had been.

PHYSICAL DISTRIBUTION

Actually getting goods from point of manufacture to consumers, via any number of intermediate mechanisms like wholesalers. Very important, and a neglected part of the firm's DELIVERY SYSTEM. Very often the customer's greatest contact is with the person who delivers the product, and the perception of the firm may be powerfully influenced by how efficient and pleasant the delivery experience is.

PIECEWORK
Pay by volume produced.

PIE CHART
Overused display showing a circle with slices to represent percentage splits (revenues by country, profits by product etc), beloved by elderly management consultants and designers of annual reports. Much more exciting are BUBBLE CHARTS.

PIMS (Profit Impact of Market Strategy)
A co-operative DATABASE originating from research by GE in the USA that collects data from member firms about market share, profitability, and a variety of other variables (like R&D spend) that might be expected to influence profits. The data is confidential but aggregate results are fed back to members so that they can see how to raise profits. Some of the research has been published and demonstrated beyond reasonable doubt that high market share correlates with high profits, though there are significant industry variations. Two problems with the approach are that it accepts the firm's own segment definitions, which may not correctly describe BUSINESS SEGMENTATION or be sufficiently disaggregated; and that it pays insufficient attention to relative market share. See BCG MATRIX, RMS, OPPORTUNITY/VULNERABILITY MATRIX.

PIONEERS
Companies that develop great technical expertise and introduce new products. May not end up as the market leaders if they fail to maintain the lowest costs and/or have too high corporate overheads and/or maintain too broad a product line that they get CHERRY-PICKED by lower cost specialists.

PIRATE
Unbranded consumable supplies that go into a branded product, such as razor blades going into a branded razor. Pirate supplies are used because they are cheaper.

PISTONNAGE
Use of a freemasonry-like business network to reciprocate personal favours. The EC bureaucracy is riddled with it.

PLACING
Also called placement, PRIVATE PLACEMENT, private placing. When a NEW ISSUE goes to selected INVESTMENT INSTITUTIONS rather than being offered

for sale to the public. Often quicker and cheaper, but ought to be banned above a certain size to give private investors a chance to participate.

PLAIN VANILLA

Standard product without any bells or whistles. Same meaning also attaches to VANILLA without the 'plain'.

PLANT

One of BELBIN's 8 team roles. The plant is a quiet introvert who will come out with the best and most original new ideas, if only other team members will prompt and listen.

PLC, plc, (Public Limited Company)

British acronym corresponding to French SA, Dutch NV, etc. A common misperception is that PLCs have to be QUOTED COMPANIES: most PLCs are not. The just have slightly more onerous PAID-UP CAPITAL and REPORTING requirements than limited companies.

POLITICAL RISK

The risk of investing in unstable countries or those that may default on obligations to shareholders, bond holders or joint venture partners. Agencies rate individual countries on their perceived political risk. Has generally declined since the collapse of Communism in the Eastern bloc.

POLYCENTRIC

Many-centred; the idea that the modern TRANSNATIONAL CORPORATION should have a number of centres, not just one called head office.

PORCUPINE PROVISION

Same as SHARK REPELLANT.

PORTER, MICHAEL (b. 1947)

The second highest paid management lecturer after Tom PETERS: Harvard Business School professor, consultant, and the star of corporate strategy worldwide. Porter even talks about the 'Porter brand'. In two books, *Competitive Strategy: Techniques for Analysing Industries and Competitors* (1980) and *Competitive Advantage* (1985), Porter summarises and builds on the main concepts of corporate strategy. A brilliant synthesiser, formulator and packager. Porter defines two kinds of competitive advantage: low cost, or differentiation. He places a firm in the context of its industry (see PORTER's FIVE COMPETITIVE FORCES) and identifies the firm's own VALUE CHAIN (all the ways it adds value from start to finish by activity) systematically. Since the mid-1980s he has looked at global competition and the comparative advantage of nations, building on work done earlier by Ira MAGAZINER. He stresses the need for clusters of mutually supporting industries (see also

KEIRETSU) and comes as close as a mainstream American could to recommending INDUSTRIAL POLICY. *The Competitive Advantage of Nations* (1990) should be compulsory reading for all politicians. Like PETERS, Porter has come up with some useful and insightful strategic prescriptions, including:

- Sell to the most demanding buyers, as they will set standards for your people.
- Seek buyers with the most difficult needs, so they become your R&D lab.
- Establish norms exceeding the world's toughest regulations.
- Source from the world's best suppliers: scour the world for them.
- Treat employees as permanent partners.
- Use outstanding competitors as motivators.

Precisely.

Porter's competitive analysis, *Competitive Strategy* (1980) codified how to gain competitive advantage. His analysis suggests four diagnostic components of looking at any specific competitor: (1) Future goals: what are they trying to achieve, including their ambitions in terms of market leadership and technology; (2) Assumptions: how does the competitor perceive himself, and what assumptions does he make about the industry and his competition?; (3) Current Strategy; and (4) Opportunities: what do they think they have? Armed with this framework, one can then construct scenarios about competitors' possible reactions to any action by one's firm.

PORTER'S FIVE COMPETITIVE FORCES

Porter was an innovator in structural analysis of markets, which previously, even with BCG, tended to focus largely on direct competition in the industry, without looking systematically at the context in other stages of the industry VALUE CHAIN. Porter's five forces to analyse are:

1. Threat of potential new entrants.
2. Threat from substitutes using different technology.
3. Bargaining power of customers.
4. Bargaining power of suppliers.
5. Competition amongst existing suppliers.

The interactions amongst the five forces are shown in Figure 37.

From this Porter builds a useful model of industry attractiveness and how this might change over time, both because of objective economic changes and also because of the ambitions of the players themselves.

POISON PILL

Provisions in a company's articles or other actions by management that make it unattractive to an acquiror, and thus unpleasant to swallow. Such provisions might stipulate that in the event of a takeover, management or existing shareholders are to receive large payments; or a firm under threat of takeover may make a STRATEGIC ALLIANCE with the would-be acquiror's major competitor, that would give that competitor major rights in the event of a takeover. Poison pills are frowned upon or illegal in many countries, including the UK, but different US states allow varying degrees of poison pills to operate. A blatant display of the MANAGERIAL HERESY that ought to be totally illegal everywhere.

PORTABLE PENSION
One that can be carried by an individual from one company to another.

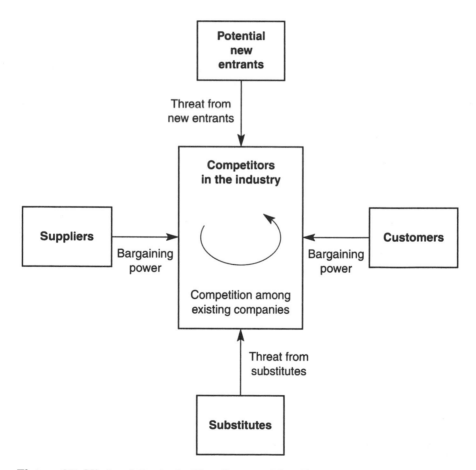

Figure 37 Michael Porter's Five Competitive Forces

PORTFOLIO

A very useful word, but confusing because it has so many different meanings, depending on the context. **1.** An investor's portfolio is his or her holdings of shares, the idea being that holding several shares (a portfolio) is lower risk than holding just one or two. **2.** A firm's portfolio is its RELATIVE MARKET SHARE positions in different BUSINESS SEGMENTS (see BCG MATRIX), or, more loosely, its spread of activities. **3.** An individual's work portfolio is all the different activities he or she has, particularly if self-employed and working with or for several clients. Idea comes from Charles HANDY, who believes that knowledge workers will have shorter careers in more firms and will increasingly divide their time into two, three or more areas that they choose themselves: see, KNOWLEDGE WORKERS and SHAMROCK ORGANISATION.

PORTFOLIO MANAGEMENT

How a portfolio in any of the senses above is managed. In sense **1**, it refers to effective DIVERSIFICATION OF RISK by holding about a dozen or 15 different shares: see CAPITAL ASSET PRICING MODEL. In sense **2**, it refers to management of the firm's business portfolio along lines indicated by the BCG MATRIX or any other way a firm decides to handle the transfer of cash and other scarce resources between its businesses.

PORTFOLIO MARRIAGE

A very useful theory about how one's marriage should adapt to the jobs and roles of the two partners, and vice versa, under different circumstances, so that the demands of both the job and the marriage can be reconciled. Invented by Charles HANDY. Since slightly adapted into PORTFOLIO PARTNERSHIP: see below.

PORTFOLIO PARTNERSHIP

Slight adaptation of HANDY's theory of PORTFOLIO MARRIAGE to include the primary relationships of two people living together, irrespective of whether they are actually married.

Handy's research identified four types of personality or behaviour based on two dimensions:

- Achievement and Dominance (the need to succeed, and have power and influence), which could either be high or low;
- Succourance and Nurturance (the desire to help and support, and take care of someone) versus autonomy (the desire to do your own thing).

He then created a matrix to typify four different types (Figure 38).

Type A, the Involved, are both achieving and dominant, but also interested in helping and caring for people. Type B, the Thrusters, are archetypal yuppies, ambitious, hard working, but with little time or inclination to help others and strong drive towards autonomy. Type C, the Loners, score low on everything except autonomy: unambitious, but not social or caring either. Type D, the Carers, are not interested in personal achievement or dominance but want to help others.

Without worrying about who comes first in the sequence (you or your partner) there are ten possible combinations for you and your partner. These are AA, AB, AC, AD, BB, BC, BD, CC, CD, DD.

The most common patterns are BD, AA, and BB. The classic BD pattern, of one B (Thruster) and one D (Carer), works well, until either the B ceases to be successful at work or the D wants to start or restart a career. The AA pattern, of two involved people, usually presents a major time challenge: time to pursue two careers and also have a full and rewarding home life for both parties. The key to success here is to avoid excessive work-related time and travel commitments, and to use outside domestic help for the less rewarding home tasks. The BB pattern of dual income thrusters needs to rely even more on outsider services that minimise the extent of housework. For a fuller discussion of portfolio partnership, see *The Successful Boss's First 100 Days* by Richard Koch (1994), pp. 1–14.

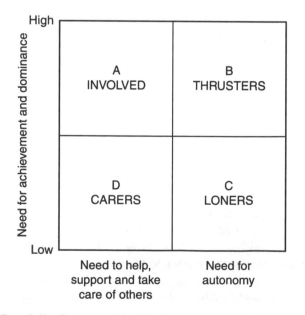

Figure 38 Portfolio Partnership Matrix

Source: Adapted from Charles Handy, *The Age of Unreason (1989)*

PORTFOLIO THEORY

1. Usually refers to the financial theory advocating diversification of an investor's portfolio. See PORTFOLIO (1) and PORTFOLIO MANAGEMENT (1).
2. Can refer to the BCG MATRIX theory.

POS (Point of Sale)

1. The place where customers pay for goods, where it is most effective to merchandise other small goods. **2.** Merchandising material to go at the point of sale. **3.** Electronic cash register, see also EPOS.

POSITIONING

Finding a marketing position for a product or a company that differentiates it from competitors and occupies a 'slot in the brain'. This may be entirely emotional and subjective rather than defined by product or verifiable criteria. For example, British Airways was repositioned as 'the world's favourite airline' to let travellers know that the cabin crew no longer bit their heads off or ignored them. An interesting positioning technique for a new entrant or a follower is to draw a veiled contrast with the market leader, as in Avis' successful slogan 'We're Number Two. We Try Harder', or 'Carlsberg, probably the best lager in the world', as opposed to the biggest or the strongest. Positioning is partly a matter of understanding the most appropriate battleground for a product, but it is also a highly creative process of identifying vacant ground and finding an emotionally warm pitch. Positioning is far more art than science.

POSITIVE-SUM GAME

Where two or more players have some mutual interests and do not have to make the other party or parties lose in order to win themselves. Opposite of the more commonly used ZERO-SUM GAME.

POST ACQUISITION MANAGEMENT

The very important process of integrating acquisitions. Post acquisition management should be planned long before the acquisition is even attempted, in order to see whether it will work: and if it seems difficult, the bid should not be made. The process involves thinking through in great detail what changes will be made to the acquired company (and parts of the acquiror) in order to improve performance and realise SYNERGIES. Changes in CULTURE will be necessary and should also be carefully planned.

POST BALANCE SHEET EVENT

Anything important that happens after a BALANCE SHEET DATE but before an ANNUAL REPORT is posted, and that shareholders need to know in order to have a full and fair view of the company's financial position.

POSTING
Making an entry in a firm's BALANCE SHEET or intermediate record.

POWER
The study of power in organisations has generally been neglected. It is a very important subject, and rarely corresponds to the naïve assumptions made in most management books. One scholar who has greatly contributed to the area is Andrew Pettigrew.

POWER OF ATTORNEY
Legal document appointing one person to act, within defined limits, on behalf of another.

POWER RETAILER
See POWER STRIP and DESTINATION RETAILING.

POWER STRIP
US STRIP MALL (shopping complex alongside a highway) comprising several POWER RETAILERS (specialist CATEGORY KILLERS like Toys R Us). See DESTINATION RETAILING.

PPM
See PRODUCT PORTFOLIO MANAGEMENT and BCG MATRIX.

PR (Public Relations)
1. A firm's activities designed to put it in the most favourable light with consumers, government, regulators, and the public at large. Means used include press releases, annual reports and other corporate literature, corporate lobbying, company videos and in-house magazines, as well as attempts to place favourable articles in the financial press, and fend off unwelcome ones. 2. The internal department and/or external consultants that provide the service. PR is trying to upgrade itself from its journalistic origins and become a proper 'profession'. See also INVESTOR RELATIONS, (IR), for the most serious part of PR.

PREDATOR
1. A firm (or individual) that stalks a bid target or launches a BID. 2. A firm engaging in PREDATORY PRICING to try to force a competitor out of business. Predatory pricing is probably beneficial to customers and society as well as shareholders (of the predator) and is not practised as much as it should be. The words have an unfortunately sinister connotation.

PREDATOR PRICING
See PREDATOR 2.

PRE-EMPTION RIGHTS
Right to do something (usually buy shares) before other people.

PREFERENCE DIVIDEND
DIVIDEND payable on a PREFERENCE SHARE.

PREFERENCE SHARE, PREFERRED STOCK
Share that has a right to a DIVIDEND that must be paid in full before any dividends can be paid on ORDINARY SHARES.

PREFERENTIAL CREDITOR
One that has rights to rank ahead of other creditors in the event of a LIQUIDATION.

PREMIUM OF MARKET TO BOOK
When a company's stockmarket value exceeds its book value. See MARKET TO BOOK RATIO, TOBIN'S Q and SERVICE-COMPETENCY VALUES.

PREPAYMENT
A deposit or other payment made in advance of receiving goods or services.

PRESENTATION
Formal event when consultants or executives present findings about an area they have investigated and make recommendations. Presentations often use an overhead projector and are nearly always too long.

PRESENT VALUE (PV)
See NPV (Net Present Value), DCF (Discounted Cash Flow).

PRESIDENT
North American term usually denoting a firm's chief executive, who will normally be called President and CEO.

PRICE DISCRIMINATION
Term used by economists but only rarely by managers to mean the segregation of markets by price to maximise revenue, as with first class, club, full fare economy and discounted economy flights. See also MARKET SKIMMING.

PRICE EARNINGS GROWTH FACTOR
See PEG.

PRICE EARNINGS RATIO
See PE.

PRICE LEADERSHIP

When one firm in an industry sets the pattern of price increases (more rarely price cuts). Tends to happen in uncompetitive markets like retail banking. Ultimately of dubious value: firms would be better off in the long run by cutting costs and cutting prices unilaterally, to gain competitive advantage.

PRICE REALISATION

Slightly pretentious way of saying the actual price received, net of discounts etc.

PRICE-SENSITIVE INFORMATION

Information about a company's prospects that could cause a material change in its share price. Usually INSIDER INFORMATION.

PRICE UMBRELLA

Colourful term meaning a high general price level in an industry or product, held over all competitors to stop the rain of competition spoiling anyone's day. Although it leads to short term profits, it is usually a mistake for the market leader to hold out a price umbrella, as it prevents more marginal competitors exiting the business and makes it possible for them to build up experience and lower their costs, thus becoming more viable. See EXPERIENCE CURVE and OPPORTUNITY/VULNERABILITY MATRIX.

PRICE WAR

When one supplier cuts price dramatically and others are forced to follow. Price wars are hated by most businessmen and by stock market analysts, but often lead to long-term success for the low-cost competitor who can wage war longest.

PRICING STRATEGY

1. Setting prices in order to gain a long-term competitive advantage, rather than to maximise short-term profits. There are three main rules: (1) in introducing a product, price at or below cost in order to gain volume, cut costs, and deter competitors; (2) in fighting competition, especially when the market is still growing, consider sudden, startlingly short price cuts, so that the price is immediately perceived as low by the consumer, and as too low to match by competitors; and (3) ensure that the true costs of all products are known, including all overhead costs, and that the more complex, special products are not under-priced and the standard, high-volume products under-priced. See EXPERIENCE CURVE, AVERAGE COSTING, AVERAGE PRICING and BCG MATRIX. 2. More broadly, the major decisions made on pricing.

PRINCETON TEST

See GMAT.

PRINCIPAL

1. In management, the owner or person deciding an issue. 2. In finance, the amount of a loan, its initial value, excluding interest.

PRINCIPAL-ONLY BOND

Same as ZERO COUPON BOND: pays no interest but rewards with capital gain on maturity.

PRIOR CHARGES

Interest payments on bonds and loanstock that must be paid before ordinary shareholders can receive a DIVIDEND.

PRIOR YEAR ADJUSTMENT

A change to last year's BALANCE SHEET as a result of a change in the firm's accounting principles, so that the new figures can be compared to last year's consistently.

PRIVATE BANKING

1. Originally, a bank privately owned by its partners, such as Brown Brothers Harriman in New York, Lombard Odier in Geneva, or C Hoare & Co in London. 2. Now generally used to mean a bank for HIGH NET WORTH INDIVIDUALS offering an all-round bespoke service with instant access to a personal manager who can sort out any financial need.

PRIVATE LABEL

See OWN LABEL.

PRIVATE PLACEMENT

Issue of new shares to investing institutions (and a few large private clients) rather than through an offer to the public.

PRIVATISATION

World-wide movement started by the then Mrs Thatcher. Had been advocated years before by Peter DRUCKER, though he called it RE-PRIVATISATION (and, incidentally, he wanted to privatise all sorts of non-business organisations such as universities). Though it takes many years to change the CULTURE of a newly privatised organisation, the effects of doing so can be massive improvements in service to consumers and decreases in cost, though much of the benefits of the latter tend to go to shareholders. In general privatisation in the UK (where they have been first) have given investors high returns, at least partly because the scale of previous over-manning had been seriously under-estimated.

PROBABILITY

1. The likelihood that an uncertain event will occur. Probability is usually estimated, sometimes on the basis of historic data. The convention is to estimate probabilities on a scale of 0.0 to 1.0, where the former means it cannot happen and the latter means it definitely will. A probability of 0.54 means that there is thought to be a 54% chance of it happening. Probability can be made to equate to the odds that bookmakers offer: a 0.50 probability equates to evens, a 0.33 probability to 2–1 against, a 0.80 probability to four to one on (written as 1–4). Bookies are much better at estimating probabilities than most forecasters. **2.** The branch of mathematics dealing with probability theory.

PROCESS DESIGN, PROCESS RE-DESIGN

See BPR (Business Process Re-engineering).

PROCESS INNOVATION

Changing the way in which a service is provided to the customer, rather than changing the structural DELIVERY SYSTEM. Process innovation is the less common phenomenon, but can lower costs and raise value simultaneously. Examples of process innovation include the whole self-service revolution in supermarkets and service stations. A generation ago, you queued to be served: most consumers prefer the new system, and it generates much higher throughput at lower unit cost. Similarly, you used to have to go through the operator to make a long-distance telephone call. Other examples include the shuttle between Boston and New York, or the Gatwick express, where you can buy tickets on board; and the UK catalogue stores, Argos and Index, where a small selection is on display in the stores along with a large catalogue, and the goods are picked from a warehouse behind the store after the customer has paid. Delivery system process innovation is an opportunity waiting to happen in many industries: it can raise industry profitability (as has clearly happened in the supermarket, service station and telephone examples, as well as give a market share advantage to the FIRST MOVER. Could you create a process innovation in your industry? See also DELIVERY SYSTEM.

PROCESS/PRODUCT-BASED ORGANISATION

The opposite of FUNCTIONAL ORGANISATIONS and increasingly believed to be better. The benefits are better co-ordination and integration of work, faster response to customers and quicker TIME TO MARKET, simpler control systems, fewer people, and greater employee fulfilment and creativity. Functional organisations, on the other hand, may lead to greater skill development and ease of attracting the best specialists. It should not be automatically assumed that the process/product-based organisation is always better, though it usually is. BPR (Business Process Re-engineering) usually includes abolition of functional organisations and greater stress on the product/process flow. See WORKFLOW.

PROCUREMENT
See PURCHASING.

PRODUCT CHAMPION
Manager who is an enthusiast for a particular product (often in the development stage, when the product could be aborted) and will not countenance competitive defeat. Often, but not always, a marketing person. The main champion of the Sony Walkman was the head of Sony, Akio Morita, who insisted on the product being launched despite consistently negative market research.

PRODUCT DEVELOPMENT
See NPD.

PRODUCT FAMILY
A particular supplier's product range targeted at different parts of the market (mass market cars being an example).

PRODUCTION
Process of manufacturing. Must be integrated with the rest of the customer-satisfying process. See BPR, COSTS OF COMPLEXITY, DELIVERY SYSTEM, JUST-IN-TIME, MAKE VERSUS BUY DECISION, PROCESS INNOVATION, EVA, and QUALITY.

PRODUCTION BUDGET
Annual plan specifying production targets and planned inputs to production-like materials, direct labour and factory overhead.

PRODUCTION MANAGEMENT
See OPERATIONS MANAGEMENT.

PRODUCTION ORIENTATION
Being manufacturing rather than marketing or customer drive. A bad thing. See MARKETING MYOPIA for the classic denunciation.

PRODUCTION SCHEDULING
Planning production to avoid BOTTLENECKS and DOWNTIME and attain production targets. See BUFFER STOCKS, BOTTLENECKS and JUST-IN-TIME.

PRODUCTIVITY
Any measure of output divided by a measure of input (e.g. profit per pound of capital employed). Productivity is not a clear end in itself: it depends on the measure adopted and why. See EVA for a very good measure in many circumstances.

PRODUCT LIABILITY
Legal responsibility of a supplier for ill-effects caused by a product.

PRODUCT LIFE CYCLE

Ludicrous but once well-respected theory that all products go through a life analogous to that of animals: birth/launch; youth/growth; maturity; decline and death. Curves resembling mountains (or mole hills) could then be drawn looking at sales over time with the aim of discovering which stage the product was at and therefore what policy was most appropriate. Contributed towards the neglect and even euthanasia of allegedly DECLINING MARKETS. In fact, the product life cycle is a pernicious myth. Some markets grow, contract, grow again, contract again, and so on. Some, including most service businesses, just go on growing, albeit with recession-driven interruptions. Several markets have come back from the dead by imaginative NPD (New Product Development) and new customer-focused strategies. For some examples and more proof that the product life cycle is bunkum, see DECLINING INDUSTRIES and MARKETING MYOPIA.

PRODUCT LINE

Can mean one supplier's PRODUCT FAMILY within a particular product category (e.g. a range of refrigerators of different sizes and features); can also mean all the products that a firm supplies, including ones in quite different product categories.

PRODUCT LINE PROFITABILITY

Much neglected, highly useful analysis of how much money a firm makes (fully costed) on each of its products or services. Usually throws up results that surprise managers, often showing that a majority of products lose money on a fully costed basis, and 100% or more than 100% of the profits are made by a small proportion of exceptional money spinners. No-one has yet standardised a universally applicable way of conducting this analysis. Traditional accounting systems make it very difficult, and accurate product line profitability is nearly always supplied by outside consultants. See ABC ANALYSIS.

PRODUCT-MARKET MATRIX

1. The ANSOFF MATRIX. 2. The BCG MATRIX.

PRODUCT MIX

1. Same as PRODUCT LINE. 2. A firm's percentage distribution of products by turnover.

PRODUCT PORTFOLIO MANAGEMENT (PPM)

Techniques developed in the 1970s for the CENTRE, a division, or a standalone SBU (Strategic Business Unit) to develop different strategies for different types of businesses, usually involving giving higher priority (in terms of investment and management resources) to some businesses than to others. For the original and best guide to PPM, see BCG MATRIX. See also

BUSINESS ATTRACTIVENESS for a rival matrix that is also useful. Poor use of portfolio management and some dubious assumptions about cash management led to the technique becoming discredited in the late 1970s and early 1980s, but the thinking behind PPM is valuable and any firm with a large number of different products can benefit by dusting off the old techniques and thinking anew about priorities.

PRODUCT RANGE

1. PRODUCT LINE. 2. The extent to which a supplier has a broad or a narrow range. See RANGE VERSUS FOCUS, COSTS OF COMPLEXITY and ECONOMIES OF SCOPE.

PRODUCT SEGMENTATION

Trying to fit a firm's products to defined MARKET SEGMENTS, or vice versa. See MARKET SEGMENTATION, and also BUSINESS SEGMENTATION, which is broader, taking into account non-product dimensions like customers, and also taking competitors into account. Business segmentation is much more useful than product or market segmentation alone.

PRODUCT STRATEGY

See BCG MATRIX.

PRODUCT WIDTH

Means PRODUCT RANGE, definition 2.

PROFESSIONAL CORE

The key people within a firm who command and create its knowledge, and on whom its success depends. See SHAMROCK and CORE WORKERS.

PROFESSIONALISM

Generally connotes high standards of technical or managerial expertise, as opposed to the 'Old Guard' of amateur managers from upper-middle class backgrounds. Nowadays every function (such as PERSONNEL or PR) wants to be seen as professional, and has its own professional body or bodies to ape the older professions and appear to raise standards. Fortunately most of the new professional bodies do not have any power with which to oppress the public or shareholders.

PROFIT AFTER TAX

Profit after all expenses including interest and tax (but before deduction of dividends). In the UK also called EARNINGS.

PROFIT AND LOSS ACCOUNT

See P&L.

PROFIT BEFORE INTEREST AND TAX
See EBIT, PBIT.

PROFIT BEFORE TAX
See PBT.

PROFIT CENTRE
Unit of a firm where the manager in charge is responsible for meeting a profit budget. The preferred term nowadays is SBU (Strategic Business Unit): all SBUs are profit centres, though not all profit centres would pass the strict definition of SBU.

PROFIT FOR THE YEAR
Profit attributable to ordinary shareholders (i.e., after tax, minority interests, extraordinary items and PREFERENCE DIVIDENDS). What is left for the shareholders, some of which will normally be taken in the form of dividends and some of which will normally be retained.

PROFITABILITY
The amount of profit made for each pound or dollar of capital invested. Normally expressed as RETURN ON CAPITAL EMPLOYED (ROCE) and/or RETURN ON EQUITY (ROE).

PROFIT IMPACT OF MARKET STRATEGY
See PIMS.

PROFIT MAXIMISATION, PROFIT OPTIMISATION
Words commonly used but woolly and unsatisfactory. There are three main issues: (1) which profits? Many would say EPS (earnings per share), as these drive share prices and hence shareholder wealth. But EPS can be manipulated, and need not turn into cash, which is all that matters ultimately; (2) which time period? The shareholders are a constantly changing body in a quoted company, so which shareholders should one be trying to satisfy? Does a high share price next year have a higher or lower priority than a high share price in 30 years' time? To increase profits and share price long term may require actions like market share gain or price cuts that will hurt in the short term: see SHORT-TERMISM; and (3) many argue that shareholders should not be the only, or even the main, CONSTITUENCY that managers should be trying to satisfy: customers, employees, or the long-term health of the firm itself may be other important constituencies (see STAKEHOLDERS and STAKEHOLDER THEORY). In practice, few firms and their top managers are really trying to maximise profits, whatever they say. See MANAGERIAL HERESY.

PROFIT RELATED PAY (PRP)
A particular form of PERFORMANCE-RELATED PAY which in the UK has significant tax advantages to employees.

PRO FORMA
Standard form.

PROGRAMME EVALUATION AND REVIEW TECHNIQUE
See PERT.

PROGRAMME TRADING
Buying or selling of shares by computers when an event (like a market fall or rise of x%) is triggered. Increasingly common, leading to greater market volatility. Based, though, on the sound idea that market trends are likely to continue until there is a clear change of direction, and that such changes of direction can be discerned according to fixed formulae.

PROJECT FINANCE
The activity of financing major infrastructure projects, usually in the Third World, and the people in investment banks who arrange such finance.

PROJECT MANAGEMENT
Managing change in an organisation by means of an ad hoc, temporary group (often called a TASKFORCE) drawn from different areas and disciplines, in order to achieve specific objectives. Once these have been attained the project management team is disbanded. Some countries are better at this than others: managers in the USA and UK are generally better able to deal with the ambiguity and fluidity involved than French executives, for example. See also ATHENA.

PROJECT TEAM
1. A temporary TASKFORCE within a firm to solve a particular problem, drawn from people of different backgrounds or functional areas. Very useful.
2. A group of between 3–12 people comprising a semi-permanent organisational unit. See NUMEROLOGY.

PROMISCUITY
Term used in marketing to indicate consumers who shop around without having consistent brand loyalty; a market is also said to be promiscuous when most consumers have little brand loyalty. Promiscuity tends to be negatively correlated with the extent of brand premium over OWN LABEL goods.

PROPRIETARY BRANDS
Those of manufacturers rather than retailers. See BRANDS and contrast OWN LABEL.

PROSPECTUS
Formal financial document containing information on a company about to be floated on the stock exchange where there is a general OFFER FOR SALE and the public are invited to subscribe.

PROSPECTIVE PE

The PE ratio calculated on the best estimate of forward earnings, that is, the earnings for the current year rather than for the last year actuals (which is the HISTORIC PE). The historic PE is the one quoted in newspapers, but stock market analysts attach more weight to the prospective PE (also called the FORWARD PE).

PROSUMER

Alvin TOFFLER'S contraction of 'proactive consumer'; a consumer who hepls in new product delvelopment and design. See TOFFLER.

PROVISION

An expense recognised in a particular accounting period for a future expected loss. If the provision proves not to be needed it may be reversed by being WRITTEN BACK. Ample provisions are often taken after major rationalisations or acquisitions in order to give room for manoeuvre later. See CREATIVE ACCOUNTING.

PROXY

Authorisation for someone else to vote in place of another.

PROXY FIGHT

Common US practice whereby dissident shareholders dissatisfied with the Board of a corporation and its performance can solicit proxies from shareholders for resolutions to change specific aspects of corporate policy, including firing the Board and installing new executives. Greatly used in the 1980s by strategic investors and those contemplating a bid: a way of gaining control, or at least removing those currently in control, without majority ownership. Almost unheard of in the UK, though technically possible. On balance, a good thing.

PRUDENCE CONCEPT

Basic accounting principle: when in doubt, be conservative.

PSYCHOLOGICAL CONTRACT

Term invented by Ed SCHEIN meaning the implicit agreement between an individual and his firm about his role and the way he is treated, and the extent of his obligations to the firm. If the contract is to work long-term, the implicit assumptions in the contract must be consistently observed by both sides.

PSYCHOLOGICAL TESTING

Using tests drawn from psychology using standardised samples of behaviour to help appraise candidates for recruitment or promotion. See OCCUPATIONAL TESTING.

PSYCHOMETRIC TESTING

Use of tests of aptitudes and abilities. Often used alone for applicants for junior level jobs, and in conjunction with PSYCHOLOGICAL TESTING on applicants for middle and senior level jobs. See OCCUPATIONAL TESTING.

PUBLIC LIMITED COMPANY

See PLC.

PUBLIC RELATIONS

See PR.

PULL STRATEGY

Trying to pull demand through from the consumer end via advertising and promotions. Contrast PUSH STRATEGY.

PUMP PRIMING

Term originally from US public policy, indicating the willingness of the US government in the Depression of the early 1930s to use public works to 'prime the pump' of private enterprise, that is, get it working again. Rarely used in business to indicate help given to a new business.

PURCHASING

The activity and department in a firm that obtains all bought in goods and services. Crucial element of the VALUE CHAIN. Most firms do not make sufficient use of outside suppliers nor build close enough relationships with them. See: MAKE VERSUS BUY DECISION, COSTS OF COMPLEXITY, KEIRETSU, SUPPLIERS.

PURCHASING POWER PARITY (PPP)

Calculation of standard of living by comparing the cost in different countries of a basket of goods. The PPP may show that, by this criterion, a currency appears to be over-valued or under-valued against another. For example, PPP studies comparing the USA and the UK consistently show that more goods can be purchased in the USA with a given amount of money than in the UK (i.e. that the pound is over-valued against the dollar).

PURPOSE

Why a company exists, what its purpose in life is. Purpose is usually defined in one of four ways: (1) to serve a particular group of STAKEHOLDERS, like customers (a good purpose) or shareholders (rarely satisfactory); (2) to serve more than one stakeholder's interests, as with The Body Shop's purpose, 'We exist to provide cosmetics that don't hurt animals or the environment'; (3) reaching a future goal, like a level of turnover or profit, ranking in the industry, or becoming larger than a specific competitor; or (4) reaching a higher ideal, in terms of technical excellence or service to customers or service to customers or society in some way. See also MISSION and VISION.

PUSH STRATEGY

Trying to increase sales by controlling the channels of distribution, so that goods are pushed out to consumers rather than pulled through by their demand (the latter being a PULL STRATEGY).

PUT, PUT OPTION

The right to sell shares or other financial instruments at a fixed price at some future time, thus giving protection against a fall in the value of the instruments.

PYRAMID SELLING

Stimulating demand for a product by giving franchisees rights to sell the product; the franchisees then sub-license the next level of distributors, and so forth. Similar to a chain letter, equally certain to fail ultimately, and of equally dubious ethics.

Q

QC

See QUALITY CIRCLE and QUALITY CONTROL: different but use the same acronym.

QUALITY

Along with low costs and high service, quality is the third member of the trilogy holding the key to customer satisfaction, competitive advantage, and long term corporate success. Arguably, quality is the most important of the three. Without quality, a low-cost position will mean low prices and low margins; without quality, high service will not satisfy customers. Quality is more and more important the greater the value added and product complexity. Quality is also crucial when a product is part of a bigger product or business system, which is increasingly the case.

Quality is uncompromising; it is almost an absolute, demanding no faults at all, or faults so rare that finding one is a major event. Quality insists on its own terms. It confounds the fantasies of micro-economists, whose idea of perfect competition is vitiated once quality is not consistent across all suppliers. Consumers will increasingly buy the highest quality product, not the cheapest; and if they have to choose and have limited resources, they will buy fewer but better. Quality brings its own VIRTUOUS CIRCLE, of high quality, high employee pride, high customer satisfaction, high market share, high revenues, low costs, high profits, high re-investment, even higher quality, and so on in an ever increasing spiral. Quality compounds itself, and in doing so compounds competitive advantage. Quality is not just free: before long, it has a negative cost. Quality is also exclusive, and the biggest BARRIER TO ENTRY ever invented. Quality soon becomes not an optional extra, or even a source of competitive advantage, but a way of excluding those of lower standards from the market altogether. Who, given a free choice, would buy a car from the un-reconstructed Eastern bloc, at any price, when he or she could buy a cheap, compact Japanese car? Quality is a demanding way of life: RIGHT FIRST TIME, no mistakes, no compromise, constant striving for that accretion of small steps that will raise quality for ever. Quality is monastic in its intensity, a secular religion in the service of mankind.

Quality was the great business revolution of the West in the 1980s, but of Japan in the 1950s and 1960s. Quality came from the West, but has found its most prolific breeding ground in Asia, and now not just in Japan. Quality is an integral part of a management approach, not a box on its own. Quality should not be inspected, it should be in-built; it should not be a department, but the loving responsibility of all employees. Quality should not be part of a process, or a step, or a function, or an area of expertise: it should be the inside and the outside of any product produced, the core that runs through everything, the glue that binds everything, the commitment to the customer that unites the whole firm and binds each individual to each group, each group to the firm, and the firm to the customer.

Quality cannot be practised properly in a firm that has resented hierarchy, alienation, imperfect communications, sectional interests, or lack of commitment of people to the firm and its PURPOSE. Quality cannot be practised without a passion for quality; conscientious, rational behaviour is not enough. Quality means constantly striving to do things better, to make current standards of excellence obsolete, to push oneself and one's colleagues to the edge of achievement. Quality is not easy.

Quality should not be viewed as a series of techniques, like QUALITY CIRCLES of TQM (Total Quality Management), though these can start to change behaviour. Quality is in the hearts and minds of the workforce. See also DEMING, JURAN, and JAPAN.

QUALIFICATION (OF ACCOUNTS), QUALIFIED OPINION, QUALIFIED AUDITORS' REPORT

When the auditors cannot say that the accounts represent a 'true and fair' picture without making a qualification, because of some reservations or lack of data about the business. Generally very bad news.

QUALITY CIRCLE (QC)

System that became popular in Japan and has since spread extensively where groups of workers meet to discuss how to raise quality. A genuinely participative technique that requires full commitment from employees if it is to work well. Not all Western QCs have been a success, in some cases being seen as a manipulative attempt by management to extract more from its workers. QCs still exist but are now generally seen as part of TQM (Total Quality Management). See QUALITY, DEMING and JURAN.

QUALITY CONTROL (QC)

Refers both to the process of controlling quality and the department and people who do it. QC departments used to be popular, but were based on a false idea: that quality was external to production and the way to get higher quality was to inspect and reject poor quality items. People now realise that quality must be built into the product at the start and that quality is the responsibility of everyone in the firm. Quality control makes no more sense than 'service control'.

QUALITY OF WORKING LIFE

Rather wet term first used extensively in the 1960s. The subject is important. See HUMAN RELATIONS SCHOOL and EMPOWERMENT for earlier and later embodiments of the concept respectively. Sometimes abbreviated to QWL.

QUANGO

British term: abbreviation of 'quasi-autonomous non-governmental organisation'. Neither a good description, nor a good thing. Most quangos are under the patronage of the government: it appoints the great and the good to sit on these things. Also, they are devices for restricting either wealth creation or the exercise of personal liberty, or both. Their origins go back a long way, certainly into the 18th century, reflecting the penchant of the ruling classes for boards of control on which gentlemen could sit and think that they were usefully employed. All quangos should be abolished forthwith.

QUANTITY DISCOUNTS

Discount based on order size or on total purchases during a year, or both. The latter are usually called OVERRIDERS.

QUANT JOCK

US colloquialism meaning 'quantitative jockey', one who gets his or her rocks off by playing with numbers. Common in computer departments, OR, quantitative business schools like MIT, and quantitative consulting firms like LEK. A quant jock is not necessarily a NERD, but likely to be. See also ROCKET SCIENTIST, an advanced form of quant jock.

QUARTILES

The first, second, third and fourth 25% of observations in a FREQUENCY DISTRIBUTION.

QUESTION MARK

A firm's position in a BUSINESS SEGMENT where the market is growing fast (expected future volume growth of 10% or more per annum) but the firm is a FOLLOWER, that is, has a RELATIVE MARKET SHARE of less than 1.0x. One of the four positions on the BCG MATRIX. Unlike two of the others, very well named: there is a real question about such businesses that must be faced up to. Should the corporation invest a lot of cash and management talent to try to drive that business to a leading position, hence becoming a STAR (high market growth, high relative market share) and eventually a much bigger and highly positive CASH COW? Or should the business be sold for a HIGH PRICE EARNINGS RATIO, because people pay highly for 'growth' businesses without usually thinking too hard about the relative market share position? There is another option, which is usually taken, and usually wrong: putting *some* cash into the business but not enough to drive it to a leading position. The BCG theory and observation both lead to the conclusion that this will tend to give a poor return on the cash invested: the business will eventually become a DOG, and though it may throw off rather more cash in this state than the original BCG theory, it is unlikely to show a very good return (IRR) on the cash invested.

So is it to be investment to drive to leadership, or a quick and lucrative sale? It depends, of course, on the sums of cash involved, but particularly on whether you think leadership is attainable at acceptable cost. And then it depends on the reaction of the current leader, who has the star position: he ought to defend it to the death, but may not. Getting into this kind of battle is unpredictable and like playing poker: once started, you have to keep upping the ante to persuade your opponent that you will win in the end; and if you are to cut your losses at any stage, you had better do it early. What is the size of your pot of cash compared to his? The strength of your hand versus his is also very important: do you have the knack of satisfying customers better or higher quality or better people or better technology or just greater will power and commitment, or preferably all of the above?

Star positions are enormously valuable once obtained and defended. But most attempts to back question-marks fail to turn them into stars. Unless you are determined to win and have a better than evens chance, sale is usually the option that will better enhance shareholder wealth. As a shareholder you had better hope that the latter consideration weighs more heavily with the management than wanting to stay in a glamorous growth business. See BCG MATRIX.

QUEUING THEORY

OPERATIONS RESEARCH tool for working out how frequently and when to provide a service that will keep queues to an acceptable level while not incurring unacceptable cost. Nifty device that is clearly not used by most mass transit systems.

QUICK ASSETS

See LIQUID ASSETS.

QUICK RATIO

CURRENT ASSETS less STOCK divided by CURRENT LIABILITIES. Also called CURRENT RATIO.

QUID PRO QUO

Something in return for something else.

QUORUM

The minimum number of participants required to make a BOARD or similar body's deliberations legally valid.

QUOTA

Ceiling set on production or imports.

QUOTA SAMPLING

Market research technique aimed at getting a representative sample of a population before interviewing the sample. The technique is to describe the population by a number of variables (such as socio-economic class, sex and age) and make sure that the quota to be interviewed correspond to the population as a whole along these dimensions. Better than not using such an approach, and less expensive than increasing the sample size.

QUOTATION, QUOTE

Obtaining or being a QUOTED COMPANY.

QUOTED COMPANY

One listed on the stock exchange. Also called LISTED COMPANY.

QUOTED PRICE

The MID-MARKET PRICE of a share or other FINANCIAL INSTRUMENT.

QWL

See QUALITY OF WORKING LIFE.

R

R&D (Research and Development)

Key department of firm in a KNOWLEDGE INDUSTRY like pharmaceuticals or any high tech business, and many others. The quality of the R&D staff and its culture, and the degree to which it is keyed into marketing and customers, may be the most important competitive advantage in such a firm. Why is it that some smallish pharmaceuticals firms like Astra (of Sweden) are able over long periods to come up with a stream of brilliant drugs that half of the top ten drug companies in the world cannot match? The answer is in the Astra R&D culture and its links with universities.

Spending on R&D is thus at best half the battle. The bang for the buck in R&D is crucial. That involves recruiting the best scientists by providing an attractive working environment and a sense that they are central to the company, as well as nurturing the R&D culture over time. This may seem obvious, but few firms behave as though they understand it. Those that do should prosper mightily over the next century.

R&D STRATEGY

This can describe the effectiveness of the R&D function and how it is managed (see R&D above), but it can also describe the corporate use of whatever R&D provides. Many companies forget that they have a choice re R&D strategy. Many years ago, BCG characterised two useful R&D strategy extremes. One, called Hit and Run, relies heavily on invention, followed by a sequence of MARKET SKIMMING, loss of cost advantage over other competitors as they take market share, neglect or abandonment of the product once profit margins become thin and the product turns into a 'commodity', and replacement with a new invention.

The alternative, and much better, strategy was called Bet on Success. Here the inventor sets a moderate initial price and reduces it in line with costs, discourages new entrants by making it impossible for them to make a profit, pursues a high debt/equity position in order to make returns for shareholders acceptable despite narrow margins, and retains earnings in order to finance new inventions. The sequence eventually leads to a big CASH COW, and maybe the only one that can justify the high initial research costs. See also INVENTION, INNOVATION, PIONEERS, PRICING STRATEGY and EXPERIENCE CURVE.

RAIDER, CORPORATE RAIDER

Person or firm that is highly acquisitive and preys on under-performing companies. See ARBITRAGEUR and PREDATOR.

RAIDER MENTALITY

When a firm that might come under attack from a BID thinks through how a RAIDER (predator) might look at the firm, and what it would do (such as sell off businesses that are worth more to others than to the owner). A very useful way of preventative defence (if action is taken accordingly).

RAINCHECK, TAKE A RAINCHECK

Postpone until another (unspecified) occasion.

RALLY

Stock market or currency market term for an increase after a period of decline. A TECHNICAL RALLY is one where the market (or a share or individual currency) goes up, but for technical rather than underlying reasons, perhaps because of activities in the FUTURES MARKET, or because one player with SHORT POSITIONS decides to liquidate them and take a profit. A technical rally may be short-lived.

RAM (Random Access Memory)

Computer memory device incorporated in microchips enabling a user to go straight to any part of the memory.

RAMP

To manipulate a share price upward.

RANDOM ACCESS MEMORY

See RAM.

RANDOM-WALK THEORY

Idea that shares move regardless of historic patterns, and therefore that CHARTISM is nonsense. Also associated with the EFFICIENT MARKET HYPOTHESIS.

RANGE

PRODUCT RANGE, or the extent to which a supplier 'covers the waterfront' or specialises.

RANGE CLARITY

The right range for the customer.

RANGE VERSUS FOCUS

The dilemma of whether to expand the number of products by line extension and/or entering ADJACENT SEGMENTS, in order to realise ECONOMIES OF

SCOPE, or alternatively to focus very tightly in order to reduce or avoid the COSTS OF COMPLEXITY. There is no generally right answer, but it is a crucial question for a firm's management to keep asking itself. One approach is to go for range, but avoid excess costs of complexity by OUTSOURCING all or most non-core components and activities, and by having very close relationships with suppliers and distributors, so that the firm is very focused in the part of the VALUE CHAIN where its expertise lies, but can continue to realise ECONOMIES OF SCOPE. See PRODUCT RANGE, ECONOMIES OF SCOPE, DELIVERY SYSTEM, COSTS OF COMPLEXITY, FOCUS and OUTSOURCING.

RATCHET

A change to move things up or down a gear: pay can be ratcheted up by inflation, the REWARDS of an MBO to the managers can be ratcheted up by reaching a certain profit threshold, and so on. A ratchet is usually permanent and irreversible.

RATE CARD

List price, especially for media advertising. Often discounted heavily.

RATE OF RETURN

1. The IRR (Internal Rate of Return) on an investment. **2.** Sometimes used loosely to mean either RETURN ON CAPITAL EMPLOYED (ROCE) or RETURN ON EQUITY (ROE).

RATING

1. Independent assessment of the quality of a company's debt. **2.** CREDIT RATING.

RATIO ANALYSIS

Use of accounting ratios.

RATIONALISATION

1. Cutting costs and DELAYERING an organisation by removing a large number of employees. **2.** Making something simpler and cleaner, like product line rationalisation, which means cutting out slow-selling or unprofitable lines. **3.** Industry rationalisation, which means removing capacity unilaterally or by agreement with other suppliers. See DOWNSIZING (use **1**), the word now favoured.

RCP (Relative Cost Position)

The cost position of a firm in a product relative to that of a competitor. For example, if it costs Heinz 10p to manufacture a can of beans, and it costs Crosse & Blackwell 11p for the same can, Heinz has an RCP advantage of about 10%, or an RCP of 91 (C&B = 100). Classical economics assumes that firms in an industry will come to have the same cost position, but in the real world this is almost never true. RCP can be quite difficult to establish (usually requiring the use of specialist consultants) but it is often not what managers imagined, and the differences between competitors usually emerge as much greater than previously thought. It is useful (and necessary anyway, to arrive at the total answer) to look at RCP at each stage of the VALUE CHAIN: for example, X may have a 30% cost advantage in production but have an inefficient salesforce, and be at a 10% cost disadvantage in selling. Relative cost advantage is often, but by no means always, related to scale or experience advantages (expressed in RMS (Relative Market Share)).

RCP analysis is not invalidated by differences in quality, or the fact that one supplier may have a better brand. The cost position can be looked at with the PRICE REALISATION of each supplier indexed at 100, so that if Heinz receives 12p for its can of beans and C&B only 10p, Heinz's total and sub-divided costs can be looked at relative to the 12p, and C&B's relative to the 10p that they receive. On this basis, Heinz would have a total cost of 83 (10/12) and C&B a total cost of 110 (11/10): Heinz would be making a profit margin of 17% but C&B would be losing 10%. The real cost difference between the two firms (adjusted for price realisation) would be 27% (110 minus 83). Heinz might be spending more on marketing, to help capture the extra price realisation, but the analysis would show this as well.

RCP analysis is expensive and only worth doing when there is a lot of turnover in the products being compared and there is a good chance that it will reveal things that can be acted upon, or help to set a competitive strategy in a battle worth winning. RCP analysis can lead to cost savings through imitation: for example, a competitor may miss out a process step altogether that the firm can also eliminate; or lead to a dramatic redesign of production to take out perhaps 30% of cost.

RCP is little practised but where it has been used it has generally been extremely insightful and effective, saving tens of millions of pounds and giving a return of about 20–50 times the amount paid for the analysis (which will be several hundred thousand pounds). RCP cannot be conducted *vis-à-vis* most Japanese competitors, because it is impossible to discover their real costs, partly because of deliberate obfuscation, and partly because of the KEIRETSU system. See also RPP (Relative Price Position), and EXPERIENCE CURVE.

RCR (Relative Customer Retention)

How well a firm retains its customers relative to its competitors. A key influence on relative profitability. See CUSTOMER RETENTION.

RDC (Regional Distribution Centre)

A distribution depot in a HUB AND SPOKE system serving a number of delivery points in the region.

REACH

Marketing term meaning the percentage of a target market that an advertiser reaches at least once during an advertising campaign.

READ ONLY MEMORY

See ROM.

REAL

1. Something not distorted by inflation, as in REAL MONEY. **2.** Realistic, as in 'get real': face up to the facts, rejoin the human race.

REAL ACCOUNTS

Ledgers or accounts that deal with ASSETS and LIABILITIES. Contrast NOMINAL ACCOUNT.

REALISATION

1. Selling something; turning an asset into cash. **2.** What is actually realised, as in PRICE REALISATION: price received, not list price or asking price.

REAL MONEY

Money adjusted for inflation, so you can compare over time without this distortion. A firm's sales may have gone up from £100m in 1989 to £130m in 1994, but if inflation averaged 5% over this period, the £100m was worth £127.6m in 1994 pounds, so in real money terms there has been scarcely any growth.

REAL TIME

Computer term meaning doing something now, interactively, as when a package holiday is booked and logged into the hotel and plane reservation computers while the customer waits; also used more broadly to mean something done spontaneously, without planning or delay. But what is false time?

REALTOR

American for estate agent.

REAL VALUE, REAL VALUES

See REAL MONEY.

REAL WAGES

Wages adjusted for inflation.

RECALL TEST

Marketing research test to see how many people can recall an advertisement and what they remember of it.

RECEIVER

Someone who takes charge of a LIQUIDATION.

RECESSION
Period of negative growth in GNP. See BUSINESS CYCLE.

RECIPROCITY
Bilateral trade agreement.

RECOGNITION
An event (like a sale or expense) is recognised when it finds its way on to a company's BALANCE SHEET.

RECOMMENDED RESALE PRICE, RECOMMENDED RETAIL PRICE (RRR)
List price from which most retailers will discount.

RECONCILIATION
Accounting term: making a firm's books balance with each other and ensure that they are all correct.

RECONSTRUCTION
Financial reconstruction: change in a firm's CAPITAL STRUCTURE, usually to help it to survive. Reconstruction may involve banks converting debt to equity (thus subjecting the shareholders in many cases to DILUTION OUT OF SIGHT), rescheduling of debt, or the transfer of useful assets into a more viable new company in which the shareholders and bankers may be given equity and debt respectively.

RECOVERY
Coming out of a recession: when GNP growth turns positive. Often heralded (GREEN SHOOTS) but slow to materialise. See BUSINESS CYCLE.

RECOVERY STOCK
Share bought in the hope that its share price will rise after a sustained fall, or share that is likely to benefit disproportionately from an economic RECOVERY.

RECRUITMENT
Technically, hiring from outside an organisation. Often used to include 'internal recruitment', more properly called SELECTION. See ADVERTISED RECRUITMENT and HEADHUNTING.

RECYCLING PETRODOLLARS
In the 1970s oil exporting countries had more money than they could spend, as a result of the surge in oil prices. They lent the money to banks, who then recycled the so-called petrodollars, mainly by lending to Third World countries, many of which later defaulted on the debt.

REDEEMABLE FINANCIAL SECURITY

A PREFERENCE SHARE, BOND, or DEBENTURE with a fixed term, repayable on maturity.

REDEMPTION YIELD

The total average annual YIELD of a bond if held until MATURITY, including both interest and capital gain.

RED GOODS

US term for FMCG (fast moving consumer goods), e.g. most grocery items.

RED QUEEN SYNDROME

Improvement is not enough; it is improvement relative to competition that matters. Based on Lewis Carroll: 'The Red Queen said, "Now, *here*, it takes all the running *you* can do to keep in the same place. If you want to get somewhere else, you must run at least twice as fast as that!"' As competitors adjust to each other and to customers, a BUSINESS SEGMENT itself changes. Segmentation is thus constantly in flux.

RED TAPE

Unnecessary rules and procedures in a firm or society: see BUREAUCRACY.

REDUNDANCY

1. British term for firing people or agreeing to pay them off (the latter being 'agreed redundancy', usually euphemised as 'early retirement'). Confusing word for Americans, who do not use it in this sense. **2**. Something no longer needed.

REFERENCE GROUP

A group that an individual is or wishes to be part of, that will be a touchstone for his or her behaviour ('would the group approve if I did this?', 'what would the group norm be in this situation?'). See BELONGING.

REFINANCING

Swapping new debt for old, hopefully at a lower interest rate or with less onerous conditions. Can also mean refunding a business in trouble: see RECONSTRUCTION.

REGIONAL DISTRIBUTION CENTRE

See RDC.

REGIONAL POLICY

Attempts to revive depressed areas by offering subsidies or other incentives to incoming business. One of the few forms of intervention in industry that most observers agree works.

REGISTERED OFFICE

The official address of a firm. Not necessarily where it has its main, or any, operations.

REGRESSION ANALYSIS

Statistical device for estimating what is correlated with what, in the hope of finding 'drivers' of desiderata. Regression analysis finds the BEST FIT between variables, for example, the success of sales executives is most highly correlated (has the best fit) with their years of experience and the amount of training received. Regression analysis can describe mathematically the extent to which any variable is associated with any other. It is a useful technique, though it must be remembered that correlation does not necessarily imply causation. See CORRELATION.

REGULATION

Government or quasi-governmental ordering of a market, especially in relation to large private monopolies such as utilities; government or self-governing body rules to ensure probity and ordered behaviour.

REINSURANCE

When one insurer lays off the risk of policies with another insurer, as when bookies lay off large bets with other bookies.

RE-INTERMEDIATION

When financial institutions get their noses back in the trough by acting as a financial intermediary. Opposite of the more beneficial trend, DISINTERMEDIATION.

RELATED COMPANY

See ASSOCIATED COMPANY.

RELATEDNESS

The extent to which businesses are similar and may benefit from direct or indirect SYNERGY if they are put together by acquisition.

RELATIONAL DATABASE

A database which incorporates clever software, enabling it to be organised or recalled easily in any way desired, not just in the way it has been put in. More flexible than the traditional hierarchical database. Relational databases are made up from 'flat files', two-dimensional tables that effectively serve as an index to anything else. Relational databases can be expensive to construct, although cheap and efficient to use.

RELATIONSHIP MARKETING

Understanding your customers and *their* customers so that you can provide the most effective product or service and ensure that its role is properly appreciated.

RELATIVE COST POSITION
See RCP.

RELATIVE CUSTOMER RETENTION
See RCR.

RELATIVE MARKET SHARE
See RMS.

RELATIVE PRICE POSITION
See RPP.

RELAUNCH
Marketing a product once it has been improved or REPOSITIONED, usually with the help of a big one-off marketing and advertising campaign.

RELUCTANT MANAGER
One who is alienated from his firm, usually a large BUREAUCRACY, who feels and generates stress and works poorly.

REMAINDER
To sell off surplus stock extremely cheaply, as with books.

RENEWABLE RESOURCE
Natural resource that can be replenished at least as fast as it is used, such as solar energy.

RENUNCIATION
When shareholders do not take up their RIGHTS.

REORDER LEVEL
When STOCK falls to this level it is reordered. Also called ORDER QUANTITY and OPTIMAL ORDER QUANTITY (the latter when correctly calculated using a formula).

REORGANISATION
1. Changing reporting relationships and possibly the whole way the firm is organised: see CENTRE, DECENTRALISATION, ORGANISATION ANALYSIS and MANAGEMENT STYLES. 2. A euphemism for DOWNSIZING or REDUNDANCY.

REPACKAGING
FINANCIAL ENGINEERING to change a SECURITY, perhaps by splitting up different attributes to appeal to different types of investor.

REPEAT PURCHASES, REPEAT PURCHASE RATE
The proportion of customers who, having made a purchase, buy from the same supplier. A key indicator of customer satisfaction. Where repeat pur-

chasing is low, as in car retailing (less than half of customers buy the next car from the same garage), it means that the service is poor and that there is great potential benefit from improving it.

REPLACEMENT COST
The cost of replenishing STOCK or replacing a FIXED ASSET. Replacement cost should be borne in mind when pricing.

REPOSITIONED, REPOSITIONING
Marketing term meaning the process of moving a product (or even a whole industry) from one consumer perception to another. A popular (but not always successful or profitable) move a few years ago was to try to 'move upmarket' in terms of product status and price. Repositioning is always somewhat difficult and risky, because the new position may not be reached, and the old one destroyed in the process. For instance, Lowndes Queensway, the British carpet and furniture retailer, tried to reposition itself away from the 'cheap and cheerful' perception of Harris Queensway but never found a convincing market proposition as an alternative. On the other hand, there have been some very interesting and successful repositioning attempts. In the UK drinks industry, for example, Guinness was successfully repositioned in the early 1980s as a drink consumed by young as well as older people, a trick repeated with even greater success in the past few years by the cider industry, largely as a result of new initiatives by Taunton Cider.

RE-PRIVATISATION
Peter DRUCKER'S original term for restoring firms and other institutions (such as universities) to the private, commercial sector. More apt than the generally accepted term PRIVATISATION, though never normally used today. See PRIVATISATION.

REQUIRED RATE OF RETURN
See HURDLE RATE.

RESCHEDULING
Allowing a new, more elongated, programme for repayment of debt, especially Third World debt.

RESEARCH AND DEVELOPMENT
See R&D.

RE-SEGMENT
To redefine a market to your firm's advantage, to create a new segment, based on a detailed understanding of why a particular group of consumers buys a product. See SEGMENTATION and OHMAE.

RESERVE

Accounting term meaning an account giving SHAREHOLDERS a claim over some ASSETS of a firm. Examples of reserves are RETAINED PROFIT and REVALUATION RESERVE.

RESERVE PRICE

The lowest price a seller will accept in an auction: known until bidding has finished only by the auctioneer.

RESIDENCE

Where a firm or individual is domiciled. Increasingly multinational companies and supranational bodies such as the EC and NAFTA are trying to escape from the idea that a firm is 'British', 'American' or 'Dutch'. Both legal and cultural recidivism is frustrating such attempts at the moment. See MULTINATIONAL ENTERPRISE.

RESIDUAL VALUE

Scrap value, or what is left of a depleting resource, such as the residual value of a coal mine or of a lease.

RESOURCE ALLOCATION

The way an organisation allocates resources, principally money. See BCG MATRIX.

RESOURCE-INVESTIGATOR

BELBIN's name for the team member who likes, and has a talent for meeting new people and finding ideas and solutions from elsewhere, and who introduces them to the group.

RESOURCES

1. Term used in ABC ANALYSIS, meaning things like people, machines or computer systems that perform work and cost money. 2. Things available to central management which can be channelled to or taken from businesses. The 'things' are usually cash, people, technology, and other assets. See BCG MATRIX for such a view of resource allocation.

RESTRAINT OF TRADE

Legal or illegal device preventing free trade or restricting competition in a market.

RESTRICTIVE COVENANT

Term in an employment contract or other agreement that restricts the future freedom of action of one of the parties, such as an agreement not to work for a competitor for a year after termination of an employment contract. If too restrictive, may not be enforceable.

RESTRUCTURING

A CAPITAL RE-ORGANISATION for companies or debtors, often involving banks agreeing to swap debt for equity.

RÉSUMÉ

French word which is American for CV (Curriculum Vitae). Odd.

RETAIL BANK

US term for CLEARING BANK.

RETAILING

One of the few industries where Britain is world class, though its impact on the balance of payments may not be positive. See GLOBAL VILLAGE.

RETAINED EARNINGS, RETAINED PROFIT

1. Profit after tax in any year not distributed to SHAREHOLDERS in DIVIDENDS, but retained in the business. 2. The total amount of such profits that has accumulated over time.

RETENTION RATIO

The proportion of earnings in a year that is RETAINED PROFIT rather than distributed in DIVIDENDS. If a firm makes £5m after tax and £2m is distributed in dividends, the retention ratio is $3/5 = 60\%$.

RETIREMENT

Leaving a business, generally implying leaving the world of work altogether at the end of a career. Increasingly this does not happen at a point in time, but we do not yet have adequate and commonly used words to describe what does happen. See PORTFOLIO (meaning 3).

RETURN ON ASSETS (ROA)

Operating profit divided by net assets. Not a good measure of performance.

RETURN ON CAPITAL EMPLOYED (ROCE)

Increasingly actually called 'ROCE', as though it were one Italian word. One of the best measures of profitability: OPERATING PROFIT divided by CAPITAL EMPLOYED. See also EVA (Economic Value Added).

RETURN ON EQUITY (ROE)

A good measure of corporate profitability: PROFIT BEFORE TAX (or sometimes PROFIT AFTER TAX) divided by SHAREHOLDERS' EQUITY. It thus takes into account the extent to which GEARING (leverage) is used, and is the best measure of how productively the most scarce resource from shareholders' point of view, their money, is being used. Also called RETURN ON SHAREHOLDERS' FUNDS.

313

RETURN ON INVESTMENT
See ROI.

RETURN ON NET ASSETS
See RONA. Same as RETURN ON ASSETS (ROA).

RETURN ON SALES
OPERATING PROFIT (*not* PROFIT BEFORE TAX) divided by SALES. Also called ROS.

RETURN ON SHAREHOLDERS' FUNDS
See RETURN ON EQUITY.

RETURNS TO SCALE
See ECONOMIES OF SCALE and RMS.

REVALUATION
Process to increase (or, rarely, decrease) the value of an ASSET to reflect a change in its market value. The change in value is reflected on the BALANCE SHEET by a change in the firm's RESERVES.

REVALUATION RESERVE
See REVALUATION.

REVANS, REG (b. 1907)
Obscure British educationalist and consultant who invented ACTION LEARNING, the title also of his 1974 book. The book was remaindered but Action Learning had a better fate as a movement. Well ahead of his time and unjustly neglected.

REVENUE
1. The amount that is paid or due to firm for supplying goods or services, and recorded in its books. Revenue is usually stated net of sales taxes such as VAT, that is, after deducting (or before adding on) the tax. 2. The total annual amount of money received by a firm for its goods or services: a synonym for TURNOVER. Note that revenue does *not* mean 'profit', though it is occasionally confused with it.

REVERSE ENGINEERING
Breaking down a competitor's product to see how it was made and analyse its costs. See TEAR-DOWN ANALYSIS, its modern name.

REVERSE TAKEOVER
1. When a smaller company (usually measured by MARKET CAPITALISATION) takes over a bigger one. 2. When the management of an acquired company emerges on top in the new entity.

REVERSE YIELD GAP
When the YIELD on equities is lower than that on government FIXED-INTEREST STOCKS. See YIELD GAP.

REVOLVING CREDIT
A line of credit from a bank that has no fixed term but revolves continuously (until cancelled).

REWARD
Usually means to pay someone, generally in an American firm. The linguistic preference partly reflects the awfulness of one American word, compensate, but partly also the desire to link pay to performance.

REWARD SYSTEMS
See PAY SYSTEMS.

RICE OF INDUSTRY
Felicitous Japanese term for electronic components (often specifically applied to VLSI (very large scale integrated) circuits that 'feed' most industries of importance in Japan.

RIGHT BRAIN PROCESSES
The creative and intuitive part of the brain. See LEFT BRAIN PROCESSES.

RIGHT FIRST TIME
The idea that goods should not need to be inspected for quality, because the objective should be to build quality in and ensure that all product is of high quality the first (and only) time round. Not only increases quality, but decreases cost and speeds up TIME TO MARKET. See QUALITY.

RIGHTS ISSUE
When a firm issues new shares and the existing shareholders have the right to buy them before they are offered to new shareholders, thus avoiding DILUTION. In practice, rights issues are often bad news for existing shareholders, for at least two reasons: (1) they usually depress the price of the shares, because in order to 'get the shares away' it is thought necessary to price them 5–15% below the previously prevailing share price: new supply depresses the price; and (2) rights issues are often undertaken either because a company is in financial difficulties, or in order to finance future takeovers, which may be thought likely to detract from shareholder value. If a shareholder cannot or does not want to take up the rights, the shares will go to someone else and he or she will be 'diluted', that is, have lower voting rights and a smaller share of the company.

RIGHTS

Shareholders' entitlement to new shares in exchange for cash. Sounds good, but often bad news. See RIGHTS ISSUE.

RIGHTSIZING

Newspeak-type word for DOWNSIZING or REDUNDANCY.

RING

Group of conspirators trying to rig a market or form a CARTEL.

RISK ANALYSIS

Systematic review of any business risk, for example of doing business with a new customer, or entering a new market, or of making a large investment.

RISK ARBITRAGE

Buying the shares of a company rumoured to be the target of a future bid, or after the bid has been announced, in the hope of selling out at a higher price in the near future. At times risk arbitrageurs have relied upon INSIDER TRADING, but there is a perfectly respectable branch of the activity too.

RISK CAPITAL

Another name for shareholders' EQUITY investments, emphasising the greater degree of risk attached to this class of instrument.

RISK PREMIUM

The amount being paid or necessary to be paid over and above a riskless investment such as a government security. If the US government is paying investors 3% per annum, but a company can only issue commercial paper at a 7% interest rate, the risk premium is 4%. The risk premium will vary from time to time and from investment to investment. The term is also used more loosely, to indicate any additional amount received or required because of higher risk. See also CAPITAL ASSET PRICING MODEL.

RMS (Relative Market Share)

The share of a firm in a BUSINESS SEGMENT divided by the share of the largest competitor that the firm has. Much more important than MARKET SHARE as an absolute number. For example, if Sony's nearest competitor in making Walkman-type products is one-tenth the size, Sony will have an RMS of 10 times (written as 10x, or 10.0x, or sometimes simply 10). The competitor, on the other hand, will have an RMS that is the reciprocal of this: it will have an RMS of 0.1x. One more example will suffice: if Coca-Cola in one national market has a market share of 60%, and Pepsi-Cola, 30%, then Coke has an RMS of 2x, and Pepsi 0.5x.

Relative market share should correlate with profitability. If it does not, one (or more) of five things is happening: either (1) the business segment has been defined incorrectly; or (2) the smaller competitor is much cleverer than the bigger: the leader is not using his potential advantage properly, and/or the follower has found a nifty way to lower costs or raise prices that has overcome the advantages of scale and experience; or (3) the leader is deliberately forfeiting profit now by expense reinvestment that will compound his advantage in the future, and lead to much higher profits then; or (4) there is over-capacity in the industry, so that the key concern is capacity utilisation, and the bigger competitors may simply have too much of the excess; or (5) it is a business not susceptible to normal scale, status and experience effects.

Let us take each of these in turn. (1) Incorrect business definition: more often than not, this is the reason. In most cases, the segment will not have been defined in a sufficiently disaggregated way. See BUSINESS DEFINITION. (2) A clever follower. This does happen, and is usually manifest in a refusal to play by the usual RULES OF THE GAME. See MAVERICK, DELIVERY SYSTEM and INNOVATION. (3) Long term compounding strategy by the leader. May be true if it is Japanese or Korean, almost certainly not otherwise. (4) Excess capacity: yes, sometimes. (5) Industry and business not susceptible to scale, experience or status: very rare. Even service businesses generally are skewed in favour of the bigger players, who have greater advantages in terms of branding, reputation, lower marketing and selling costs, and greater expertise and ability to attract the best recruits.

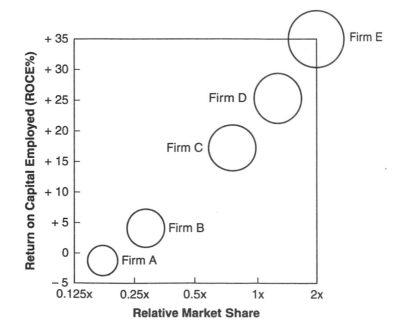

Figure 39 Typical pattern of profitability by RMS

One of the most useful charts to draw for any business, if the data can be collected, is shown in Figure 39, which looks at the profitability (in terms of ROS or ROCE) of different competitors in a business segment.

The chart shows a typical pattern, but the beauty of the method is that empirical data can be displayed to see whether and how far the expected pattern applies. If there is deviance from the normal pattern, the reasons given in (1) to (5) above can be systematically investigated.

The chart stops at 2x (two times) RMS only because in this case the leader had a 2 × RMS. In other examples the relationship has been observed to continue working over whatever range of RMS applies: businesses with a 10x RMS really do make very high ROCE: normally in the 60–90% range.

Observation of this relationship led to the development of a very useful tool – the OPPORTUNITY/VULNERABILITY MATRIX. See this entry for the action implications of RMS and profit relationships. See also EXPERIENCE CURVE, BCG MATRIX, MARKET SHARE and RCP.

ROBOT

Tools that make products: automated, mechanical production workers. Robots were first used in the car industry, but can be used for any purpose, including artistic creation, but are most used in industry, and fast growing. Robots have many advantages: lower and decreasing cost relative to humans, greater quality, greater strength, greater precision, and ability to work in environments that are dangerous or unpleasant to humans. Given their universal advantages, it is stunning (but on reflection not surprising) how skewed the use of robots is in different countries. In 1987, the top 14 countries using robots had a total of 103,209; by 1990 this had gone up to 243,931, an annual increase of 33%. Japan leads the world as by far the largest user of robots: with over four-and-a-half times as many as the USA, and 61% of the total used. Germany is third, Italy and France almost together in fourth and fifth (with rapid growth in both countries), followed by Britain, Sweden and Spain.

The constructive role that government can play in industry is well illustrated by robots. They are expensive for small and medium-sized firms and rapidly become obsolescent. The Japanese government got round this problem by buying the output of robot producers and then leasing them to users, replacing them with the latest technology whenever required.

ROBOTICS

The technology of making robots; the study and practice of designing, making and using robots.

ROCE

See RETURN ON CAPITAL EMPLOYED.

ROCKET SCIENTIST

Mathematical, computer or technical expert who is a dab hand at complex calculations. Also used more broadly to indicate someone who is of high intelligence.

ROLE

Part someone is expected to play; job specification, but carrying a bit more flexibility than this usually connotes. See JOB DESCRIPTION.

ROLE PLAYING

Acting the part of a competitor, another executive, or anybody else, in order to gain insight into the expected behaviour of others and/or to increase interpersonal skill and sensitivity.

ROLLOUT

Implementation of a plan, or replication of a model in a large number of areas, as with the rollout of a fast food chain.

ROI (Return On Investment)

US term used as a synonym for RETURN ON CAPITAL EMPLOYED (ROCE).

ROM (Read Only Memory)

Computer memory that can be read but not added to. Clearly less useful than a RAM (Random Access Memory).

RONA (Return on Net Assets)

Operating profit divided by NET ASSETS, expressed as a percentage. See also EVA (Economic Value-Added).

ROS (Return on Sales)

Operating profit over sales.

ROYALTIES

Stream of income from sale of intellectual property, or amount received by a business for LICENSING a technology.

RPP (Relative Price Position)

A complement to RCP (Relative Cost Position). RPP looks at the PRICE REALISATION for two or more competitors in the same product or service. If two identical packets of crisps are sold in the same outlet, one under the KP brand, and one a retailer's private label, and the former is 20p and the latter 18p, then the KP RPP is 20/18 = 111 and the RPP of the retailer's brand is 18/20 = 90. RPP shows how far there is a brand, quality or distribution advantage.

RULES OF THE GAME

The conventional way of competing, often broken by a MAVERICK firm to the great discomfort of established competitors. Breaking the rules of the game is often rewarding.

RUN

1. To start a computer program going. 2. Panic withdrawal of cash from banks.

S

SA
Société Anonyme, the French for PLC.

SACK
To fire, dismiss.

SALE AND LEASEBACK
When an organisation that owns its own freehold property sells it to a property company for a lump sum, but agrees to stay where it is and make annual rent payments for a defined period. The organisation frees up cash and the property company is assured a tenant at a specified rent.

SALES
1. The total REVENUES or TURNOVER of a firm in a period. 2. The sales department in a firm, or its selling activities.

SALES FORCE, SALESFORCE
The total group conducting sales activities, including reps (representatives) covering a region, key account salesmen, TELESALES staff, demonstrators and merchandisers, sales management and general management.

SALES LEDGER
A computer program (or book) detailing customers and amounts owed by them.

SALES PER EMPLOYEE
A ratio: total sales in a year divided by the average number of FULL-TIME EQUIVALENT employees during the year.

SALES PER SQUARE FOOT
Until DPP (Direct Product Profitability) came along, sales per square foot was a ratio widely used by retailers (along with profit per square foot).

SAMPLE
A sub-set of a population chosen randomly (or randomly within strata) in order to conduct market research and make inferences about the whole population. See also QUOTA SAMPLE.

SAMURAI BOND
Bond issued in yen in Japan by a foreign issuer.

S&Ls (Savings & Loans)
US financial institution that originated as a MUTUAL SAVINGS BANK (owned by its customers) and may still be that, or may have gone public. Basically a small retail bank.

SARL (Société à Responsabilité Limitée)
French for private limited company.

SATELLITE BANKING
Where one big branch has a number of smaller 'satellites' offering a more limited range of services.

SATISFICING
Willingness to settle for a satisfactory result, not striving for the optimum. Managers will often satisfice, particularly when the 'optimum' (which is a theological concept) is not simply and clearly defined. Part of the MANAGERIAL HERESY too.

SATISFACTION
See JOB SATISFACTION and MOTIVATION.

SATURATION LEVEL
When a new product or service has penetrated all possible buyers; when demand becomes replacement demand rather than new purchase demand. See S-CURVE.

SAVINGS & LOANS
See S&Ls.

SBU (Strategic Business Unit)
A PROFIT CENTRE within a firm that is organised as an autonomous unit and that corresponds roughly to one particular market. SBUs originated in the 1970s and have proved popular since then. The story of how they came about is interesting. In 1970 Fred Borch, head of the American GE, decided to decentralise, abolish or curtail staff functions, and reorganise on the basis of stand-alone SBUs. GE set up the following criteria required for a group to be a pukka SBU:

- An SBU must have an external, rather than an internal, market: must have a set of external customers.
- It should have a clear set of external competitors it is trying to beat.

- It should have control over its own destiny: decide what products to offer, how to obtain supplies, and whether or not to use shared corporate resources like R&D.
- It must be a profit centre, with performance measured by its profits.

The move to SBUs in GE and other Western countries has on the whole been positive. The drawback with an SBU structure is that it does not encourage (though it does not prevent) full use of the common skill base and technology that a corporation may have. The SBU structure is not well equipped to deal with the challenge of Japanese companies who not only draw fully on common internal skills derived from and serving a variety of products, but also benefit from each other's skills in an interlocking way. See M-FORM ORGANISATION and KEIRETSU.

SCAB
Pejorative term for worker who disregards a strike and carries on working.

SCALAR
Word used by the SCIENTIFIC MANAGEMENT school to describe a boss.

SCALAR CHAIN
The management hierarchy, with each person responsible to a boss who has other subordinates, with the pattern repeated up and down the CHAIN OF COMMAND.

SCALE, SCALE FIRM
One that has reached the minimum economic size to spread fixed costs and have a low cost position. See ECONOMIES OF SCALE. A firm that has not reached the requisite size is SUB-SCALE.

SCAM
US term for a fraud, a fraudulent scheme.

SCENARIO
Term made popular by Royal Dutch/Shell for an imagined future. Planners would construct several scenarios for how important variables (like demand for oil, the oil price, the cost of production, and so on) might unfold, taking different assumptions in each scenario about the variables, and then working out possible responses to each scenario, sometimes also assigning probabilities to each scenario so that the optimal policy could be worked out covering all scenarios. The point was to be open to the possible implications of a very wide range of possible scenarios.

SCENARIO PLANNING, SCENARIO WRITING

Activity using computers to construct alternative futures and their implications. Scenario planning was most popular in the period 1965–90. See
SCENARIO.

SCHEDULE

Timetable or list of appointments.

SCHEIN, EDGAR H

Edgar H 'Ed' Schein is a distinguished and commercially astute American
social psychologist based at MIT. He is 'well networked', having worked
with and been influenced by Doug McGREGOR, as well as having close links
with Warren BENNIS, Chris ARGYRIS and Charles HANDY, whom he taught.
Schein was one of the first to focus on PROCESS CONSULTING, the title of his
1969 book, which involves looking at how a firm operates and its CULTURE
and helping it be more effective, rather than supplying expert content-ori-
ented consulting. Schein has been influential for the past 20 years, and has
added three concepts to management language: besides process consulting,
there are also the PSYCHOLOGICAL CONTRACT and the CAREER ANCHOR.

The 'PSYCHOLOGICAL CONTRACT' is the bargain struck between employees and the firm, covering not only the normal economic contractual terms
but what is expected more broadly, both by the firm and the employee, of
each other. Unless the terms of the psychological contract are understood
(at least intuitively) by each side, the basis for a long-term relationship does
not exist, and there may be unexpected friction in the short-term. The psychological contract related to trust and expected patterns of behaviour.

The 'CAREER ANCHOR' is the self-image of an individual in an organisation that holds him or her in place. Early on in a career the individual may
develop (or fail to develop) a sense of worth, satisfaction and confidence in
his or her role in the organisation. Without the anchor, the individual may
strive for a new role inside or outside the organisation.

Schein was an early writer on corporate culture, which he defines as 'what [an
organisation] has learned as a total social unit over the course of its history'. He
stressed the importance of VALUES, modes of behaviour, and ARTEFACTS (the
external manifestations of a firm's CULTURE, like Mars' white coats and clock-
ing-in, IBM's white shirts, open-plan or compartmentalised offices, the way that
people in the firm talk to each other, and so on). Schein emphasises also the role
of LEADERSHIP in CHANGE MANAGEMENT. See MISSION.

SCHONBERGER, RICHARD J (b. 1937)

Interesting and creative American industrial engineer and the author of the
two best-selling books on manufacturing: *Japanese Manufacturing
Techniques* (1982) and *World Class Manufacturing* (1986). Introduced JUST-

IN-TIME and other techniques used in Japan to the US market in the early 1980s. But his most interesting book is *Building a Chain of Customers* (1990), which argues boldly that world-class business can only be built if each function in a business is viewed as the customer of the preceding stage, all the way to the final customer. Each part of the corporation must satisfy its (internal or external) customer's four needs: 'ever-better quality, ever-lower costs, ever-increasing flexibility, and ever-quicker response'. Schonberger packaged the idea of CELLULAR MANUFACTURING as the way to meet these needs: clusters of employees and the operations are deployed according to the work flow rather than on artificial functional or departmental lines. Schonberger thus laid the foundations for BUSINESS PROCESS RE-ENGINEERING and for the recent theories of Tom PETERS and other prophets of customer obsession.

SCHUMACHER, E F (1911-77)

Fritz Schumacher will be for ever associated with the phrase 'Small is Beautiful', actually coined for him by the publishers of his collection of essays *Small is Beautiful* in 1973; the subtitle was also intriguing: *A Study of Economics As If People Mattered*. He was a German economist who was a socialist and worked for the British National Coal Board between 1950 and 1970. Some have commented that his reputation rests on pretty slender foundations, since his writing was neither extensive nor detailed, and he himself was a pretty odd bird.

On the other hand, he did come up with one-and-a-half Big Ideas, and if he was lucky to be influential, we too are fortunate that he was. Small is Beautiful was an interesting idea, not just because it ran counter to the prevailing corporatist mentality, but because Schumacher was the first explicitly to urge that big organisations should try to simulate smallness. He did not advocate breaking up the National Coal Board, for example, but claimed that it could be seen as a federation of semi-autonomous units, each with its own feel and CULTURE. He thus harked back both to Alfred SLOAN, who had decentralised General Motors in the early 1920s, and forward to Jack Welch and the efforts to make GE a 'big/small' organisation. He can also be seen as the forerunner of the EMPOWERMENT school of thought, though in many ways he remained an unreconstructed public sector enthusiast that modern writers would find frankly anachronistic.

The 'one half' Big Idea was INTERMEDIATE TECHNOLOGY: the idea that developing countries should eschew replication of smokestack industry and the assembly line and go for simpler, smaller and less expensive uses of technology.

SCIENCE PARK

An industrial estate, often of high-or mid-tech companies, usually located near a university. Also called a BUSINESS PARK.

SCIENTIFIC MANAGEMENT

The body of knowledge and practice associated with F W TAYLOR (1856–1917) that was the first systematic attempt to make management a profession based on clear principles. Taylor took up the theme of specialisation first celebrated in Adam Smith's pin factory and conducted experiments at Bethlehem Steel in Pittsburgh showing how efficiency could be raised if each element of a process was broken down into separate tasks, and one worker made 'first-class' at each task. Scientific management was thus the forerunner of TIME AND MOTION STUDY. Scientific management was a comprehensive and internally coherent set of principles, designed to motivate employees by specialisation and performance-related incentives, training, and mutual co-operation between management and workers based on clear expectations, rewards and discipline.

Scientific management no longer has any supporters. It is a soft target for all modern schools of thought. The most serious criticisms relate to its mechanical, atomistic, analytical and non-holistic nature. But the criticism is over-done and fails to place Scientific Management in its proper historical context. Scientific Management was a great improvement on unscientific management, and the choice at the time was between authoritarian bad management and Taylor's invention, authoritarian good management. Taylor's principles were suited to the time, and have foreshadowed in some ways not only WORK STUDY, but also theories of MOTIVATION, TRAINING, and the knotty question of how to reconcile the interests of workers and owners. In his own way, Taylor was the first exponent of corporate excellence and using the talents of the workforce to the full. Scientific Management lasted for about a century and throughout that time was always at the progressive and humanistic end of the spectrum.

SCOPE

The range of activities or products that a firm has: see ECONOMIES OF SCOPE.

SCORCHED EARTH DEFENCE

A defence against takeover that involves destroying the value that a bidder sees in the company, either by selling what he wants (see CROWN JEWELS), or ensuring that it will not be available to him (perhaps by an announcement that the key knowledge workers will resign if the takeover is successful). A defence that is rarely practised and almost impossible to justify ethically.

SCRIP ISSUE

Issue of bonus shares to shareholders, usually in order to increase LIQUIDITY in the market and decrease the average price of the shares. In the absence of other developments, a scrip issue should be broadly neutral for shareholders' wealth: if one new share is issued to supplement each existing share ('a one-for-one' scrip issue), then the share price should halve, leaving the holder neither better nor worse off than before.

S-CURVE

The growth pattern resembling an S: slow to pick up, followed by a period of maximum growth, then a point of inflection leading to gradually slower growth. Study of the 1665 Plague in England led to the conclusion that the spread of disease followed a mathematically predictable path, and the same methodology has been used with some success to predict the rate at which a new product will penetrate into any given population, given the early experience. If, for example, you knew that the penetration of dishwashers into Korea was 1% in the first year, 2% in the second year and 4.5% in the third year, you could calculate a prediction for future years. The formula to be used to calculate each year's observation is f/1–f, where:

f	=	the penetration (expressed as a fraction: e.g. 1% = 0.01), and
1–f	=	one minus the penetration fraction (e.g. 1 – 0.01 = 0.99)
f/1–f	=	0.0101 in this case, or for the 2% observation
	=	0.02/0.98
	=	0.0204

If the observations are plotted on SEMI-LOG paper and a straight line is drawn through the observations, predictions for future years emerge in the form of the 'answer' above (e.g. 0.0204), which can then be converted by algebra into the percentage prediction. A simple computer program will perform the calculations without the need to resort to plotting on semi-log paper.

The same procedure can be used in modified form where you know that there will be a SATURATION level at a given point. With dishwashers in Korea, for example, you may know from similar cases that no-one below a certain income level will ever own a dishwasher. Let us assume that this cuts out 40% of the population: the saturation level is therefore 60%. Instead of using 1.0 as the maximum point, therefore, we would use 0.6, the saturation point (s). The calculation would then be f/s–f, and the first observation (at 1%) would become:

$$0.01/.6–0.01 = 0.1695.$$

Many people are sceptical of the power of this methodology until they actually use it. It is not, of course, a magic predictor, but it does enable you to calculate what the answer would be if the current momentum persists. It will work out when the growth will slow because there is a diminishing pool of people to be 'converted' to the new product.

SDF
See STRATEGIC DEGREES OF FREEDOM.

SDR (Special Drawing Right)
Form of currency invented in 1967 and now a basket of five leading currencies. Sometimes Certificates of Deposit (CDs) and bonds are denominated in SDRs.

SEARCH
1. Research to find a new executive, usually by a headhunter. **2.** Legal or accounting examination of records, for example, to find a firm's filed accounts.

SEASONAL ADJUSTMENT
Adjusting the pattern of demand or sales for the season in order to see the underlying trend.

SECONDARY BRAND
A brand that is not the primary brand (brand leader) in its product category. Less profitable than primary brands and vulnerable to retailers restricting or removing its SHELF SPACE.

SECOND MORTGAGE
Loan secured on a property, ranking after the first mortgage.

SECULAR TREND
The basic long-term trend after ironing out short-term fluctuations.

SECURITISATION, SECURITIZATION
1. The conversion of a bank loan for a company into a marketable security, such as commercial paper, a note or other negotiable debt instrument. **2.** Since the mid-1980s, securitisation has also been used (and this is now the more common usage) to mean the process of making a new tradeable security out of any collection of financial instruments that were not previously traded, usually by bulking together a large number of individual small transactions into one sizeable entity. Examples of securitisation include mortgages, where original lenders to individuals have collected together a large number of individual mortgages into one security and then sold on the collective mortgage debt to another financial institution, thus freeing up the balance sheet of the first lender and enabling it to originate new business, while giving the buyer of the securitised paper exposure to the mortgage market without having to originate the business himself. The buyer could then, if he wished, sell on the securitised paper to a third buyer, and so on. Another example of securitisation is collections of insurance policies, and in theory any individual financial transactions

could be grouped together and made into a securitised instrument. A clever and useful piece of FINANCIAL ENGINEERING.

SECURITISED PAPER

The negotiable instrument resulting from the process of SECURITISATION (in both senses: 1 and 2).

SECURITY

1. A financial instrument like shares or bonds. 2. Rights over assets given in return for a loan.

SEED CAPITAL, SEED MONEY

The first, small investment of venture capital in a project to establish its feasibility and lead to the ability to attract a second round of financing that will then launch the business proper.

SEGMENT

Part of a market identified by one or more firms as a target. A sharp distinction should be drawn between MARKET SEGMENTS, which are defined by marketeers and very often have at best tactical significance, and BUSINESS SEGMENTS, that are arenas within which a firm can establish a COMPETITIVE ADVANTAGE. A small, defensible business segment is sometimes called a NICHE. See SEGMENTATION.

SEGMENTAL REPORTING

Reporting by a company of its revenues and profits broken down into broad categories like geography (by country) and activity or major product line. Most annual reports in the UK and USA provide such information, and it is of some interest, but it is usually too aggregated (and sometimes deliberately constructed to be unhelpful) to draw attention to the really interesting differences in PRODUCT LINE PROFITABILITY. Although it is called 'segmental', it bears only a very pale resemblance to real BUSINESS SEGMENTS, which are usually many, many times the number of reported segments.

SEGMENTATION

Most usefully, the process of analysing customers, costs and competitors in order to decide where and how to wage the competitive battle; or a description of the competitive map according to the contours of the business segments. Sadly, segmentation is often used to describe a more limited (and often misleading) exercise in dividing up customer groups. See SEGMENT, BUSINESS SEGMENT and MARKET SEGMENT. Proper segmentation only takes place at the level of identifying the business segments: this is at the root of any firm's business strategy. Segmentation in this most useful sense is what is discussed below.

It is crucial for any firm to know which segments it is operating in, to know its relative market share in those segments, and to focus on those segments where it has or can build a leadership position. A segment is a competitive system, or arena, where it is possible to build BARRIERS against other firms, by having lower costs or customer satisfying differentiation (which will be expressed in higher prices, and/or in higher customer volume which itself will lead to lower costs). A segment can be a particular product, or a particular customer group being sold a standard product, or a particular customer group being sold a SPECIAL product or provided with a special service, or a particular distribution channel or region, or any combination of the above. What matters is that the following conditions for a genuine segment are *all* satisfied:

1. The segment must be capable of clear distinction, so that there is no doubt what customers and products fall inside and outside the segment.
2. The segment must have a clear and limited set of competitors that serve it.
3. It must be possible to organise supply of a product or service to the segment in a way that represents some specialisation, and is differentiated from supply to another or other segments.
4. The segment must have purchase criteria that are different in important ways from other segments.
5. The segment must be one where competitors specialise, and where there is a characteristic market share ranking that can be described.
6. The segment must be capable of giving at least one competitor a profitability advantage, either by having lower costs, or higher prices, than other competitors, or both.
7. It must be possible to build barriers around the segment to deter new entrants.

Segmentation may change over time. To take the example of the motor car, Henry Ford created his own segment around the black Model-T Ford: the mass produced, standard automobile. Initially, he had 100% of this segment, and it satisfied all of the rules above. Then it became possible to provide other colours at relatively low cost, and General Motors changed the mass automobile market to include any colour, standard car: the 'black car' segment ceased to exist and became part of a wider competitive arena. Subsequently new segments emerged, based on sports/high performance criteria, and later on 'compact' low fuel consumption cars.

Geography is a fascinating and changing dimension of segmentation. Most products and services start out by having a very limited geographical reach: one region or one country. The UK crisp (what Americans call potato chips) market is an interesting example. At one time the market was dominated by Smiths, then by Golden Wonder (who innovated with a range of flavours), both national competitors. Slowly but surely a new regional competitor, Walkers, emerged, based on superior quality. Initially the segment boundaries of Walkers were very restricted, based around the Midlands where the company was based. Within these regions the national segmentation did not rule: Walkers was the number one supplier by a long way, although nationally very small. Gradually, with greater production and improved distribution, Walkers became a national competitor, and for a time market leader, again causing the segmentation to revert to a national level.

An increasing number of markets are global: the battle between Pepsi and Coke is fought out beyond the boundaries of individual countries. Nevertheless, segment RELATIVE MARKET SHARE positions often vary significantly in different countries: if Pepsi outsells Coke in one national market, against the global trend, that national market is today a separate segment. If, on the other hand, relative market shares around the world converge, the whole world can become one segment for cola drinks. Economics comes into this as well. To take one far-fetched example: assuming that Coke came to have a two-to-one advantage over Pepsi everywhere in the world except New Zealand, where Pepsi was by far the leader, it would be correct to speak of New Zealand as a separate segment, but the rest of the world would be one segment and the marketing scale advantage enjoyed by Coke everywhere else would make New Zealand a barely tenable separate segment for Pepsi: at some point, the most interesting segmentation would have become global, even if national segment enclaves temporarily continued to exist.

Similarly, segments can be carved out or relinquished within a product range. At one time, British motorcycles were the market leaders throughout the world whatever type or power of bike was being considered: motorcycles were one global segment. Then the Japanese began to develop bikes, based around the low-powered bikes for which there was greatest domestic demand. What happened first was that this low c.c. market became a separate segment in Japan, because the market leaders (Honda and Yamaha) were different from the leaders in the rest of the world market (and in Japan in mid- and high-performance bikes). Then the Japanese companies, by trial and error, managed to develop a market for these low c.c. bikes in America, and later throughout the world, so that low c.c. bikes became a separate global segment. Later, using modular designs and high cost sharing, the Japanese suppliers entered mid-size bikes, became market leaders in these, thus changing the segmentation around the world by annexing the mid market, so that there were two global segments: the low-to-mid segment (dominated by the Japanese), and the high performance segment, still dominated by Norton and BSA. Then, in the early 1970s, the Japanese began to edge their way into the high performance segment, and BMW created a separate high-comfort, high-safety segment, so that the world motorcycle market had two major segments: the 'BMW' segment, and the rest (the majority) of the market, served largely by Japanese competitors.

In diagnosing what segments you are in today – whether the market is one big segment or several small ones – the best way is to set up hypotheses that X market is a separate segment from Y market, and then test according to the following rules. The short set of rules, that will give you the correct answer 95% of the time, is to ask just two questions:

1. Are there separate competitors, with significant market share, in segment X that do not participate in segment Y? If so, it is a separate segment.
2. Are the relative market share positions in market X different from those in market Y, even if the same competitors compete? If so, it is a separate segment. For example, Heinz and HP compete in both the red sauce (ketchup) and thick brown sauce markets in the UK, but in the first Heinz is miles ahead of HP, and in the latter HP is way ahead: so they are separate segments.

To be absolutely sure, apply the following additional rules:

3. Is your firm's profitability different in market X from market Y? If so, even if it is the same product being supplied to different customers, it may be a separate segment.
4. Are the COST STRUCTURES different in the two markets?
5. Are there technological barriers between the two markets that only some competitors can surmount?
6. Are prices different (for the same product or service) in the different markets?
7. Is it possible to gain an economic advantage by specialising in one of the markets, by gaining lower costs or higher prices in that market.

Because segmentation changes over time, it is interesting to look both at the EMPIRICAL SEGMENTATION today, which is defined particularly by the first two questions above, and also at potential segmentation based on the economics of the business: what is called ECONOMIC SEGMENTATION. Economic segmentation applies questions (3) to (7) above to ask, not just whether the segmentation is distinct today, but whether it could be distinct. Economic segmentation can be used as a technique to RE-SEGMENT a market, either by creating a new, smaller segment out of an existing segment (as with the initial Japanese move to create a below-250c.c. motor-cycle segment), or to merge two segments together (as with the later annexation of first the mid and then the high performance motorcycle segments) in order to realise ECONOMIES OF SCALE. Economic segmentation asks: could we obtain lower costs or higher prices or both by redefining the segment and changing the RULES OF THE GAME?

SEGMENT RETREAT

Policy of retiring from a particular market segment, conceding it to competitors, and focusing on other segments. Tends to be a continuous, sad process. One classic example is the UK motorcycle industry in the early 1970s, which, faced with the onslaught of Japanese competition, retreated first of all from the small bikes segment, then the mid-bikes segment, so that it was left at the 'high end' of large and super-bikes. The problem was that the Japanese advanced just as the British retreated, and, given the high shared component cost between the segments, Japanese dominance in the lower end product eventually fed dominance in all segments. If pursuing a strategy of segment retreat, it is essential to build solid BARRIERS against the advance, or the retreat will turn into a rout.

SELECTION

Often used as a synonym for RECRUITMENT, although technically selection means recruiting from within an organisation.

SELF-ACTUALISATION

An individual's efforts at fulfilling his or her potential in the widest possible sense: see MASLOW who coined the phrase.

SELF-CONTAINED WORK GROUP

A team of people within an organisation, usually 7–10 in number, who do everything (hiring and firing, purchasing, production, selling, planning) in relation to their product. Effectively a firm within a firm. See NUMEROLOGY.

SELF-FINANCING

Does not require external capital.

SELF-STARTER

Inner directed person who can be relied upon to do things without external supervision.

SELLER'S MARKET

A market favouring selling, where there are more buyers than sellers.

SELL INTO STRENGTH

Stockbrokers' jargon for selling a share which is expected to perform strongly in the near future, but then decline. The shares should be sold, but not until they are in strong demand and the price is rising.

SEMI-LOG SCALE, SEMI-LOG PAPER

Graph paper that has a normal horizontal axis (used mainly for time), but has a logarithmic vertical axis, so that each doubling of the measure (usually money or an index) takes an equal distance. Consider the sales of a company increasing from £1m in 1994 to £2m in 1995, £4m in 1996 and £7m in 1997 (Figure 40).

Drawn on a 'normal', linear scale it looks as though growth is accelerating throughout the period, whereas in fact the rate of growth is constant in the first two years (doubling each year) and then declines (to a 75% rather than 100% increase in 1997). Semi-log paper enables you to see this at a glance: a straight diagonal line represents a constant rate of growth, a move up represents an acceleration, a flattening of the growth lines represents a deceleration. Graphs of stock-market performance over time should always be expressed on a semi-log scale; otherwise it looks as if the recent growth is more impressive than it is. See also LOG-LOG SCALE.

SENGE, PETER M

American writer, academic and consultant based at MIT and proponent of the LEARNING ORGANISATION. His 1990 book, *The Fifth Discipline*, stressed five 'competent technologies' needed to build learning organisations: (1) SYSTEMS THINKING; (2) Personal Master for individuals, who approach life as a creative work; (3) Mental Models to overthrow the basic disease of management hierarchy (see PARADIGMS OF MANAGEMENT); (4) Shared Vision (see VALUES and VISION); and (5) Team Learning (see TEAMWORK). *The Fifth Discipline* is a good synthesis of these themes.

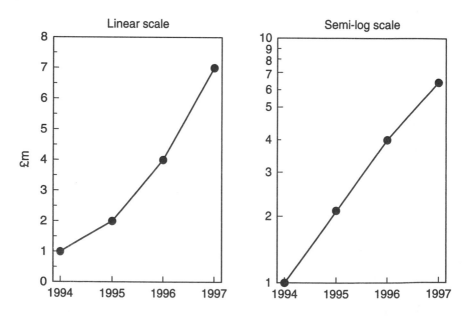

Figure 40 Company Growth drawn on linear and semi-log paper

SENIOR DEBT
The highest-ranking form of debt, that has the first call on assets in a liquidation. Contrast SUBORDINATED DEBT.

SENIORITY
Length of tenure with a firm.

SENSITIVITY ANALYSIS
Showing the extent to which results (usually in a plan or projection) would differ if a key assumption were to be varied. Attention should focus on the key assumptions, where a small change in such variables could make a large difference to the outcome.

SENSITIVITY TRAINING
Touchy-feely techniques to improve interpersonal and group effectiveness, used by industrial psychologists. See ENCOUNTER GROUPS and T-GROUPS.

SEQUENTIAL MANAGEMENT
Traditional management method of doing one thing at a time: time is the enemy, a long, straight line leading to death. Stresses time commitments, short-term relationships, 'first-come-first-served', and the PRODUCT LIFE-CYCLE. Contrast the much more appropriate approach of SYNCHRONISING MANAGEMENT.

SEQUESTRATION
Confiscation of an organisation's assets by a court.

SELECTION
Recruitment from inside an organisation, often by internal advertising of the position.

SERVICE
1. A business that does not provide a product, but something intangible or something that changes a product that is valued. **2.** The quality of customer care and responsiveness provided by any business that is a key competitive weapon in most markets, leading both to market share and profit gains.

SERVICE-COMPETENCY VALUES
The market value of an acquisition or quoted company minus the book value of its assets: in other words, the value of its intangibles, the knowledge and skill of its people and the firm's service relationships. It is quite common nowadays to have service-competency values that are greater than (sometimes several times) the book value. At the time of writing, for example, Microsoft has a 7-to-1 ratio of market value to book value, or, expressed another way,

its service-competency value is 600% of its book value. Another way of saying this is that its SOFT VALUE greatly exceeds its hard value.

SERVICE CONTRACT

A contract of employment for senior managers, often containing a GOLDEN PARACHUTE.

SETTLEMENT DAY

The day on which share or other financial instruments recently bought must be paid for, and when the broker must pay for shares sold.

SET-UP COST,

The cost to change production from one product to another; or more loosely the start-up costs of any operations.

SEVEN S, 7S FRAMEWORK

A framework for thinking about a firm's personality; a diagnostic tool for describing any company, developed by PETERS and Waterman and their then colleagues in MCKINSEY around 1980. Seven elements of an organisation, all beginning with S – strategy, structure, systems, style, skills, staff and shared values – can be used as a checklist. Do the Ss fit well together, or are they inconsistent or unclear? When the Ss fit well together and reinforce each other, the organisation is likely to be moving forward purposefully; where the Ss are in conflict, it is likely to lack unity and momentum. The Seven Ss are shown in Figure 41.

Note, however, that an organisation with seven consistent Ss will be much harder to change than one where the Ss are visibly in disarray.

SEXUAL HARASSMENT

Actual, attempted or alleged abuse of one employee by another (usually a boss) which includes a sexual element: usually of women by men. An American invention, spreading slowly to Europe, still unknown in Japan.

SGR

See SUSTAINABLE GROWTH RATE.

SHADOW DIRECTOR

A person who is not a director of a company, but who behaves as though he were and has influence; someone from whom the directors are accustomed to take advice and instruction. A shadow director may be deemed to have some or all of the responsibilities of actual directors.

SHADOW ORGANISATION

See INFORMAL ORGANISATION.

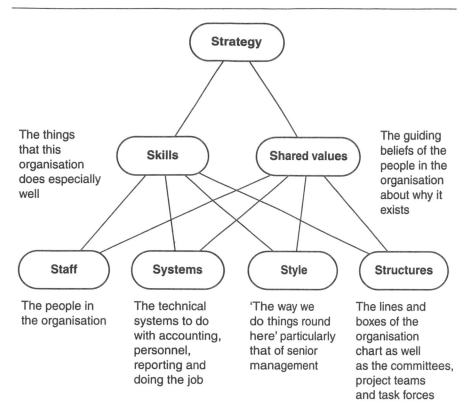

Figure 41 The Seven Ss

SHADOW PRICE
A price imputed when a proper market is not in existence; the best guess at a real price or cost.

SHALLOW ORGANISATION
A FLAT ORGANISATION with few layers.

SHAMROCK, SHAMROCK ORGANISATION
A form of organisation described by Charles HANDY using the Irish national emblem, a three-leaved clover. According to Handy, today's organisation is increasingly like a shamrock, made up of three distinct but interlocking parts. The first leaf represents the CORE WORKERS or PROFESSIONAL CORE, the people who hold the knowledge of the organisation and are essential to its success. The core must be looked after and treated as partners, but this is expensive, so the answer is to have a much more selective and smaller core, and rely increasingly for less essential input on the other two 'leaves' of the shamrock. The second leaf is the CONTRACTUAL

FRINGE: specialists outside the organisation who are experts in a particular part of the work and have a close relationship with the firm, but who are not on its payroll. All work which need not be performed in-house should therefore be CONTRACTED OUT to lower cost specialists. The third leaf of the shamrock is the FLEXIBLE LABOUR FORCE, part-time and temporary workers who come and go as required, and are an increasing proportion of the total. Many of this third group will not want full-time employment, and will be young, female or 'retired'. The organisation may invest in some elements of the flexible labour force, for example by giving training and some privileges, but this third tranche of labour will never have the commitment or ambition of the core.

Handy believes that the shamrock organisation has increased, is increasing, and ought to be further increased, with a realisation that each part of the shamrock needs to be treated differently. Eventually the dominance of the shamrock organisation could change accepted patterns of behaviour, abolishing traditional views about work and career, leading many more people to take a PORTFOLIO of different sorts of work, significantly reducing the incidence of wasteful commuting, and making only a minority of people, the highly motivated professional core, really committed to their companies. This last group, however, must really believe in what the organisation does and be zealots for it.

There is no doubt that this is the wave of the future.

SHAPER

The extrovert team member who supplies an initial focus to the discussion and gets everyone excited; slapdash, impatient, broad picture merchant and shooter-from-the-hip. See BELBIN.

SHARE CAPITAL

1. Funding raised by a company in return for shares. 2. The nominal value of the shares issued by a firm.

SHAREHOLDERS

Those who own a company. Can be individuals or INSTITUTIONS. See also FAMILY FIRM, and STAKEHOLDERS.

SHAREHOLDERS' EQUITY, SHAREHOLDERS' FUNDS

The share of a firm's assets that are due to shareholders, comprising share capital, share premium, retained profit and any other reserves. For the purposes of financial analysis, dividends can be included in shareholders' equity.

SHAREHOLDER VALUE, SHAREHOLDER WEALTH

Phrase often used to mean what is in shareholders' interests, as in 'create shareholder value'. Often means 'get the share price as high as sustainably possible', and includes a sense of medium- and long-term value creation rather than short-term share price maximisation (or manipulation). Generally not a neutral term: the users tend to imply that the main or exclusive responsibility of top management is to maximise shareholder value rather than worry about other STAKEHOLDERS' (e.g. customers' or employees') interests. Most US firms and many UK ones claim that shareholder value is their main objective; few mean it. See also STAKEHOLDERS and STAKEHOLDER THEORY.

SHARE ISSUE
When new shares are issued. Usually refers to the initial FLOTATION of a company, what the Americans call an IPO (Initial Public Offering).

SHARE OF VOICE
See SOV.

SHARE OPTIONS, EXECUTIVE SHARE OPTIONS
Rights granted to valuable employees to buy shares in the future at today's price and, thus, if the shares perform well, to make a potentially large capital gain sometimes amounting to millions of dollars or pounds for top executives. Share options are widely used in the UK and USA and form an important part of top managers' pay packages. They often give a return quite disproportionate to a proper reward, if the stock market generally performs well, lifting with it the value of the managers' firms' shares.

SHARE PREMIUM
The difference between the issue price of shares and their par or nominal value. A matter of interest only to accountants.

SHARE PRICE INDEX, SHARE INDEX
A basket of shares against which individual shares or the performance of a portfolio can be judged. Most FUND MANAGERS fail to match the increase in the index, hence the popularity of INDEX (TRACKER) FUNDS. To some extent the index is skewed to show a good return, because most indices have provisions forcing under-performing shares out of the index from time to time and replacing them with better-performing shares. Each country has several different indices, so be careful about which is being referred to.

SHARE SPLIT, STOCK SPLIT
A form of SCRIP ISSUE using a round number.

SHARK
1. A PREDATOR or ARBITRAGEUR scenting blood before or during a takeover BID. **2.** Exploiter, as in 'loan shark' (lending money at very high rates of interest).

SHARK REPELLENT

Measure taken by a company to discourage a bid, such as changing the rules to make takeover more difficult. Sometimes used when a company makes itself less attractive to a specific predator, though more properly the latter is a POISON PILL.

SHARK WATCHER

Consultant who helps identify and repel SHARKS.

SHARP END

The front line, where the action is (the Japanese call it the GENBA).

SHELF SPACE

The amount of space allocated to a particular product on supermarket (or other retail outlet) shelves. The battle for shelf space is a key step in the battle for market share. It gives retailers considerable power and bargaining leverage over suppliers, particularly of SECONDARY BRANDS, where the threat to DE-LIST a product (refuse it shelf space) can be highly potent.

SHELL, SHELL COMPANY

A QUOTED COMPANY but one which has few or no trading activities and where much or all of the value of the company is in its QUOTE. Nearly always a PENNY SHARE. Speculators like to spot 'shells' that will benefit from the INJECTION OF ASSETS by someone acquiring control of the company or buying a large slice of its shares. Many stocks that performed brilliantly well (at least for a time) like Polly Peck and WPP started life as shells. Most shells, however, remain shells for ever.

SHIP

To send goods (by land, air or sea).

SHOP

1. Retail outlet 2. A production or maintenance department within a firm.

SHOPFLOOR

Production-related, place where production takes place.

SHOPFLOOR WORKER

Blue-collar, production or maintenance worker.

SHORT POSITION

When a market maker believes that the price of an instrument he trades will fall, and consequently runs down his stock, or sells more than he has, in the expectation of being able to buy back later more cheaply. Contrast LONG POSITION.

SHORTS
Short-dated securities, usually government bonds with less than five years to maturity.

SHORT-TERM
Generally means something within a 1–2 year horizon.

SHORT-TERMISM
Tendency to think more about the short term (and especially this year, half-year or quarter's financial results) than about the long term. Generally recognised to be a major problem with Anglo-Saxon business. A poll of international managers conducted by Charles HAMPDEN-TURNER showed that American managers came 18th out of 30 in their capacity to take a long-term view, while Japanese managers came first. Related to the SEQUENTIAL MANAGEMENT view.

SHORT-TERM LOAN
A loan due to be repaid within 12 months.

SHORT TIME, SHORT TIME WORKING
Reduced working week and pay as a result of weak demand, which it is hoped will be temporary and not require loss of jobs.

SHRINKAGE
Amount lost by a retailer in shoplifting or theft by employees.

SICK BUILDING SYNDROME
Late 1980s invention: claim that certain large buildings cause minor sicknesses because of poor ventilation, lighting etc. May be a reaction to the unpleasantness of working in a huge firm with little exposure to natural light.

SIDE DEAL
Private arrangement between two people as a supplement to a more major transaction, rather than as part of it.

SIGHT DEPOSIT
Instant access bank account.

SILENT PARTNER
See SLEEPING PARTNER.

SIMPLEX METHOD
Method in LINEAR PROGRAMMING, which takes account of more than two constraints to produce an optimal solution.

SIMULATION

OPERATIONS RESEARCH technique for estimating the outcome of an event by replicating ('simulating') a large number of possible real life outcomes, nearly always using computers. An early and fun example is MONTE CARLO SIMULATION.

SINGLE MARKET, SINGLE EUROPEAN MARKET

The idea that the European Community should become one market rather than a series of national ones. The Single European Market Act of 1986 was implemented at the end of 1992, removing many but not all barriers to free trade within the EC. The Single Market is an ideal, not a reality, but will gradually become one by the early years of the 21st century.

SINGLE STATUS FIRM

One that does not distinguish between BLUE-COLLAR and WHITE-COLLAR employees, or between 'workers' and 'managers'; it has a single category of employee, and the same benefits and facilities (e.g. one canteen). Will single status be sustainable though, in the SHAMROCK ORGANISATION.

SITTING NEXT TO NELLIE

On-the-job training by observation.

SITUATIONAL STRUCTURES

The organisational view that prevailed in the 1960s: there was no one best organisational structure: it depended on circumstances and the firm's strategy. Associated with the CONTINGENCY SCHOOL of organisational design.

SIZE OF FIRMS

It is interesting to look at the average size of firms over time, in terms of the number of employees. Data are available for Germany, the USA and the UK. After rising in all three countries between 1930 and 1970, the average has fallen significantly in the USA, and sharply in Britain (from about 95 in 1980 to just over 30 in 1990). In Germany the decline started later, in 1980, and has been less steep. The decline is due to the start-up of many very small businesses and the increasing focus of companies on one part of the VALUE-ADDED CHAIN, with increased NETWORKING and OUTSOURCING.

SKIMMING

See MARKET SKIMMING.

SKINNER, B F (1904-90)

American psychologist who had some influence on industry with his theories of 'behaviourism': how to condition people's behaviour. May not have had the influence he wanted, however, as there was at least an opposite reaction to his chilling celebration of manipulation, leading many to critique and avoid the 'rat race'.

SKU (Stock Keeping Unit)

A product kept in stock; the number of variants of a product line. Reduction of SKUs is a frequent tactic to reduce stock-keeping costs and complexity.

SKUNK WORKS

US term for an unofficial and unsanctioned group of employees who take the initiative on any project of their own. Similar to a PROJECT TEAM or TASKFORCE except that it is the individuals, rather than the management, who set the ball rolling. May receive an allocation of budget but generally not. Skunk works can be very useful: one at 3M developed the Post-It note.

SLACK

See ORGANISATIONAL SLACK.

SLEEPER

A product that becomes a big success but only a long time after it has been available and after it has been promoted. An example is the Filofax: personal organisers were available from the 1920s but only became popular from the 1980s.

SLEEPING BEAUTY

A product or service that will be a winner in the future (similar to a SLEEPER, although the latter term usually implies that the success has already come), or a company that has enormous unrealised potential and just needs a prince (in the form of a new leader or owner) to wake it up .

SLEEPING PARTNER

A co-owner who provides capital but is not executive within a business. Strictly speaking relates to partnerships but much more commonly used of private limited companies, or, more loosely, of any corporate structure. In partnerships, often now called a LIMITED PARTNER, that is, one for whom it is possible to procure limited liability.

SLOAN, ALFRED P (1875–1966)

One of the very few industrialists to be referred to as an authority on management; head of General Motors from 1923 to 1955; author of *My Years with General Motors* (1963) and notable for three reasons. First, he virtually invented the decentralised, divisionalised firm, establishing what he called FEDERAL DECENTRALISATION, when he transformed General Motors in the early 1920s from a mass of untidy and overlapping entities, with sporadic but ineffective central control, into eight separate divisions (five car divisions and three component divisions) which were treated as though they were separate businesses, but which were subject to professional controls on finance and policy from the Centre.

Second, Sloan changed the structure of the car industry and its SEG-MENTATION, and provided a model for how other firms could do the same. When he took over, there were just two car segments in the USA: the mass market, dominated by the black Ford Model T, which had 60% of the total car market volume; and the very low-volume, high-class market. Sloan aimed to plug the gap between these two markets by creating five price and performance segments and aiming that the five markets so created should be dominated by one of the new five GM car ranges: the Chevrolet, Oldsmobile, Pontiac, Buick and Cadillac (this represented a range rationalisation for GM from eight competing models). He turned Ford's no choice policy on its head by introducing a range of colours and features so that cars could be 'customised' at relatively little extra cost, as well as introducing new models each year to encourage trading up.

The SEGMENTATION fitted neatly with the divisionalisation: each of the five car segments and models had its own division, thus inventing the idea of the SBU (Strategic Business Unit) about 50 years before GE actually articulated it.

Sloan's third innovation was to establish the three component divisions as separate profit centres that supplied not only the five car divisions but also outside customers. Again, this concept has had to wait 50–70 years before its virtues became fully appreciated.

Sloan is fascinating because he had a foot in the old management camp of SCIENTIFIC MANAGEMENT, drawing on many of the 19th-century ideas of Henri FAYOL, as well as anticipating some of the tenets of very contemporary theory, including decentralisation, segmentation as a basis for organisation, and the value of creative dissent. The latter side can, however, be exaggerated: Sloan was at heart a mechanistic autocrat who was also a marketing genius, and to expect him to be a liberation manager into the bargain is to expect too much. MIT named its business school after him, a fitting tribute for both.

SLOT IN THE BRAIN

The effective POSITIONING of a product or service can result in it coming to occupy a unique and memorable 'slot in the brain' as with the Avis slogan, 'we try harder'. See BRAND.

SLOW-MOVING LINE

A product that sells slowly; it may be unprofitable because of the stock-keeping cost and because it adds to complexity generally.

SLUMP

Extreme recession or depression. Consigned to the dustbin of history?

SMALL FIRM

There is no accepted definition of what is a small firm. Nowadays the preferred terminology is DEVELOPING FIRM or SME (Small and Medium-sized Enterprises).

SMALL IS BEAUTIFUL

See E F SCHUMACHER.

SMART

Interactive, intelligent: attribute of a computer or chip controlled component.

SMART CARD

An interactive card like a debit card that is linked on-line to a computer; often used in security systems.

SME (Small and Medium-Sized Enterprises)

Small firms are usually started by entrepreneurs who may find the transition to professional management difficult. See ENTREPRENEUR.

SMOKESTACK INDUSTRY

US term for heavy industry from the first industrial revolution, usually with major environmental issues and often operating in declining markets and/or under severe competition from Third World countries with lower labour costs. More specific term than SUNSET INDUSTRY, which is an industry alleged to be in decline.

SNIP

A bargain.

SOCIAL ACCOUNTING

Trying to account for social costs and benefits of projects: see COST-BENEFIT ANALYSIS.

SOCIAL RESPONSIBILITY

A trend that cannot be ignored. See CORPORATE RESPONSIBILITY.

SOCIO-ECONOMIC GROUP

The more modern, subtle and cumbersome word for 'class'. Traditionally divided into the fatuous groups of A, B, C1, C2, D, and E.

SOCIO-TECHNICAL SYSTEM

Phrase used by the TAVISTOCK INSTITUTE and especially Eric TRIST to describe the workplace: both a technical and a social system. See also SYSTEMS THINKING.

SOFT BENEFITS

Benefits from a project or acquisition that cannot be quantified but are expected to be beneficial, like gaining additional management experience or a wider range of contacts.

SOFT CURRENCY

One that is weak. If floating, it will be falling; if at a fixed exchange rate, it will be vulnerable to speculative selling, so that it is likely to be forced to devalue. Opposite is a HARD CURRENCY.

SOFT LOAN

One at a subsidised rate of interest.

SOFT OPTION

Line of least resistance.

SOFT VALUE

See SERVICE-COMPETENCY VALUES.

SOFTWARE

Program enabling a computer to perform particular analysis and generate particular types of output.

SOLE TRADER

1. Individual businessman owning 100% of his concern. 2. By extension, someone in a firm, especially a professional firm like a solicitor's, who behaves as though he or she is a one-person business, and tries to ignore responsibilities to partners or other colleagues.

SOLUS

Without competition: solus status means that no other competitor is allowed access; a solus advert is one where competitors are not allowed near.

SOLVENCY

Being able to meet trading obligations and pay one's debts.

SOURCING

Procurement or purchasing. A key function. See PURCHASING.

SOV (Share Of Voice)

A product's share of total advertising in its category.

SPACE MANAGEMENT

The process of setting up and managing office layout in order to change managerial interactions and behaviour. Important. See NON-TERRITORIAL OFFICE.

SPAN OF CONTROL

The number of people who report to a boss. Traditional thinking is that six or seven is about right. A rather mechanistic concept that does not take into account the usual and necessary ambiguity in reporting relationships. Some organisational theorists now argue that the FLAT ORGANISATION should have typical spans of control of 7–20.

SPECIAL

Non-standard product requiring extra overhead. See AVERAGE COSTING.

SPECIALISATION

See FOCUS.

SPECIALITY, SPECIALITY GOODS, SPECIALS

1. Product that is customised or has extra value added. See AVERAGE COSTING. **2.** Special UPMARKET consumer goods.

SPECIALTY, SPECIALTY GOODS

American for 'speciality', increasingly used in English too.

SPECIFIC RISK

See DIVERSIFIABLE RISK.

SPECULATION

Gambling.

SPECULATIVE BUY

Stockbrokerese for 'you might want to buy but don't blame me if you lose your money'.

SPELLCHECK

Useful computer facility to check and correct mis-spellings. Many spellcheck facilities appear to have American and/or restricted vocabularies.

SPIDER'S WEB ORGANISATION

One that radiates out from the Centre or the leader and is a complex, informal network rather than a traditional hierarchy. A spider's web has no top or bottom.

SPIN-OFF, SPINOFF

1. To take a subsidiary and make a separate company, usually a publicly quoted one, out of it. This is a frequent practice in the USA, where the original owner usually retains a stake but sells a majority of the equity to a third party. Management often obtains a small stake in the business. If ownership does not change at all, a spin-off is more correctly called a DEMERGER. **2.** Used rather more loosely to indicate a splinter group that leaves one firm and sets up its own business, usually without the original firm having a stake in the new one, and in competition with the first firm. Most often used in professional services, especially in consulting and investment banking: for example, Bain & Company was a spin-off from the Boston Consulting Group. **3.** Also describes incidental benefits from a project, development or technology, as in 'the project achieved its goals, but also had unforeseen spin-off benefits'.

SPONSOR

1. BROKER or MERCHANT BANKER who assists in the FLOTATION (IPO) of a firm on the stockmarket. **2.** Protagonist or CHAMPION of a particular project or person within a firm. **3.** Firm providing SPONSORSHIP.

SPONSORSHIP

1. A form of promotion where a company sponsors a sports or cultural event in return for publicity: now big business. **2.** Financial support from firms for students, especially MBAs.

SPOT GOODS

Commodities available for delivery within two days.

SPOT MARKET

The here-and-now market for immediate delivery, as opposed to the FUTURES MARKET.

SPOT PRICE

Current price for immediate delivery.

SPREAD

The difference between buy (BID) and sell (OFFER) prices for a financial security. Spreads can be quite large on shares with low LIQUIDITY, such as PENNY SHARES or EMERGING MARKET shares, making it expensive to deal.

SPREADSHEET

Computer program for analysing numbers in rows and columns, which is clumsy and difficult in normal word processing packages.

SPU (Strategic Planning Unit)

A product-market segment that requires its own strategy, even though organisationally it may be part of a larger grouping, the SBU (Strategic Business Unit). 'Sauces', for example, may be an SPU, even though just part of a Dry Groceries SBU. SPUs may (indeed, generally should) be purely conceptual entities, meaning that line management recognises the need to think specifically about strategy for the product-market segment. The term is not without its uses, though little used nowadays (unlike SBU).

SQUARE BOOK

See BALANCED BOOK.

STAFF

Generally used to mean either salaried as opposed to shopfloor workers, or people in support as opposed to operational jobs. See LINE AND STAFF.

STAG

Person who applies for a large number of shares in an IPO or NEW ISSUE and intends to sell them quickly at a profit; to act in this way.

STAGFLATION

Combination of inflation and stagnation: now rare in developed economies.

STAKEHOLDER

Loaded term now widely used to mean someone who has a real or psychological 'stake' in an organisation: used to include anyone who has significant dealings with it, such as customers, employees, suppliers, distributors, joint venture partners, the local community, bankers and shareholders. It is generally a normative rather than a descriptive term, implying that the user believes that a number of stakeholders have a right to determine what happens within an organisation, and more particularly in a firm, rather than just the owners. See STAKEHOLDER THEORY.

STAKEHOLDER THEORY

The theory that a firm should be run in the interests of all its STAKE-HOLDERS (customers, employees, suppliers, distributors, society, bankers and shareholders) rather than just the SHAREHOLDERS. The 'stakeholder' name was invented by academics to help counter the view that the main responsibility of top management was to maximise SHAREHOLDER VALUE.

The stakeholder theory has no legal validity (yet). At one level it is banal (for what sensible management can afford to ride roughshod over the interests of customers or suppliers?). At another level it is practically useless, since it cannot tell management how to trade off the interests of one group against another when there is a conflict of interest: should management prioritise the stakeholders, or just aim to keep each in a mild state of discontent? A firm should not be some great creaking empire like nineteenth-century Austro-Hungary or the modern European Community where the main job is balancing different interest groups. Few firms are really run like this and none successfully.

Certainly management should think hard about its relationships with each stakeholder group. For a particular firm at a particular time, some of the stakeholders (and some individual stakeholders within each common class) will be of greater importance than others, and will need to be cultivated to a greater or lesser degree. To the extent that stakeholder theory causes such thought to take place, it may have some use. It is generally accepted (even by shareholder value enthusiasts) that firms should be close to their customers, even obsessed by them, and that satisfying customers is crucial; but no firm gives away its goods for long, or is entirely careless of its commercial interests. It is also accepted that in KNOWLEDGE INDUSTRIES and increasingly in all industries, competition for the best employees may be more important than, and a primary cause of, market share (competition for customers). Similarly, the success of many Japanese companies can be attributed to a large degree to close relationship with SUPPLIERS. When it comes to consider how important shareholders are to the success of a firm, as a matter of day-to-day reality rather than theory, the conclusion must often be: not very. The owners are generally less critical to the success and future of a firm than customers, employees or suppliers. If the owners are family, and close to the business, they may be important, but if they are mainly investment INSTITUTIONS, they may know little about the business and have very limited commitment to it: they may sell their shares next week or next year.

The trouble with stakeholder theory is not that it is wholly wrong, but that it is vague and intellectually soggy. Fundamentally, it attempts to answer the wrong question: in whose interests should a firm be run? This is a precise, legal question requiring a precise, legal answer: the shareholders, provided others' legal rights have been met. But the question itself is unhelpful, as anyone who has worked in a firm can testify. Do managers sit around thinking about stakeholder priorities before acting? No, nor should they. Instead, they do things, partly responding to commercial pressures, but (if they are good) trying to drive the firm forward to 'more and better': higher standards, better products and services, closer relationships with individuals (of whatever stakeholder stripe) that are important and valuable to the firm, greater quality, higher market share, higher sustainable profits, higher employee quality, longer lasting customer and supplier relationships, the repulsion of competitors, and a whole series of mixed-up, interlocking objectives that have concrete manifestation in action and a sense of progress. To the extent that managers and everyone in a firm need an 'over-arching' objective, sense of PURPOSE, CAUSE or MISSION, that is far better satisfied by a concrete goal (such as become larger than X, a competitor, or achieve product breakthrough Y, or reach Z level of sales and profits) than a theoretical construct about whom the firm is serving. When Henry Ford was asked the purpose of his company in 1909, he did not blabber about stakeholders (a term not yet invented) or shareholders (invented but not yet made into a god), but said, simply, to 'democratise the automobile'. He served the customer, employees and shareholders, but not by thinking about them: instead, by achieving something of real value.

See also: LOYALTY, MOMENTUM, CORPORATE RESPONSIBILITY and SYSTEMS THINKING.

STALEMATE, STALEMATED MARKET

A market that has ossified, where competitor market shares are stagnant, customers' expectations are rigid, and innovation has ceased. The argument advanced by some writers (e.g. Kenichi OHMAE) is that it is expensive to gain or even hold share in a stalemated market, and that the best strategy may be to HARVEST the business, that is, take cash out by losing market share, and reinvest in a more promising market. The only alternative strategy, so it is argued, is to go in for major INNOVATION to transform the market. Actually, transformation by innovation is generally a good idea, particularly for a market FOLLOWER. But there is little empirical evidence that so-called stalemated markets need be unprofitable for the market leader, especially if other players give up on the market. The concept of stalemate, like that of DECLINING INDUSTRY, is flawed.

STANDARD COST

Budgeted product cost at budgeted volume. See ABC ANALYSIS and ABSORPTION.

STANDARD DEVIATION

A statistical measure of the degree to which observations within a group vary from each other. In a group of numbers, it is the square root of the average of the squared deviations of the numbers from their average. To take a simple example, the standard deviation of 1, 2, 3 is the square root of (1-2) squared, (2-2) squared and (3-2) squared, that is, the square root of (1×1) plus (0×0) plus $(1 \times 1) = 1$.

STAR

The most exciting of the four positions on the BCG MATRIX. A star is a business which is the market leader (has the highest relative market share) in a high growth business (generally over 10% per annum anticipated future volume growth rate in the next 3–5 years). The star business is immensely valuable if it keeps its leadership position, because the market growth will make it much bigger and because it should be very profitable, having higher prices or lower costs than lower market share competitors. The star business may not yet be very cash positive, in fact the usual expectation is that it will be broadly cash neutral, since although it earns a lot of profits it will require reinvestment in new facilities and working capital to continue to grow. But when the market growth slows, if the leadership position has been successfully defended, the business will become a large CASH COW and provide a high proportion of cash for the whole business portfolio.

It is said that there are three policy rules for looking after stars: 'invest, invest and invest'. Almost no investment is too great; whatever the financial projections say, any investment is likely to show an excellent return. The worst possible thing to happen to stars is that they lose their leadership position to someone else's QUESTION-MARK (which then becomes the new star, relegating the erstwhile star to the position of a question-mark and eventually, as growth slows, a DOG). If leadership is lost, the cash previously invested in building up the (former) star may never be recovered, and for all the glamour the business would have proved a CASH TRAP. Hence the necessity to invest to hold the star's leadership position, and if possible further extend it, so that competitors can never catch up. This may require very rapid growth, perhaps up to 40–50% per annum, which requires skilful management and possibly large amounts of cash.

Star businesses are very rare. But star businesses that are well managed and that keep their leadership positions are even rarer. The Model-T Ford was once a star, but then lost its leadership position, became a question-mark and eventually a dog. The Xerox range of photocopiers, Kodak cameras, TI (US) semiconductor chips, Du Pont synthetic fibres, Gestetner office machines, and Hilton hotels are all examples of one-time stars that became dogs, and never yielded the anticipated returns to investors. On the other hand, McDonalds hamburger restaurants, the Sony Walkman, and Coca-Cola are all examples of former stars that held their star status until the market growth slowed, and have since become enormous cash cows and given fantastic returns to shareholders. Filofax is an example of a business that lost its star position in personal organisers (outside the USA), but then recovered it again. It is interesting that in all these cases the stock market fortunes of the companies reflected what BCG said would happen, with a time lag. All of these businesses were highly valued by the stock-market when they were stars, often on PEs of 50 or over. Those businesses that lost share and ended up as dogs were over-valued and never fulfilled the implied promise; those that held on to leadership amply justified the confidence of investors.

The BCG theory really works, especially in relation to stars. What an irony that BCG almost never uses it these days! See BCG MATRIX.

START-UP
A new business, a GREENFIELD INVESTMENT.

START-UP COST
The initial investment required for a new business. See VENTURE CAPITAL.

STATE-OF-THE-ART
Most modern, best practice.

STEADY STATE
The long-term, normal outcome, usually after a period of growth: thus steady state demand is long-term expected annual demand.

STICKY
Slow to respond to new conditions: for example, the price of coffee in the shops may be sticky, not changing much despite a fall in the world price of coffee as a commodity.

STOCK

1. In accounting and production management, raw material, WORK IN PROGRESS and finished goods (ready for sale). Also called STOCKS. 2. American word for shares.

STOCKBROKING

Literally the broking of stock (shares), now applied to any dealing in financial securities. Same as MARKET MAKING.

STOCK CONTROL

Controlling STOCK in order to keep the cost of keeping them low while ensuring that production is not lost through unavailability. See also BUFFER STOCKS.

STOCK DIVIDEND

A dividend paid in extra stock (shares) rather than cash. Increasingly popular option in the UK that can have tax advantages for the firm.

STOCKHOLDER

See SHAREHOLDER.

STOCKHOLDING MODEL

A formula used in production management to minimise stockholding costs. Same as ECONOMIC ORDER QUANTITY model.

STOCKIST

Retailer or wholesaler who carries a particular product line.

STOCK-KEEPING UNIT

See SKU.

STOCKPILING

Building up a high level of stock in anticipation of a shortage or price rise.

STOCKS

See STOCK.

STOCK SPLIT

Same as SCRIP ISSUE: increasing the number of shares held by existing shareholders.

STOCKTAKING

Audit process to check physical stock against records.

STOCKTURN, STOCK-TURNOVER, STOCK-TURNOVER RATIO

Period sales divided by end period STOCK: how fast the stock is turned over.

STOCK VALUATION

Valuing stock, usually by one of two methods: see FIFO and LIFO.

STOP ORDER

Instruction to a stockbroker to buy or sell shares when and if they reach a certain price (the STOP PRICE).

STOP PRICE

The price at which stockbrokers are instructed to buy or sell shares for a client.

STRADDLE

Buying both CALL and PUT OPTIONS, either to reduce risk, or to make a speculative gain in the expectation that the shares will move sharply up or down from their current level. Can work but incurs heavy transactions costs.

STRAIGHT-LINE

At a constant rate over a period. For example, an estimate that a share would see 'straight-line' appreciation over a year from 100p to 200p would imply a mid-year estimate of 150p.

STRAIGHT-LINE DEPRECIATION

Depreciating an asset by the same amount each year.

STRATEGIC ADVANTAGE

See COMPETITIVE ADVANTAGE.

STRATEGIC ALLIANCE

A mutual commitment by two or more independent companies to co-operate together for specific commercial objectives, usually because the cost of development is too high for a single company, and/or because the companies have complementary technologies or competences. A strategic alliance is different from a JOINT VENTURE in that no legal entity is set up, and the scope of co-operation can be both broader and deeper, despite (or perhaps because of) the absence of tight contractual definitions of the partners' obligations. Strategic alliances can take place between competitors in the same business, as with that of Grundig and Philips to join their video and cordless phone businesses, or co-operation between Honda and Rover (but see below); between particular suppliers and their customers (Marks & Spencer has informal strategic alliances with many of its textile and food suppliers, which date from long before strategic alliances were fashionable, and supplier/customer links are hugely important in Japan: see KEIRETSU); or between different firms that are not competitors but can each use a particular technology in their respective markets, as in the case of the alliance between France Telecom and Deutsche Telecom.

Strategic alliances are already important; they will become one of the major global competitive weapons in the 21st century, and could conceivably lead to a new form of corporate organisation then too. But strategic alliances require a long-term orientation and appropriate behaviour, the developing and cementing of trust, and above all the will from the top and middle of the partners to make them work. A recent example where a strategic alliance fell down was between Honda and Rover, where the alliance had been working extremely well and to enormous benefit for both parties. Then, in early 1994, British Aerospace, the owner of Rover, decided that it wanted to sell its majority stake in Rover (Honda held 20%). Honda was not prepared to buy the whole of Rover, so British Aerospace sold its stake to give control to BMW. Honda executives were furious and could not believe that their trust would be violated in this way; the top brass at British Aerospace were surprised at the reaction, and believed that they had served their shareholders well. Two mutually uncomprehending cultures collided. Two things are clear: one, that Honda would never have behaved in a comparable way with a strategic partner; and two, that it will be much more difficult in the future for Japanese companies to trust British firms enough to enter strategic alliances with them. Strategic alliances are a passport to success, but the ability to receive passports may be restricted for British firms.

STRATEGIC BUSINESS UNIT

See SBU.

STRATEGIC CONTROL

One of the three main MANAGEMENT STYLES defined by GOOLD and CAMPBELL (the other two are FINANCIAL CONTROL and STRATEGIC PLANNING). Strategic Control companies are half-way between the other two styles: in the Strategic Control company, the CENTRE realises the importance of a co-ordinated strategy but leaves the initiative in developing plans to the business unit managers. The Centre will then critique the plans, and may agree strategic targets to be met (such as market share gains), and will attach importance to these. The Centre may forgive failure to meet financial budgets if it can be shown that market imperatives required lower short-term profits, but will control and reward business unit managers on the basis of strategic and financial success. Strategic Control companies combine moderate planning influence with tight strategic controls. At the time of their research (the mid to later 1980s), Goold and Campbell gave as examples Courtaulds, ICI, the Imperial Group, Plessey and Vickers.

Goold and Campbell concluded that the style had real advantages, notably portfolio rationalisation, business unit motivation (through increased decentralisation) and enhancement of strategic planning capability at the SBU level, and improved communication between the Centre and divisions, as well as the ability to pursue strategic objectives even at the expense of short-term profit. But they also drew attention to the drawbacks: the difficulty of defining clear strategic control variables; the distance of the Centre from understanding strategic issues; the unwillingness to commit easily to major takeovers, and the lack of clarity between financial and strategic objectives. In 1993, Goold and Campbell revisited the question of whether the Strategic Control style was tenable, in light of the fact that two of their five companies exhibiting the style (Imperial and Plessey) had been taken over in hostile bids, that one of the others (Vickers) was struggling, and that a fourth (ICI) had de-merged under pressure from a bid. They concluded that the style could not cope with too diverse a portfolio of businesses, but was viable where the strategic characteristics of the different businesses were sufficiently homogeneous to allow the Centre to have a good feel for and understanding of each of them.

STRATEGIC DEGREES OF FREEDOM (SDF)

The dimensions along which a strategy can be radically reworked. Kenichi OHMAE insists that the dimensions of product improvement, for example, should not be viewed too narrowly or imitatively. If General Electric has brought out a coffee percolator that makes coffee in ten minutes, its competitors should not aim to bring out one that takes seven minutes. People drink coffee for the taste, but the taste depends most of all on water quality. The strategic degree of freedom here is finding ways to improve the taste via the water quality: and this leads straight to the conclusion that the percolator had to have a de-chlorinating function. See also INNOVATION and SEGMENTATION.

STRATEGIC FIT

The extent to which a firm's strategy fits its capabilities.

STRATEGIC GROUP

A number of companies in an industry pursuing roughly similar strategies.

STRATEGIC HEDGING

Use of an investment bank by industrial firms, for example, oil companies, to hedge against fluctuation in the price of an important commodity or component.

STRATEGIC INTENT

The overall medium- to long term strategic objective of a company. Like a CAUSE, often expressed in a snappy form, like Henry Ford's aim in 1909 to 'democratise the automobile', Coke's objective of having its drink 'within arm's length of every consumer in the world', or Honda's desire to 'smash Yamaha'; but strategic intent usually has a timeframe of at least ten years, whereas a Cause should be attainable within 2–4 years.

STRATEGIC PENTANGLE

The 5Cs: company, customer, competition, currency and country. See
STRATEGIC TRIANGLE.

STRATEGIC PLANNING

One of GOOLD and CAMPBELL's three main MANAGEMENT STYLES, and the
one that gives the CENTRE the greatest role in planning the firm's strategy
and ensuring that it is carried through. Strategic Planning companies have
relatively few core businesses, and seek to establish long term competitive
advantage in each of these by means of co-ordinated, global strategies. The
Centre works with the divisional or SBU managers to develop strategy, and
has a major influence both on business unit strategy and on the overall corporate strategy, which is usually much more than just the addition of the SBU
strategies. The Centre often pays great attention to encouraging synergies
between the divisions and developing and nurturing a common winning culture. Annual financial targets are less important than longer term strategic
objectives. Examples of such companies included (c. 1985–7) BOC, BP,
Cadbury Schweppes, Lex, STC and UB.

Strategic planning companies are able to make bold strategic moves because
of support (and in some cases initiation) from the Centre. The main drawbacks
are that the Centre can lose objectivity, and therefore not exercise proper strategic control; that its success depends on the skill and understanding of the
Centre; and that it can lead to time-consuming planning and demotivation of
divisional staff. See also the other two main styles, STRATEGIC CONTROL and
FINANCIAL CONTROL, and two variants of Strategic Planning (two sub-styles):
STRATEGIC PROGRAMMING and STRATEGIC VENTURING.

STRATEGIC PLANNING UNIT

See SPU.

STRATEGIC PROGRAMMING

One of GOOLD and CAMPBELL's minor MANAGEMENT STYLES, a variant of
STRATEGIC PLANNING that takes it further, with the CENTRE trying to set
clear performance targets and to enforce them. Detailed planning, central
direction of strategy and tight control against both financial targets and
strategic milestones are characteristics of Strategic Programming. In practice
it is very difficult to make this style work: unforeseen events intrude, often
making the strategic targets unsuitable; and the style can degenerate into CEN-
TRALISED MANAGEMENT, which is inefficient, demotivating and unworkable.

STRATEGIC STAKE

Significant shareholding (usually 10–30%) taken in a company by
another firm or ARBITRAGEUR with the intention of changing its policy,
developing a trading relationship, or catalysing a bid. See ARBITRAGEUR
and GREENMAIL.

STRATEGIC TRIANGLE

Kenichi OHMAE's original '3 Cs': company, customer and competition. In 1990 he added two more Cs: currency and country, arguing that major companies needed to neutralise the impact of currency fluctuation and also move deeply into all their major markets to achieve GLOBAL LOCALISATION. Though he did not bother to rename it, his strategic triangle has become a useful STRATEGIC PENTANGLE.

STRATEGIC VENTURING

Another infrequent MANAGEMENT STYLE described by GOOLD and CAMPBELL, also associated with STRATEGIC PLANNING. The CENTRE is a bit like a venture capitalist: very interested in the business, concerned to get the right team in place, leaving the business to get on with it, but having fairly frequent contact and monitoring the attainment of medium term objectives. In addition, higher priority is placed on strategic than on financial goals (which is not true of venture capitalists!). The style may be appropriate for new growth opportunities, where the Centre knows little about the new business, but is not much practised.

STRATEGY

Over-used word, and one that commonly confuses what a company *should* be doing (and sometimes, indeed, what it says it is doing), with what it is *actually* doing: the word strategy can and is applied in both cases. To differentiate, the word is defined below in these two separate senses.

1. in the normative sense, a good strategy is the commercial logic of a business, that defines why a firm can have COMPETITIVE ADVANTAGE and a place in the sun. To be complete, a strategy must include a definition of the domain – the lines of business, types of customer and geographical reach – in which the firm competes. It must also include a definition of the firm's distinctive COMPETENCES and the competitive advantage that gives the firm a special hold on the chosen business domain.

For example, is the firm especially good at low cost production? If so, of what type of product and for what type of customer? Or is the secret a service oriented culture, a special relationship with suppliers or with a particular client base? Is it the ability to command high prices because of a terrific and renewed brand franchise? Or great skill in innovation and commercialising new products?

Defining strategy is particularly difficult in the multibusiness company. A useful distinction can be drawn in this case between the BUSINESS UNIT STRATEGY for each SBU (which must answer the questions above) and the overall CORPORATE STRATEGY, which is concerned with integrating the business unit strategies, ensuring that synergies between the SBUs are fully exploited, allocating resources (cash, technology and management) between the businesses, deciding whether to buy or sell businesses, and developing the culture of the whole firm, and providing the overall sense of direction and momentum. For further discussion of these roles see the CENTRE, PARENTING and PARENTING ADVANTAGE.

A useful checklist for deciding whether you have a complete strategy is to force yourself to answer the questions in Figure 42.

1. Who are your five most important competitiors?

2. Are you more or less profitable than these firms?.

3. Do you generally have higher or lower prices than these firms, for equivalent product/service offering? Is this difference due mainly to the mix of customers, to different costs, or to different requirements for profit?

4. Do you have higher or lower relative costs than your main competitors? Where in the COST STRUCTURE (for example, cost of raw materials, cost of production, cost of selling, cost of distributing, cost of advertising and marketing) are the differences most pronounced?

5. Define the different BUSINESS SEGMENTS which account for 80% of your profits. Be careful to apply the segmentation criteria given in the entry for SEGMENTATION above. You will probably find that you are in many more segments than you thought, and that their profit variability is much greater. If you cannot define the segments that constitute 80% of your total profits, you need to conduct a detailed PRODUCT LINE PROFITABILITY review.

6. In each of the business segments defined above, how large are you relative to the largest of your competitors? Position each of the businesses on the BCG MATRIX and the OPPORTUNITY/VULNERABILITY MATRIX. Are you gaining or losing relative market share? Why?

7. In each of your important business segments what are your customers' and potential customers' most important purchase criteria?

8. How do you and your main competitors in each segment rate on these market purchase criteria? (see COMB ANALYSIS).

9. What are the main strengths of the company as a whole, based on aggregating customers' views of your firm in the segments that comprise most of your profits? What other COMPETENCES do you believe the firm has, and why do they not seem to be appreciated by the market?

10. Which are your priority segments, where it is most important to the firm as a whole that you gain market share? How confident are you that you will achieve this, given that other firms may have targeted the same segments for share gain? What is your competitive advantage in these segments and how sure are you that this advantage is real rather than imagined (if you are not gaining relative market share the advantage is probably illusory)?

Figure 42 – Do you have a good strategy?

Few businesses can answer these questions convincingly. Few have a really well thought through strategy.

2. Strategy also means what a company does, how it actually positions itself commercially and conducts the competitive battle. You can always attempt to describe a competitor's strategy, whether or not you think it is sound. In this sense, a strategy is what a firm does, not what it says it does, or what its strategy documents propound. Which markets is the firm targeting most? Where is it putting its discretionary investment funds? Is it making an attempt to exploit its technology or salesforce or brands in new products or markets? What relationships does it have with suppliers or other collaborators? How much is it investing, where, and why? Is it trying to beat specific competitors, and how is it faring? A company may not think very much, but all companies act, and the commercial actions define the strategy.

STREAM

Business unit or product of one type. Cadbury Schweppes has two streams (of business): confectionery and soft drinks.

STRIKE PRICE

1. The price at which a new security is issued in a TENDER OFFER. 2. The BASIS PRICE (or EXERCISE PRICE) at which an option can be exercised.

STRIP

1. An interest in all elements of a security's financial structure, hence a strip including some risk equity, some MEZZANINE, some SENIOR DEBT, and some SUBORDINATED DEBT, or whatever the relevant entities are. 2. Almost the opposite meaning, when a bond is split into its capital element (the ZERO COUPON BOND) and an interest-only instrument. An American acronym from Separate Trading of Registered Interest and Principal of Securities.

STRIP MALL

US shopping complex arranged alongside a highway in the form of a strip parallel to the road.

STRONG FOLLOWER

Business that is between 70% and 99% the size of the segment leader. See MARKET CHALLENGER.

STRUCTURAL SYNERGY

See SYNERGY.

STRUCTURE

1. Organisation structure: see ORGANISATION CHART. The generally accepted view now (first propounded by Peter DRUCKER) is that 'structure should follow strategy', that is, first determine the strategy, and then ensure

that the structure is fully aligned with it. In practice, structure and strategy may be determined simultaneously, as with Alfred SLOAN and General Motors in the early 1920s: a new marketing strategy based on innovative SEGMENTATION was introduced alongside a new divisional structure to implement the strategy. Tom PETERS takes a third view: that Chandler was 100% wrong. Peters holds that the structure of a firm will determine a firm's strategy, and certainly will prevent it changing radically. Firms like MCKINSEY, Goldman Sachs, CNN or EDS can change because their structures allow 'reinvention'; most industrial firms' structures do not. **2.** Market structure, see PORTER'S FIVE COMPETITIVE FORCES.

STRUCTURED INTERVIEW

Market research using a predetermined questionnaire and pre-coded possible responses. Quick, cheap and often misleading.

STS (Socio-Technical System)

Term invented by Eric TRIST and the TAVISTOCK INSTITUTE to describe companies. See SYSTEMS THINKING.

SUBCONTRACTING

Increasingly becoming a way of life for firms. See NETWORKS and OUTSOURCING.

SUBCONTRACTOR

See CONTRACTOR.

SUBCULTURE

A particular CULTURE in part of a firm, such as a department or a group of close colleagues.

SUBORDINATED DEBT, SUBORDINATED LOANSTOCK

A long-term loan that ranks behind other creditors. In a liquidation, all other creditors must be paid in full before the holders of subordinated debt receive anything. Contrast SENIOR DEBT

SUB-SCALE, SUB-SCALE FIRM

One that is too small in a particular industry or product to enjoy reasonable ECONOMIES OF SCALE. A sub-scale firm will be at a cost disadvantage relative to scale competitors, and will need either to grow its size considerably or to sell the business to a larger industry player.

SUBSIDIARITY

The doctrine of decentralisation and pushing responsibility down to the lowest level possible. Reaffirmed by Pope Pius XI in 1941: 'it is a grave evil . . . for a large and higher organisation to arrogate to itself functions which can be performed efficiently by smaller and lower bodies'.

SUBSIDIARY, SUBSIDIARY UNDERTAKING

Company that is part of a group and owned by a PARENT; a company where the parent owns more than 50% of the voting rights or can exercise effective control.

SUBSTITUTION

A firm should always be aware of potential threats from substitutes. See PORTER'S FIVE COMPETITIVE FORCES: substitution is one of them.

SUCCESSION PLANNING

The very important task of ensuring that there is a nominated or implicit successor for each key manager. One leading US investment bank carries this to an extreme, by having two people for each job. In the USA it is not uncommon to have a HORSE RACE, where two or three candidates are told that they are competing for the top job. Not surprisingly, this often leads the beaten horses to leave, which may or may not benefit the corporation.

SUNK COST

Cost that has already been incurred and should not be taken into account when thinking of whether to continue with a project or product.

SUNRISE INDUSTRY

US term for high growth, emerging industry.

SUNSET INDUSTRY

American expression for DECLINING INDUSTRY (but see that entry for caveats about the usefulness of the term).

SUPER-STAR

Very successful investment, especially in VENTURE CAPITAL or DEVELOPMENT CAPITAL. Generally used for investments that give at least a ten-fold return.

SUPERVISOR

A boss. Usually refers to a foreman or someone in charge of a group of shopfloor workers. Not a fashionable term or concept: many firms prefer 'team leader', or to do away with supervisors altogether.

SUPERVISORY BOARD

Top board of many large companies in Germany, Holland and Scandinavia that exercises general supervision over the firm's affairs and is responsible for appointing and removing members of the EXECUTIVE BOARD. Supervisory boards are generally elected by a combination of shareholders and trade unions. See also *AUFSICHTSRAT* (the German name for a supervisory board) and DIRECTOR.

SUPPLIER

1. A firm that supplies another with raw materials, components, or goods in a semi-finished (or even completed) form. Companies have always had suppliers but their importance has never been as great as today and it is only recently that firms have recognised how important suppliers can be and that there are often critical choices to be made in selecting suppliers and developing relationships with them. Sometimes the way supplier relationships are organised can be completely different in different countries and the basis of competitive advantage. For example, European car makers have looser and less important relationships with their suppliers than their Japanese competitors. Fiat, Renault, Ford, GM and PSA all make many of their own components, and each firm makes between 50 and 65% of the total value of a car in-house. In contrast, Japanese car firms make few of their own components: they make between 34% (Nissan) and 42% (Honda) of the total value of a car themselves. Instead, the Japanese car makers have very close relationships with their suppliers and support them carefully, while concentrating their energies on design, efficient assembly and customer care. See MAKE OR BUY DECISION, OUTSOURCING, CONTRACTORS, COMPETENCES, VALUE CHAIN and OEM. 2. Also used as a synonym for 'manufacturer': someone who supplies a product to a customer.

SUPPLY CHAIN

The relationships between customers, distributors and suppliers.

SUPPLY SIDE

1. Emphasis on what suppliers provide and initiatives they take, rather than on the demand side, what customers require. Many innovations take root not because of articulated consumer demand, but because of persistent faith on the part of the suppliers: the refrigerator and the Sony Walkman are two examples. 2. A school of economics in favour of removing restrictions on business, in order to free up the supply side.

SURRENDER VALUE

What is given for cashing in a fixed-term investment (especially a life insurance policy) early; usually a rip-off.

SUSTAINABLE GROWTH RATE (SGR)

Concept invented by BCG in the early 1970s to measure and demonstrate the effects of leverage and the proportion of earnings retained on the rate at which a company could grow. The point was that a firm could be constrained from growing (in the absence of new equity) if it had too little debt or retained too low a proportion of its earnings (that is, if dividends were too high a proportion of earnings). Since BCG believed (correctly) that the successful firm should aim to grow market share in its major markets, it tended to use the SGR to urge firms to become high debt, low dividend corporations, channelling as much money as possible back into investment. For the algebraicly inclined, the SGR formula is:

$$SGR \quad = \quad D/E\,(R - i)p + Rp$$

where:

D/E	=	Debt/Equity
R	=	return on assets, after tax
i	=	interest rate, after tax
p	=	percent of earnings retained.

The SGR is more an interesting curiosity than a useful management tool, except where firms are competing pretty much head to head in a single segment business. The flaw in the thinking is that very few firms are that: there are usually a very large number of businesses and funds for one can come from one or more other businesses, or from the sale of one or more businesses. It is rarely the case that financial policy constrains growth.

SUSTAINABLE PROFITS
The level of profits or profitability that can be reached and sustained indefinitely in STEADY STATE. For example, most engineering businesses cannot return more than 15% return on sales on a sustainable basis, and very few businesses can earn over 20% return on sales sustainably. If these levels are exceeded, it may be a warning that necessary expense investment is being neglected in the interests of short-term profits.

SWAP
1. To BARTER. 2. An exchange of debt. Some swaps are highly-complex pieces of FINANCIAL ENGINEERING that only the most sophisticated players should contemplate.

SWEATING ASSETS
Making assets work hard, using capital productively, raising ROCE by such means as adding a third shift or obtaining third-party business to put through one's own facility and raise capacity utilisation.

SWEETHEART UNION
A trade union effectively under the control of management or sympathetic to management. Also called a COMPANY UNION.

SWING
1. Variation from previous position: for example, if a business went from losses of $5m to profits of $2m, that would be a swing of $7m. 2. Shareholding or supplier that holds the balance of power: for example, if a firm is owned by

three parties in the proportions 49%, 49% and 2%, the latter is the swing shareholder; or in a cartel, the swing producer is the one who is most able to influence the overall production level (in this case, usually the largest producer or the one with most political clout).

SWITCHBOARD, THE CORPORATION AS SWITCHBOARD

Metaphor used by Rosabeth Moss KANTER to describe when a small CENTRE helps to direct other parts of a diversified organisation in order to realise synergies.

SWOT ANALYSIS

An overview of a company's prospects, generally undertaken in a loose and qualitative way by collecting management opinions about the company's Strengths, Weaknesses, Opportunities and Threats. The first two should always be thought about relative to competition. Opportunities should include developing closer relationships with customers and suppliers, STRATEGIC ALLIANCES with other firms (including competitors), increased use of OUTSOURCING, and ways to upgrade the firm's core COMPETENCES, as well as specific market and product initiatives. Threats should include not only new competitor initiatives, but also possible threats from the bargaining power of customers and suppliers, the threat of substitution from new technologies (or the application of existing technologies to the firm's market for the first time), the threat of potential new entrants, and requirements to protect the environment. SWOT analysis is rarely conducted rigorously and extensively: if it is, it should include consideration of competitive costs (RCP) and prices (RPP) and market share (RMS) trends, as well as a review of PRODUCT LINE and SEGMENT PROFITABILITY. SWOT analysis can be useful even if it is not rigorous: it has the advantages of being participative and holistic. See also OPPORTUNITY/VULNERABILITY MATRIX, RCP, RPP, ANSOFF MATRIX, MAKE OR BUY DECISION and OUTSOURCING.

SYMBIOSIS

Term from biology describing constructive relationship between two or more organisms. Used in management to describe such relationships between firms and their customers, or firms and other partners in a NETWORK.

SYNCHRONISATION

Process of running operations in parallel as much as possible, rather than in sequence (one after the other). Often a key to getting product to customers quickly, which in turn is a key influence on profitability. See TIME TO MARKET and SYNCHRONISING MANAGEMENT.

SYNCHRONISING MANAGEMENT

Management that does many things at once, sees time as elastic, welcomes interruptions of the real world, and thinks in terms of cycles, renewable products and developing long-term relationships. Contrast SEQUENTIAL MANAGEMENT.

SYNDICATED LOAN

A large loan, usually in the EUROMARKET, shared among several banks.

SYNDICATED RESEARCH

Multi-client market research.

SYNERGY

2 + 2 = 5 (or more), rather than 4, or 3 (negative synergy). Usually used in the context of an acquisition: if there is no synergy expected, it is difficult to justify paying a premium for an acquisition; and even if it is a merger with no premium, why bother unless there is some synergy? There is often a great deal of cynicism about the reality of claimed synergies, and the word is certainly overused, but it is a key concept.

There are really two different types of synergy: STRUCTURAL SYNERGY, where the synergy derives from combining resources to lower costs or raise revenues; and MANAGEMENT SYNERGY, where the improvement is due to better management, without structural change. Some people only use synergy in the structural sense. Examples are when two sales forces can be combined, saving costs; or when one company's products can be sold through the other's distribution network, both raising revenues and lowering the unit cost of sales. Structural synergy is clearly greatest where two firms are engaged in the same or adjacent products and markets, but where they have different in-going configurations. It is not unusual to see cost reductions of the order of 15–25% or revenue gains of 20–30% as a result of acquisitions pregnant with such structural synergy.

MANAGEMENT SYNERGY exists when an acquiror runs a company better than the previous management, as when a new financial control system is put in to raise returns (as with BTR, Hanson, Tomkins or Williams Holdings), when managers are given greater responsibility and compulsion to meet budgets, when unnecessary costs are cut (without structural synergy), or when non-core businesses are sold to someone else who will pay more than their value to the seller. Management synergy can produce large cost reductions, though more rarely significant revenue increases.

Synergy can also exist independent of acquisitions: for example in JOINT VENTURES, in STRATEGIC ALLIANCES, in closer relationships with SUPPLIERS, from realising synergies within an existing group of companies, by getting managers to help each other. Such synergies could be called 'cheap synergies' because they do not involve paying an acquisition premium: they should be looked at before acquisitions. Synergy is any unrealised potential open to a group from mixing and matching resources better.

SYSTEM

Any combination of people and economic resources in a specific setting. Firms are systems, living organisms, not machines.

SYSTEM 4

A democratic management style advocated by Rensis LIKERT. He also invented Systems 1, 2 and 3 and imagined a System 5. See LIKERT.

SYSTEMATIC RISK

See CAPITAL ASSETS PRICING MODEL.

SYSTEMS, SYSTEMS ANALYSIS

Department/activity within an organisation dealing with computer systems. See also IT and MIS.

SYSTEMS THINKING

The creative branch of OPERATIONS RESEARCH: a school of thought especially associated with Igor ANSOFF and Eric TRIST that stressed the firm as an STS, (Socio-Technical System), especially in the late 1960s and 1970s. A business should be regarded as a system, which may or may not be in equilibrium. The term 'socio-technical system' is not used much now, but is at the root of such creative thinkers as MINTZBERG, OHMAE, HANDY and Rosabeth Moss KANTER.

T

TA
See TRANSACTIONAL ANALYSIS.

TACHISTOSCOPE
Projection technique used to register the extent to which different versions of an advertisement register with samples of consumers, prior to selecting the final advertisement to be run.

TAGUCHI METHODOLOGY
A useful quality technique developed by the eponymous Japanese engineer, which stresses product design and practical engineering. See QUALITY.

TAKE-HOME PAY
Pay after tax and insurance deductions.

TAKE-OUT
To remove a competitor, to force him out of a particular business or into bankruptcy.

TAKEOVER
Acquisition.

TAKEOVER BID
Attempt at takeover. See also AGREED BID and HOSTILE BID.

TAKEOVER DEFENCE
A management's attempt, invariably with expensive professional advisers such as merchant bankers, PR people and consultants, to defend a firm against a so-called HOSTILE BID. Many specific tactics may be adopted, especially in the USA (see CROWN JEWELS, PAC-MAN DEFENCE, POISON PILL, SCORCHED EARTH DEFENCE, and SHARK REPELLENT), but in general defence must follow one or two tactics, depending on what is being offered by the bidder:

- If the bidder is offering mainly or exclusively his own paper (i.e. shares in his company in exchange for existing shares), the main issues are (a) how well his company is run relative to yours, and (b) are his shares overvalued? Thus in a famous defence against Hanson, the Imperial Group tried to prove that the quality of Hanson's earnings were low, that Hanson's earnings per share only went up because of acquisitions and short-term profit maximisation, and that future acquisitions could not continue this trend, because the size of the required future acquisitions advanced exponentially. This elegant and well-researched defence ultimately failed to save the old Imperial management (though it did give shareholders a lot more money than the original bid), but it probably did damage Hanson's rating in the market for a few years thereafter.

- If the bidder is offering 100% cash (or a cash alternative), the defence must either focus on the firm's prospects, so that the key thing is a large profit forecast for next year and preparing good arguments why medium-term earnings growth is better than appreciated; or if this line of argument will not wash, incumbent management must find a WHITE KNIGHT who will pay more than the original bidder. The latter tactic is usually more effective, but also more dangerous for the management, because the white knight may turn out to have a distinctly off-white, grey or even black undercoat once the bid has been completed. See GREY KNIGHT. See also DEFENCE AGAINST TAKEOVER

TAKER

The buyer of an OPTION.

TAKING PRIVATE

Expression generally used in preference to 'privatisation' (which generally means something almost opposite) to mean the process of taking a publicly quoted company off the stock exchange and making it a private company (again). This is done by one large investor (often the manager) offering to buy everyone else's shares at a certain price. This manoeuvre is very common in the USA but rather rare in the UK, as fewer individuals are in a position to buy out their public shareholders and the investing institutions are generally suspicious that they will be given less than the company is worth. Richard Branson successfully took Virgin private, however, arguing that the stock market could not value the company correctly, while Alan Sugar was rebuffed in his attempts to take Amstrad private.

TALENT BANK

In an industry heavily dependent on individual talent (such as pop music or films), someone (like an agent) who controls or can make available the best performers has a 'talent bank'. Some day soon headhunters will start calling themselves 'talent bankers' or 'talent brokers'.

TALENT PACKAGER

An agent, venture capitalist or other entrepreneur who puts together a whole deal on an ad hoc basis and sells it to a conventional company for execution. For example, a Hollywood independent producer may come to a studio with a total deal, comprising script and screen-play, stars, director and financing.

In high tech or knowledge industries the talent packager may be more important than the studio ostensibly supplying the service.

TALL ORGANISATION

One with many levels: opposite of FLAT ORGANISATION. Tall organisations in the West are usually bureaucratic and inefficient; in Japan there are many examples of successful tall organisations.

TANGIBLE FIXED ASSET

Property, plant or equipment that can be pointed to and touched.

TARGET

Usually means company that is the target of a bid, whether or not this has yet been announced.

TARGET MARKET

See SEGMENTS, SEGMENTATION.

TARGET-PROFIT PRICING

The same as COST-BASED PRICING.

TASK CULTURE

The culture found in one of Charles HANDY's four GODS OF MANAGEMENT: a task culture follows the god ATHENA. The culture is meritocratic, authority is based on expertise and professionalism, with problem-solving TASK-FORCES that cut across functions and organisational barriers. The culture is popular with able people and is commonly found in consulting, advertising and investment banking, and in some KNOWLEDGE INDUSTRIES like pharmaceutical and high-tech business. For most other firms, a task culture may be an expensive way of operating, though pressure from the best employees will increasingly require any business where the quality of people is key to move towards this culture.

TASK FORCE, TASKFORCE

A short-term team put together to solve a particular problem. The team is usually drawn from different parts of an organisation, cutting across functional and national lines of command, and sometimes involves an outside catalyst as well. Very useful mechanism that works well in Anglo-Saxon cultures. Often found inside ATHENA organisations that have a TASK CULTURE, but can be adopted by any type of firm as a short-term expedient. Taskforces are disbanded once their task has been accomplished.

TAVISTOCK INSTITUTE

Much of the best early work on the sociology of industry was conducted by the Tavistock Institute of Human Relations in London in the years between

1945 and 1970. See HUMAN RELATIONS SCHOOL, Elliott JACQUES, Eric TRIST and SYSTEMS THINKING.

TAXABLE INCOME
The income on which a tax authority decides to base its calculation of corporate tax liability.

TAX AVOIDANCE
Legitimate actions to lower tax paid: good tax planning.

TAX CREDIT
Document received along with dividends that states the amount of tax already deducted from the dividend.

TAX EVASION
Illegal actions taken to attempt to pay less tax than is legally required.

TAX HAVEN
A country with very low or zero rates of personal and corporate income tax and capital gains tax. Examples include Andorra, some cantons of Switzerland, Monaco, the Cayman Islands, Bermuda, Liechtenstein, Hong Kong, Singapore, and (to a lesser degree) the Channel Islands and the Isle of Man. The best tax havens are warm, sunny and large enough to be interesting.

TAX HOLIDAY
Period during which a firm pays no tax.

TAX LOSS
A loss which it is hoped will be of use in offsetting future profits.

TAX POINT
A taxable entity that must report on a particular sort of tax, for example, VAT.

TAX SHELTER
US originated term, now commonly used to describe legislation or device enabling income or capital gains taxes to be avoided. Examples of tax shelters include pensions, PEPS (personal equity plans), charitable donations, accelerated depreciation and investment in government-approved start-up businesses.

TAYLOR, FREDERICK WINSLOW (1856–1915)
American Quaker who invented SCIENTIFIC MANAGEMENT in 1911. The father of industrial engineering and best-practice manufacturing, based on division of labour, specialisation, time targets and stopwatches, financial incentives (including piece rates) and penalties for the workforce, the blending of workers' and managerial initiatives to raise production levels and

quality, and functional management. Now a hate figure for all progressive management integrators, who correctly point out the flaws in excessive role specialisation and atomistic, analytical thinking, and quite incorrectly allege that Taylor ignored or trampled down the human element. Taylor was ahead of his time, and always a progressive in contemporary society, and is rarely given his due. See SCIENTIFIC MANAGEMENT for a fuller discussion.

TAYLORISM
TAYLOR's school of thought or SCIENTIFIC MANAGEMENT.

TEAM BUILDING
The practice of encouraging individuals to work productively in teams and of making particular groups of workers effective as a team. Good team building requires differentiation of roles within a team and a good fit of each individual to the particular role (see BELBIN), as well as good communication within the team. See also ADAIR, JAQUES, MAYO, REVANS and TEAMWORK.

TEAM CAREER, CAREER TEAM
See TEAMWORK.

TEAM PLAYER
An executive who is concerned about the effectiveness and welfare of the team as a whole, rather than just his or her individual interests.

TEAMWORK
Magical concept more talked about than practised: when individuals complement each other and demonstrate team SYNERGY. Nearly all successful firms demonstrate a high degree of teamwork; nearly all unsuccessful ones do not, at least in their upper reaches. Increasingly, the team rather than the individual should be the basic unit that is accountable for achieving objectives. Some pioneering firms are experimenting with the idea of CAREER TEAMS, groups of individuals who move through an organisation together and have a collective career. This substantially reduces learning costs and helps liberate talent and build commitment in a way that conventional organisations simply cannot do. See also BELBIN.

TEAM WORKER
One of BELBIN's eight team roles: the person whose main contribution is keeping individual team members happy and ensuring that the team works effectively, rather than in contributing ideas, solutions or administration.

TEAR-DOWN ANALYSIS
Graphic Japanese phrase for what used to be called REVERSE ENGINEERING. Companies such as Isuzu, Nissan or Honda systematically take apart com-

petitors' products, analysing the materials used, the way they have been moulded, the process used to assemble the product, and therefore the likely cost. The aim is to take any ideas that are lower cost and ensure that your firm is both lower cost and higher quality than the competitors.

TECHNICAL ANALYSIS

The study of share and commodity prices in order to discern trends and likely future market direction: see CHARTISM. Technical analysis contrasts with FUNDAMENTAL ANALYSIS, which is the study of the companies or the economics of the commodities rather than the study of their prices.

TECHNICAL RALLY

When a stock market or other financial market recovers following a sharp fall, but the rally is due to technical factors and not as a result of better news or a basic change in sentiment; when the rally is called technical it means that dealers expect the fall to resume soon.

TECHNOLOGICAL OBSOLESCENCE

When technological advance renders the previous (and often very recent) technology obsolete, because it is higher cost or lower performance than the new generation of technology. Can inhibit investment and tends to favour large over small firms, and particularly STRATEGIC ALLIANCES between firms to share the costs of developing and implementing new technologies. A particular problem in robotics, which the Japanese government has circumvented by leasing robots to small and medium firms and allowing them to trade-in the last version of robots for the new version at no extra cost.

TECHNOLOGY

The application of scientific knowledge to economic activity. Firms are often divided into LOW-TECH (firms where technology is stable and predictable, like quarrying or bricks), MID-TECH (e.g. most engineering businesses) and HIGH-TECH (industries like computers or BIOTECHNOLOGY where the ground rules are constantly shifting as a result of INNOVATION). High-tech businesses are often glamorous and highly rated, but often also risky and disappointing in terms of their commercial results. See BIOTECHNOLOGY, INNOVATION and INVENTION.

TECHNOLOGY TRANSFER

Sharing knowledge of new technologies, whether across parts of the same firm, with a strategic partner, or more broadly in society. The speed of technology transfer differs widely and can be more important than INVENTION. Some countries, like Japan, are particularly well set up for technology transfer because of their industrial structures. See KEIRETSU and STRATEGIC ALLIANCE.

TELECOMMUTING, TELECOMMUTER
Commuting by phone, fax and computer rather than 'real' commuting. A modern form of HOMEWORKING and one that has grown (millions of Americans are already telecommuters) and will spread at a faster rate in the future.

TELECONFERENCING
Using telephone and vision link-ups so that a board or other group can 'meet' in two or more places at the same time and all be able to see and hear each other. As technology improves (so that set-up is quicker and body-language can be clearly seen) and its cost falls, will be used much more extensively than today. Now it is the exception; perhaps in a generation's time the personal visit to Tokyo, Rome or Los Angeles for a single board meeting will be the curiosity. Teleconferencing is also being used to hold global brainstorming sessions, pulling in people who are not formal members of an organisation to participate in these sessions.

TELEGRAPHIC TRANSFER
See TT.

TELEPHONE SELLING
Old-fashioned and little used name for TELESALES.

TELEMARKETING
Same as TELESALES.

TELEPROCESSING
Processing data where transactions are input via remote data terminals and processed by a central computer.

TELEPUTING
Using the telephone and computer to conduct business from home rather than commuting. See TELECOMMUTING and COMMUNICOPIA.

TELESALES
Increasingly important practice of selling via the telephone rather than face to face, or using telesales staff to 'pre-qualify' prospects, that is, provide sales people with high quality leads. Telesales is a cheap and efficient way of selling any but the most expensive or personal items.

TELEWORKER
Same as HOMEWORKER or TELECOMMUTER: executive or self-employed person who works from home making full use of telephone, fax and computer links to colleagues or business partners.

TELLER
Bank clerk.

TEMP

Originally a temporary secretary; now applied to any temporary worker, a growing breed. See TEMPORARY WORK.

TEMPORARY WORK

Employment on a fixed-term contract or short-term swing employment. Increasingly important: Charles HANDY says that the FLEXIBLE LABOUR FORCE (temporary and part-time workers) will become one of the three main components of the workforce for most firms. See SHAMROCK ORGANISATION.

TENDER

1. Invitation to pitch for work alongside other suppliers, or the pitch itself. **2.** To offer a payment. **3.** To offer to buy shares at a fixed price: a TENDER OFFER.

TENDER OFFER

US term where a company offers to buy the shares of another at a fixed price, usually above the previously prevailing price.

TEN-K, 10K

Important US document which every quoted US company has to file with the SEC, and which is publicly available, containing a wealth of detailed data about the company. Any attempt at studying a US firm should start with the 10K.

TERM

Duration of a loan or other debt instrument.

TERM LOAN

A bank loan with regular interest payments required, repayable within a fixed period (typically 3–10 years).

TERMINAL

1. A computer keyboard and screen (VDU). **2.** A depot for storage.

TERMINAL BONUS

A bonus on a life insurance policy at the end of its life.

TERTIARY BRAND

An obscure manufacturer's brand sold on price, with the intention of taking spot market share away from both top brands, SECONDARY BRANDS, and retailers' OWN LABEL. Tertiary brands sell at up to 40% below the top brand prices, and are often opportunistic and short-term phenomena, cashing in on a glut in particular foodstuffs and/or excess manufacturing capacity. They are becoming increasingly important, both because some top brands have become too greedy in their price premia (see MARLBORO FRIDAY) and because value for money has become more important for consumers.

TEST MARKETING

Testing a new consumer product in one area. Very expensive and usually fails to meet expectations. Test marketing should only be undertaken once initial market research has proved positive and the product concept has been well thought through and tested via consumer panels or FOCUS GROUPS. New computer technology makes it possible to play around with the physical attributes of products and produce life-like pictures of these, so that they can be tested on small groups of consumers and lessons learnt long before a real test market is attempted.

T-GROUP

Invented by Kurt LEWIN: an early form of ENCOUNTER GROUP for encouraging colleagues to expose their true feelings about each other, in order to provide SENSITIVITY TRAINING for individuals and encourage better TEAMWORK. Can be dangerous stuff and not much used now.

THEORY W

Humorous but seriously-barbed management theory invented in 1974 to provide an alternative to THEORY X and THEORY Y. Theory W (for Whiplash) is even more primitive than Theory X, preferring the stick to the carrot. Theory W is probably the one under which most people in history have lived, and even today it is unfortunately still widely practised, although mainly in goals, prison camps and the many gulags around the world that linger and even flourish under repressive regimes.

THEORY X

Doug MCGREGOR's management construct, used to characterise the prevailing management ethos when he wrote (c. 1960). 'Theory X managers believe that people are inherently lazy and need to be energised and supervised through a combination of carrot and stick'. McGregor thought this incorrect, and advocated instead THEORY Y management.

THEORY Y

MCGREGOR's preferred management style: predicated on the belief that workers are inherently motivated, and that the manager's job is to encourage, channel and orchestrate that natural energy for the good of the firm and the individual alike.

THEORY Z

When MCGREGOR died in 1964 he was working on Theory Z, the ultimate synthesis between the good of the firm and the striving of the individual for self-realisation. The term was later used as the title of a book by William Ouchi, which focused on what the West could learn from Japan about TEAM-WORK, training and generating employee commitment. The Theory Z organisation has these Japanese characteristics: lifetime employment, concern for employees including their social life, informal control, decisions made by consensus, slow promotion, excellent transmittal of information from top to bottom and bottom to top with the help of middle management, commitment to the firm and high concern for QUALITY. See also JAPANISATION.

THERBLIGS

Coding system used (or rather, not much used) in WORK STUDY.

THIN MARKET

When there is not much LIQUIDITY in a market (especially a stock market), and when small purchases or sales may make a big difference to the price. Beware of shares that characteristically have a thin market.

THREATS

Usually part of the phrase 'threats and opportunities'. The trendier (and slightly more accurate) word more commonly used now is 'VULNERABILITIES'. See OPPORTUNITY/VULNERABILITY MATRIX.

THRIFTS, THRIFT INSTITUTIONS

US financial institutions encouraging saving, including MUTUAL SAVINGS BANKS, and S&Ls (Savings & Loans).

THROUGHPUT TIME

The total time to process a customer's order, or to get a product from the drawing board to the customer. See TIME-BASED COMPETITION.

THURSTONE'S COMPARATIVE JUDGMENT TECHNIQUE

Measurement device in market research where interviewees are asked their reaction to a statement, usually on a five-point scale running something like: agree strongly, agree, neither agree nor disagree, disagree, disagree strongly. Useful.

TICK

1. Credit. 2. The smallest price fluctuation possible in a market.

TIED INDICATOR

In sales forecasting, using one product as a LEADING INDICATOR for sales of another.

TIGHT MONEY

When it is difficult to borrow and interest rates are temporarily high.

TIME AND MOTION, TIME AND MOTION STUDY

The old name for the stop-watch element in SCIENTIFIC MANAGEMENT.
Now a part of WORK STUDY.

TIME-BASED COMPETITION

Concept invented by BCG which holds that the time it takes a firm to get a
product from conception to the customer, or to complete its tasks and provide goods or services to market can be the key to COMPETITIVE ADVANTAGE.
Time is a crucial factor in the internal and external chain of customers and
suppliers. At each internal or external customer/supplier interface there is not
just a risk, but a near certainty, that time will be wasted. And time really is
money, as well as being service to boot. The total time taken through the
chain – THROUGHPUT TIME – determines not only the firm's costs, but is also
a litmus test of the firm's responsiveness to customers. Concentration of time
to market therefore kills two birds with one concept: service and cost. If quality is free, reducing the time to market has negative costs as well as customer
benefits. Notwithstanding its importance, time-based competition is basically
a package of earlier discoveries, and it in turn has been repackaged as just a
part of BPR (Business Process Re-engineering).

It has long been realised that most of the time taken to make a product or
provide a service is generally not 'productive' time but the gaps between different stages of the process. An example is given in the entry on BPR of IBM
Credit, which at one time took seven days to process a credit application for
a would-be computer buyer: but the actual work involved took only 90 minutes. By cutting out the gaps and giving responsibility to one person, costs
can be cut, customer satisfaction and retention increased, and profits dramatically increased. Another example, this time quoted in the 'bible' of
time-based competition (*Competing Against Time: How Time-Based
Competition is Reshaping Global Markets*, by George Stalk, Jr., and Thomas
M Hout), is the 'H-Y War' in the early 1980s between Honda and Yamaha.
This revolved around the speed with which new motorcycles could be produced. Honda won the war by producing first 60 new motorcycle models in
a year, and then another 113 new models in 18 months, speed that Yamaha
could not match.

Most organisations, even well run ones like Yamaha, soak up time like a
sponge. Stalk and Hout invented the '0.05 to 5 rule', which says that most
products are receiving value for between one-half of one per cent and five
per cent of the time that they are in the value delivery system of the firm. In
other words, over 95% of the time products spend in their companies is
wasted; eliminate the wasted time, and time to market can be increased
between 20 and 200 times!

The time to market a product can be calculated and compared to that of
several competitors; the idea behind time-based competition is to become

the shortest time-to-market competitor. It is worth stopping to think through the implications for your own business.

TIME DEPOSIT

US name for a DEPOSIT ACCOUNT.

TIME ELASTICITY OF PROFITABILITY

BCG's term for the relationship between a supplier's profit and the speed with which the product is supplied (the elapsed time between the customer's decision to buy and his receipt of the product or service). Short elapsed time equals high profit; long elapsed time equals low profit. This is because the customer will pay top whack if he can obtain the product at once, but if he has to wait he will shop around and may lower the price he will pay. Customers made to wait may also cancel their orders.

The firm's value-delivery system therefore needs to be changed to speed up TIME TO MARKET. Any extra costs will be more than compensated for by higher prices and greater market share.

TIME OFF IN LIEU

Overtime rewarded not by money but by an extra holiday.

TIME MANAGEMENT

The movement started in Denmark and now much used in the West to record, monitor and improve how executives use time.

TIME MANAGER

A personal organiser used by managers who are devotees of TIME MANAGEMENT, eager to fill Kipling's 'unforgiving minute'.

TIME OUT

Metaphor from American sport which is used in meetings to propel the discussion from one topic to another, to calm conflict, or to propose a break. The person calling time out usually holds up his hands in the form of a T.

TIME SCALE

Time required to complete a project.

TIME-SERIES

Data showing comparisons over time. Much more useful than a SNAPSHOT at one point in time. If data are worth collecting, they are worth collecting over time.

TIME TO MARKET

The time taken to get a new product introduced into the market, from conception to launch; or the time taken to process and deliver a customer order. See TIME-BASED COMPETITION.

TIMES COVERED

Refers to DIVIDEND COVER or INTEREST COVER: the number of times that earnings are greater ('cover') than dividends or interest.

TIME SHARING

1. Joint use of a computer facility. **2.** Joint ownership and use of a holiday home, where ownership rights are confined to certain weeks of the year.

TIME SHEET

Document used in professional and service firms selling time, recording each employee's time and expenses by client.

TIME-SPAN OF DISCRETION

Theory invented and propagated by Elliott JACQUES in the early 1960s, that the importance of a job (and even its pay) could be measured by how long it is before its work is checked. Bizarre theory that became intellectually respectable for a time, but probably Jacques' least important or useful contribution to management theory, though Jacques himself believed it was his major breakthrough and that its universal application could replace COLLECTIVE BARGAINING and industrial strife.

TOBIN'S Q

The ratio of a quoted company's MARKET VALUE to the book value of its assets. See SERVICE-COMPETENCY VALUES.

TODAY'S MONEY

Adjusting an amount paid or invested in previous years to account for the intervening inflation, so that a fair comparison can be made 'in today's money', or in real terms. If an asset or company was bought for £10m five years ago, and inflation has averaged 5% over the period, and we have just sold it for £15m, did we make much of a profit in real terms? The answer is that £10m five years ago is (in this case) equal to a little over £12.75m in today's money, so the real profit we made is not £5m but just under £2.25m. This represents a real compounded average annual return (excluding inflation) of under 3.3%: nothing to get excited about!

TOFFLER, ALVIN

Popular and provocative futurologist whose three main books, *Future Shock, The Third Wave*, and *Power Shift*, are all worth reading or re-reading. The most prophetic and interesting is *The Third Wave*, published in 1980 and since broadly vindicated by events. In it Toffler argues that industrialisation (the Second Wave) split apart consumer and producer, which had been integrated on the land under the First Wave. *The Third Wave* includes the arrival of the 'super-industrial society' but is much more, making obsolete the nation-state, specialisation, mass production, the concept of employment, the power of political parties, traditional family values and most other assumptions of Second Wave thinking. Not all Toffler trends are soundly based but one that is is the PROSUMER, Toffler's neologism for proactive consumers who participate in the product design process: one example Toffler gives is the prosumer who sits at a computer work station at a car dealer's and makes choices fed to him on car design and features by a CAD/CAM software programme.

Toffler noted the impact of technology and information on industrial society, the rise of homeworking, the decline of the big organisation, the secular rise in unemployment, and the need for new political and social mechanisms more appropriate to the new age: all themes taken up and made more specific by Charles HANDY. The book also coined the phrase 'small-within-big is beautiful'.

TOLERANCE

The precise measurement by which an engineered product may differ from the original specification without being rejected.

TOMBSTONE

Advertisement in the FT or similar publication boasting of the completion of a financing, acquisition, divestiture, flotation or syndicated loan, listing all the arrangers, providers of finance and advisers.

TOPLESS FEDERALISM

See FEDERALISM.

TOP MANAGEMENT

Vague expression meant to encompass all very senior executives, usually comprising all executive members of a firm's top board and any particularly influential executives not thus included. 'Top management' is useful for pandering to status or obfuscation; but a more useful concept is 'those who run a company': that is, those executives (and occasionally non-executives) who have veto power over any important decision in the firm, whether or not the decision falls within 'their' area. By this definition, those who matter in most firms (sometimes also called an INNER CABINET) comprise a much smaller number than 'top management': except in the very largest firms, the number is usually within the 1–5 range. Working out how many and who runs the company tells you more about its processes than looking at an organisation chart or studying the composition of the Board.

TOP SLICING

1. Taking a profit on part of a shareholding. 2. Way of assessing tax on a life assurance policy.

TORT
Law protecting people's property or person.

TOTAL ASSETS
Gross assets of a firm, including all fixed and current assets, before deducting liabilities.

TOTAL DELIVERY SYSTEM
See DELIVERY SYSTEM.

TOTAL QUALITY MANAGEMENT
See TQM.

TOUCH
Brokers' term for the maximum spread in a financial market: the gap between the highest bid price and the lowest offer price.

TOWNSEND, ROBERT
Head of Avis who enjoyed remarkable success with his send-up of bureaucratic big business: 'Up The Organisation'. Townsend was an advocate of what is now called ADHOCRACY, though his very American obsession with the rights of the individual now seems a bit dated: commitment to a firm and its objectives can be a liberating and constructive choice.

TQM (Total Quality Management)
Technique for building quality into products by training all employees in quality and motivating them to 'do it right first time'. Contrasts with and clearly superior to earlier attempts at QUALITY CONTROL, that set up a separate department to monitor work after the fact. TQM is both a set of techniques, including QUALITY CIRCLES, and an overall philosophy of management. As such it has been generally successful: and that cannot be said of too many major management 'movements'. In the end, though, the Anglo-Saxon need for a cut-and-dried programme such as TQM can be self-defeating. What is needed is total obsession with QUALITY, and not a programme to 'take care' of it. To have this obsession requires being able to see the big picture of customers' needs and the total business system, and TQM is too much a technique and too narrowly based to be able to supply this.

TRACKER FUND
Same as INDEX FUND: one that tracks the stockmarket index. See INSTITUTIONS.

TRACKING
Monitoring, following and measuring.

TRADE ASSOCIATION
Body which firms in an industry belong to in order to share information and to lobby government and regulators.

TRADE BUYER

Someone who is in the same business as a firm up for sale. The relative attractions of a trade buyer versus, for example, a public FLOTATION, are often a subject of great interest to venture capitalists and management who are seeking an EXIT for an MBO. If the stock market is strong and PEs (price earnings ratios) are high, it may be more profitable to float than to sell, unless particular trade buyers have strong SYNERGIES with the business for sale and could therefore realise major savings or increase sales easily.

TRADE CREDIT

Normal system whereby purchasers of goods are allowed 30 days (or often 60 or 90 days in practice) before they have to pay.

TRADE CREDITORS

Same as ACCOUNTS PAYABLE: the amount a firm owes to people who have supplied goods or services.

TRADE CYCLE

See BUSINESS CYCLE.

TRADE DEBTORS

Same as ACCOUNTS RECEIVABLE: the amount a firm is owed for goods and services delivered.

TRADED OPTION

A financial instrument whereby an investor can obtain an option to buy or sell another share at a certain future price, and can trade the option (sell it on to another buyer or seller) rather than have to exercise it himself. Traded options exist in the UK and USA and in a few other countries in the largest companies.

TRADE FAIR

Exhibition of products in a particular industry. Useful for making and renewing social contact in a relaxed and agenda-free setting. Some trade fairs (like the Frankfurt book fair or the Cannes Film Festival) are focal points for the whole industry, with a fixed place on everyone's calendar.

TRADE-IN

To return old goods and receive a credit against part of the cost of a new version of the same product.

TRADE INVESTMENT

Purchase of shares in one company by another in the same industry, made for strategic reasons related to its trade, rather than purely for financial gain.

TRADE MARK

Pictorial representation of a product or firm, registered to prevent another supplier using the same or similar symbols.

TRADE-OFF

To make a choice, 'trading off' the advantages and disadvantages of alternative courses of action. For example, a decision to go to the supermarket rather than the corner shop trades off convenience against price.

TRADE PRICE

Price charged to wholesalers or retailers (who will then sell at a higher price to their customers); by extension, price for a large quantity entitling someone who is not really a trade customer to purchase at the trade rate.

TRADE SHOW

See TRADE FAIR.

TRADE UNION, TRADES UNION

Organisation of employees to negotiate with employers. Strictly speaking, a trade union is confined to a single industry (like the NUM in the UK: the National Union of Mineworkers), whereas a trades union comprises employees in different industries. In practice both kinds are usually called trade unions.

TRADE WAR

Imposition of reciprocal trade barriers like high tariffs, quotas or import bans by two or more countries.

TRADING ACCOUNT

1. The top of a P&L showing sales revenue, cost of sales and gross profit. **2.** Term used by stockbrokers to mean the period during which credit is extended on sale or purchase of stock, to be paid on SETTLEMENT DAY, a few days after the end of the account.

TRADING PERIOD

The period between two sets of accounts (e.g. a month or a year).

TRADING PROFIT

The same as PBIT (Profit Before Interest & Tax) or EBIT; the profit from trading before taking account of interest paid or received and before paying tax. Usually the best guide to the underlying performance of a business.

TRADING STAMP

Very little seen today but a generation ago Green Shield trading stamps were all the rage, with many retail outlets supplying little green stamps which were then stuck into books and could be redeemed for goods chosen from a catalogue. Intended to encourage customer loyalty, but by the time many competing suppliers offered trading stamps the advantage accrued to the trading stamp company (and just possibly to the consumer) but not to the retailer giving the stamps. Now such loyalty schemes tend to be from single supplier or non-competing groups of suppliers, like Air Miles.

TRADING VOLUME

The daily total of shares bought and sold on the stock market for individual shares and the market as a whole. Volume can be as important as the direction of the market in helping to divine future trends.

TRAINING

One very important key to national and firm success. See MANAGEMENT DEVELOPMENT.

TRANCHE

A slice of a financial transaction, giving part of a deal but exposure to all its elements.

TRANSACTION

Anything a firm does that affects its financial position and balance sheet.

TRANSACTIONAL ANALYSIS (TA)

The 'I'm OK, You're OK' school of thought, developed in the 1960s by Eric Berne, an American psychologist, which holds that people can only work together (as two people or a group) if each member of the group accepts and appreciates the other members. If I accept that you are basically 'OK' (i.e. I value and respect you as a human being and am on your side), and you reciprocate, we can criticise each other for specific actions without arousing unhelpful defence mechanisms or anger. If any member of the group is held to be 'not OK', the team will not work at all, or only by excluding that individual from anything important. TA also looks at characteristic interactions between people in organisations, pointing out that we all tend to use (at different times) 'parent', 'child' or 'adult' type patterns of speech and thought. TA contains a few extremely useful insights, but the need to generate books about TA means (as with much else on management) that what could be written down in fewer than a thousand words stretches to several hundred thousand.

TRANSACTIONAL LEADERSHIP

Style concerned more with immediate events and tactics than with long-term direction or MISSION.

TRANSACTION COSTS

Costs associated with the act of buying or selling (shares, a house, any asset), that may make it uneconomic to buy and sell very often.

TRANSDUCERS
Method of inputting data into computers via device that converts signals into electromagnetic impulses.

TRANSFER DEED
Document recording change of ownership of shares.

TRANSFER PAYMENT
Redistribution of wealth by the state from one person or group to another. Usually creates more wasteful bureaucracy than is warranted by the net value of the transfer.

TRANSFER PRICE
Price charged by one part of a firm to another. See ARMS-LENGTH PRICING.

TRANSFORMATION
Changing an organisation's culture and behaviour, so that it ascends to a new level of financial and market performance. Not surprisingly, transformation is difficult: 75% of all attempts fail. There do seem, however, to be six conditions of successful transformation, which are always present in successful transformations:

1. They are driven by demanding and inspiring leaders, and one person embodies the transformation ethic.
2. The top team (those who really run the company: see TOP MANAGEMENT) are emotionally united; they are on the same side and want to help each other personally, as well as the firm.
3. There is a slogan used as a rallying cry: either a medium-term CAUSE or a longer-term statement of STRATEGIC INTENT.
4. BARONIES are absent or destroyed.
5. The change process focuses on real business issues, changing attitudes on the back of commercial success. There are simple performance measures so that everyone knows what is expected.
6. The firm has or builds at least one world class COMPETENCE: a skill where it is as good as or better than any competitor.

TRANSFORMATIONAL LEADERSHIP
Leadership style oriented to making long term changes in a firm, providing VISION and inspiration to employees. Contrast TRANSACTIONAL LEADERSHIP.

TRANSLATION EXPOSURE
Same as EXCHANGE RATE EXPOSURE: a firm's risk if exchange rates change.

TRANSLATION PROFIT OR LOSS

Same as EXCHANGE PROFIT OR LOSS: the profit or loss caused as a result of a shift in the exchange rate between the currency where a firm is domiciled and one or more other currencies. Usually firms only report the mechanistic financial profit or loss; behind this, and usually not costed, is the difference that exchange rates make to a firm's factor costs in foreign countries.

TRANSNATIONAL CORPORATION

Term used by Fons TROMPENAARS and others to describe an ideal for the international corporation: polycentric, flattish in structure, drawing on a multiplicity of expertise centres, with each country within the corporation specialising in what it does best, but linked together in an unbeatable product or service. See also LOCAL GLOBALISATION and MULTILOCALS.

TRANSPARENCY

Extent to which dealings in a financial market can be freely observed to ensure open competition.

TRANSPORTATION MODEL

A LINEAR PROGRAMME showing how to minimise transport costs.

TRANSPORTATION TABLEAU

Technique in transportation planning: a matrix with one row for each factory and one for each warehouse or depot.

TREASURY

Accounting department in a firm or bank that handles short term cash and borrowing.

TREND

Something that is becoming more prevalent, the way that things are going. Looking at trends, particularly those that are coming up fast in the 'rear-view mirror', is an excellent and much under-used way of gaining insight into the future. Trends are sometimes reversed, of course, but much less often than they are reinforced and extended.

TREND ANALYSIS

Formal analysis of TRENDS, particularly those related to a firm's performance over time, using mathematical and/or graphical analysis. Useful.

TREND FITTING

Making a projection of future demand (or another variable) based on an extrapolation of past data.

TRENDY

Curiously, a pejorative word, describing a fad or fashion expected to be short-lived.

TRIAD

The group of three most powerful economic blocs: North America (now including Mexico); Europe; and Japan/Asia. See Kenichi OHMAE, whose books *Triad Power: the Coming Shape of Global Competition* (1985) and *The Borderless World* (1990) argue that major corporations need to have a centre of gravity in each of the triad and should be perceived as being equidistant from any important competitor. The first business school to absorb the lesson of triad power and make it work will have a huge competitive advantage.

TRIAL BALANCE

A very detailed balance sheet: a list of all the NOMINAL ACCOUNTS a firm has, showing the balance in each.

TRIPLE I ORGANISATION

Charles HANDY's formula (expressed in *The Age of Unreason*, 1988) for organisational effectiveness: I-cubed, where I = Intelligence × Information × Ideas. In the Triple I Organisation, everyone (including even the machines) is paid to do and to think.

TRIPLE WITCHING HOUR

Colourful US expression for trading session when three US markets expire simultaneously: the stock index futures, options on these, and options in individual stocks. Can cause volatility as computer programs feed on one another and sometimes go haywire.

TRIST, ERIC

British systems thinker who was one of the leading lights of the TAVISTOCK INSTITUTE in London in the 1960s before working at The Wharton School in Philadelphia. Invented the concept of the SOCIO-TECHNICAL SYSTEM, which began to edge management thinking away from mechanistic models and asserted the importance of the social element and effective TEAMWORK. Trist derived the idea of the Socio-Technical System from his pioneering work in Britain's coal industry (described in his 1963 book, *Organisational Choice*). He showed that the co-operation required between the three main groups of workers – those performing cutting, filling and conveyor moving – was hampered by their being organised as three discrete units. When the interdependent nature of the tasks was realised, they were reorganised into one total work group, leading to greater co-operation and higher productivity. Trist's general point was that, as in the UK coal industry, traditional management tended to optimise purely technical factors, without looking at the social system. Influential among fellow academics, his mild manner concealed a creative intelligence and deeply felt humanism. Under-rated.

TROMPENAARS, FONS

Dutch expert on international cultural differences between managers. Co-author with Charles HAMPDEN-TURNER of the excellent *Seven Cultures of Capitalism*, and author of *Riding the Waves of Culture* (1993) that covers some of the same ground but focuses particularly on how the TRANSNATIONAL CORPORATION should maximise effective co-operation between operations in different countries and between these and the CENTRE. Trompenaars insists that cultural diversity must be recognised and that the transnational corporation is 'polycentric' rather than a hub and spoke from the Centre. The transnational corporation must synthesise the advantages of all the national cultures and facilitate communication, but leave local operations free to reward their people in the way most effective for their culture. An important message from an increasingly prominent guru.

See GLOBAL LOCALISATION, MULTILOCALS, SYNCHRONISING MANAGEMENT, CULTURE, FLAT ORGANISATION and COMPETITIVE ADVANTAGE.

TROUBLESHOOTER

Term made popular in the UK by Sir John Harvey-Jones' TV series of the same name; means a consultant able to swoop into an organisation and quickly recommend major changes. Sometimes also used (incorrectly) to mean an INTERIM MANAGER or COMPANY DOCTOR.

TROUGH

Low point in a cycle, the bottom of a market.

TRUE AND FAIR VIEW

Important boilerplate phrase in an auditor's opinion giving the accounts the thumbs up. Usually 'unqualified' by any reservation; if these exist, it is a QUALIFIED OPINION which is very bad news.

TRUNKING

Delivering goods by road over a long distance, for subsequent local distribution from a depot.

TRUST

1. A way of organising assets, often for ESTATE PLANNING and/or TAX AVOIDANCE purposes, so that the assets are looked after ('held in trust') by professional TRUSTEES on behalf of the owners or beneficiaries. 2. US word for INVESTMENT HOLDING COMPANY. 3. Confidence, the glue essential for TEAMWORK or successful commercial relations. Trust is rare and precious; to be earned, it must be absolute. You cannot be half trusting or half trusted, any more than you can be half pregnant. Creating trust where none currently exists requires radical change and total sincerity. 4. (Rare) a UNIT TRUST.

TRUSTEE
Lawyer, accountant or other professional who manages a TRUST (1).

TRUSTEESHIP
Share workers own a firm via an employee trust, which owns the company on their behalf, or where the worker-owners delegate management to an elected council (as the UK's John Lewis Partnership).

TT (Telegraphic Transfer)
Inter-bank transfer of funds by cable.

TUNNEL VISION
A narrow and blinkered approach to an issue.

TURNAROUND
A company that has recovered from severe crisis and losses to sustainable profits, or one that is in the process of 'being turned around'. There are four important points to remember re turnarounds:

1. They are difficult. Warren Buffett, the legendary US investor, has commented that 'when a new management team, with a reputation for brilliance, is brought into a firm with a reputation of trouble, it is usually the reputation of the firm that remains intact'. Investors should steer clear of turnarounds, unless they are very rich, very brave and know something everyone else doesn't, until the time that the turnaround can be seen to be working. For whatever reason, many firms become BAD BUSINESSES, ones that are beyond redemption, where they have suffered from under-investment, HARVESTING of market share, long-suffering of their customers (so that only the most idle or least demanding customers remain), loss of the most qualified and ambitious employees, low quality, high-cost position, poor service, poor brand image, a losing culture and a large burden of debt and charges from bankers and other vultures. Beyond a certain point (which is difficult to call), the firm goes into a downward spiral, and nothing short of a miracle can call it back.
2. It is almost impossible to conduct a successful turnaround without replacing top management. Otherwise there is no hope of the CULTURE and ways of working changing in a sufficiently decisive way.
3. Turnarounds fail because (or when) the company runs out of cash. Cash management on a daily basis must become your number one obsession.
4. Anyone attempting a turnaround must ask one fundamental question: Is the base business salvageable with the investment I can afford to make? In making this judgement, you should look at relative market share (RMS) and the trend, whether it would be possible to reverse the trend, the relative cost position (RCP) against competitors, at what customers think of the firm's products relative to competition (COMB ANALYSIS), and at whether

your stronger competitors are trying to drive you out of the business or are pursuing policies (like holding up a PRICE UMBRELLA of high prices) that are helping you stay afloat. You should look at whether there is a particular NICHE or small SEGMENT you could aim to dominate profitably, within the total market. You should be realistic: either you can come up with a better CUSTOMER PROPOSITION than competition for a particular segment (or segments), or a lower cost position, or you are sunk.

You must decide either that the base business (with necessary re-segmentation) is salvageable, or that it is not. If you decide yes, focus everyone's efforts on what needs to be done there (and set yourself objectives for the next three months. If you do not achieve the objectives, you should decide in three months that you were wrong, and give up on the base business).

If the base business is wrecked beyond repair, there may still be hope. You now need to look at everything that the business has outside or around the base business, which with a radical change of tack might offer you salvation. Does the firm have assets that could be sold (even if they are essential for the base business) to realise some cash? Could you sell the base business itself to a competitor who could turn it around more easily than you and/or realise SYNERGIES? Do you have access to tolerant shareholders or bankers who would give you more cash for a good purpose? Do any of your smaller businesses, which are already profitable, offer you the prospect of expansion if all available funds were channelled there? There are many examples of firms that turned around by adopting extreme volte-face policies. Gestetner abandoned production of photocopiers in the early 1980s and used its distribution network to sell Japanese machines. Firestone decided at about the same time to get out of tyre production (which constituted 80% of sales) and focus exclusively on service and retail segments. Both firms survived and prospered as a result of giving up on the base business.

TURNAROUND SITUATION

A troubled company that has not yet been turned around, but one where someone else wants you to believe it will. See TURNAROUND and the notes of caution therein.

TURNAROUND TIME

Nothing to do with TURNAROUNDS in the sense above. Turnaround time is the time to get something completed, from arrival in the in-tray to delivery to customer, or the time taken to undertake one specific task (such as the time it takes a typist to complete a report).

TURNKEY PROJECT

A major public works or construction project where a single firm is responsible for co-ordinating all suppliers and activities. See PROJECT FINANCE.

TURNOVER

1. Annual sales revenue. **2.** Annual rate at which labour, stocks or anything else 'turns over': see LABOUR TURNOVER and STOCK TURN respectively. **3.** The total value of stock exchange transactions.

TWELVE MONTH MOVING AVERAGE

A very useful measure of the trend in sales, profits or any other important variable. See MOVING AVERAGE and Z-CHART.

TWILIGHT SHIFT

From late afternoon to mid or late night, often involving part-time workers (perhaps a four-hour shift).

TYCOON

Rather old-fashioned slang for a rich industrialist.

TYPE 1, TYPE ONE EXECUTIVE

A very useful typology of people into three types (1, 2 and 3), invented by Harold Leavitt. Type ones are Visionaries: bold, charismatic, original, often eccentric, brilliant and uncompromising, someone who offers a clean break with the past and a new heaven and earth. Historical examples include Jesus Christ, Churchill, Garibaldi, Ghandi, Gladstone, Hitler, John F Kennedy, the Ayatollah Khomeni, Martin Luther King, and Margaret Thatcher. Type ones have insights and inspire followers, they follow their instincts, led by heart more than head, and they can see the destination so clearly that they are often impractical about the obstacles en route. They can be extremely impractical and bad at getting things done. Understanding whether you (or close colleagues) are type 1, 2 or 3 can be of practical value, for two reasons. First, you should aim to move your job in the direction where the skills of your particular type can be deployed most fully and effectively. Second, you should aim to team up with and rely on close colleagues who exemplify the two types different from your own, to provide a balanced ticket and the skills you lack. See also TYPE 2 and TYPE 3.

TYPE 2, TYPE TWO EXECUTIVE

See TYPE 1. Type 2 executives are Analysts. They deal with numbers and facts, not opinions; they are rationalists, calculators and controllers. They deal in black and white, not grey: there is always a right answer. The analyst par excellence uses numbers and accounting to control a vast empire: to run a FINANCIAL CONTROL company. Examples include Clement Atlee and Sir Owen Green, Robert Macnamara, [Lord] Arnold Weinstock, Harold Geneen, and from further back in history, Pitt the Younger, Sir Robert Peel and Jimmy Carter. Type twos are great systematisers and control system users. See also TYPE 3.

TYPE 3, TYPE THREE EXECUTIVE

See TYPE 1 and TYPE 2. Type threes are Doers, successful men of action, implementers, fixers, pragmatists. Generally unencumbered by either vision or analysis, the type 3 leader revels in arm-twisting, lining people up to do his will, leading troops into battle, and all the hurly-burly of business. Historical type threes include Noah, Attila the Hun, Alexander the Great, Julius Caesar, Louis XIV, Napoleon, Bismarck, Lloyd George, Lenin, Stalin, Eisenhower, James Callaghan and Lyndon Johnson. Type threes need a programme or vision from a type 1 and the calculation of a type 2 as supplements to increase their own effectiveness.

U

ULTRA VIRES
Literally, 'beyond the powers of': when an individual or firm does something unauthorised.

UMBRELLA
1. 'Under the umbrella of XYZ corporation' means under its auspices, where something that may not formally belong to a firm is conducted by it or regarded as part of it. **2.** An UMBRELLA ORGANISATION is a large one that incorporates several smaller ones, like the United Nations. **3.** Sometimes shorthand for a PRICE UMBRELLA, that is, where the largest competitor prices highly for short-term profits and thus holds out an umbrella protecting smaller and higher cost competitors, who can still make a profit because of the high prices maintained by the leader.

UMBRELLA FUND
A fund of funds.

UMBRELLA ORGANISATION
See UMBRELLA (**2**).

UNBUNDLING
1. When a firm (especially after a takeover) decides to sell off non-core businesses and focus on just one or two core businesses. Sometimes less politely called ASSET STRIPPING. **2.** Process of SEGMENTATION whereby customers are offered the chance to buy individual parts or modules of a product, rather than having to buy everything together. For example, investors used to buy a bundled service from stockbrokers, comprising advice and execution; now, execution-only services exist for those who do not need advice. Every supplier should ask whether there is an opportunity or threat from unbundling. See BUSINESS SEGMENT and SEGMENTATION.

UNCALLED CAPITAL
Same as UNISSUED CAPITAL.

UNCONDITIONAL
Usually refers to a takeover bid; when it goes unconditional it means that it has been accepted by the requisite majority (often 90%) of shareholders, and that its original conditions no longer obtain. In practice it means that

minority shareholders are pressured into accepting the offer, because the takeover can now be regarded as a fait accompli. A case where the practice describes pretty much the opposite of the commonplace use of the word.

UNCONVENTIONAL COMPETITION

When one industry player (usually a new entrant) refuses to play by the established RULES OF THE GAME and sets up his own rules. IKEA is an excellent example in the furniture industry; so too was Apple in computers. Unconventional competitors are to be feared. Why not try to be unconventional yourself? See MAVERICK and, for the IKEA example, DELIVERY SYSTEM.

UNCOVERED DIVIDEND

One where what is paid to shareholders is provided wholly or partly from reserves and not from current earnings. A danger signal.

UNDERCAPITALISED

Where a firm has insufficient capital. May need to be RECAPITALISED by the injection of new funds.

UNDERCUT

Offer cheaper.

UNDEREMPLOYMENT

Where employees are insufficiently stretched; a form of disguised unemployment often evident in the public sector.

UNDERLEASE

Lease from a tenant to another tenant, not the head (original) lease.

UNDERLYING OPERATION

The basic business of a company, its operations, regardless of the funding structure. The underlying operations of a debt-ridden company may be profitable, whereas the company may not be able to meet its interest obligations.

UNDERMANNING

The rare case where a firm has too few employees.

UNDER-SUBSCRIPTION

When a new issue of shares is not fully sold and the unsold shares are left with the UNDERWRITERS. Likely to depress the share price for some time. Contrast OVER-SUBSCRIPTION.

UNDERWEIGHT

Expression used by fund managers to indicate that they have less invested in a particular sector, country or other category of firm than they would normally have. Indicates caution about the prospects for share prices in the sector. Contrast OVERWEIGIIT.

UNDERWRITING

When an investment bank or other financial institution guarantees a financing transaction by offering to buy shares that are not sold to others, or where an insurance company provides cover and assumes risks.

UNDIFFERENTIATED MARKETING

Targeting the whole market and ignoring MARKET SEGMENTS. In some ways this is the idea, on a global scale, of the UNIVERSAL PRODUCT. On the other hand, most broad market suppliers still break the market up into different segments, with a product for each category (for example, Ford or General Motors in cars).

UNDISTRIBUTED PROFIT, UNDISTRIBUTED EARNINGS

Earnings retained in a business and not distributed to shareholders in dividends.

UNEARNED INCOME

Income from investments rather than from employment.

UNFAIR COMPETITION

Usually a bleat about DUMPING or PREDATORY PRICING: selling below cost, in order to help force a competitor out of business. In practice it usually means that the bleater has over-estimated the competitor's true costs, and is complaining about competition per se.

UNFAIR DISMISSAL

Unjustified firing for which compensation must be paid.

UNFUNDED PENSION

One where a reserve fund does not exist, or does not fully exist, to cover payment; where today's pensions are paid out of today's contributions from those in work.

UNFAIR DISMISSAL

Concept invented by labour law in the UK and elsewhere. The law sets up certain procedures that must be complied with before firing employees; if the procedures are not met, the dismissal is deemed unfair and compensation must be paid.

UNGEARED

Without debt. Ungeared companies are usually doing their shareholders no favours: the return on equity could be higher and the competitive strategy more aggressive if the firm took on some debt.

UNILATERAL

One-sided; a unilateral capacity reduction is when one supplier closes a facility without negotiating the same from his competitors.

UNIQUE SELLING POINT, UNIQUE SELLING PROPOSITION

See USP.

UNISSUED CAPITAL

Share capital that is authorised but has not yet been sold or allocated.

UNITARY TAXATION

Tax assessed on a multi-national enterprise for overseas operations by the tax authorities of the country where it is domiciled. Can lead to DOUBLE TAXATION; unfair and discourages inward investment.

UNIT COST

The cost of producing one unit of a good or service; the average cost per unit.

UNITISATION

Changing an investment trust into a unit trust.

UNIT LABOUR COST

The cost of labour per unit of output.

UNIT-LINKED POLICY

Life-assurance policy linked to performance of a share portfolio.

UNIT PRICING

Showing the price per unit for a multi-unit package in a supermarket.

UNIT TRUST

UK financial institution: a fund that invests in shares and other instruments and quotes a price to buy or sell 'units' from/to individuals. A stockbroker is not required to buy and sell units, but the SPREAD between bid and offer prices is usually quite high (currently around 6.4%), which makes it uneconomic for short-term investment. INVESTMENT TRUSTS will normally provide the same sort of service but with lower transaction costs, though a stockbroker is required.

UNITY

The number one.

UNITY OF COMMAND

One employee, one boss.

UNIVERSAL PRODUCT

One that is sold in the same form throughout the world, like the original Model-T Ford, or Coca-Cola, the Mars bar or the Big Mac, or indeed, the Macintosh computer. In many ways this is the American dream: a standard product, made up of defined and highly controlled parts (thus the servant of analysis), high quality and low cost, capable of being rolled out around the world for ever. The two keys are the widest possible product appeal, based on the insight that people around the world may be different, but consumers are the same; and standardised manufacture, so that the product can be produced cheaply and to the same standards anywhere around the world. In a way the whole concept of business strategy *à la* BCG or PORTER is a vision of a Universal Product, battling against the cultural peculiarities of different nations. Note that the idea of a Universal Product could never have originated in France or Germany, and these countries have a poor record in producing Universal Products. See GLOBAL BRAND and UNIVERSALISM.

UNIVERSALISM

The school of management thinking that treats all cultures as if they were or will become the same; that believes that people and their needs are basically the same everywhere; that believes in universal management prescriptions and styles; that believes that the world will be made in the image of the home country (usually the USA). Universalism is easy to deride, but its simplifying optimism has supplied great energy and notched up some notable successes, thus proving that ignorance is more potent than knowledge. For example, companies like Ford and Mars treated Europe as one market from the 1920s and 1930s, when more sophisticated marketeers would have realised that there was no such thing as Europe. But on the whole the naïve universalists of Detroit and Langley have proved their point: their reach may exceed the grasp, but gives it a good head start. See also GLOBALISATION and LOCAL GLOBALISATION.

UNLEVERAGED

1. Without debt: same as UNGEARED. **2.** An executive is unleveraged if he or she does not have subordinates or lower cost colleagues who can take on the less demanding parts of the executive's job.

UNLIMITED LIABILITY

Partnerships and a few other entities have unlimited liability, that is, liability is not limited to what is in the business; creditors can ask for the partners' houses if they are not paid.

UNLISTED SHARES, UNLISTED SECURITIES

Shares that are quoted but not on the official or main market. See USM.

UNLISTED SECURITIES MARKET
See USM.

UNQUOTED SHARES, UNQUOTED SECURITIES
Shares in a private company, not listed on any stock exchange.

UNRELIEVED ACT
A quirk of British taxation of dividends: Advance Corporation Tax (ACT) that cannot be offset against mainstream corporation tax. Can happen when a British company draws most of its profits from overseas, and therefore does not have enough UK corporation tax liability to set against the ACT. Will normally result in an above-average total tax liability.

UNSECURED CREDITOR
Someone who is owed money or goods but does not have any security in the event of default.

UNSECURED DEBENTURES
See UNSECURED LOANSTOCK.

UNSECURED LOAN
Money borrowed without having to offer any security. The banker in this case is an UNSECURED CREDITOR.

UNSTRUCTURED INTERVIEW
Technique used in market research where customers are asked open-ended questions and the questioning follows the areas of most interest to the customer, rather than following a structured list of questions.

UNSOCIAL HOURS
Shift or night work.

UNSYSTEMATIC RISK
Refers to investors' risk in buying shares: the risk that belongs to an individual company or share, and that can be diversified away by holding a PORTFOLIO of shares. See CAPITAL ASSET PRICING MODEL.

UPFRONT
In advance.

UPGRADE
To improve, particularly in respect of computers, where it means to replace a machine with a more powerful model.

UPLEGATION

The opposite of DELEGATION; the bizarre tendency of many responsibilities to move up an organisation, when individuals do not exercise initiative, but instead rely on the boss to see that things happen. Often the consequence of a boss not trusting subordinates and double-checking on what they do, so that the subordinate knows that he or she can rely on the boss to do it. Causes major management bottlenecks because the boss is more busy than the subordinates, whereas the reverse should be true.

UPMARKET, UP MARKET

The more expensive, higher quality or feature part of any market. The generic strategy of 'moving up market' has been tried by many suppliers, to capture a greater share of the value added; but if the customer proposition and service and brand image do not fit, this can be an expensive mistake. Contrast DOWNMARKET.

UPSIDE

1. The best reasonable expectation from a project or business. **2.** Monetary quantification of that expectation. Contrast DOWNSIDE.

UPSTREAM

Near the start of the VALUE CHAIN, that is, nearer to raw materials than to the consumer. Contrast DOWNSTREAM.

UPSTREAM INTEGRATION

VERTICAL INTEGRATION backwards, that is, buying a supplier.

USEFUL ECONOMIC LIFE

The period over which a product is depreciated. Usually selected on accounting rather than technical grounds. If a firm wants to bolster its balance sheet, it will make the useful economic life as long as possible; if it wants to reduce tax liability, as short as possible.

USER FRIENDLY

Cute phrase originally used to mean a computer that could be easily used, especially by an ordinary user; now extended to mean anything that makes life easy for the customer, and further extended to describe people's behaviour. Someone who is 'not user friendly' is too technical or awkward.

USER INTERFACE

The way of producing two-way communication between a computer and its user.

USM

The UK junior stock market, confusingly called the Unlisted Securities Market. Soon to be abolished, although it is unclear what will replace it.

USP (Unique Selling Point, Unique Selling Proposition)

The CUSTOMER PROPOSITION – what the customer is being offered – that differentiates one firm's product or service from a competitor's. Many commodity products do not have a USP. Unless a product has a USP, or is lower cost and lower price than competing products, its market share and profitability will be vulnerable.

UNSYSTEMATIC RISK

See CAPITAL ASSET PRICING MODEL.

UTILISATION

The extent to which an individual or firm is operating at full capacity.

UTILITY, CUSTOMER UTILITY

The value to a customer of a product or service.

U-TURN

Volte-face, reversal of policy.

V

VA

See VALUE ANALYSIS.

VALUATION METHODS

Valuation of companies falls into two types: market-based approaches, which are used by the stock market; and intrinsic value methods, that are used to evaluate acquisitions (although some acquisitions are evaluated by ARBITRAGEURS according to the BREAK-UP VALUE, which is a market-based method). The market-based method relies upon placing a multiple on the firm's earnings: see PE RATIO. The intrinsic methods are based either on NET ASSETS, or more normally on a DCF (Discounted Cash Flow) model. There are flaws in all these approaches, but a consistent methodology at least allows a sensible ranking of different options. In considering acquisitions, the most important point to consider is the extent of the SYNERGY.

VALUE ADDED

What a firm adds in value; the firm's turnover minus the cost of bought-in raw materials and services. The concept of value-added is becoming a little less useful, because sometimes a lot of the value accrues from good relationships with suppliers, and this falls outside the technical definition of value added. See OUTSOURCING.

VALUE ADDED CHAIN

See VALUE CHAIN.

VALUE ADDED NETWORK (VAN)

Distributed data-processing system that adds in something extra of value like E-MAIL (Electronic Mail) or data interchange services.

VALUE ADDED RATIO

Value added per employee: i.e. VALUE ADDED, divided by number of employees.

VALUE ADDED STATEMENT

Statement which shows where the value added of a firm goes: usually depicted in a pie chart, showing the amount going to employees, to government, to bankers, to shareholders, and retention in the business.

VALUE ADDED TAX
See VAT.

VALUE ANALYSIS (VA)
Analysis of whether costs (especially of bought in materials and components) are reasonable relative to the product price, and whether they can be
reduced by VALUE ENGINEERING.

VALUE CHAIN
A firm's co-ordinated set of activities to satisfy customer needs, starting with
relationships with suppliers and procurement, going through production,
selling and marketing, and delivery to the customer. Each stage of the value
chain is linked with the next stage, and looks forward to the customer's
needs, and backwards from the customer too. Each link in the value chain
must seek COMPETITIVE ADVANTAGE: it must either be lower cost than the
corresponding link in competing firms, or add more value by superior quality or differentiated features. The basic idea behind the value chain has been
around ever since the concept of value-added and COST STRUCTURES, but
was first made explicit by Michael PORTER in 1980.

VALUE ENGINEERING (VE)
Analysis of purchased raw materials and components to determine whether
their quality and reliability are right for a particular product design and
function and whether the cost could be reduced, either by taking a different
type of component, or by buying from another supplier.

VALUE FOR MONEY
See VFM.

VALUE GAP
The difference between the value a potential seller places on a company and
the value placed on it by a potential buyer. Very often a matter of shadow-
boxing: the stated values may not be the 'real' reserve values of each side.

VALUE GRAPH
Two-by-two matrix which compares the cost to supply an item with customer perceptions of its value.

VALUES
The set of cultural norms, ways of behaving, beliefs, objectives, relationships,
methods of control, view of the outside world, style, character and business
philosophy shared by those in a firm; what the executives believe in at the
deepest level and what conditions their behaviour. Firms in the same industry often have radically different values. It is useful to break values down
into six separate categories:

1. Objectives. Firms may or may not exhibit the following values: results orientation, devotion to quality, profit driven, sales driven, service focus, growth driven, technology driven, fighting for good causes.
2. Relationships. Possible values include being: co-operative, carries passengers, us and them, political, sink or swim, club culture, fair, formal, sexist, protect employees, egalitarian, warm, driven by peer respect, promises kept, unforgiving, competitive.
3. Organisation and control, including: visible top management, meritocratic, small is beautiful, bureaucratic, professional ethos, hierarchical, management by culture not rules, anything goes, lean, chaotic, avoid conflict, financially controlled.
4. Social values, including: integrity, support suppliers, open, crusading, cuts corners, respectable, strong local roots, a national institution, drives hard bargains, internationalist.
5. Style and character, including: thrifty, hard-working, alienated, problem-solving, we're winners, we're survivors, beat competitors, exuberant, high energy, inventive, exploitative, rational, entrepreneurial, time is money, dependable, chameleon-like, global, American, Dutch, iconoclastic, improvising, disciplined, mediocre, young, well organised, maverick, creative, persevering, high standards, realistic, smart dress standards, homogeneous, conservative.
6. Business philosophy, including: stick to knitting, diversify, acquisitive, short-termist, avoid debt, pay well, opportunistic, be astute traders, use muscle through market dominance, innovate, copy innovators, create synergy, use strategic alliances, win because best products, slave drivers, get timing right, bring quality to mass market.

Senior managers considering values should first diagnose the values currently prevalent in the firm, and then consider what values they would like the firm to manifest in the future. Evolution based on commercial success – proving that the new values work in practice, changing belief by changing behaviour – is the way to change values: by action, not words. Values cannot be changed radically except by a new top management team at a time of crisis, but gradual adjustment of values can take place at any time, provided there is genuine top management commitment to the new values. See also MISSION and BEHAVIOUR STANDARDS.

VANILLA
Standard product without bells or whistles. Same as PLAIN-VANILLA.

VARIABLE
Something that is not fixed, that can be changed.

VARIABLE COST

An expense that changes even with small changes in volume, for example, raw material costs.

VARIABLE RATE

American for FLOATING RATE interest.

VARIANCE

The difference between budget and actual.

VARIANCE ANALYSIS

Breaking down the reasons for VARIANCES so that corrective action may be taken.

VARIANT PROCESS PLANNING

A form of COMPUTER-AIDED PROCESS PLANNING (CAPP) in which process plans are stored in digital form to allow modifications to be made easily.

VARIATION

The extent to which products or processes are non-standard or special. W E DEMING claimed that high quality and low cost was mainly due to 'reducing variation'. See AVERAGE COSTING, SPECIALS and COSTS OF COMPLEXITY.

VARIETY

How wide or narrow a product range is. See COSTS OF COMPLEXITY.

VARIETY REDUCTION

Analysing a product or component range in order to reduce the number of products, parts, materials or processes. A key to both cost reduction and QUALITY improvement.

VAT

British tax on each stage in the value-added chain; a bureaucrat's dream. Insidious and expensive to collect.

VCR

Videocassette recorder.

VDU (Visual Display Unit)

Computer screen.

VE

See VALUE ENGINEERING.

VENDOR PLACING

When an acquisition is funded effectively by placing shares with selected institutions. Called a vendor placing, because the vendor of the company being acquired is given shares, and these shares are then mainly or totally placed on behalf of the vendor with institutions. In practice the acquiror arranges the whole deal through its brokers. Vendor placings may take place at a small discount to the prevailing market price and are a good way for institutions to acquire cheap shares. See also BOUGHT DEAL.

VENTURE CAPITAL (VC)

Provision of finance to new or small companies in the form of risk (equity) capital, in return for a high proportion of the shares. Venture capital is technically the highest risk part of this activity, financing start-ups; helping small firms grow and financing MBOs (Management Buy Outs) is technically DEVELOPMENT CAPITAL. This distinction is not always made, however, and 'venture capital' is used to describe both activities. (In fact, the great majority of VC funds go to development capital). Venture capital firms raise funds from large investors and then make investments (typically in the £1–50m range, though sometimes much larger) in firms which they believe have growth potential. The venture capitalists tend to react to DEAL FLOW from managers seeking funds, and will evaluate whether they can obtain (with the help of GEARING) a return on their equity of 35–40% per annum compounded. Venture capitalists place great stress on the personal qualities of the managers concerned, and usually ensure that the managers have a strong financial interest (both incentive and penalty) in the success of the business. The venture capital firm will normally control the firm and have frequent informal contact with it, but generally leave the managers alone to deliver the goods and only step in if the financial milestones are not being attained, when they may sack the entire top management and find a new team. Venture capital is almost always a transitional stage in a company's financing: the venture capitalists know that they cannot compound earnings at 35% per annum for very long and are constantly reviewing when the business can be sold (the 'EXIT') as a lower risk proposition to buyers who have less exorbitant return requirements. The typical VC holding is sold 2–4 years after acquisition, either to a TRADE BUYER or by means of public FLOTATION.

Two pieces of VC folklore still hold good. One is that 'lemons mature before plums', in other words, that some businesses will collapse pretty quickly, but it will take time for the best businesses to develop so that they can be sold for the optimal return. The other is that of ten VC investments, only three will fully meet projected returns, but one will be a SUPERSTAR that will return ten or more times the original investment. The secret of being a good venture capitalist is not to avoid failures (for these are inevitable), but to spot an above-average number of superstars.

VENTURE CAPITALIST
Executive in a VENTURE CAPITAL firm.

VERTICAL INTEGRATION
Moving to cover a greater part of the total industry VALUE CHAIN, by buying or competing with suppliers (BACKWARD INTEGRATION or UPSTREAM INTEGRATION) or customers (FORWARD INTEGRATION or DOWNSTREAM INTEGRATION).

VERTICAL MARKETING SYSTEM (VMS)
A vertically integrated firm controlling a number of channels of distribution, and having its own wholesaling and retailing.

VFM (Value For Money)
The foundation of mass market retailing and manufacture. Suppliers who position themselves to give better VFM than their competitors have a secure foundation. Very obvious, but very often neglected.

VICE PRESIDENT
US term for a senior executive; but some firms have hundreds of them.

VICIOUS CIRCLE
A downward spiral that can often attack a weak competitor. Consultants tend to refer to a DOOM LOOP, the industrial equivalent of a vicious circle.

VIDEOCONFERENCING
See TELECONFERENCING.

VIDEOTEXT SYSTEMS
Also called 'viewdata' and 'teletext'. Provision of financial and other data on TV screens by calling up relevant pages, which are constantly updated.

VIOLENT MARKET-INJECTION STRATEGIES
Tom PETERS' name for when ruthless competitors turn an industry upside-down by innovation. Peters stresses the role of anarchy, mess, confusion, destructive competition. Examples he gives of violent (no-nonsense) market-injection strategies include:

- Selling off all or part of new units.
- Licensing the most advanced technology to all-comers.
- Destroying the firm's most profitable products by cannibalisation.
- Insisting that each element of a firm demonstrates its fitness to compete by having outside customers.
- Sub-contract extensively.

The idea is to keep employees and competitors on their toes by continuous revolution. All his examples come from young and generally high-tech companies, and it is not clear whether his prescriptions are relevant outside this maelstrom.

VIRTUAL CORPORATION
A NETWORK model of a company, where it relies more on outside contractors and relationships than on the few people actually on the payroll.

VIRTUAL REALITY
Computer simulation devices and software that can devise new products and 'smarten' everything, even check connections between one atom and another. It will change the world by the start of the next century. The most relevant industrial applications thus far have been the use of advanced and interactive CAD/CAM systems to devise new products with the help of consumers. See PROSUMERS.

VIRTUOUS CIRCLE
The opposite of a DOOM LOOP: when a firm is able to continuously reinforce a strong position. Figure 42 shows how a virtuous circle can operate:

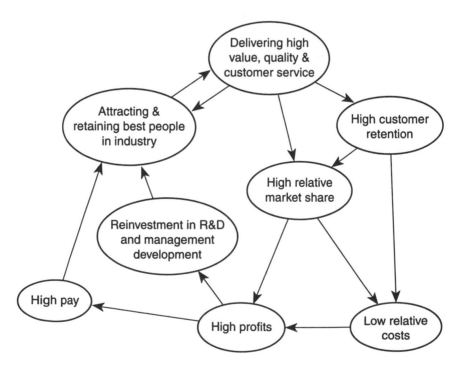

Figure 43 Illustration of a Virtuous Circle

VISION

An inspiring view of what a company could become, a dream about its future shape and success, a picture of a potential future for a firm, a glimpse into its Promised Land. A vision is the long-term aspiration of a leader for his or her firm, that can be described to colleagues and that will urge them on through the desert.

The word vision is often used as a synonym for MISSION, particularly in non-English speaking countries, where 'mission' is difficult to translate. But the two concepts are different. Mission is why a firm exists, its role in life. Vision is a view of what the firm could become, imagining a desired future.

Vision may be thought of as reaching a future goal. A good example of a vision that was fulfilled was President Kennedy's preposterous pledge in 1961 of 'achieving the goal, before this decade is out, of landing a man on the Moon and returning him safely to Earth'. An industrial equivalent may be the number 26 in the world league table of drug companies aiming to reach the top five by the year 2000. Another popular vision is for a regional (say, European) company to become 'truly global', where this is defined as having at least 25% of sales and profits in each TRIAD of the world (North America, Asia and Europe). Another vision is for a small company to become larger than its largest competitor, or for a derided airline to become 'the world's favourite'. It was a vision of Marvin Bower in the 1940s to think that MCKINSEY, a small, regional US consultancy, could become a huge firm with offices all around the world and with a reputation for developing professional management. Likewise, it was Henry Ford's vision in 1909 to 'democratise the automobile'. Steve Jobs' vision at Apple was to change work habits by making PCs user friendly to normal executives. The vision at IKEA was to change for ever the structure of the furniture market, become the first and leading global competitor in an industry previously dominated by separate national leaders. And so on.

Many writers imply that a new leader should have a ready-made vision from the start or in the early stages of the TRANSFORMATION process. This is wrong. The best visions evolve from experience during the first five years of a transformation process. In the early stages it is best to concentrate on making a break with the past, developing a cadre of supporters of the change process, modifying values, and obtaining early commercial successes with the new approach. Once real progress has been made, the leader should lift up his or her eyes, and identify the vision.

See also TYPE 1, VALUES and LEADERSHIP.

VLSI CIRCUITS

Very large scale integrated circuits, called by the Japanese the RICE OF INDUSTRY.

VOCATIONAL GUIDANCE
Helping school-leavers, the unemployed or those considering a career switch to assess what they are best suited to.

VOICECOM
Advanced telephone system for leaving and accessing messages from colleagues on a user network.

VOICE MESSAGING
See VOICECOM.

VOLUME VARIANCE
When product volumes are either higher or lower than budgeted.

VOLUNTARY ARRANGEMENT
When a firm or individual agrees with creditors to a scheme of postponed or reduced payments, in order to avoid bankruptcy and continue to provide earnings to pay off debts.

VOLUNTARY REDUNDANCY
When job cuts are made by inviting employees to apply for redundancy on generous terms and no-one is forced to resign or fired.

VOLUNTARY WINDING-UP
When a firm decides of its own volition to wind itself up and pay off creditors.

VORSTAND
German executive board. Contrast *AUFSICHTSRAT*, the supervisory board required additionally for certain German companies.

VOUCHER
Document supporting an entry in accounting books, or a receipt.

VULNERABILITY
The extent to which a firm faces threats; the degree to which sales and profits may come under attack. Vulnerability is not the opposite of profitability; rather, it is its soft underbelly. Many very profitable firms are highly vulnerable. Vulnerability exists when any of the following conditions apply:

- When high profitability (measured by ROS or ROCE) co-exists with a poor relative market share (RMS) position.
- When a firm is more profitable than competitors yet has lower productivity per employee.
- When RMS is being lost to at least one more aggressive competitor.
- When depreciation exceeds new capital investment over a sustained period.

- When the rate of investment in new capacity is lower than that of one or more competitors.
- When expense investment in R&D, marketing and management development is lower than that of competitors.
- When competitors have access to greater cost sharing, shared technological development, a superior supplier network, or better distribution.
- When some of the best people have been leaving, for whatever reasons.
- When it is difficult to recruit the best people in the industry into the firm.
- When the firm is locked into SEGMENT RETREAT, conceding more and more markets and focusing on a narrower customer base.
- When competitors can bring out new products faster.
- When competitors have owners that will accept a lower rate of investment return or lower dividends.

Vulnerability exists, in short, when a business has been HARVESTING its position, preferring short-term profits to long-term reinvestment, or, conversely, when a competitor has been doing the reverse, investing for the future, to a greater extent. Systematic identification of when companies are vulnerable, or the opposite (what we may perhaps call LATENT OPPORTUNITY), is the key to identifying shifts in relative market share and is a leading indicator of future swings in shareholder value. See OPPORTUNITY/VULNERABILITY MATRIX.

W

WAGE DRIFT
When actual earnings increase faster than wage rates, because of special productivity or other deals giving bonuses or overtime. A problem in the late 1960s in the UK; not so much an issue when unemployment is high and total pay is constrained.

WAITING TIME
See DOWNTIME (1).

WAIVER
Voluntary relinquishment of rights in a contract.

WANTS
What consumers want and will pay for. Sometimes used interchangeably with NEEDS; sometimes relegated to a less urgent category of discretionary spending.

WAREHOUSE CLUB
US and UK retailing hard discount format, where shoppers pay an annual fee and then can buy groceries and other goods at large discounts to supermarket prices. A very successful US sales channel and one that will become increasingly important in the UK and elsewhere. Traditional supermarkets will be forced to introduce their own warehouse club formats or face losing major market share.

WARRANT
Quoted share instrument giving the right to buy particular shares (usually in investment trusts) at a particular price (the EXERCISE PRICE) in the future; an interesting geared investment which can multiply several times if the underlying shares do well, or become worthless if the shares decline and stay below the exercise price. Warrants are speculative but generally better value than PENNY SHARES or TRADED OPTIONS. Warrants are ideally suited to rich private investors, though even these should never allocate more than a small proportion (say 5–10%) of their total portfolio to warrants.

WARRANTY
1. Guarantee. 2. Affirmation that a document is correct. Warranties are often required by buyers of a private business giving them a come-back to the sellers if all is not as warranted.

WASTAGE

Generally called NATURAL WASTAGE: loss of employees through retirement or resignation.

WASTING ASSET

One being used up.

WATERMAN, ROBERT H WATERMAN JR (b. 1936)

Forever linked with Tom PETERS as joint author of *In Search of Excellence* (1982), Waterman is the older, more reflective and, many would say, more original of the two writers. A laid-back Californian, he has written two outstanding books since: *The Renewal Factor* and *Adhocracy: the Power to Change*. Both are concerned with how organisations learn, manage change and chaos, use TASKFORCES and develop their distinctive roles in life. Waterman has pointed out that most managers still live in the shadow of TAYLOR, and practise the opposite of what they preach. Waterman's latest (1994) book, called *What America Does Right* in the US edition, and *The Frontiers of Excellence* in the UK, looks at ten US organisations that 'put people first', including Federal Express, Levi Strauss, Motorola, Procter & Gamble and Rubbermaid. It is a useful and enjoyable read that asserts that the most successful companies do not put shareholders first, paying primary attention to customers and employees. A side-effect is excellent stock-market performance. The case examples are fresh, but a little rose-tinted; the general argument is not original, but well argued and broadly correct.

WEAKNESSES

See VULNERABILITIES.

WEAR OUT PERIOD

Period towards the end of its life when a machine may fail. See FAILURE RATE CURVE.

WEBER, MAX (1864–1920)

The prophet of BUREAUCRACY, which he saw as the best prototype for the modern organisation. He saw the role-determined organisation – where everyone knew what they were supposed to do, and reported upwards through a boss with greater responsibility, promotion was by merit and the whole thing could operate as a smooth machine – as indubitably the most efficient and even liberating model. He contrasted it with two other forms: the traditional, hereditary system, where authority was inherited and required deference, as in the family firm; and the charismatic, which relies upon an outstanding individual like Henry Ford, and was likely to disintegrate or transmute to another style when the charismatic leader retired. (Weber was the first writer to clearly define the charismatic leader and his type of company, and rejuvenated the word 'charisma' that had lain dormant since the fall of Greece.)

Weber was right: bureaucracy was best at that time, and was the engine of wealth creation. The idea led to the formation of big business empires and the MULTINATIONAL CORPORATION, organised on bureaucratic lines. Even today, the role-type culture may be the most efficient in slow-changing markets such as insurance, as even Charles HANDY concedes. In his book GODS OF MANAGEMENT, Handy gives an even-handed account of the modern form of bureaucracy, which he calls APOLLO).

Weber cannot be blamed for not living another 25 or 75 years. Since the Second World War it has become increasingly clear that bureaucracy is not enough, and even in its original sense is an albatross for any firm facing volatile markets, demanding customers and fearsome competitors. Fast response requires ADHOCRACY, roughly the opposite of bureaucracy. Moreover, as the people in companies who comprise its knowledge have become increasingly central, and demanding, the role of the charismatic leader has become much more important, even in many cases necessary. Finally, Weber could not be expected to see the damaging effects of MANAGERIALISM and the absentee landlords in the form of investing institutions. The divorce of ownership from management, and the short-term view of Western investors, has led the Anglo-Saxon corporation to be ill-equipped to deal with the Japanese challenge, where investors are more central and long term. The German medium-sized family firm, with its own network of local financial support, has proved to be much more resilient and valuable than the feudal family firm of Weber's time. Weber would have been the first to turn his ideas on their head in response to changed circumstances.

WEIGHTED AVERAGE

Average of observations, weighted to reflect their relative importance. For example, if a firm has two products, one with return on sales of 5% and the other with 15%, it might seem that the average return on sales was 10%; but if the first product was 80% of sales and the second 20%, the weighted average would be only $(0.8 \times 5) + (0.2 \times 15) = 7\%$.

WEIGHTED AVERAGE COST OF CAPITAL

A special form of weighted average much beloved by financial analysts. It is the weighted average of the cost of EQUITY (the return required by shareholders, which is usually quite high) and the cost of DEBT (the interest on a loan, which varies widely across the cycle but is usually significantly lower than the cost of equity). The weighted average clearly depends not only on the cost of equity and debt but also on the mix. A highly-geared company will generally have a much lower weighted average cost of capital than a company with low gearing.

Curiously, many, perhaps even most, UK and US companies maintain HURDLE RATES for investment that are well above the weighted average cost of capital, particularly when the cost of debt has come down but the hurdle rate has not been lowered. This suggests that they do not believe the projections of their managers and want some slack in the system. The result is often chronic under-investment.

WEIGHTING
Additional pay for work in a high-cost city.

WHITE COLLAR
Clerical and managerial; contrast BLUE COLLAR (shop floor). Insidious and disappearing distinction.

WHITE COLLAR CRIME
Covers a multitude of clerical and managerial misdeeds, from stealing paper clips to fraud.

WHITE GOODS
Consumer durables in a white cabinet like washing machines, tumbledriers, cookers, dishwashers and refrigerators. Contrast BROWN GOODS.

WHITE KNIGHT
Friendly bidder who rides to rescue a firm from a HOSTILE BID. White knights may not win the bid, or may only do so at a high cost, if an auction develops between the original bidder and the white knight.

WIDE AREA NETWORK
Distributed data-processing system for widespread public or private organisation.

WIDGET
Mythical unit of a standard product.

WINCHESTER DISK
Hard disk for computers sealed in an airtight container.

WHOLE-LIFE INSURANCE
Payment of a fixed premium each year in return for a payment on death.

WHOLESALE DEPOSIT
Large deposit from one bank or large corporation to another.

WHOLESALE MARKET
The MONEY MARKET between banks (and sometimes corporate and rich individual depositors/lenders) for large short-term loans.

WHOLESALER

Someone who buys from a manufacturer (or other wholesaler), breaks bulk, aggregates orders and delivers to a retailer (or other wholesaler).

WILDCAT

BCG's original name for QUESTION-MARKS (a firm's businesses that are in high growth markets, but not the market leader). See QUESTION-MARKS and BCG MATRIX.

WILDCAT STRIKE

Unofficial strike.

WINDFALL PROFIT

One due to exceptional circumstances, unlikely to be repeated.

WINDING-UP

To put a company into liquidation.

WINDOW

1. Time-slot in an American's schedule, into (through?) which you may be squeezed as a special favour. **2.** Short for WINDOW OF OPPORTUNITY. **3.** A short period during which funds are available, often from a central bank.

WINDOW DRESSING

Making use of laxity in accounting rules to make the P&L and BALANCE SHEET look better than they really are, without actually breaking the law. Some firms characteristically engage in more (and 'better') window-dressing than others; their shares are to be avoided. One type of CREATIVE ACCOUNTING.

WINDOW GUIDANCE

Bank of Japan 'advice' to banks on lending policy.

WINDOW OF OPPORTUNITY

A time when the iron is hot and you should strike; a limited period beyond which the opportunity may diminish or disappear. Often used in an attempt to get you to do something quickly and without thinking about the consequences; in practice windows rarely close as predictably or fully as is implied.

WIND UP

Liquidate a company; cease trading.

WITHHOLDING TAX

1. Tax deducted at source from dividends and interest payment, especially where payments are made to non-residents. Can sometimes be offset against taxes of the non-resident in their own country, but may lead to double taxation. **2.** US income tax deducted from gross pay.

WORD PROCESSING
Using a WORD PROCESSOR to write, manipulate, store and recall text. Has revolutionised office work.

WORD PROCESSOR (WP)
1. A PC equipped with a software package like Word Perfect that makes text and document preparation easy and quick. **2.** Sometimes used to refer to the software package itself.

WORKAHOLIC
Someone addicted to work who works very long hours.

WORKER DIRECTOR, WORKING DIRECTOR
A worker who also serves on a company's board: common in Germany and many other Continental countries. See also CO-DETERMINATION.

WORKFARE
The system of putting unemployed people into special jobs and paying them for work rather than doling out welfare. Controversial in the UK but works well in Sweden.

WORK FLOW, WORKFLOW
The series of work sequences in producing a product or service. An original and useful view of workflow has been given by Taichi Ohno in respect of the Toyota production system, which he compares to a series of race circuits in which each runner hands on the baton to the next runner, with the speed and stamina of each runner perfectly balanced for smooth transitions. Ohno contrasts this 'work flow' with the normal factory, where work is forced to flow, against normal volition. Good work flow synchronises activities as much as possible so that they overlap and flow naturally.

There is evidence that where an operation has many work steps, natural synchronisation of work flow is both more important, and more difficult for Western as opposed to Japanese competitors. Jim Abegglen and George Stalk of BCG's Tokyo office found that in industries with only around 20 work steps (like shirt-making and steel and paper mills) American firms' labour hours were similar to those in Japanese firms. But in making car engines, with over 200 steps, US firms used 60% more labour hours, while in work with more than 1,000 steps, like car assembly, the US firms used 80–100% more labour. The more complex the work, the more crucial SYN-CHRONISATION becomes.

WORK IN PROGRESS
Goods or services being prepared for sale but not yet FINISHED GOODS. Recorded on the BALANCE SHEET as an ASSET.

WORKING CAPITAL
Funding required for day-to-day operations to cover the gap between payment for inputs (raw materials, labour etc) and the time that customers pay. Working capital plus FIXED ASSETS equal CAPITAL EMPLOYED.

WORKING CAPITAL PRODUCTIVITY
SALES divided by WORKING CAPITAL.

WORK MEASUREMENT
A form of WORK STUDY.

WORKPLACE BARGAINING
Negotiations between management and unions at the local plant level, rather than nationwide. Less likely to lead to wage escalation.

WORK SHARING
When two part-time workers share one job.

WORK STATION, WORKSTATION
Place where work is done, usually with a machine and a person stationed there (though sometimes the human moves around from one work station to another). Originally confined to factories, now applied also to offices, where a PC and desk may constitute a work station.

WORK STUDY
General name for analysis to improve efficiency which derives from the SCIENTIFIC MANAGEMENT school (TAYLORISM). Includes METHOD STUDY (analysis and improvement of the way jobs are done) and WORK MEASUREMENT (which dates from Taylor's stopwatch and includes TIME AND MOTION STUDY and its slightly more sophisticated derivatives. Not much practised now.

WORLD ENTERPRISE
Term coined in 1959 by Gilbert Clee of McKINSEY. The idea was to buy raw materials around the globe wherever cheapest, manufacture where labour was cheapest, and sell wherever the prices were highest. The concept led many US firms to become MNEs (Multi-National Enterprises) with operations in Europe and Asia. The idea of the world enterprise was path-breaking, but now needs modification. Most industries are now capital- and knowledge- rather than labour-intensive. See also Kenichi OHMAE, and his concept of the world being 'borderless' but still having distinct and different local markets.

WP

See WORD PROCESSOR.

WRIT

Legal document from a court that must be responded to or complied with.

WRITE DOWN

Decrease the value of an ASSET on the BALANCE SHEET.

WRITE OFF

Take an ASSET off the BALANCE SHEET; declare it worthless.

WRITER

Someone who writes (issues) an option, similar to a bookmaker who accepts a bet.

WRITE UP

Revalue an ASSET, such as land, which may have appreciated in value.

WRITTEN BACK

Accounting PROVISIONS are written back when it is safe to assume that they will never be required.

WRITTEN DOWN VALUE

The value to which an ASSET has been depreciated; its NET BOOK VALUE.

WRONGFUL DISMISSAL

Same as UNLAWFUL DISMISSAL: firing that was unjustified and that must be compensated.

WRONGFUL TRADING

Continuing to trade when a firm is unable to meet its obligations. A serious misdemeanour for directors, who can be held personally liable to creditors. Directors must liquidate a company rather than risk the imputation of wrongful trading. In practice it is a grey area that is highly unsatisfactory, giving extra employment to lawyers and often causing the closure of businesses because directors cannot afford to be other than extremely conservative in avoiding any risk of being deemed to have traded wrongfully.

X

XD

Ex dividend, share price quoted without the latest dividend.

X-INEFFICIENCY

The extent to which a plant or other part of a firm falls below the efficiency of the best comparable unit within the firm. See BEST DEMONSTRATED PRACTICE (BDP).

XEROX

Popular word for 'to photocopy': mainly on Japanese rather than Xerox machines.

XEROGRAPHY

Commercial process for reproducing documents cheaply (actually a distinct process from photocopying). A good example of how the inventor of a market (Xerox Corporation) lost global market leadership to lower cost and latterly better quality and better featured Japanese machines. Even after the threat was already apparent, in the early 1970s, Xerox sold on a PE of over 35, yet it should (with the benefit of hindsight) have sold on a PE of only 6.8 times earnings. The earnings disappointed because Xerox lost its STAR position and ended up a DOG. See BCG MATRIX.

Y

YANKEE BOND

Bond issued in the US in dollars by a foreign company or bank. Contrast EUROBOND.

YANKEES

US shares or other financial instruments.

YARDSTICK

Measurement that is useful for comparing one company or unit's performance with another. Used in BDP (Best Demonstrated Practice) and other BENCHMARKING techniques.

YARDSTICKING

Another (rather rare) name for BENCHMARKING; or the process of using a yardstick in a benchmarking activity.

YELLOW GOODS

A term covering both BROWN and WHITE GOODS (brown + white = yellow): HIGH TICKET ITEMS bought infrequently. Contrast RED GOODS (frequent purchases) and compare ORANGE GOODS (bought moderately often).

YIELD

The return on shares, bank deposits or other financial instruments. It is the interest or dividend received annually divided by the current market price (not the cost paid by an investor) of the instrument. Some shares are bought principally for the yield: these are generally companies where earnings have declined, but where the dividend has not (yet) been cut. There are two dangers with such shares: (1) the yield may never be received, since it is always quoted on the basis of last year's dividend, which may be cut; and (2) the share price may fall if earnings continue to decline or the dividend is cut. Conversely, however, if the dividend is held and the earnings look like recovering, the investor may receive not only a large yield but also healthy capital appreciation through a share price increase. Some investors and investment trusts specialise in high yield shares, trying to pick the less risky ones and those with greatest recovery potential. All that can safely be generalised about high yield instruments is that they have above average risk.

YIELD CURVE

Graph showing the yield of fixed-interest securities according to the length of their maturity: normally slopes gently up to reflect premium expected for long-term funds. If it slopes down at some point, this indicates the expectation that medium term interest rates will fall.

YIELD GAP

The difference between the YIELD on risk-free government stock and the average yield on shares. In the UK, from the mid-nineteenth to the mid-twentieth centuries, the normal expectation was that the yield on shares should be higher than that on government securities (gilts). The absence or reversal of this yield gap (that is, whenever shares yielded the same as or less than gilts) was a reliable 'sell' indicator for shares.

But once Harold Macmillan ushered in the 'never had it so good' world, and inflation became a significant and persistent feature of the economy, this inflation obscured the old relationship. Only in 1981, with the invention of Index Linked Gilts, was it possible to reconstruct a reliable new yield gap measure without inflation confusing the picture. Since 1981 the yield on shares has generally been above that on Index Linked Gilts: which makes sense, because shares carry some risk and gilts do not. Only in 1987, when the share prices soared, did the yield on shares fall below (and well below) the yield on Index Linked Gilts, thus creating a REVERSE YIELD GAP. This gave a reliable, though generally ignored, 'sell' signal. Investors who want to avoid buying shares at the top of the market should avoid buying them when the yield gap is only 0.5% or less (and especially when the yield gap becomes negative).

YIELD TO MATURITY

Same as YIELD TO REDEMPTION or REDEMPTION YIELD.

YIELD TO REDEMPTION

The total annual average yield to the end of a fixed-interest security's life, comprising the interest yield plus the annual capital gain (or minus the annual capital loss). The best measure of the security's total return.

YUPPIE

Mysterious breed that multiplied in the late 1980s and is now in hibernation: young, upwardly mobile, professional, and usually rather greedy.

Z

ZAIBATSU

Old name for the groupings of Japanese banks, trading and industrial companies in affiliated combines with extensive cross-shareholdings. The modern form, based on changes in Japanese law after 1945, is KEIRETSU. Not all large Japanese companies participate in Keiretsu, though those that do not like Canon, Sony and Toyota tend to be more focused in their product lines than the majority of large Japanese companies that are in such combines. For the latter there are major benefits in terms of close supplier and customer relationships, shared technological development and the ability to take a long term view of commercial policy.

ZAITECH

Japanese term meaning financial profits arising from good financial management.

ZANINESS

Tom PETERS has single-handedly put this word on the management map: he claims it is an essential requirement for success or sometimes corporate survival, despite the fact that few corporate leaders are (or allow themselves to be) at all zany. In *Liberation Management*, Peters comments: 'Zany leaders for zany times. To wit: If you don't feel crazy, you're not in touch with the times . . . Nutty organisations, nutty people, capable of dealing with the fast, fleeting, fickle, are a requisite for survival'.

Z CHART

Useful device for tracking the progress of sales over time. Figure 43 shows an example: the term Z comes from the rough shape of the three main lines.

ZEBRA

Special sort of ZERO-COUPON BOND, where the accrued income is taxed annually instead of at the end of its life. Only for investors with odd tax needs.

ZEITGEIST

Prevailing culture or spirit of the times: German term sometimes applied to a firm, an industry or society as a whole.

Figure 44 Example of a Z chart

ZERO-BASED BUDGETING (ZBB)
Budgeting with a clean sheet of paper, disregarding historical costs, in order to remove any unnecessary costs. A useful discipline but not often done, except as a one-off exercise by consultants.

ZERO BASED PRODUCTION
Design of a product from scratch to standards acceptable to consumers, combined with VALUE ANALYSIS and VALUE ENGINEERING and production analysis to ensure that the cost for this standard is as low as possible. The basis of success for many Japanese products, including the Honda Civic and Ricoh's copiers, as well as Toyota and Nissan cars.

ZERO DEFECTS
The idea that quality should be absolute: 99.9% is not enough. See QUALITY.

ZEROES, ZERO-COUPON BONDS
A loan or share instrument that pays no interest. Instead, investors are rewarded at the end of its life with a larger amount than they subscribed, usually on a pre-determined schedule, provided there are enough net assets to pay the designated amount. Zero-coupon shares are generally one class of shares in quoted investment trusts. The holder of zero-coupon shares can

take a capital gain in lieu of interest, which is of value to higher rate tax-payers who effectively 'roll up' the implied annual gain, and may be able to avoid some or all of the eventual capital gain tax. Because zero-coupon shares are generally quoted on the stock exchange, it is not necessary to wait until the end of the period (which may be many years) before taking a profit.

ZERO-SUM GAME

The idea derived from GAME THEORY that if I gain you must lose: there is a finite amount of goodies in a market and if one competitor grabs some it must be at the expense of the other competitors. In general, in competitive markets (that is, in the absence of a cartel), it may be the best assumption that it is a zero-sum game in the short term. If Coke wins, Pepsi loses; if Canon wins in photocopiers, Xerox suffers. There are, however, two impor-tant qualifications to the zero-sum game concept. First, a sub-set of competitors may co-operate on some issues, such as market development or sharing technology, to their mutual advantage and to everyone else's detri-ment. This still represents a zero-sum game between the bloc of collaborators and all others, but a POSITIVE-SUM GAME for competitors within the bloc. Groupings such as the EC and NAFTA may be seen in this way. The second qualification is that competitors within an industry may have a mutual interest in increasing the size of the market for their product, or in increasing the size and health of the economy as a whole. A simple illustration of this is when someone slaps down a service station next to another at a cross-roads; this may actually increase demand for the first sta-tion, by making the area the place where you fill up. In practice, life and competition are never zero-sum games: competitors help each other by encouraging higher standards, which in turn enlarges the market and con-duces towards a richer society. The concept of zero-sum competition is, nevertheless, of great value, and in the short-term broadly correct; and longer-term, the concept itself helps us create its opposite.

ZEUS

One of Charles HANDY's four GODS OF MANAGEMENT. A Zeus culture is a club based around one leader, so that the organisation can best be depicted not as a normal hierarchy (as on a pyramid-like organisation chart) but as a series of lines running into the centre, where the leader (Zeus) sits; or as a web radiating out from this centre. The concentric lines closest to the centre represent the greatest power (apart from Zeus himself); power and influence are measured by the amount of time that Zeus spends with each executive and the regard in which Zeus holds him or her.

The culture is the norm in young, entrepreneurial firms, and also in investment banks, BOUTIQUES of all sorts, small and medium-sized brokers, any small professional service firms, in politics, sport and the performing arts.

The great advantages of the Zeus culture are (1) speed of decision-taking; (2) empathy, trust and emotional commitment ('what would Zeus do in this circumstance?'); and (3) lean and economical structure and absence of bureaucracy (no memos, committees or corporate politics).

Zeus organisations can be amateur, blinkered, inequitable, cruel, and riddled with courtiers rather than good professional managers. But equally, with high quality people, Zeus organisations can exhibit great flair, unleash enormous energy and commitment, and change the world. Microsoft is a Zeus organisation; so too are (or were) The Body Shop (with the more dominant Zeus being female), Egon Zehnder, GEC, Filofax, Hanson, LL Bean, Mars, Maxwell Communications Corporation, MCKINSEY, Polly Peck and Virgin. Lonrho was a Zeus organisation before Tiny Rowland ceded power to Dieter Bock. Succession is always a major issue.

Zeus organisations flout all the laws of SCIENTIFIC MANAGEMENT and most of the classic management principles that we still implicitly believe in. Zeus organisations are the wave of the past but also the wave of the future. See also FAMILY FIRM, ATHENA, APOLLO and DIONYSUS.

ZIGGURAT

Hierarchical organisation. Contrast FLAT ORGANISATION.

ZIP CODE

US post-code.

ZIPF'S LAW

G K Zipf's 'Principle of least effort': serious, mathematical 'proof' that mankind strives to produce any given outcome with the minimum amount of work. The basis of productivity and increases in wealth.

ZONING

US term for categorising areas according to planning permission rights (e.g. industrial, residential).

Z-SCORE

A single number, based on a number of accounting ratios, indicating the risk of a firm going bust. Useful as one input to risk assessment.